Your All-in-One Resource

On the CD that accompanies this book, you'll find additional resources to extend your learning.

The reference library includes the following fully searchable titles:

- *Microsoft Computer Dictionary*, 5th ed.
- *First Look 2007 Microsoft Office System* by Katherine Murray
- Windows Vista Product Guide

Also provided are a sample chapter and poster from *Look Both Ways: Help Protect Your Family on the Internet* by Linda Criddle

The CD interface has a new look. You can use the tabs for an assortment of tasks:

- Check for book updates (if you have Internet access)
- Install the book's practice file
- Go online for product support or CD support
- Send us feedback

The following screen shot gives you a glimpse of the new interface.

Microsoft

Microsoft® Office Accounting Professional 2007 Step by Step

Curtis Frye
William E. Pearson III

PUBLISHED BY
Microsoft Press
A Division of Microsoft Corporation
One Microsoft Way
Redmond, Washington 98052-6399

Library of Congress Control Number: 2007934744

Printed and bound in the United States of America.

1 2 3 4 5 6 7 8 9   QWT   2 1 0 9 8 7

Distributed in Canada by H.B. Fenn and Company Ltd.

A CIP catalogue record for this book is available from the British Library.

Microsoft Press books are available through booksellers and distributors worldwide. For further information about international editions, contact your local Microsoft Corporation office or contact Microsoft Press International directly at fax (425) 936-7329. Visit our Web site at www.microsoft.com/mspress. Send comments to mspinput@microsoft.com.

Acquisitions Editor: Juliana Aldous Atkinson
Developmental Editor: Sandra Haynes
Project Editor: Valerie Woolley
Editorial Production: Online Training Solutions, Inc.
Technical Reviewer: Mitch Tulloch; Technical Review services provided by Content Master, a member of CM Group, Ltd.

Body Part No. X14-06997

Contents

R0413801590

CHICAGO PUBLIC LIBRARY

What do you think of this book? We want to hear from you!

Microsoft is interested in hearing your feedback so we can continually improve our books and learning resources for you. To participate in a brief online survey, please visit:

www.microsoft.com/learning/booksurvey/

14   Managing Bank Accounts and Transactions   285

On the CD

What do you think of this book? We want to hear from you!

Microsoft is interested in hearing your feedback so we can continually improve our books and learning resources for you. To participate in a brief online survey, please visit:

www.microsoft.com/learning/booksurvey/

Introducing Accounting 2007

Microsoft Office Accounting 2007 is an accounting program that enables small businesses to manage financial tasks, organize their records, and grow their business online. Accounting 2007 uses the familiar Microsoft Office interface, which lets you dive right in and use the program immediately. Furthermore, you can use Accounting 2007 in conjunction with other programs in the 2007 Microsoft Office system, which makes information-sharing simple and helps boost productivity.

Accounting 2007 is available in two editions: Express and Professional. Accounting Express 2007 provides all of the basic functionality you need to run a small business, such as managing customer records, selling products online, and accepting credit card payments. Accounting Professional 2007 greatly expands your ability to manage your business information by offering additional capabilities such as enhanced reporting capabilities, greater flexibility in managing products and services to offer to your customers, and the ability to generate quotes and sales orders.

Navigating Within Accounting 2007

Accounting 2007 uses the familiar Microsoft Office user interface, so you will have no trouble using the program immediately. The controls in Accounting 2007 are divided into groups, represented by buttons in the Navigation Pane.

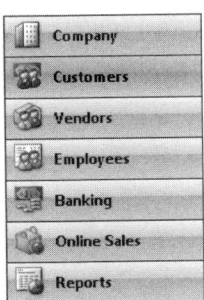

Clicking any of these buttons displays the corresponding home page containing commands that you can use to perform tasks relevant to the home page's focus. For example, clicking the Customers button displays the Customers home page.

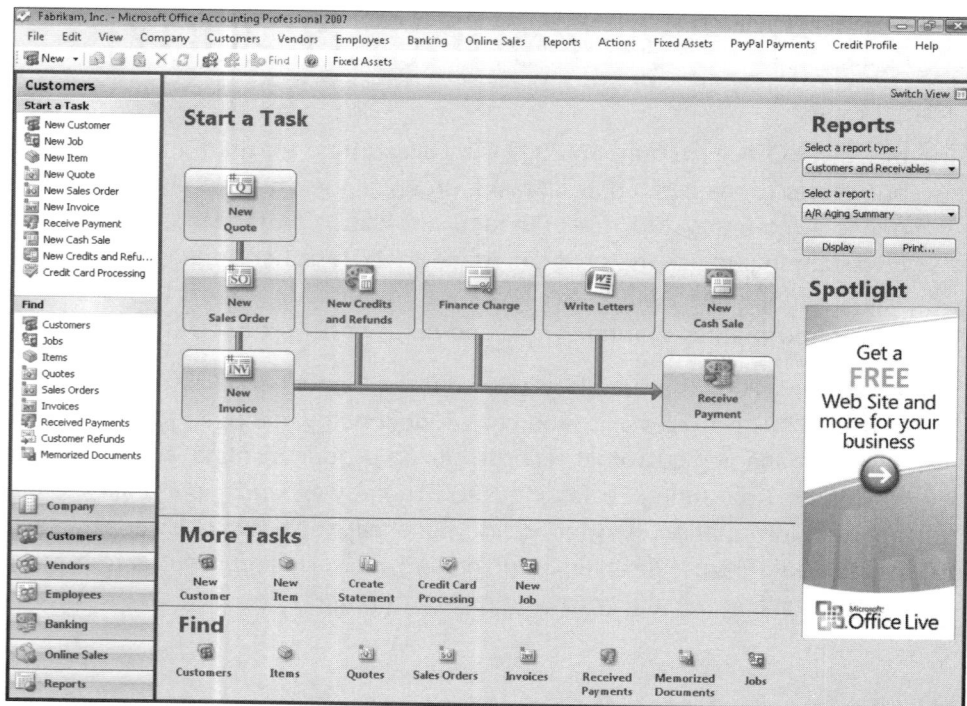

You can use the commands on the Customers home page to create new customer records in your company file, generate quotes and invoices, accept cash payments, and define items for sale.

Accounting 2007 maintains lists of customers, items for sale, invoices, and other business objects you define within the company file. For example, the Item List contains the details of every item you have created.

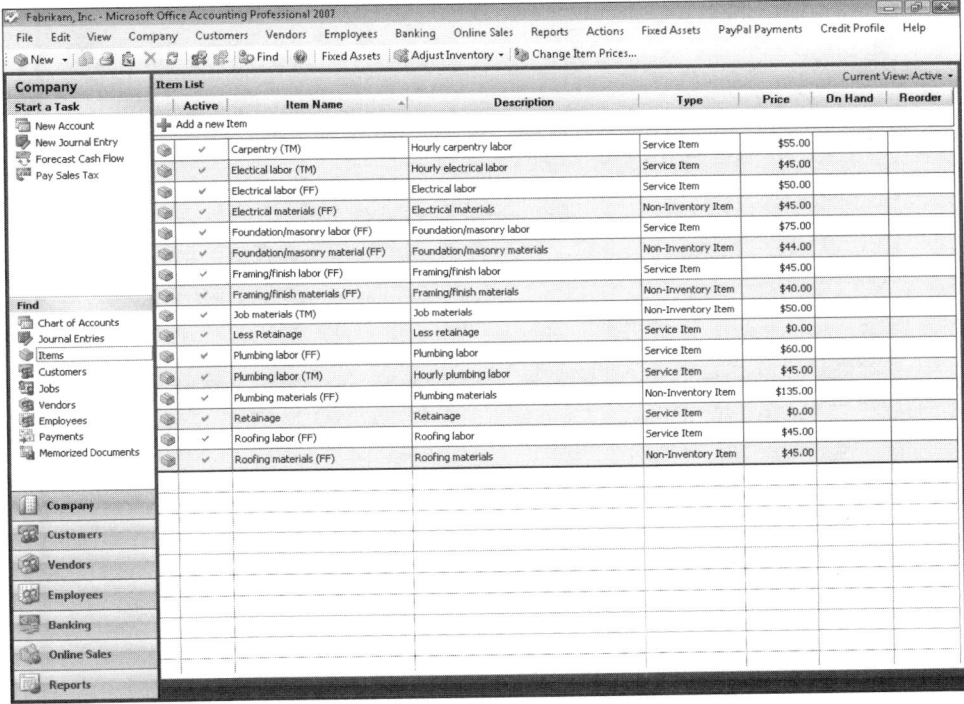

Lists organize data effectively, but their data doesn't always fit on one screen. Double-clicking a list entry displays the entry's details in a user-friendly form. In addition to viewing the form's contents, you can update the information it contains to reflect an item's new price, a customer's new address, or a vendor's new phone number.

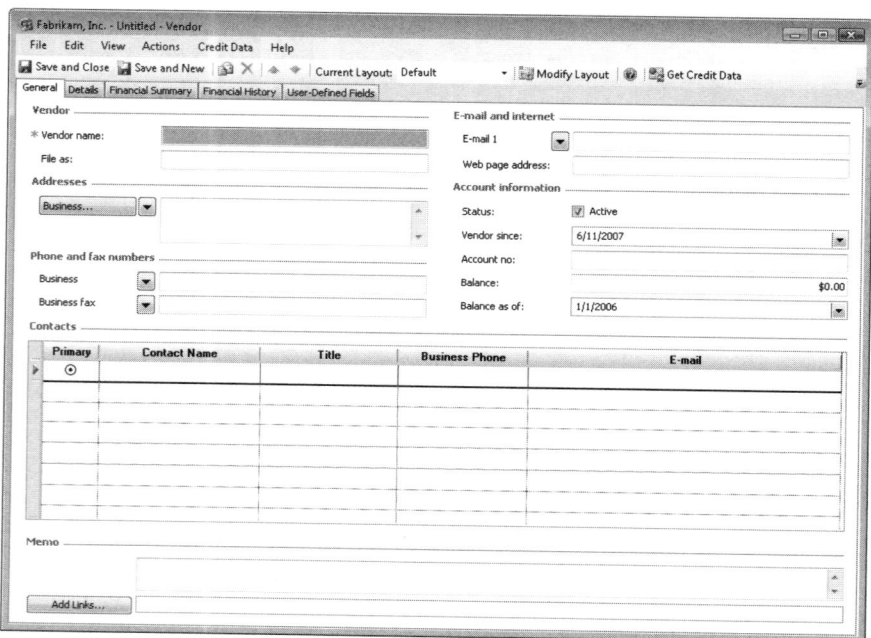

Managing Your Business

With Accounting 2007, you can keep a close watch on your bank accounts, derive business intelligence from the data you collect, and work closely with your accountant. You can view the activity for each of your bank accounts in an account register, where you can also add and edit transactions. You can initiate banking tasks such as writing and printing checks, depositing and transferring funds, and recording credit card charges, all from the Banking home page.

With Accounting 2007, you can bank online, provided that you have an Internet connection, and the financial institution where you bank offers online banking. After you set up your accounts for online banking, you can download transactions from your online accounts and match your bank's records with the records you keep in Accounting.

Accounting 2007 comes with a wide range of reports built into the product. Each of these reports is useful for discovering important business intelligence, reviewing past performance, and planning your future ventures. You can analyze your company's performance by viewing and printing the built-in reports as Accounting presents them, or you can focus on specific data within the reports by sorting and filtering the reports' contents.

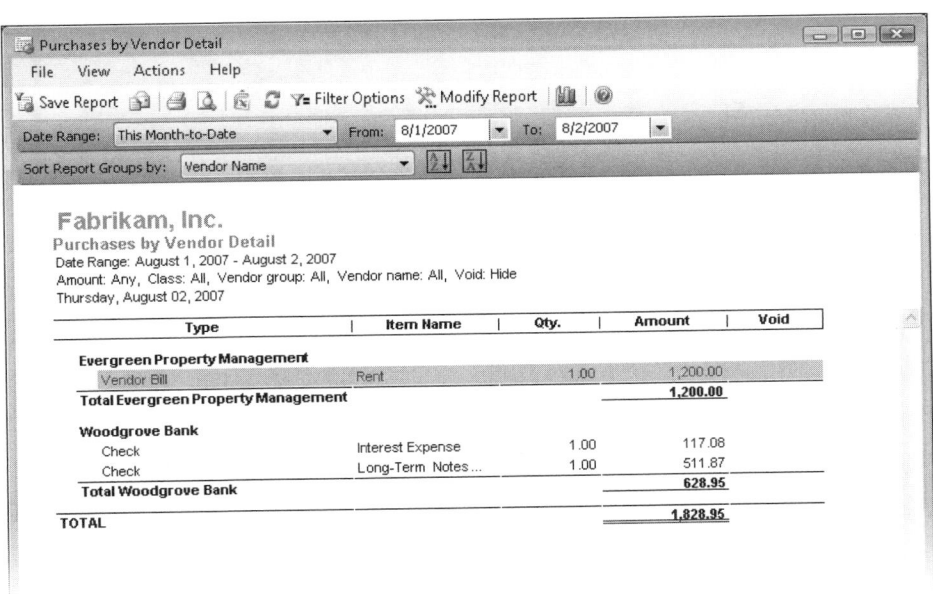

You should, of course, share all of your data with your accountant. Small-business owners excel at their chosen field, but often don't have the rigorous background in accounting and business analysis that a trained accountant possesses. Learning how to work effectively with an accountant can help you manage current operations, understand your tax and payroll responsibilities, and plan your company's future.

Information for Readers Running Windows XP

The graphics and the operating system–related instructions in this book reflect the Windows Vista user interface, but you can also use a computer running Windows XP with Service Pack 2 (SP2) installed.

Most of the differences you will encounter when working through the exercises in this book on a Windows XP computer relate to appearance rather than functionality. For example, the Windows Vista Start button is round rather than rectangular and is not labeled with the word *Start*; window frames and window-management buttons look different; and if your system supports Windows Aero, the window frames might be transparent. In addition, file system dialog boxes and some file system paths are different between the two platforms. For example, the *My Documents* folder in Windows XP is named *Documents* in Windows Vista.

In this section, we provide steps for navigating to or through menus and dialog boxes in Windows XP that differ from those provided in the exercises in this book. For the most part, these differences are small enough that you will have no difficulty in completing the exercises.

Using the Start Menu

Folders on the Windows Vista Start menu expand vertically. Folders on the Windows XP Start menu expand horizontally. However, the steps to access a command on the Start menu are identical on both systems.

To start Microsoft Office Accounting 2007 on a Windows XP computer:

 → Click the **Start** button, point to **All Programs**, click **Microsoft Office**, and then click **Microsoft Office Accounting 2007**.

Navigating Dialog Boxes

On a computer running Windows XP, some of the dialog boxes you will work with in the exercises not only look different from the graphics shown in this book but also work differently. These dialog boxes are primarily those that act as an interface between Accounting and the operating system, including any dialog box in which you navigate to a specific location.

For example, to navigate to the *My Pictures* folder in Windows XP:

→ On the **Places** bar, click **My Documents**. Then in the folder content pane, double-click **My Pictures**.

To move back to the *My Documents* folder in Windows XP:

Up One Level

→ On the toolbar, click the **Up One Level** button.

Features and Conventions of This Book

This book has been designed to lead you step by step through all the tasks you are most likely to want to perform in Microsoft Accounting 2007. If you start at the beginning and work your way through all the exercises, you will gain enough proficiency to be able to create quite elaborate publications with Accounting. However, each topic is self contained. If you have worked with a previous version of Accounting, or if you completed all the exercises and later need help remembering how to perform a procedure, the following features of this book will help you locate specific information:

- **Detailed table of contents.** A listing of the topics and sidebars within each chapter.
- **Chapter thumb tabs.** Easily locate the beginning of the chapter you want.
- **Topic-specific running heads.** Within a chapter, quickly locate the topic you want by looking at the running head of odd-numbered pages.
- **Detailed index.** Look up specific tasks and features and general concepts in the index, which has been carefully crafted with the reader in mind.
- **Companion CD.** Contains additional book content as well as a fully searchable electronic version of this book, and other useful resources..

In addition, we provide a glossary of terms for those times when you need to look up the meaning of a word or the definition of a concept.

You can save time when you use this book by understanding how the *Step by Step* series shows special instructions, keys to press, buttons to click, and so on.

Convention	Meaning
USE	This paragraph preceding a step-by-step exercise indicates the practice files or programs that you will use when working through the exercise.
BE SURE TO	This paragraph preceding or following a step-by-step exercise indicates any requirements you should attend to before beginning the exercise or actions you should take to restore your system after completing the exercise.
OPEN	This paragraph preceding a step-by-step exercise indicates files that you should open before beginning the exercise.
CLOSE	This paragraph following a step-by-step exercise provides instructions for closing open files or programs before moving on to another topic.
1 2	Blue numbered steps guide you through hands-on exercises in each topic.
1 2	Black numbered steps guide you through procedures in sidebars and in expository text.
→	An arrow indicates a procedure that has only one step.
Tip Note	These paragraphs provide a helpful hint or shortcut that makes working through a task easier, or information about other available options.
Important	These paragraphs point out information that you need to know to complete a procedure.
Troubleshooting	These paragraphs warn you of potential missteps that might prevent you from continuing with the exercise.
See Also	These paragraphs direct you to more information about a given topic in this book or elsewhere.
Enter	In step-by-step exercises, keys you must press appear as they would on a keyboard.
Ctrl + Tab	A plus sign (+) between two key names means that you must hold down the first key while you press the second key. For example, "Press Ctrl+Tab" means "hold down the Ctrl key while you press the Tab key."
Program interface elements	In steps, the names of program elements, such as buttons, commands, and dialog boxes, are shown in black bold characters.
User input	Text that you are supposed to type is shown in blue bold characters.
Glossary terms	Terms explained in the glossary are shown in blue italic type.
Paths and emphasized words	Folder paths, URLs, and emphasized words are shown in italic characters.

Using the Book's CD

The companion CD included with this book contains valuable resources and downloads along with a selection of additional electronic books (eBooks) to help you get the most out of your Microsoft Office Accounting 2007 experience.

What's on the CD?

No external practice files, other than those supplied with Accounting 2007, are necessary to complete the exercises in this book.

The CD contains this additional material that didn't fit in the book, but will help you use Microsoft Office Accounting 2007 effectively:

- Chapter 16, "Managing Employee Time and Payroll"
- Chapter 17, "Interacting with Other 2007 Microsoft Office System Applications"
- Chapter 18, "Interacting with Your Accountant"

In addition to the bonus content, the CD contains the following resources:

- *Microsoft Office Accounting Professional 2007* in eBook format
- *Microsoft Computer Dictionary*, 5th edition eBook
- *First Look 2007 Microsoft Office System* (Katherine Murray, 2006) eBook
- *Windows Vista Product Guide* in XPS format
- Microsoft Office Fluent Ribbon Quick Reference

> **Important** The companion CD for this book does not contain the Accounting 2007 software. You should purchase and install that software before using this book.

Minimum System Requirements

To perform the exercises in this book, your computer should meet the following requirements:

- **Processor.** Pentium 1 gigahertz (GHz) or higher; 2 GHz recommended
- **Memory.** 512 megabytes (MB) of RAM; 1 gigabyte (GB) recommended
- **Hard disk.** For the eBooks and downloads, we recommend 3 GB of available hard disk space with 2 GB on the hard disk where the operating system is installed.

> **Tip** Hard disk space requirements will vary depending on configuration; custom installation choices might require more or less hard disk space.

- **Operating System.** Windows Vista or later, Windows XP with Service Pack 2 (SP2), or Windows Server 2003 with Service Pack 1 (SP1) or later
- **Drive.** CD or DVD drive
- **Display.** Monitor with 1024×768 or higher screen resolution and 16-bit or higher color depth
- **Software.** Windows Internet Explorer 7 or later, or Microsoft Internet Explorer 6 with service packs; Microsoft Office Word 2007, Microsoft Office Excel 2007, Microsoft Office Access 2007, and Microsoft Office Outlook 2007 recommended, but you can create templates and perform other tasks by using Microsoft Office 2003 Small Business Edition or later

Installing the Practice Files

The exercises in *Microsoft Office Accounting 2007 Step by Step* use the sample databases that are included when you install Accounting 2007. (Accounting Express 2007 has one sample database; Accounting Professional 2007 has two.) Follow these steps to open a sample database.

1. Start Accounting.

2. In the **Start** dialog box, click **Open a Sample Company**.

3. If you are running Accounting Professional 2007, in the **Select Sample Company** dialog box, click the type of sample file you want to open, and then click **OK**.

Using the Practice Files

Each exercise is preceded by a paragraph or paragraphs that list the sample company files needed for that exercise and explain any preparation you need to take care of before you start working through the exercise, as shown here:

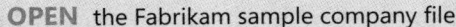

> OPEN the Fabrikam sample company file.

Wherever possible, we made the exercises independent of each other. However, if you choose to do exercises in a sequence other than that presented in the book, be aware that there are exercises in some chapters that depend on other exercises performed earlier in the book. If this is the case, we will tell you where in the book the prerequisite exercises are located.

Reinstalling the Practice Files

If you would like to reinstall the Fabrikam or, in Accounting Professional 2007, Northwind Traders sample company files, you can do so by following these steps:

1. Start Accounting and close any open company files.
2. On the **Start** screen, click **Delete a Company**.
3. In the **Select a Company to Delete** dialog box, click the company file you want to delete, and then click **Open**.
4. In the message box that appears, click **Yes** to verify the deletion.
5. In the **Select a Company to Delete** dialog box, click **Close**.
6. On the **Start** screen, click **Open a Sample Company**.
7. In the **Select Sample Company** dialog box, click the option representing the sample company you want to open, and then click **OK**.

   Accounting creates a new sample company file on your computer.

> **Note** You might also be required to walk through the Upgrade Company wizard in order to re-create the deleted company file.

Getting Help

Every effort has been made to ensure the accuracy of this book and the contents of its CD. If you run into problems, please contact the appropriate source, listed in the following sections, for help and assistance.

Getting Help with This Book and Its Companion CD

If your question or issue concerns the content of this book or its companion CD, please first search the online Microsoft Press Knowledge Base, which provides support information for known errors in or corrections to this book, at the following Web site:

www.microsoft.com/mspress/support/search.asp

If you do not find your answer in the online Knowledge Base, send your comments or questions to Microsoft Learning Technical Support at:

mspinput@microsoft.com

Getting Help with Microsoft Office Accounting 2007

If your question is about Accounting 2007, and not about the content of this Microsoft Press book, please search the Microsoft Help and Support Center or the Microsoft Knowledge Base at:

support.microsoft.com

In the United States, Microsoft software product support issues not covered by the Microsoft Knowledge Base are addressed by Microsoft Product Support Services. The Microsoft software support options available from Microsoft Product Support Services are listed at:

www.microsoft.com/services/microsoftservices/srv_support.mspx

Outside the United States, for support information specific to your location, please refer to the Worldwide Support menu on the Microsoft Help And Support Web site for the site specific to your country:

support.microsoft.com/common/international.aspx

Chapter at a Glance

Tour a sample company in Accounting Express 2007, **page 2**

Tour a sample company in Accounting Professional 2007, **page 6**

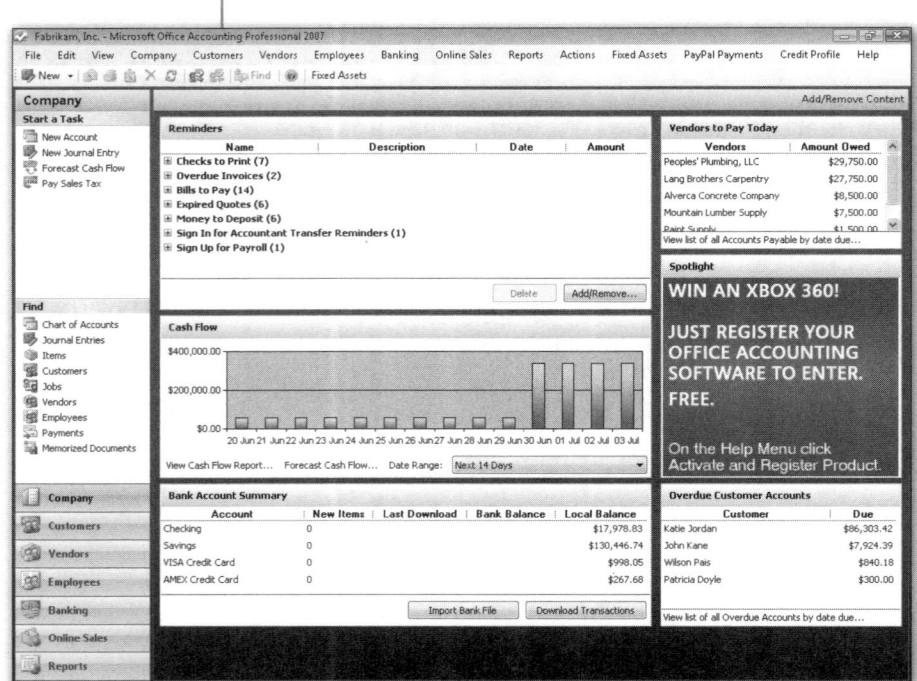

1 Touring a Sample Company

In this chapter, you will:

✔ Tour a sample company in Accounting Express 2007.

✔ Tour a sample company in Accounting Professional 2007.

Microsoft Office Accounting Express 2007 and Microsoft Office Accounting Professional 2007 organize data around companies, creating a set of accounts and reports you can use to manage inventory, track bank transactions, and create quotes. Company files can contain a lot of details that might seem overwhelming to a new user, but a quick look through a sample company file that comes with the program will build your familiarity with Accounting 2007 and show how it helps you manage your business. And, because Accounting 2007 uses the familiar Microsoft Office user interface, you'll be able to learn how to use the application quickly.

In this chapter, you will take a brief tour of both Accounting Express 2007 and Accounting Professional 2007. The goal isn't to show you everything both versions of the program can do; rather, you should come away with an understanding of the capabilities of Accounting Express 2007 and how Accounting Professional 2007 extends those abilities and enables you to manage any type of small to medium-sized business effectively.

> **Important** Accounting Professional 2007 comes with two sample company files: one for a service-based company (Fabrikam, a construction company), and one for a product-based company (Northwind Traders). Accounting Express 2007 comes with only the Fabrikam sample service-based company file.

> **Troubleshooting** Graphics and operating system–related instructions in this book reflect the Windows Vista user interface. If your computer is running Windows XP and you experience trouble following the instructions as written, please refer to the "Information for Readers Running Windows XP" section at the beginning of this book.

Touring a Sample Company in Accounting Express 2007

Though not as powerful as Accounting Professional 2007, Accounting Express 2007 provides a wide range of tools you can use to manage the finances of your small business.

After you enter your business's information into Accounting Express, you'll be able to create quotes, invoices, and receipts, as well as derive important business intelligence by using reports. Furthermore, you'll be able to view, organize, and filter important lists of data, such as the items that you sell or purchase, your customers, and the vendors from whom you purchase goods and services.

In this exercise, you will open a sample company file and view some of the reports, summaries, and projections you can create in Accounting Express.

> **USE** the sample company file supplied with Accounting Express.

1. On the **Start** menu, point to **All Programs**, point to **Microsoft Office**, and then click **Microsoft Office Accounting 2007**.

2. In the **Start** window, click **Open a sample company**. Then on the upgrade screen that appears, click **Close**.

> **Note** Accounting Express might need to convert the sample data file to the current year. If so, the program displays a message box indicating it needs to convert the data; click OK to convert the data, and then restart Accounting Professional.

3. In the **Navigation Pane**, click the **Customers** button.

4. In the **Find** section of the **Customers** home page, click **Customers**.

   The Customer List displays the sample company's active customers.

Customer List								Current View: Active ▾
Active	**Customer Name** ▲	**Address**	**City**	**State**	**Zip Code**	**Phone**	**Fax**	**Balance**
➕ Add a new Customer								
✓	A Datum Corporation	678 Elm Street	Redmond	WA	11052	701 555-0143	701 555-0144	$0.00
✓	Adventure Works	555 Walnut Street	Redmond	WA	11052	701 555-0145	701 555-0146	$0.00
✓	Alpine Ski House	355 Washington Avenue	Bellevue	WA	11054	701 555-0147	701 555-0148	($174.08)
✓	Baldwin Museum of Scie...	989 Technology Way	Redmond	WA	11052	701 555-0148	701 555-0149	$0.00
✓	Blue Yonder Airlines	134 Ash Street	Covington	WA	11056	701 555-0150	701 555-0151	$0.00
✓	Brenda Diaz	5568 Sequoia Road	Lake Forest...	WA	11052	701 555-0154		$0.00
✓	City Power & Light	111 Technology Way	Redmond	WA	11052	701 555-0152	701 555-0153	$200.00
✓	Coho Vineyard	688 Grape Street	Redmond	WA	11052	701 555-0154	701 555-0155	$0.00
✓	Coho Winery	686 Grape Street	Redmond	WA	11052	701 555-0154	701 555-0155	$0.00
✓	Consolidated Messenger	331 Walnut Street	Redmond	WA	11052	701 555-0158	701 555-0159	$0.00
✓	Contoso Pharmaceuticals	5559 Princeton Boulevard	Lake Forest...	WA	11050	701 555-0156	701 555-0157	$0.00
✓	Fourth Coffee	6677 Main Street	Redmond	WA	11052	701 555-0160	701 555-0161	$0.00
✓	Graphic Design Institute	7777 Technology Way	Redmond	WA	11052	701 555-0162	701 555-0163	$0.00
✓	Heidi Steen	1226 Willow Avenue	Redmond	WA	11052	701 555-0134		$360.00
✓	Jeff Low	7815 Poplar Street	Redmond	WA	11052	701 555-0168		$17,038.08
✓	John Kane	1174 Juniper Avenue	Redmond	WA	11052	701 555-0127		$8,652.67
✓	Katherine Berger	7812 Woody Creek	Covington	WA	11054	701 555-0111		$360.00
✓	Katie Jordan	5582 Hemlock Avenue	Redmond	WA	11052	701 555-0126		$94,128.86
✓	Kevin Casselman	8901 Pecan Street	Redmond	WA	11052	701 555-0129		$0.00
✓	Litware, Inc.	6678 Adams Way	Redmond	WA	11052	701 555-0166	701 555-0167	$0.00
✓	Lucerne Publishing	5600 Quail Run	Medina	WA	11058	701 555-0168	701 555-0169	$0.00
✓	Margie's Travel	6788 Main Street	New Castle	WA	11055	701 555-0170	701 555-0171	$0.00
✓	Mark Bebbington	6681 Chestnut Street	Redmond	WA	11052	701 555-0125		$0.00
✓	Northwind Traders	4500 Technology Way	Redmond	WA	11052	701 555-0172	701 555-0173	$0.00
✓	Olivier Lee	7753 Sycamore Street	Redmond	WA	11052	701 555-0165		$0.00
✓	Patricia Doyle	777 Black Oak Drive	Lake Forest...	WA	11052	701 555-0112		$300.00

> **Important** What you see on your screen might not match the graphics in this book exactly. The screens in this book were captured at a resolution of 1024 × 768 pixels with the Windows Vista Basic color scheme. The Windows taskbar is hidden to increase the space available for the program window.

5. In the upper-right corner of the **Customer List**, click the **Current View** button, and then in the list, click **Inactive**.

The Customer List displays only inactive customers.

6. In the **Current View** list, click **Active**.

The Customer List redisplays only active customers.

7. In the **Navigation Pane**, click the **Vendors** button.

The Vendors home page appears.

8. In the **Find** section of the **Vendors** home page, click **Items**.

    The Item List displays items that the sample company currently purchases from vendors.

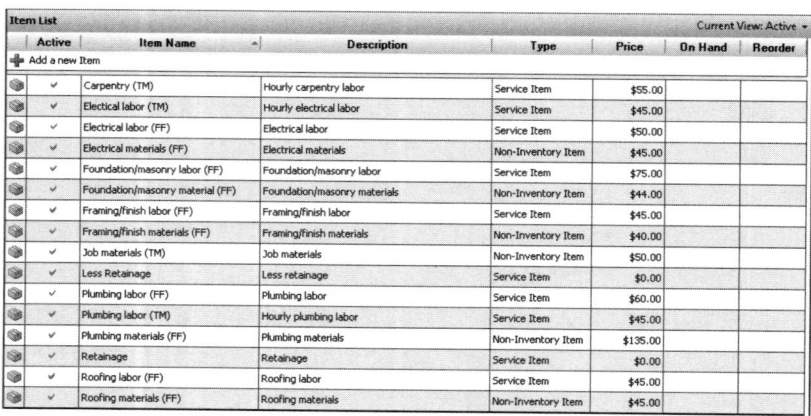

9. In the **Item List**, double-click **Plumbing labor (FF)**.

    The Plumbing Labor (FF) – Service Item form opens.

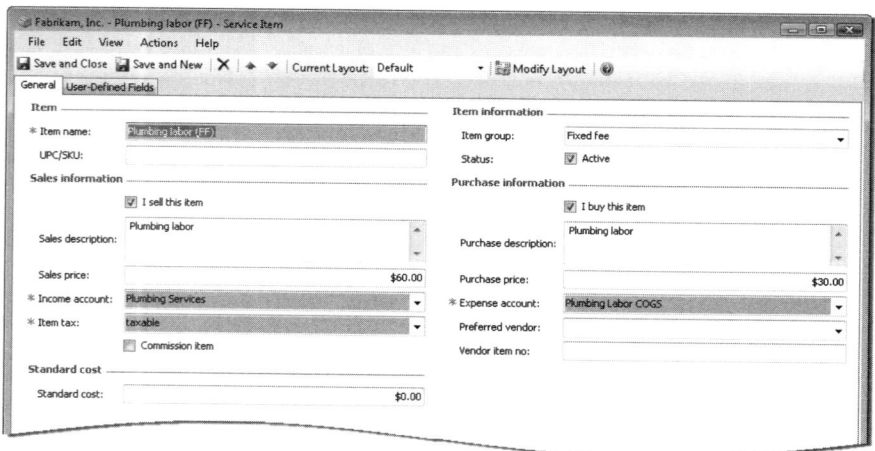

10. On the form window toolbar, click the **Save and Close** button.

    The Service Item form closes.

11. In the **Navigation Pane**, click the **Banking** button.

    The Banking home page appears.

12. In the **More Tasks** section of the **Banking** home page, click **Pay Bills**.

    The Pay Bills dialog box opens, displaying the sample company's current bills.

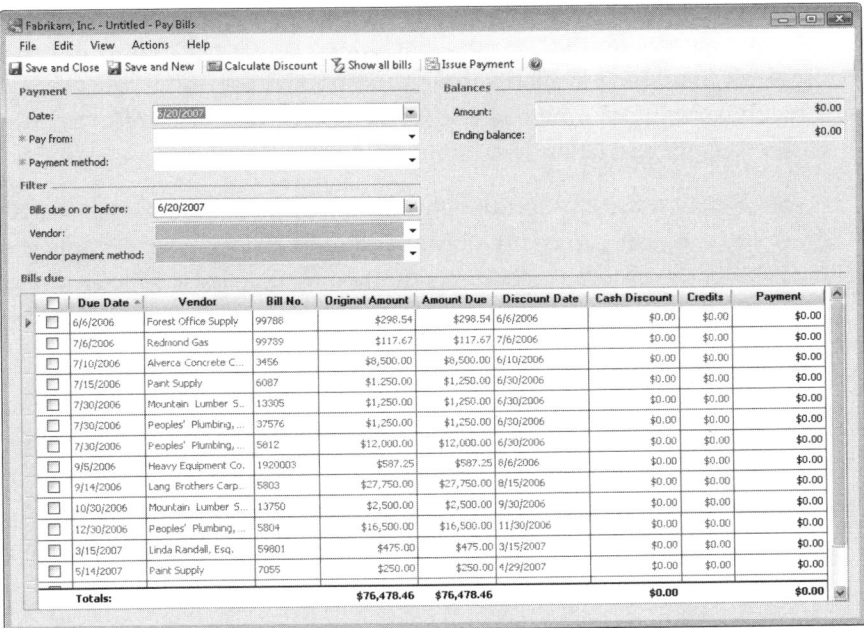

13. In the **Pay Bills** dialog box, click the **Close** button.

Close

14. In the **Find** section of the **Banking** home page, click **Payments**.

    The Payment List appears.

15. In the **Navigation Pane**, click the **Customers** button.

    The Customers home page reappears.

16. On the **File** menu, click **Close Company**.

    The sample company file closes.

Touring a Sample Company in Accounting Professional 2007

Although Accounting Express 2007 will be sufficient for some businesses, investing in Accounting Professional 2007 will greatly enhance your ability to discover actionable business intelligence from your data and to manage your company's operations. For example, Accounting Professional includes a suite of cash flow forecasting and reporting tools that aren't available in Accounting Express. With the cash flow tools, you can look ahead and determine where to focus your collection efforts, how to manage your cash on hand, and when to take on new work.

If you're in a business that routinely bids for work, you'll find that Accounting Professional gives you the ability to create quotes and sales orders, which enable you to record your bids within the program and turn a quote into an invoice directly. You can also record which quotes are rejected and compare the rejected quotes to those that were accepted to facilitate your bidding process.

Accounting Professional also gives you much more flexibility in defining and pricing the goods and services you offer for sale. For example, you can define multiple pricing levels for a single product, which gives you the ability to set prices for your best customers and not have to remember to assign a discount to individual items. If you work with foreign clients, you can handle incoming and outgoing payments in foreign currencies. You can also group a set of items into a single job, which enables you to bill your clients as you reach project milestones.

In this exercise, you will open a sample company file and view some of the reports, summaries, and projections you can create in Accounting Professional.

> **USE** the sample company file supplied with Accounting Professional.
> **BE SURE TO** start Accounting Professional before beginning this exercise.

1. In the **Start** window, click **Open a sample company**.

   The Select Sample Company dialog box opens.

2. In the **Select Sample Company** dialog box, with the **Service based sample company** option selected, click **OK**.

The Fabrikam, Inc. sample data appears. The data file is generated dynamically to fit the current year, so you might see a different summary screen than the one shown here.

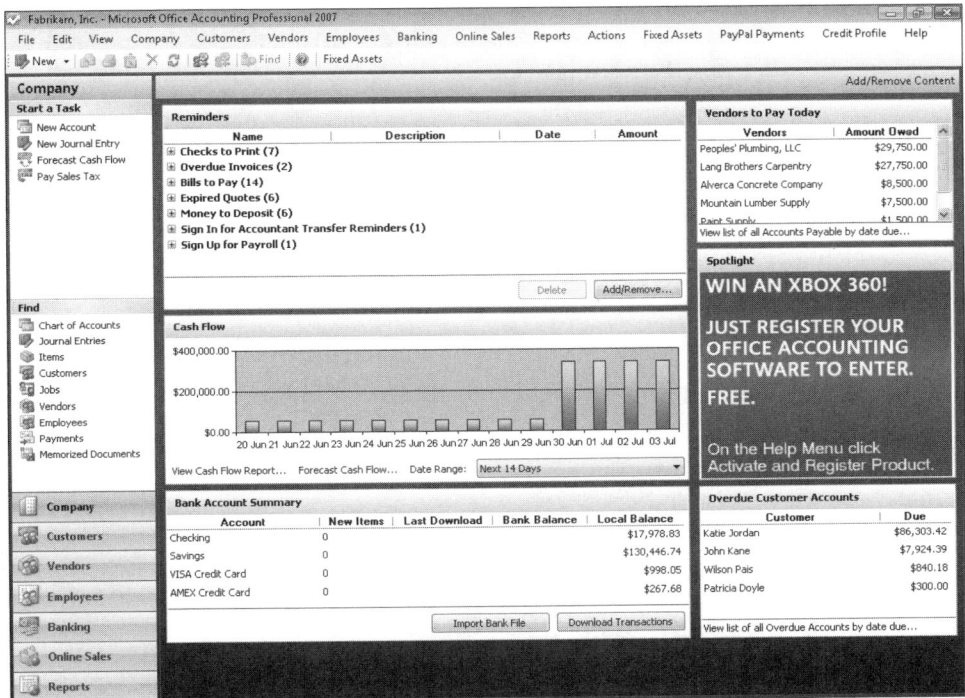

> **Note** Accounting Professional might need to convert the sample data file to the current year. If so, the program displays a message box indicating it needs to convert the data; click OK to convert the data, and then restart Accounting Professional.

3. On the **Company** home page, in the **Cash Flow** pane, click the **Date Range** arrow, and then in the list, click **Next 2 Months**.

The Cash Flow graph changes to reflect the selected time frame.

4. In the **Reminders** pane, expand **Bills to Pay** by clicking the **Show Detail** control (the plus sign).

   Accounting Professional displays the outstanding bills in the Reminders pane.

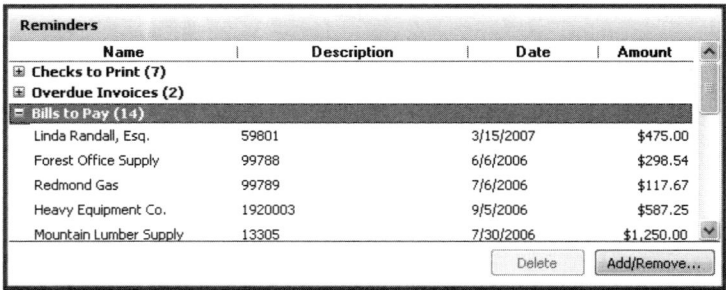

5. In the **Navigation Pane**, click the **Customers** button.

   The Customers home page appears.

6. In the **Find** section of the **Customers** home page, click **Jobs**.

   The Job List appears.

7. Double-click the job for **Brenda Diaz**.

   The Job form opens.

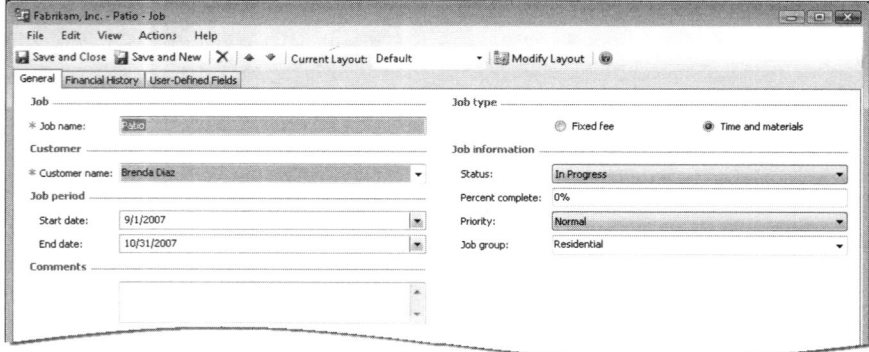

Close

8. In the **Job** form, click the **Close** button.

9. In the **Navigation Pane**, click the **Reports** button.

   The Reports home page appears.

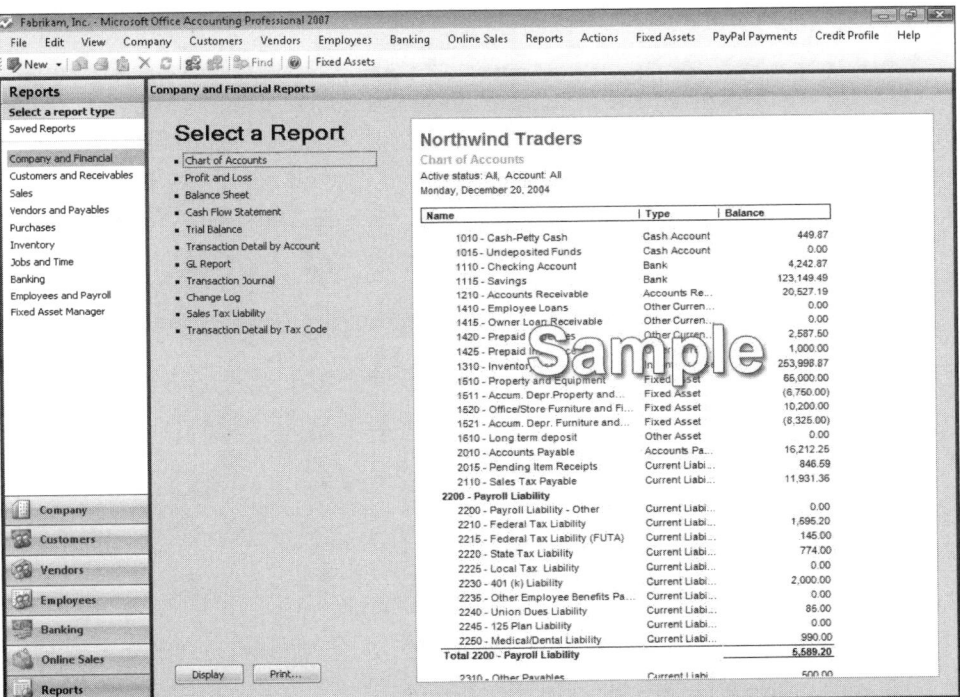

10. In the **Reports** pane, under **Select a report type**, click **Jobs and Time**.

    The Jobs And Time Reports pane displays a list of available reports.

11. Under **Select a Report**, click **Job Estimates vs. Actuals Summary**.

    A sample version of the selected report appears in the preview pane.

12. In the lower-left corner of the **Jobs and Time Reports** pane, click the **Display** button.

Accounting Professional generates the selected report for the sample company.

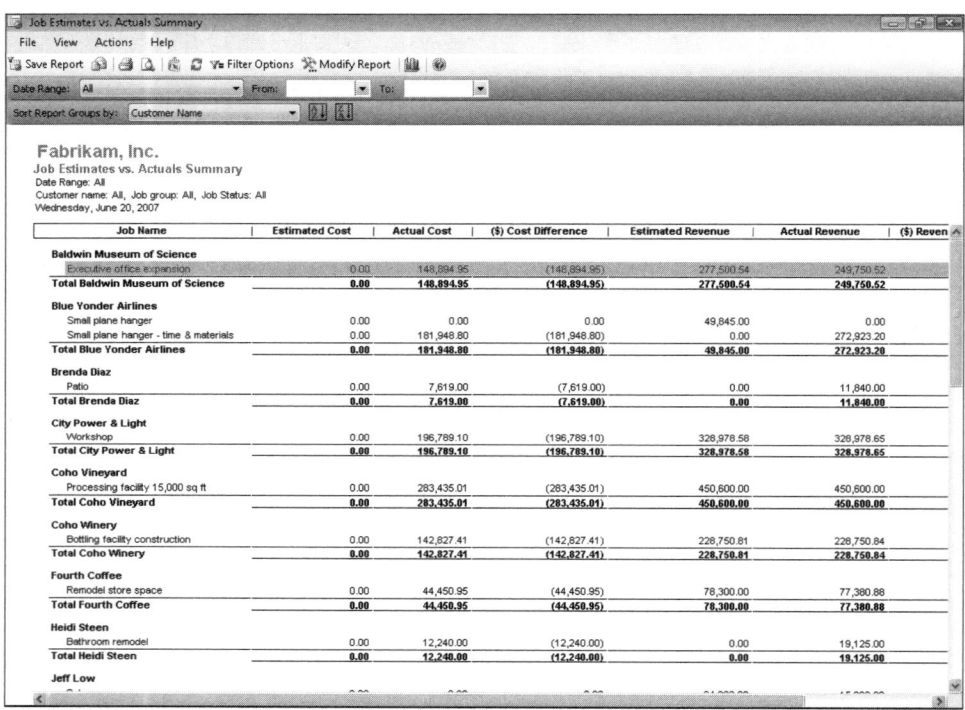

13. On the report window **File** menu, click **Close**.

CLOSE the sample company file, and if you are not continuing on to the next chapter, quit Accounting Professional 2007.

Key Points

- The Navigation Pane provides easy access to the tasks and lists you'll need most often in Accounting 2007.

- You can search for customers, goods and services, vendors, and other business objects by using the lists built into Accounting 2007.

- Accounting Express 2007 provides the basic functionality you need to track a company's finances, but it lacks some advanced capabilities.

- Accounting Professional 2007 offers a complete range of capabilities that help you manage your business effectively.

Chapter at a Glance

Create a company file,
page 20

Manage company data,
page 26

Protect your data files,
page 35

2 Setting Up a New Company

In this chapter, you will learn to:

- ✔ Prepare to set up the accounting system.
- ✔ Create a company file.
- ✔ Manage company data.
- ✔ Protect your data files.

Before you can begin entering your company's financial information into Microsoft Office Accounting 2007, you need to create a file to hold the data. In Accounting 2007, you use the Startup Wizard to create a new company file that contains all of the tools you will need to manage your company's finances. After you create your company file, you can customize it, add user accounts to give your employees access to the data they need to do their jobs, and back up your files to prevent data loss that could cost you many thousands of dollars, and days or weeks of time, to return your company to order.

In this chapter, you will learn what information you need to set up a company, and how to view data from a sample company, create a new company, import data from other programs, manage your company data, and protect your data files.

> **Troubleshooting** Graphics and operating system–related instructions in this book reflect the Windows Vista user interface. If your computer is running Windows XP and you experience trouble following the instructions as written, please refer to the "Information for Readers Running Windows XP" section at the beginning of this book.

Preparing to Set Up the Accounting System (What You'll Need)

After you install Office Accounting 2007, your first step in using the program is to set up a company file. You will use the Company Setup wizard to create your new company file. The wizard will help you establish accurate customer and vendor balances, a complete list of the products and services that you sell, and all the financial account balances necessary for your business. Before you begin working with the Company Setup wizard, though, you need to complete the following three primary preparation steps to assemble data about your company:

- Determine a fiscal year and start date.
- Prepare a trial balance.
- Gather the information that will be required by the Company Setup wizard.

You might be tempted to simply begin setting up your company. But if you prepare before doing so, you'll minimize errors and be up and running much faster, with the best possible accounting system. Let's take a look at each of these steps, examining the information you need and the steps you need to take to assemble it.

Determining a Fiscal Year and Start Date

You should determine the fiscal year and start date of your company, as your earliest step of preparation and before beginning any company set up. This important date will be the date "as of" which you will begin keeping your financial records within Accounting 2007. Your start date will impact the usefulness of the financial information that you collect and put into your new system. The specific point in time that you choose will also determine the extent of the work that you have to do to get Accounting 2007 into shape to benefit your company the most, as you'll see in this section.

The start date you choose should represent a point in time for which you can easily assemble or calculate all the company's financial account balances. Because the start date will serve as the "beginning point" for your accounting system, you can easily see that reports, transactional details, and the like for activities before the start date will not be available from your system. You will enter beginning balances as of the start date you choose, and then you'll add all the transactions that have taken place from the start date up to the current date. If you do this entry correctly, the transactions, added to the beginning balances in each account, will accumulate to complete and accurate current totals.

There are a couple of possibilities that you'll want to consider in choosing your start date. By far, the best choice of a start date to use in setting up your new company is the beginning of an accounting year. While many small businesses' fiscal years are the same as the calendar year, yours may differ based upon the nature of your business or other considerations.

The reason that it is best to use the beginning of your company's accounting year as its start date is that this approach will mean you have the complete financial information for the beginning year in a single accounting system—and you won't have to reconcile data from the previous system with data in Accounting 2007 when preparing reports, filing taxes, and performing other activities that focus on details about a given year's operations. So whatever fiscal year you choose to begin using Accounting 2007, it is best to try to contain that complete year within the single system.

A less attractive, although quite possible, option is to set up your company in Accounting 2007 beginning with a start date of, for example, the beginning of a month other than the first month of your fiscal year. Although this is done fairly often, you can see that it makes for cumbersome reporting of your operations over the fiscal year in question. This is because you have to work with both the old and the new system, somehow, to obtain year-to-date income and expense information, as well as other metrics. This approach is better than simply jumping into a new system on a totally arbitrary date, but keep in mind that it virtually guarantees extra work, cost, and confusion.

Moving to Accounting 2007 at the beginning of an accounting year is the best bet for ease of reporting and other factors. If you have decided to move to Accounting 2007 and are still relatively early within your current business year, it might be easiest to make the cutover retroactively, as of the first of the current year. If you are well into your current year and coming up on a new year soon, it might be best to wait until the first of the year to begin working with the new accounting system. Finally, if you are, for example, somewhere around halfway into your fiscal year, you might want to consider making the jump to Accounting 2007 as of an intermediate beginning date (still targeting the first day of the month), like July 1. This might allow you to get your conversion underway sooner, but keep in mind the considerations you've discovered about this less-than-ideal approach.

Preparing a Trial Balance

Before posting beginning balances in your new company setup, you need to calculate balances "as of" the start date you have chosen—complete and accurate balances that include, for example, amounts you owe vendors and other creditors as of the close of business on that date, and excluding payments that may have come in from customers after the close of business on that date. Your goal, of course, is to capture all transactions (payments you've received, invoices you've created, checks you've written, and so on, summarized by the financial accounts to which they belong) up to and through the close of business on the start date. This way, you can ensure that all activity up to the start date is reflected in each of the balances you post as beginning balances.

You can accumulate your beginning balances in many ways. After you select a fiscal year and start date for your company, you should assemble a trial balance to help you with setup. A trial balance is a worksheet and not a formal financial statement. It serves as a convenient, central place where you can record your beginning balance sheet and income statement account balances. After you assemble this "list of balances," you can easily post one after another to the respective accounts during company setup in Accounting 2007.

You will use your trial balance to record your assets, liabilities, and owner's equity account balances, as well as the year-to-date totals of your income and expense accounts, as of the start date you have chosen for your company. After you capture this information (and balance it, as a further confirmation of its accuracy and completeness), you're ready to begin the process of completing the steps through which the Company Setup wizard guides you. The information in the trial balance can also help you with additional steps you may need to perform after completing the steps of the wizard.

With Accounting 2007 (both Express and Professional), you can import data from your existing accounting application if you are using Intuit QuickBooks. If you do a direct import, from a complete and accurate QuickBooks company that is already in place, then your company will be largely set up for you in Accounting 2007. If you are using QuickBooks, and for some reason are not doing a direct import, or if you are using another small-business accounting system that you believe is completely and accurately set up, you can take a shortcut by generating a trial balance report as of your new start date, and use that information (with perhaps a little tweaking after a good review) either as a complete trial balance or as a tool to help you create a complete trial balance quickly.

See Also For definitions of the accounting terms used in the following discussion, see "Key Accounting Terms and Definitions" in Chapter 3, "Accounting: A Quick Overview."

If you already know your previous accounting system to be incomplete, informal, cash basis only (and you want to move to an accrual system), or some such, you will have to make an effort to accumulate missing or incomplete information. Although you can take many approaches to accomplish this, the following tips surrounding things that most companies have in common might be helpful to you here:

- You'll probably need to perform bank reconciliation(s) as of your chosen start date to get accurate cash balance(s).

- You'll need to perform a summary total of your customers' outstanding invoices to get an accurate and complete accounts receivable balance.

- You'll need to determine historical cost values for most of your other asset accounts, particularly for fixed assets. In addition to knowing the original cost, you should either calculate accumulated depreciation (if you have never done so) or determine the previously reported accumulated depreciation that has been booked against your depreciable assets. (The combination of each asset account and its related "contra-asset," or accumulated depreciation account, gives the net book value of the asset.)

- You'll need to determine what you owe each creditor to assemble the balances of your various liability accounts. Most of these balances can be obtained from the invoice or other statement whose date most closely precedes your start date—with appropriate payment or other adjustments for activity that has transpired between the date of the invoice and your chosen start date.

- You'll often be able to use previous year's tax records (as well as the trial balance your accountant will likely have prepared, with adjustments for things like depreciation, as part of assembling them) as a source for beginning balances, assuming you haven't kept good records before deciding to set your company up in Accounting 2007.

Another reason to ask for these records might be to ensure that the ending numbers reported on the returns agree to the beginning numbers that will wind up in your tax returns for the current year.

> **Tip** You can get your company up and running quickly if you focus on entering only customers and vendors with outstanding balances. This also helps to pare down what might be a huge "graveyard" of customer and vendor accounts upon which no action has occurred for years. The end result, a list of currently active accounts, will help you to "start fresh" with a clean and nimble accounting system.

In general, you calculate the account balances on your trial balance as of the chosen start date, beginning with a statement from the bank, vendor, credit card issuer or other entity. With accounts receivable, you can perform the same process with the latest statement you have sent the customer (or, for customer(s) with which you have recently begun to conduct business, you can simply summarize payments and charges on the account, up to and including your start date), to get to the balance outstanding as of your start date within Accounting 2007.

The best statements to select for this exercise will be those that summarize a period before, but as close as possible to, your start date. You'll then add all transactions that have occurred between the statement date (that is, those payments you have made or transactions you have completed that are not included in the statement balance) and the start date you have selected.

You've probably already become aware of this, but another benefit you realize when you pick a start date that coincides with the beginning of a new year is this: year-to-date income and expense accounts will be at zero, saving you time and effort as you calculate the balances for every other account within your chart of accounts. This is yet another factor that makes it easy to see how much work you can save yourself by choosing a start date that is the first day of a new fiscal year, as opposed to having to calculate all income and expense account balances if the start date falls somewhere in the year other than its first day.

You can find myriad examples of trial balances on the Web, as well as within accounting and other texts. (You can perhaps even find one that is tailored to the kind of business you run.) Small-business resources abound, as well, to provide advice in this and other arenas. Finally, don't overlook your accountant, even if you are paying one only to complete your tax returns each year, for the reasons you've discovered in this chapter as well as for the other services they can offer.

Collecting Information Before Getting Started

The wizard is going to ask you for myriad details about your company bank accounts, credit cards, unreported and unclear transactions, unpaid customer and vendor balances. Moreover, it will provide places to record your company's assets, liabilities, and equity as of the start date from which you intend to begin using Accounting 2007.

You need to collect many things before you begin setting up your company's accounting system, some of which you will be prompted for as you proceed, and some of which you have considered in earlier sections. Among the documents/files that you will almost certainly find helpful are the following:

- Outstanding invoices of your clients or customers as of your selected start date within Accounting 2007.

- Outstanding invoices owed to your vendors as of your selected start date within your new accounting system.

- Your tax returns (federal, state, county/municipal, payroll, and so on) from the prior year. Sometimes returns from more than one year back can be helpful in piecing together beginning balances for the current year and so forth. Moreover, because Accounting 2007 setup requires information about your taxpayer identification number, as well as entity type, your tax forms can be a great, central source for other information items. Finally, information from payroll tax returns can supply information that Accounting 2007 needs if you maintain an employee payroll (even if it's only for yourself).

- Other payroll-related documents from previous accounting years, such as W-2, W-4 and other statements, details about payroll tax deposits and liabilities you have accumulated since your selected start date for the new system, and so forth. Although you have several options for managing payroll within Accounting 2007, as you'll see in chapters that follow, these documents can provide some information that will be useful in more than one place within your accounting system setup.

- Information about your inventory, if applicable. Most important in these details is your cost basis in inventory items that you purchased to resell—what you paid for them, with any adjustments such as shipping and so forth. You have to have this information in your accounting system for anything you later sell, to be able to determine your profits and losses, as well as for other possible uses.

- A list of all the transactions occurring since your chosen start date—for any accounts within your new chart of accounts—to enable you to completely and accurately re-enter activity into Accounting 2007. Although taking the balances off the trial balance alone is fine if you are converting, for example, from another system on the first day of a new fiscal year, if you are converting later in the year, "as if" on the first day of the year, you will likely find the presence of all transactional data for the current year to be ideal.

If you choose to start with balances as of a date other than the beginning of the year (one of the options we discussed earlier) you can simply input the balances and then roll forward with new transactions as of your selected start date and beyond. Just keep in mind the complications this might bring to subsequent reporting for the current year. At a minimum, you might have to base reports upon two systems to get the information you need to report for the entire year.

After you decide your start date in Accounting 2007, prepare or obtain a trial balance as of that start date, and assemble the additional details that you need, you're ready to begin stepping through the Company Setup wizard.

Many steps are involved in preparing to set up your accounting system, but the rewards by far exceed the costs in your time and effort. Taking the steps above, you can make company setup as problem-free as possible. Once you get through the process of setup, you can enjoy all the benefits of your new accounting software. The increased efficiency of your accounting procedures, combined with new capabilities to track, analyze, and improve your financial health, translates directly to a more effective, profitable business. Moreover, the opportunities that Accounting 2007 offers you to add services such as credit card and payroll processing mean the capability to expand your business as it grows, continually improving it to exploit new opportunities that you discover.

Creating a Company File

When you're ready to start tracking your company's information in Accounting 2007, you can use the Startup Wizard to create the company's basic structure. After you have that structure in place, you can fill in details such as customers, products, and services.

Working Through the Accounting Professional Setup Wizard

Setting up a new company in Accounting Professional 2007 is a straightforward but somewhat lengthy affair. To make the setup process easier for you, Accounting Professional helps you define your company by stepping you through the Startup Wizard.

In this exercise, you will use the Startup Wizard to set up your company. All you need to do is answer questions about your company.

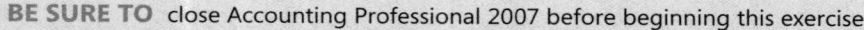

BE SURE TO close Accounting Professional 2007 before beginning this exercise.

1. Start Accounting Professional 2007.

2. In the **Start a Company** section of the **Start** dialog box, click **Set Up a New Company**.

   The Welcome To Company Setup page of the Startup Wizard appears.

3. Read the information on the page, and then click **Next** twice to display the Add Company Details page.

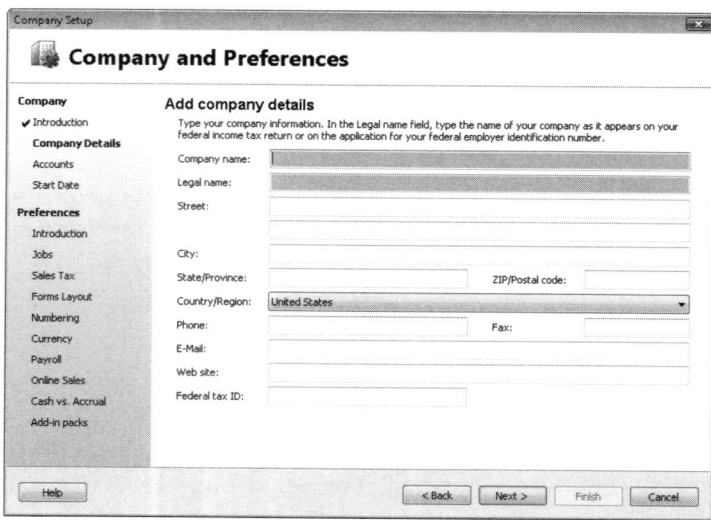

4. Fill in the requested company information, including the Federal Tax ID (also known as an Employer ID Number, or EIN), and then click **Next**.

   The Set Up Accounts page appears.

5. Verify that **Select Your Business Type and Have Accounting 2007 Suggest Accounts** is selected, and then click **Next**.

   The continuation of the Set Up Accounts page appears.

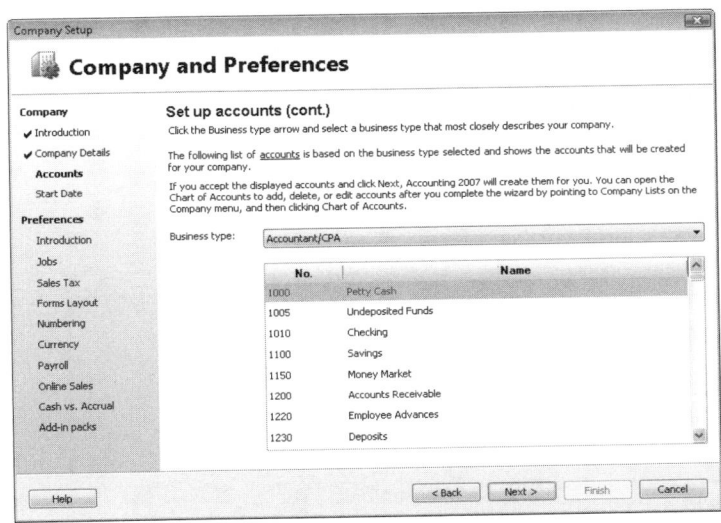

6. In the **Business Type** list, click the appropriate business type.

   The list of accounts changes to reflect your choice.

> **Tip** You might not see a change in the first few accounts (Petty Cash, Undeposited Funds, Checking, and so on), but your choice does change the accounts found later in the list.

7. Click **Next**.

   The Select A Fiscal Year And Start Date page appears.

8. In the **Beginning of the First Fiscal Year** box, select the first day of the fiscal year for which you'll use Accounting 2007.

9. In the **End of the First Fiscal Year** box, select the last day of the fiscal year for which you'll use Accounting 2007.

10. In the **Start Date** box, select the first day of transactions you'll enter into Accounting 2007.

> **Important** The Start Date must occur in the fiscal year you defined earlier.

11. Click **Next** to display the Preferences Introduction page, and again to display the Select Jobs Preferences page.

12. Click **Yes**, and then click **Next**.

    Accounting 2007 enables job tracking and displays the Select Sales Tax Preferences page.

13. Click **No**, and then click **Next**.

    The Select Form Layout Preferences dialog box opens.

14. Click the option that reflects whether your company sells services only, or a mix of products and services, and then click **Next**.

    The Select Numbering Preferences page appears.

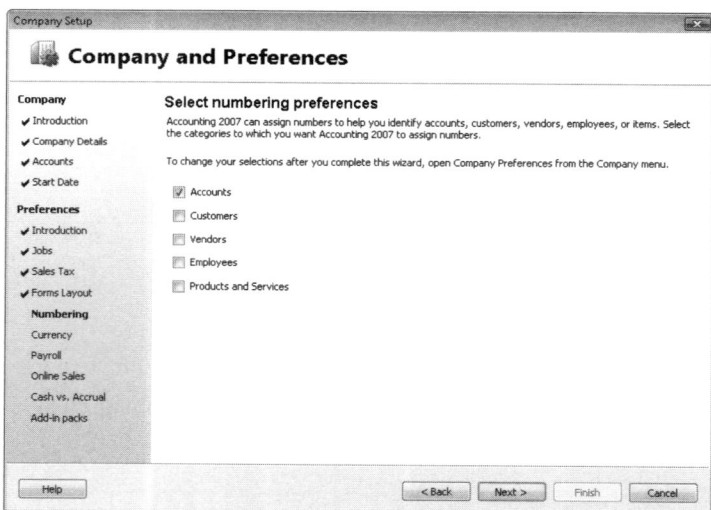

15. Select all of the check boxes on the page, and then click **Next**.

    The Currency Preferences page appears.

> **Tip** Having Accounting 2007 assign numbers to customers, vendors, employees, and products and services gives each of those elements a unique number to which you can refer if you export your data to Microsoft Office Excel or a database program. By giving each employee record a unique number, for example, you can combine a list of employee contact information with a list of sales without having to enter duplicate information into two or more lists.

16. Click **No** to use only one currency, and then click **Next**.

The Set Up Payroll page appears.

17. If you plan to use the **ADP Payroll for Small Business Accounting** service, click **Yes** to have the program remind you to set up your payroll process after you close the wizard. If not, click **No**. After you make your selection, click **Next**.

The Online Sales Preferences page appears.

18. Click **Yes, Enable Online Sales**, and then click **Next**.

The Select Cash Basis Or Accrual Basis Reporting page appears.

19. Select your desired accounting method, and then click **Next**.

The Select Add-In Packs dialog box opens.

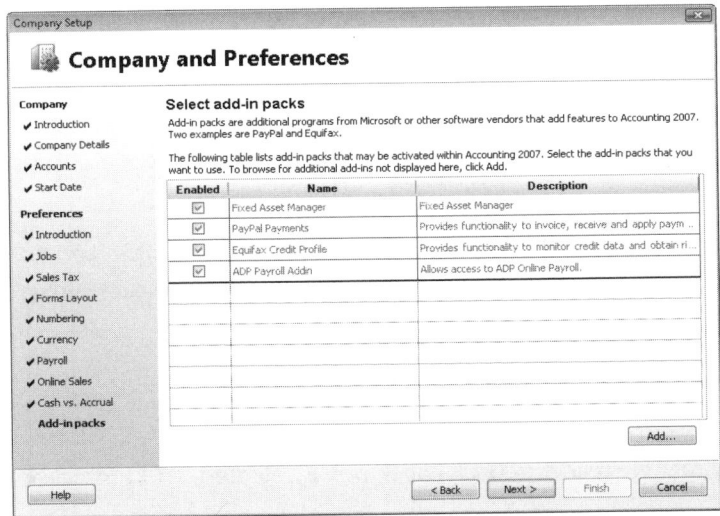

20. Verify that each add-in pack check box is selected, and then click **Next**.

The Company Details And Preferences Completed page appears.

21. Click **Finish**.

The Select Company File dialog box opens.

22. Click **Save** to accept the suggested file name.

Accounting Professional 2007 sets up your company file.

> **Tip** After you set up your company, you can display the Company Setup Checklist by clicking Company Setup on the File menu. Click the category representing the business elements you want to set up to add those elements to your company file.

Working Through the Accounting Express Setup Wizard

Like Accounting Professional, Accounting Express contains a Setup Wizard that enables you to create your company file quickly. You can customize fewer settings than in Accounting Professional, but you still have the ability to set up your company file to meet your company's needs.

In this exercise, you will set up your company by using the Accounting Express Startup Wizard.

> **BE SURE TO** close Accounting Express 2007 before beginning this exercise.

1. Start Accounting Express 2007.

2. In the **Start a Company** section of the **Start** dialog box, click **Set Up a New Company**.

   The Welcome To Company Setup page of the Startup Wizard appears.

3. Read the information on the page, and then click **Next**.

   The Add Company Details page appears.

4. Fill in the requested company information, including the Federal Tax ID (also known as an Employer ID Number, or EIN), and then click **Next**.

   The Select Sales Tax Preferences page appears.

5. Verify that **No** is selected, and then click **Next**.

   The Select Add-In Packs page appears.

6. Verify that each add-in pack check box is selected, and then click **Next**.

   The Company Details And Preferences Completed page appears.

7. Click **Finish**.

   The Select Company File dialog box opens.

8. Click **Save** to accept the suggested file name.

   Accounting Express 2007 sets up your company.

Changing Company Preferences

When you create a company, Accounting 2007 assumes that you want to do things a certain way. In many cases, Accounting remembers your choices from the Startup Wizard. For example, if you chose to assign unique identifying numbers to your accounts, that check box will be selected on the Company tab of the Company Preferences dialog box.

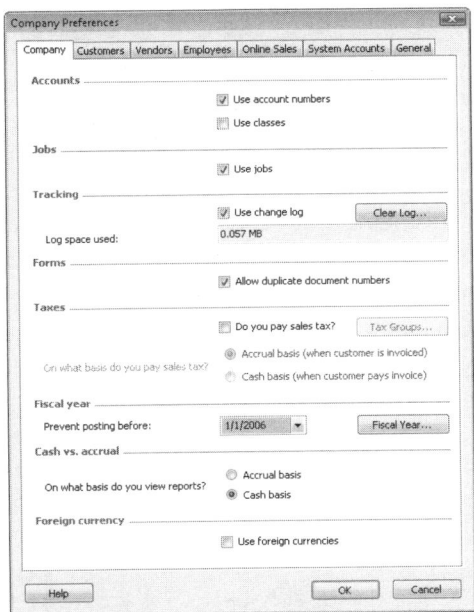

Most of the preferences you can set in the Company Preferences dialog box deal with how you handle customers, vendors, employees, and so on, so it wouldn't make much sense to go into a detailed discussion of the settings at this point. However, you will learn how to change the appropriate settings for each category in the chapters that cover those subjects later in the book.

To change your company preferences:

1. On the **Company** menu, click **Preferences**.

2. In the **Company Preferences** dialog box, use the controls to set or change your company preferences.

3. Click **OK** to save your changes.

Choosing an Entity Type for Your Business

Among many other things you need to consider in starting a new business, your choice of entity type can be very important. Common options for entity type include a sole proprietorship (sometimes called *Schedule C*, after the tax form used to report sole proprietorship earnings), a limited liability corporation (LLC), an S-Corporation, and a "regular" corporation (often referred to as a *C-Corp*). Other entity types, including partnerships, exist as well. Whatever your motivations and objectives, you should get the advice of a professional, particularly a certified public accountant (CPA), to possibly save yourself a great deal of money over the long haul.

A CPA can help you decide which entity type is right for your business. If you are a sole proprietor who seeks to protect your assets in the event of a lawsuit, you will want to consider forming an LLC or another form of corporation. Based upon your profitability, you might want to consider incorporating with an election to be an S-Corporation. This can save you money as a business owner, in addition to providing asset protection. For example, if you take the S-Corp route as a small-business owner, the corporation can pay you, its shareholder, a salary that is less than the "bottom line" you would otherwise report as a sole proprietor on a Schedule C. (A CPA can help you plan and administer a reasonable salary.) The employment taxes incurred by the business under the S-Corp approach would, of course, be computed upon the shareholder's wages, instead of being based upon the bottom line reported on the Schedule C.

Of these and other options that exist, one is probably better for your line of business and personal situation than others. You might be tempted to try to avoid the cost of consulting an expert in your selection of a business type as an inconvenient startup expense. But making the wrong choice of entity type for your business, just like choosing an inappropriate accounting method or failing to develop a good business plan, can have devastating effects on your future operations and profitability.

Managing Company Data

If you've been in business for a while, it's possible that you won't have to enter your company's data into Accounting 2007 directly. Instead, you might be able to import data from another Accounting or Small Business Accounting company file, or from a file you maintained in another accounting program. You can also export data from an Accounting 2007 or Small Business Accounting file to an XML file, which you can then import into Accounting 2007 or another program that can handle XML data.

Importing Company Data

Before you undertake the steps to import company data from another system, you should think about a couple of items first. You should consider account mapping between the previous system and your new Accounting 2007 company, and whether chart redesign is something you might want to consider while you're making changes.

Account Mapping Considerations

When you perform a direct import from one system to another, you typically recreate the same chart of accounts in the target system and populate those accounts with the transactions contained within the source system. Mapping in situations like this is straightforward—accounts are mapped to essentially identical accounts, as the original chart structure, complete with account transactions, is replicated within the new system.

However, you may find yourself importing transactional data to a company you have already set up, and that contains different accounts. As an example, accounts that do the same things may have different names, two or more accounts within the source system might be combined into a single account within the target system (for example, due to a change in the way you want to account for something prospectively), and so forth. In these cases, mapping becomes an important consideration. You have to tell Accounting 2007 where to put any transactions affected by account changes of this type.

Chart Redesign in Conjunction with Import from Another System

A redesign of your chart of accounts might make sense when converting to Accounting 2007. Reasons you might want to consider such a redesign might be to update names of accounts to more accurately reflect their meaning from a business perspective, to eliminate accounts that have historically not been used (say they were accounts within a "template" company, set up via a wizard in the previous system, which have no relevance within your business), or you may be aware of new lines of business that you expect to bring online in the current year that simply have not existed before.

Making these modifications prior to an import will afford you even more efficiency in cutting over to a new company. While the new chart of accounts will need to be created within the target system, and then properly mapped to the chart of accounts within the source system, this will certainly mean a more efficient conversion if all is planned out well. And while you might decide to take another approach entirely, a system conversion can be an opportune time to consider chart redesign.

A Word About Comparability

You will almost certainly become aware of opportunities to improve the way you account for your business as a part of converting between accounting systems. You are likely to want to make changes in your chart of accounts while you're setting up your company and, in many cases (such as eliminating accounts in the source system that contain no transactions) options for improvement become evident. Although this might be the case, you should always keep comparability in mind anytime you find yourself mapping between source and target accounts.

Regardless of which accounting system you have used in previous years, you will want reported account balances to be comparable, with regard to meaning of what the account contains. If you decide to convert your system to Accounting 2007, you will want to map your accounts so that what was, for example, classed as a certain inventory group remains in inventory (even if it is classed as another "type")—and doesn't wind up in "other assets," or the like. If you map transactions incorrectly, you might wind up with reports that are confusing, due to their incomparability to those of a prior period. Don't let this happen in your new accounting system.

Importing Data from Microsoft Money

Microsoft Money Home & Business Edition provides a wide range of tools you can use to manage your personal and small-business finances, but it lacks many of the powerful features, such as quote and online sales, that are available in Accounting 2007. If you've outgrown Microsoft Money, you can transfer your data to Accounting 2007 in just a few steps.

In this exercise, you will import data from Microsoft Money into Accounting 2007.

> **BE SURE TO** install Microsoft Money on your computer and start Accounting 2007 before beginning this exercise.

1. In the **Start** dialog box, click **Import Data from Microsoft Money**.

   The Welcome page of the Convert From Microsoft Money wizard appears.

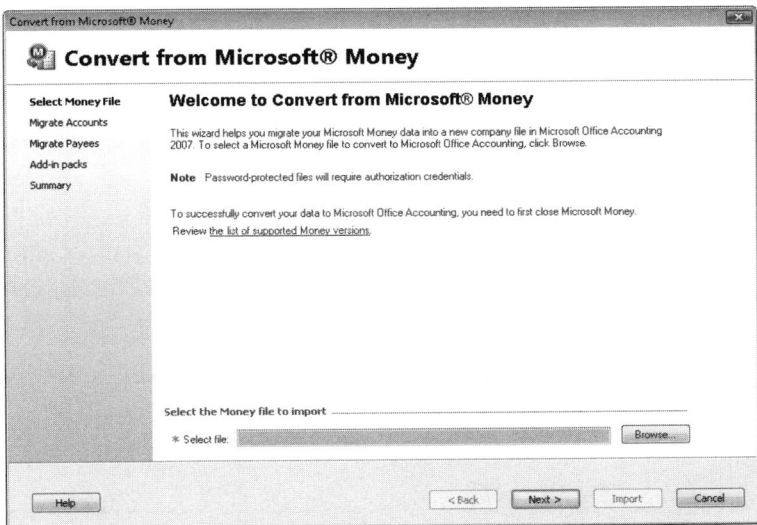

2. Click **Browse**.

   The Select File dialog box opens.

3. Navigate to the folder that contains the Microsoft Money file you want to import data from, click the file, and then click **Open**.

   The Select File dialog box closes.

4. Click **Next**.

   The Microsoft Money File Authentication dialog box opens.

5. Type your credentials in the dialog box, and then click **Sign-In**.

   The dialog box closes and the Migrate Accounts wizard page appears.

6. Select the **Migrate** check boxes for the accounts you wish to migrate, and then click **Next**.

   The Migrate Payees page appears.

7. Select the **Migrate as Vendor** or the **Migrate as Customer** check box as appropriate for each payee.

8. Click **Next**.

   The Select Add-In Packs page appears.

9. Verify that all of the check boxes are selected, and then click **Next**.

   The Data Pending Migration page appears.

10. Click **Import**.

    Accounting 2007 imports your Microsoft Money data.

Importing Data from QuickBooks

If you've previously used Intuit QuickBooks to handle your company's accounting, you'll find the transition to Accounting 2007 quick and painless. Accounting can import your data with just a few mouse clicks.

> **Important** You will need to verify within QuickBooks that you want the program to allow Accounting 2007 to access the data file. The specific messages and wizard steps you see depend on which version of QuickBooks you were using, but you should always select the option that indicates QuickBooks should allow Accounting to access its data even if QuickBooks isn't running.

In this exercise, you will use the Convert From QuickBooks wizard to import company data from QuickBooks to Accounting 2007.

> **BE SURE TO** install QuickBooks on your computer and start Accounting 2007 before beginning this exercise.

1. In the **Start** dialog box, click **Import Data from QuickBooks**.

   The Convert From QuickBooks wizard starts.

2. Click **Next**.

   The Select Master Records page appears.

3. Verify that all of the check boxes are selected, and then click **Browse**.

   The Select File dialog box opens.

4. Click the file you want to import data from, and then click **Open**.

   The Select File dialog box closes.

5. Click **Next**.

   The Access And Migrate Your Data page appears.

6. Click **Allow Access**.

   Windows runs the QuickBooks program.

7. Accept the QuickBooks security messages, allowing Accounting to access the file even if QuickBooks is not running.

8. In the **Convert from QuickBooks** wizard, click **Next**.

   The Company Details page appears.

9. Type the company's details into the available fields, and then click **Next**.

   The Select Add-In Packs page appears.

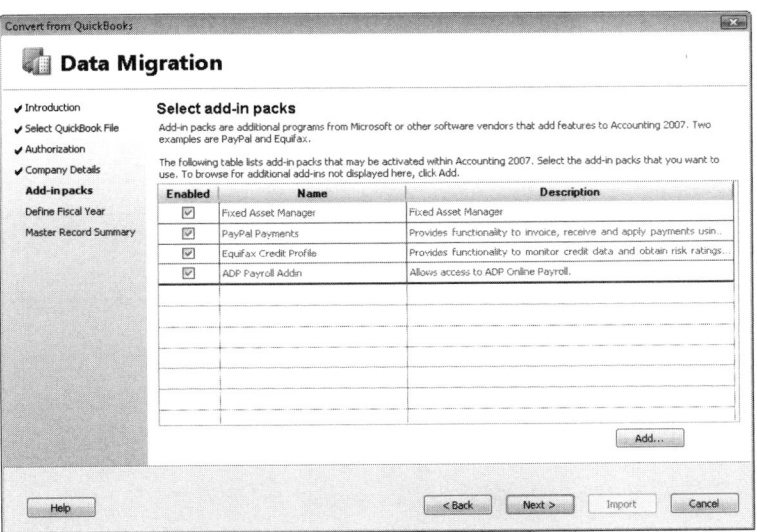

10. Verify that all four check boxes are selected, and then click **Next**.

    The Define Fiscal Year page appears.

11. In the **Beginning of the First Fiscal Year** box, select the first day of the fiscal year for which you'll use Accounting 2007.

12. In the **End of the First Fiscal Year** box, select the first day of the fiscal year for which you'll use Accounting 2007.

13. Click **Import**.

    Accounting imports your data.

14. Click **Finish**.

    Your company file now appears in Accounting 2007.

Importing Data from Excel

Many small businesses track their transactions in Microsoft Office Excel workbooks. Excel provides many powerful tools you can use to analyze your company's data, but it would take a lot of custom programming to perform in Excel even the simplest tasks you can perform in Accounting 2007. It makes more sense to record your business transactions in Accounting and export the data you want to analyze to Excel.

See Also For more information about exporting data to Excel, see Chapter 17, "Interacting with Other 2007 Microsoft Office System Applications," on the CD.

In this exercise, you will import data from Excel into Accounting 2007.

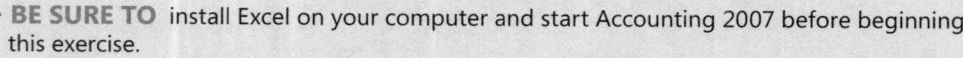

BE SURE TO install Excel on your computer and start Accounting 2007 before beginning this exercise.

1. In Accounting 2007, on the **File** menu, point to **Utilities**, and then click **Import**.

   The Import Data Wizard starts.

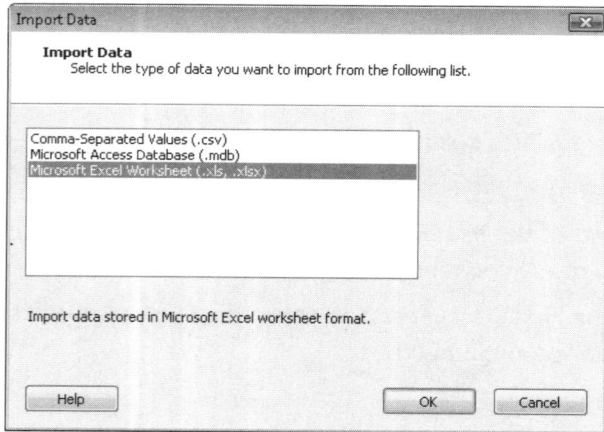

2. Click **Microsoft Excel Worksheet (.xls, .xlsx)**, and then click **OK**.

3. On the **Select source file** page, click **Browse**.

   The Select File dialog box opens.

4. Locate and click the spreadsheet that you want to import, and then click **Open** to return to the Import Data Wizard.

5. In the **Options** section of the **Select source file** page, click either the option to import duplicate records or the option to not import duplicate records, and then click **Next**.

The Select Destination Account Type page appears.

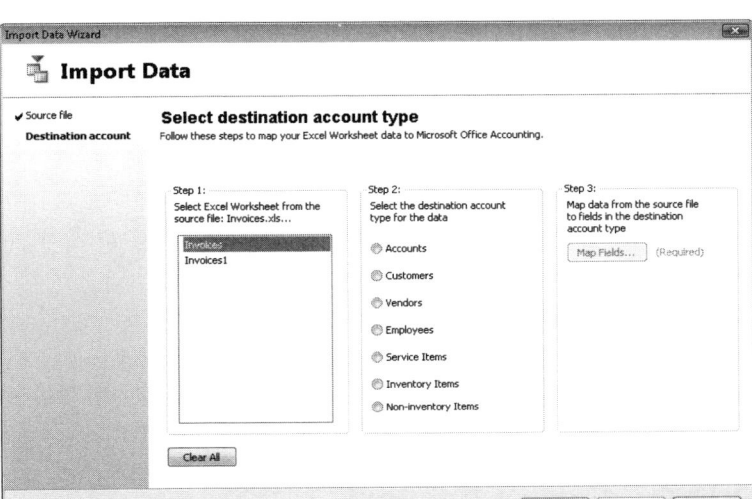

6. In the **Step 1** pane, select the worksheet that contains the account data.

7. In the **Step 2** pane, select the destination account type.

8. In the **Step 3** pane, click **Map Fields**.

   The Map Fields dialog box opens.

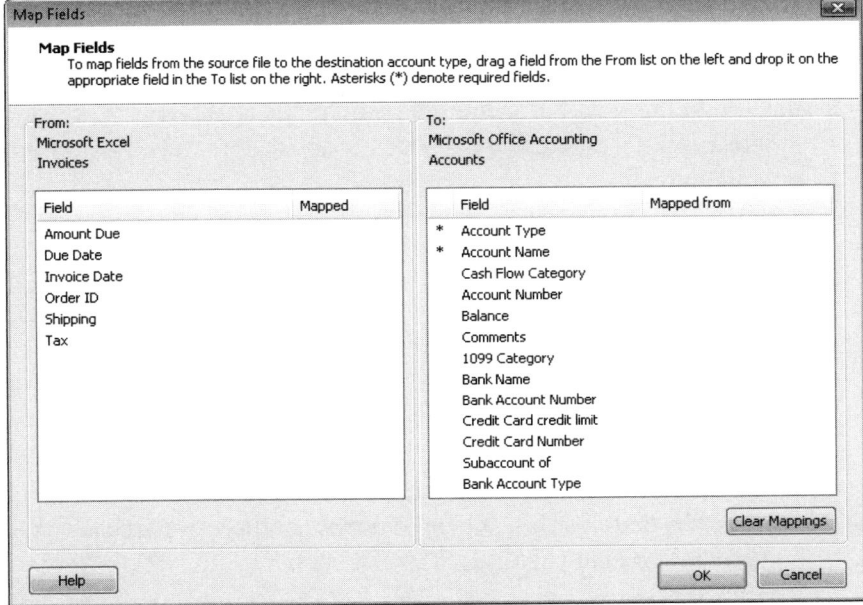

9. Drag each field you want to map from the **From** pane to the corresponding destination account in the **To** pane.

> **Tip** Accounting 2007 will try to map the fields that have the same name. When you map a field, a check mark appears under the **Mapped** column in the **From** pane. In the **To** pane, the mapped field name appears in the **Mapped From** column.

10. Click **OK** to return to the Import Data Wizard, and then click **Next**.
11. On the **Import data** page, click **Next**.

    The wizard imports your data into Accounting 2007.
12. On the **Finish import** page, click **Finish**.

    The wizard closes.

Defining Multiple Companies

With Accounting 2007, you can create multiple company files to reflect your business interests. You do need to go through the legal steps to create a separate company, but after you've done the necessary legal work, you can step through the Company Setup wizard to create a new company file.

> ### When a New Company Might Be a Good Idea
>
> The capability to have multiple companies in Accounting 2007 offers lots of flexibility as your business grows—even, perhaps, to the point of developing into more than one line of business. Sometimes there might be legal, tax, or competitive advantages in setting up a separate company to manage a certain segment of your business operations.
>
> As an example, let's consider the case of Colin, who does high-end carpentry work for relatively wealthy households on a contract basis. Wanting to maintain the business that he loves (which can be a little unpredictable), but also realizing that he needs to build sound revenue streams to provide consistent cash flow for his family, he identifies a new opportunity that, in many ways, is complementary to what he already does. He accepts an invitation to install prefabricated assemblies purchased by customers of a major building materials supplier, who agrees to refer customers to him within his geographical region, among other benefits. (The retailer wants to offer installation as an inducement to customers to purchase its out-of-the-box, home improvement solutions.)

If you encounter and exploit an opportunity like this, you might consider, as Colin soon did, setting up the new revenue stream within a separate business—instead of simply lumping it all together in a single set of books as "contractor revenue." Among other benefits, setting up the second form of contracting as separate from his more "personal" line of work might mean making it easier to meet the regular reporting requirements of the retailer—without having to back out transactions from the "other" business (which Colin wants to keep private anyway). Moreover, housing the second form of contracting within a second company might mean that Colin could set it up as a separate form of business entity—say a regular "C" corporation—for various tax and liability reasons. He could therefore leave the original business within what was, in his opinion, the more appropriate form of a Sub-S corporation, which flows directly to his personal tax return.

Protecting Your Data Files

Regardless of whether your company sells $10,000 or $10 million in products and services in a year, you must ensure that nothing happens to your company's data! If you lose your records for a year, the absolute best thing that can happen is that you have to enter the data again. Yes, that's the best case. The worst-case scenario is that you can't find some of your records and you're unable to reconstruct what happened. You need to make several backup copies of your data, not just one!

Accounting 2007 stores data in seven separate files. The following table summarizes those files' extensions and their roles in the program.

Extension	Description
.sbd	The data file, stored by default in the SQL Server folder (*Program Files\ Microsoft SQLServer\MSSQL.1\MSSQL\Data*).
.sbc	The company file, a shortcut pointing to the location of the data file, stored by default in the *Documents\Small Business Accounting\Companies* folder of the administrator who set up your company in Accounting 2007.
.sbl	An SQL log file, generated when you create a new company or restore a backup file to a new company. It is stored by default in the SQL server folder (*Program Files\Microsoft SQLServer\MSSQL.1\MSSQL\Data*).
.log	A log file, generated by migrating QuickBooks data, by repairing a data file, by upgrading your software, and by accessing online banking or payroll processing by ADP, if you have selected Log Online Activities in Company Preferences. It is stored by default in the *Documents\Small Business Accounting\Logs* folder of the administrator who set up your company in Accounting 2007.

Extension	Description
.sbb	An uncompressed backup file, generated when you upgrade your software or extracted when you open the compressed (.zip) file in the *Documents\Small Business Accounting\Backups* folder of the administrator who set up your company in Accounting 2007. Create a backup file to protect your company data, to send to your accountant, to import into a new company file, or when moving Accounting 2007 to a different computer.
.zip	A compressed backup file, stored by default in the *Documents\Small Business Accounting\Backups* folder of the administrator who set up your company in Accounting 2007.
.ate	A compressed backup file, created for the export of your company's Accounting 2007 data to your accountant and stored by default in the *Documents\Small Business Accounting\Transfers* folder of the administrator who set up your company in Accounting 2007.
.ati	A compressed backup file, created by your accountant for the transfer of updated company data back to your *Documents\Small Business Accounting\Transfers* folder.

Troubleshooting If your data file is corrupted and you cannot open it, display the Windows taskbar, click the Start button, click All Programs, click Microsoft Office, click Microsoft Office Accounting 2007 Tools, and then click Data Tools. In the Microsoft Office Accounting Data Utilities window, click Rebuild to regenerate your company data file.

Creating a Backup File

You should back up your company files daily and write the files to a CD or DVD that you store somewhere outside your office. Too many backup copies have been lost to fires that both burned the computer that contained the original data and melted the backup CD. A safe deposit box at a bank is a great place to store your backup copies.

In this exercise, you will create a backup copy of a company data file.

OPEN the Fabrikam sample company file.

1. On the **File** menu, point to **Utilities**, and then click **Data Utilities**.

   The Microsoft Office Accounting Data Utilities dialog box opens.

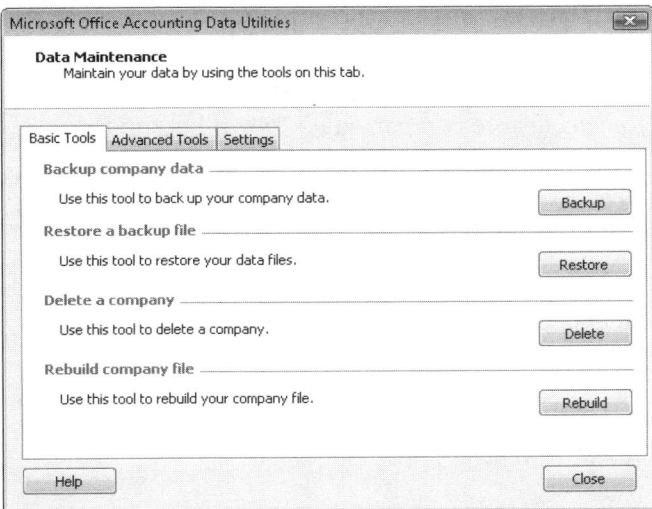

2. On the **Basic Tools** tab, click **Backup**.

   The Backup dialog box opens.

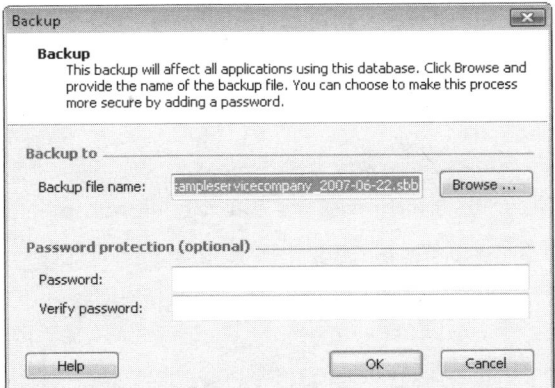

3. If desired, type a password for the file in the **Password** field, and then type the same password in the **Verify Password** field.

4. Click **OK**.

   Accounting creates a backup data file.

5. Click **OK** to dismiss the confirmation message box that appears.

6. Click **Close**.

   The Microsoft Office Accounting Data Utilities dialog box closes.

Restoring Data from a Backup File

If you need to restore your data from a backup file, you can do so quickly.

In this exercise, you will restore company data from a backup file.

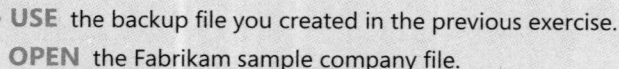

> **USE** the backup file you created in the previous exercise.
> **OPEN** the Fabrikam sample company file.

1. On the **File** menu, point to **Utilities**, and then click **Data Utilities**.

   The Microsoft Office Accounting Data Utilities dialog box opens.

2. On the **Basic Tools** tab, click **Restore**.

   The Database Restore dialog box opens.

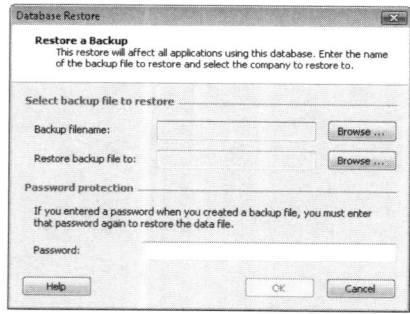

3. Click the **Browse** button to the right of the **Backup Filename** field.

   The Select Backup File To Restore dialog box opens.

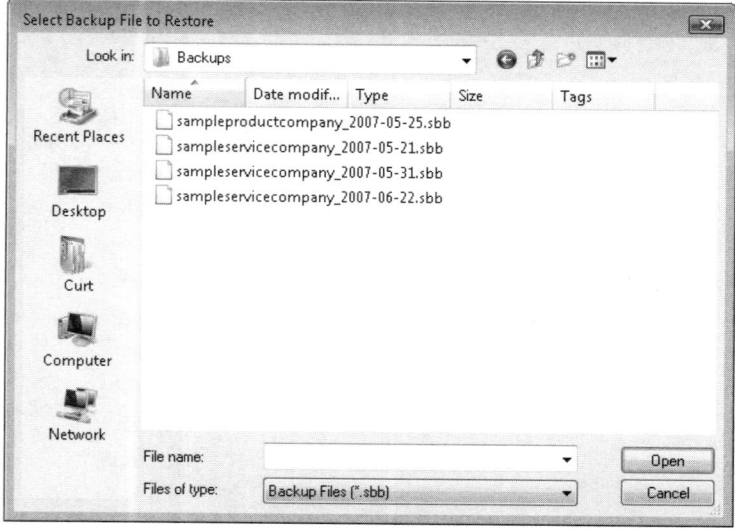

4. Click the file you want to restore, and then click **Open**.

   The Select Backup File To Restore dialog box closes.

5. Click the **Browse** button to the right of the **Restore Backup File To** field.

   The Select Company File dialog box opens.

6. Click the file you want to overwrite or type the name of a new file in the **File Name** field.

7. Click **Save**.

8. If the file is password protected, type its password in the **Password** field.

9. Click **OK**.

   Accounting restores the file. The Restore Complete message box appears.

10. Click **OK** to dismiss the confirmation box.

11. Click **Close**.

   The Microsoft Office Accounting Data Utilities dialog box closes.

Archiving Transactions from Past Fiscal Years

After you've been in business for a few years, it's likely that your Accounting company file will have become quite large. Large company files take longer to load and update, so you should consider archiving records from previous fiscal years in a separate file. However, if you refer to records from previous fiscal years frequently, you should probably not archive them.

> **Important** Running the Compress Data Wizard compresses your vendor documents and results in the loss of vendor 1099 data, which means that you can't generate accurate 1099 reports after you compress the data. You can only run the Compress Data Wizard on a closed fiscal year, but be sure that you've run all of the tax-related reports you'll need before compressing your data.

In this exercise, you will archive the previous fiscal year's transactions.

> **OPEN** the Fabrikam sample company file.

1. On the **File** menu, click **Compress Data**.

   The Compress Data wizard starts.

2. Follow the instructions in the **Compress Data** wizard.

3. Click **Finish**.

Accounting archives your transactions in a separate file.

CLOSE the sample company file, and if you are not continuing on to the next chapter, quit Accounting Professional 2007.

Data Retention Considerations

Your consistent, organized retention of important documents is an important part of managing your own business. Not only do the documents serve as a basis for much of your input into your accounting system, but many entitle you to tax deductions and other important benefits. Moreover, these documents may become critical in your defense of deductions, your justification of insurance claims, and the like. You will want to develop good record retention habits, particularly with documents related to the following areas:

- **Receipts.** You'll want to record and retain information about all receipts (whether taxable or not) to properly class them for tax and reporting purposes. Say you are paid for an asset damaged by a trucking company: it is unlikely that this receipt would be properly treated as income, and so it should be separated from regular business revenue within your accounting system. If you don't record receipts like this separately from your business revenues—and if you don't retain proof of their true nature—the IRS or state taxing authorities might come along later and class the corresponding deposits as unreported income.

- **Payments you make.** In addition to vendors and creditors, your business will likely pay employees and/or contractors, as well as others. Recording payments in detail is as critical as recording your receipts properly. Retaining support for the purchases, services, and even the relationships involved with your payments can become critical in showing proper deductibility, supporting valuations for the products you sell or depreciate as fixed assets, or supporting the values you report on W-2s or 1099s. (The value of payments to employees can also impact numerous payroll taxes and so forth, as well). The IRS uses specific guidelines to determine a person's status as an employee or a contractor. Refer to the appropriate IRS publications to understand the rules, and to ensure you retain the records required to support the way you account and report for these relationships. Be sure to consult an accountant in setting up these relationships as well, both for planning and reporting purposes.

- **Expenses.** Whether you class them as direct business expenses or "other" expenses (those "less direct" expenses, where you buy equipment, as an example, that you hope will help you to generate revenue in the future), you should always retain support for the expenses you record, noting particularly the date and type of the expense, but other details as well. It can be difficult to reconstruct the purpose of an expense at the end of a busy year, so you should make it a consistent habit to capture these details as near to the time of the expenditure as possible, and to keep the supporting documents together in a central, safe place.

- **Assets.** Your retention of supporting documents for the assets information you record in your accounting system can be critical from several perspectives. You depreciate the original cost of equipment whose life is expected to be greater than a single year to spread its cost over the time it is in operation, matching that cost to the revenue generated. Because depreciation, accumulated depreciation, and net book value (original cost less accumulated depreciation) are factors with fixed assets, you'll want to get into the habit of capturing not only specific identification information, as well as purchase date and price (including shipping, installation, and other fees required in getting the asset into operation), but you'll want to be able to support other items you report, as well. These include the date you put the asset into actual service in your company, and the amount of time the asset is used in the business (as opposed to any personal use).

Keeping records and supporting documents is important to justify your treatment of your activities in tax filings and the like. For suggested retention times, see IRS and state tax agency publications, as well as small-business sites throughout the Web.

Key Points

- Invest your time and resources by consulting a certified public accountant to determine the best entity type for your business, whether that be a sole proprietorship, subclass "S" corporation, or subclass "C" corporation.

- Be sure to gather the recommended information before you create your company. The time you spend preparing to create your company file will save you much more time in the future.

- You can import data from many other programs into Accounting.

- Back up your company data frequently, and copy your backup files to a CD or DVD that you store in a secure off-site location, such as a bank safe deposit box.

3 Accounting: A Quick Overview

In this chapter, you will learn to:

✔ Define accounting as a practical process.

✔ Use key accounting-related terms correctly.

✔ Integrate basic accounting concepts, principles and policies.

✔ Understand your recording and reporting duties as a small-business owner, and how Accounting 2007 makes the job easier.

All businesses need to keep accurate records, but these days, the complexity and sales volumes of even the smallest companies can outstrip the capabilities of paper-based and spreadsheet-based record-keeping systems. Rather than trying to bend generalized programs to your needs, you can turn to specialized software that is designed to handle your company's financial data.

Microsoft Office Accounting 2007 is a program with which you can record, analyze, and report on your company's income, assets, and expenses. For example, you can have Accounting list your total sales for a month, record the time individual employees spend on your company's projects, and identify customers who are more than 30 days late paying their bills. Accounting 2007 comes with a wide variety of reports you can use to summarize your company's operations. These summaries can help you to identify areas of interest; you can then drill down into the details to find areas where you can improve your company's operations.

In this chapter, you will learn about accounting as a process, learn key terms and concepts you'll encounter throughout this book and in general accounting literature, and learn ways in which Accounting 2007 enables you to fulfill your record-keeping duties as a small-business owner.

> **Troubleshooting** Graphics and operating system–related instructions in this book reflect the Windows Vista user interface. If your computer is running Windows XP and you experience trouble following the instructions as written, please refer to the "Information for Readers Running Windows XP" section at the beginning of this book.

What Is Accounting?

Introduced in many basic accounting texts as the "language of business," the accounting process is a tool to help your business measure results and make decisions. It enables you to establish goals, and to distill opportunities and challenges to common, understandable units. Because accounting is a universal tool, your understanding of this "language," in cluding its basic concepts and principles, is key to your success in virtually any venture you undertake.

Practical accounting is the process of recording, classifying, summarizing, reporting, and assessing a company's business transactions. By recording transactions accurately, you can analyze your company's performance, plan future endeavors, and fulfill your tax filing and payment obligations, among many other functions. Understanding fundamental concepts is vital to your effective use of any accounting system, from the simplest "set of books" (for example, a simple check register and perhaps a hand-written journal) to a small business system as powerful and flexible as Accounting 2007, which can form a complete record of all the activities of your business. Your end rewards include a system that supports you with a comprehensive view containing every aspect of your operations. This powerful business intelligence supports you in your analysis of trends and your insightful identification of future prospects and opportunities.

Because these fundamentals support your success directly, you may find a brief overview helpful before setting up and using your new accounting system.

> **Warning** Do not wait until the end of an accounting period to record your transactions! The longer you wait to record your credit card charges, payments received, and sales tax collected, the more likely it is that you'll forget something or make a mistake.

Understanding a handful of simple rules can mean insight into how things work within the universal accounting framework. Let's start with some basic accounting concepts.

The Duality Concept (Double-Entry Bookkeeping)

With your accounting system, you can record, summarize, analyze, and report the transactions of your business. After they're recorded, the myriad transactions you undertake are summarized (Accounting 2007 does much of the heavy lifting involved, of course), and from the summarized information you can perform effective analysis and reporting. But at the heart of it all is the recording of transactions, and for centuries (at least within the context of virtually any business accounting system) double-entry accounting has been behind recording itself.

Double-entry accounting classifies, or categorizes, your transactions among a system of accounts (your "chart of accounts" is the most visible portion of this system within Accounting 2007). In double-entry accounting, "every transaction has two effects." That is, every transaction affects two areas of the accounting system. Every transaction consists of at least one debit and one credit, which are contained within the accounting entry. Each entry must balance, meaning that total debits must equal total credits.

Let's review a couple of simple examples to illustrate this important concept. Suppose that your business has paid an external contractor $3,500, using a check drawn on your bank, for work performed over the previous month. You would debit your total expense to the "Outside Contractor Fees" (or similarly titled) account, within which information about transactions with outside contractors is captured. In addition to debiting this income statement account (an expense account), you would credit the same amount to your cash account (in this case, the bank account from which you wrote the check to the contractor). The cash account is a balance sheet (asset) account that keeps track of the payments made from your corporate checking account and reflects the correct cash balance within your company's year-end balance sheet.

The balancing transaction might be represented as shown in the following table.

Debit or credit?	Account	Account type	Amount
Debit	Outside Contractor Fees	Expense	$3,500
Credit	Cash	Asset	($3,500)

Another example might be as follows: Your business purchases a custom printing/collating machine for $18,000. You make a down payment of $2,500 cash, as required by the manufacturer to begin building the machine, and take out a loan of $15,500 from the manufacturer, who finances large purchases for creditworthy customers. To record this transaction, you would debit a fixed asset account (a balance sheet account where you capture the cost of the asset) instead of an expense account, for the total purchase price of $18,000. You would credit the cash account with the $2,500 down payment submitted with the purchase order, and credit the "Equipment Loans" (or similarly named) account with the remainder of the purchase price, $15,500.

The balancing transaction might be represented as shown in the following table.

Debit or credit?	Account	Account type	Amount
Debit	Fixed Assets – Printer/Collator	Asset	$18,000
Credit	Cash	Asset	($2,500)
Credit	Equipment Loans	Liability	($15,500)

You generally use a debit entry in the following scenarios:

- To increase an expense (such as a utility cost)
- To increase an asset (for example, inventory stocks or a fixed asset)
- To decrease a liability (for example, amounts owed to self-financed equipment vendors)
- To decrease capital (such as amounts you invest in the company, as reflected in the Owner's Equity account of your balance sheet)
- To decrease revenue (for example, an adjustment to a Sales account)

You generally use a credit entry in the following situations:

- To increase a liability, capital, or income
- To decrease an expense or asset

The same concepts apply to entries you would make manually (typically called *journal entries*) in your system—for example, accrual adjustments at year-end—as well as for adjustments suggested by your accountant to otherwise appropriately modify account balances for reporting, tax, and other purposes. Because all entries in a double-entry bookkeeping system should balance (this rule is enforced automatically, of course, within Accounting 2007), your books should remain in balance as a result, assuming that they were in balance from the outset. (Accounting 2007 forces balancing of all entries, including beginning balances.)

Although remembering the rules for using debits and credits within your entries might seem difficult, keep in mind that Accounting 2007 applies the rules for you as it performs double-entry bookkeeping, every time you input transactions. This allows you to move beyond the mechanics involved in recording entries and to focus on which accounts to use as you categorize your transactions. All you have to do is tell Accounting what happened, which accounts are involved, the value of the transaction, and any other details you wish to capture, and the system handles the tedium of the postings, summarizations, and other basic tasks.

The Accrual Concept

When you set up your accounting system in Accounting 2007, if your business is currently using cash-basis accounting, you should consider moving to accrual-basis accounting. The accrual concept is related to a primary accounting document—the income statement. The accrual concept is challenging to most small-business owners because small businesses, like individuals, tend to record their financial transactions on a cash basis rather than an accrual basis.

Your company, like most small businesses, might tend to think of its financial situation in light of the amount of cash, or the number and value of assets, that it possesses at any given point in time. You might also view your annual income on a gross (or perhaps after-tax) basis. Moreover, you may not factor in depreciation on the equipment you use in your daily operations, even though this is a very real cost of business.

For obvious reasons, cash-basis accounting is simple: You record revenue when you receive payment from customers, for example, and deposit the money into your bank account. When you pay your creditors, you record the expense at the same time you issue the check, rather than at the time you incur the expense for which the check is paying. Although this is acceptable in some cases (for example, when small amounts of money are involved), when you don't pair revenues with the corresponding expenses that generated them, you can't obtain a clear picture of your business results.

When you use accrual-basis accounting, you place revenues within the time period in which they were earned, instead of when they were received. You do the same thing for expenses, and when both components are thus placed within the proper time period, the net effect is a much more meaningful idea of financial results. You know how much profit you really made in a given operating month, for example. For this reason, it is almost always best to maintain your accounting system on an accrual basis. (Among the few exceptions, very small service-based companies, as well as certain businesses that are specifically allowed by the Internal Revenue Service to use the cash basis for purposes of computing their income taxes, may find advantages in using cash-basis accounting.)

What accrual-basis accounting means, in essence, is a little more work in the long haul (primarily in the form of year-end journal entries and the like) to adjust revenues and expenses to their appropriate respective periods. Typical examples you would likely encounter include journal entries to depreciate your fixed assets (for example, to adjust for the expense of using a piece of equipment in the manufacturing process during the year, to account for wear and tear), as well as to recognize expenses (utilities are a prime example) that, while incurred by your business, may not have been invoiced by their suppliers by your year-end date. After you make these general entries, your accounting system can produce an accurate trial balance, which acts as a complete list of the account balances within your system after all transactions and journal entries are considered. You or your accountant can then use this trial balance to prepare financial statements, to perform analysis on results, and to prepare tax filings.

Other Accounting Concepts and Principles

Accounting concepts and principles contribute significantly to the framework that supports the general accounting process. Accounting principles, in particular, promote characteristics that financial statements should have in common, provide operational rules with regard to how accounting is conducted and applied, and promote assumptions that consumers of financial statements should be able to make in their reliance upon a company's financial statements.

An example of this promotion of desirable characteristics is embodied within the principle that the ultimate objective of financial statements is to provide a tool that usefully supports business decisions. Characteristics that make financial statements useful include practicality and dependability. In order to be practical, statements must be capable of providing meaningful feedback, must have been prepared in a timely manner, and must promote predictability. Dependability, on the other hand, is supported by the characteristics of accuracy, verifiability, and freedom from bias. Other general characteristics promoted by accounting principles include consistency, comparability, materiality, and the provision of utility to consumers.

Examples of the operational rules established by accounting principles surround the timing of the reporting of revenue and expenses, and how expenses and revenue are matched. Other rules involve requirements for disclosure so that a financial statement consumer will completely grasp the circumstances under which information is being delivered. The principle of conservatism, which provides guidance to companies as to how to report within scenarios where choices exist that might result in the understatement or overstatement of values, is yet another illustration of a principle that establishes an operational rule.

Examples of principles that promote assumptions in statements upon which consumers can rely include provision for the fact that the business whose operations are being reported is a "going concern" that is expected to continue operations; that the information being delivered in the statement(s) under consideration is measured in specific time intervals and monetary units of measure; that the historical cost is presented where applicable, as with fixed assets and the like; and that the information being presented represents the isolated operations and characteristics of the entity being reported upon (and does not contain information that is not related to the entity concerned). Some of the most important assumptions promoted by these principles involve accounting methods used by the reporting entity.

A grasp of accounting principles and concepts is critical to understanding accounting processes and performing them correctly. Moreover, an understanding of the principles, and the characteristics, rules, and assumptions they promote, is a basic requirement for being a knowledgeable financial statement consumer.

Key Accounting Terms and Definitions

Every field uses its own specialized vocabulary to describe important concepts precisely. It might seem that accountants use technical terms to exclude you from their conversations, but in reality the accountants' goal is precision.

Each specialized term denotes something important to their profession and, by extension, to your business. The following list highlights some of the more important terms you'll encounter when you use Accounting 2007.

> **Note** You'll find a more complete glossary at the end of the book, but you'll see these terms used heavily throughout this book.

- *Account*: A "container" of financial transactions, usually grouped around a particular category that helps financial planners determine deductible expenses and taxable income. For example, you might track the cost of professional association memberships, journal subscriptions, and research materials in the "Dues, Publications, and Books" account.
- *Accounting*: The process of recording, classifying, summarizing, reporting, and assessing a company's business transactions. The overall goal of accounting is to maintain a detailed and accurate picture of the company's performance and health.
- *Asset*: A resource that the corporation owns, such as cash, inventory, buildings, or equipment.

- *Balance Sheet*: A financial statement that summarizes your company's status on a specific date (often referred to as a *snapshot*).
- *Chart of Accounts*: A list of your company's accounts.
- *Credit*: An entry that increases liabilities, equity, or income, and decreases assets or expenses. How a credit affects your bottom line depends on the type of account to which it is applied. Credits appear on the right side of an account ledger.
- *Debit*: An entry that increases assets or expenses, and decreases liabilities, equity, or income. How a debit affects your bottom line depends on the type of account to which it is applied. Debits appear on the left side of an account ledger.
- *Expense*: An amount spent on products or services related to your normal business operations, such as utilities or wages.
- *Income*: Revenue generated by selling products and services to your customers.
- *Liability*: An amount spent on products or services related to your normal business operations, such as utilities or wages.

The Importance of Accounting Policies

A sound business policy is vital to surviving in the business environment in which you will find yourself these days. Having a well-designed policy in place means you can adapt quickly to changes in that environment. In addition to a sound business policy, your company needs to have in place the appropriate accounting policies. Your accounting policies should include specific rules or guidelines that you consider when you record your company's transactions and present them, as a part of your accounting cycle, within the financial reports of the business and elsewhere. In other words, accounting policies are specific accounting principles, and methods of applying those principles in preparing and presenting financial statements.

Structuring your accounting policies to be flexible yet effective requires research, experience, and judgment. As you select and apply accounting policies within your business, you should be conservative and prudent, anticipating gains modestly but providing for all losses that seem possible. Even when you can't determine a liability or prospective loss with certainty, you should make provision for it as best you can. Moreover, you should record and report transactions with due consideration to "substance over form," seeking to present the commercial or economic realities of the transactions rather than their mere legal forms, which might be very different. Finally, you should always consider the materiality of transactions within your design and application of your accounting policies, particularly within your presentation of information within financial statements and other external reports. Policies regarding "what is material enough to report" can help you to filter out details that would not likely influence the decisions of consumers of your financial statements, and to avoid unnecessary disclosure in those reports.

Examples of accounting policies include guidelines for your valuation of volatile assets, such as stocks and bonds, at the lower of cost or market value. (For that matter, you might want to have a policy to reserve for investment value fluctuation in general, to reflect conservative values on your balance sheet.) Another policy to consider is the conservative statement of accounts receivable by making provision for questionable debts. Moreover, you need to consider a policy to expense small capital expenditures, establishing a threshold value at which you capitalize such expenditures as a standard practice. Other important accounting policies that rest upon the tandem concept of conservatism and prudence include your guidelines and rules for amortizing intangible assets (such as trademarks, patents, and goodwill), depreciating fixed assets (especially in the appropriate classification of their expected economic lives) and making it a practice to take advantage of attractive vendor discount terms.

Accounting for Your Small Business

Stated simply, your main accounting duty as a small business owner is to keep accurate records that enable you to operate your business effectively and file accurate tax reports. You should take the time to examine your income and expenses in detail, but you should also create reports that summarize your company's performance. The Securities and Exchange Commission (SEC) requires publicly traded companies to produce three reports: a balance sheet, a profit and loss statement, and a cash flow statement. Even if you haven't issued stock traded on any of the public markets, you can learn a lot about your business by examining these three reports. Accounting 2007 knows how to create these reports, and many others. Throughout this book, you will be introduced to these primary reports as well as others that might be of potential use to you in operating your business.

See Also For more information about your duties as a small business owner, download Internal Revenue Service Publication 583, "Starting a Business and Keeping Records," from *www.irs.gov/pub/irs-pdf/p583.pdf*.

In the following section, you will learn about the general steps of accounting for your business cycle to get a feel for the "big picture," and to gain an understanding of your overall accounting cycle. Next, you'll consider ongoing requirements, such as filing and reporting, from a high level. Finally, you'll consider ongoing requirements that your business will have—requirements that Accounting 2007 will help you to meet effectively and efficiently.

Accounting for Your Business Cycle

The flow of transactions required within your business to complete a sale and receive payment can be described as your "business cycle." Understanding your business cycle is a critical part of setting up Accounting 2007. You need to know what kinds of transactions are involved in your business and the accounting entries that are needed to reflect those transactions. Although Accounting will automatically construct much of the mechanism behind the entries for you, you need to be aware of the accounts affected in each to be able to tell Accounting what it needs to know to manage the setup.

Many companies would complete the steps or stages shown in the table below within their recurring business cycles. As you set up your new accounting system, you will want to ensure that all stages of your own business cycle are taken into consideration.

Business Cycle Step	Description	Accounting System Entries
Purchase materials/ inventory Enter goods into inventory	You buy the raw materials used to create your company's product (or perhaps simply the inventory you sell). You receive the goods, either paying cash or obligating the company for future payment in return.	Increase inventory account(s) Decrease cash (if you paid up front) OR Increase accounts payable (if purchased on credit)
Manufacturing or assembly process, if applicable	If you manufacture the product(s) you sell, you might transfer values between an initial inventory account, a work in process account, and a final inventory for sale account. (There are many possibilities.) All transfers can be managed via journal entries, etc., if necessary. If you simply sell inventory you purchase for resale, this step is not applicable.	Transfer materials between inventory/work-in-process/ finished inventory accounts, if applicable
Pay suppliers/ employees	You pay suppliers at some point subsequent to buying raw materials/ resale inventory on credit. You pay employees/contractors (if operating a service business).	Reduce accounts payable Decrease cash

Business Cycle Step	Description	Accounting System Entries
Sell the inventory/ services	You sell inventory (which you have manufactured or purchased for resale earlier in the business cycle). You sell services (if a service company).	Reduce inventory account(s) Increase accounts receivable OR Increase cash (if customer paid cash) Increase sales revenue
Collect accounts receivable	You collect cash for outstanding accounts receivable from customers.	Decrease accounts receivable Increase cash

Your Accounting Cycle

Your accounting cycle includes of a series of steps that are repeated every reporting period. The process starts with accounting for your recurring business cycle, where you make accounting entries for each transaction, and goes through closing the books. The general steps of your accounting cycle will likely be quite similar to the following.

During each accounting period, for each transaction that takes place, you will:

1. Identify the transaction.

   Use an original source document (such as an invoice, receipt, cancelled check, time card, deposit slip, or purchase order) that provides information about the transaction, such as the date, amount, description (business purpose), name, and address of the other party to the transaction.

2. Analyze the transaction.

   Determine which accounts are affected by the transaction, how they are affected (whether the accounts are decreased or increased), and the value that the transaction represents in dollars. (Identifying and analyzing the transactions occur within the context of the steps discussed in the previous section, "Accounting for Your Business Cycle.")

3. Record the transaction.

   Record the transaction in the accounting system. (Accounting 2007 knows where to put the debits and credits for you, based upon the way in which the company has been set up in the system).

At the end of your accounting period, you should collect the following information:

1. Trial balance

   You start with an "unadjusted" trial balance. Your primary objective is to determine that the trial balance appears to completely list all accounts and that total debits equal total credits, plain and simple. You can generate this report easily from Accounting 2007. Although the system will not allow an out-of-balance condition (Accounting 2007 automatically prevents misapplication of debits/credits, math errors, and other miscalculations, misalignment of ledgers and sub-ledgers), it is possible to have a posting error, even if the debits and credits balance. Some problems that you might not identify in your review of the trial balance are:

   - Transactions you recorded in an incorrect account.
   - Transactions you neglected to post.
   - Transactions for which you posted an incorrect value.

   Just as you've probably found to be the case with your bank reconciliations, if you prepare your trial balance consistently and frequently, you have fewer transactions to go through each time you revisit the process. This means that if there is an error, you can (usually) find it more easily. Keep in mind that you don't have to wait until the end of the accounting period to prepare your trial balance.

2. Adjusting entries

   After you have an initial trial balance, you can proceed to the next step in your accounting cycle, adjusting entries. You may want to work with your accountant or perhaps have him or her compile these entries alone. Adjusting entries are the means by which you post accrued and deferred items to your system.

3. Adjusted trial balance

   Having posted your adjusting entries, you are ready to generate an adjusted trial balance. Traditionally, you would verify that debits still equal credits, after making period-end adjustments with adjusting entries. With Accounting 2007, you can be assured that balancing is not an issue, and spend time, instead, focusing on whether all account balances appear complete and accurate.

4. Financial statements

   After you have a complete, adjusted trial balance, you're ready to prepare your financial statements. These include the income statement, balance sheet, statement of retained earnings, and statement of cash flows. You can prepare these important reports at other points in time for various reasons (say a bank requests them as a part of your application package when applying for a business line of credit), as well, with appropriate adjustments.

5. Closing entries

   You prepare closing entries to transfer the year-to-date balances from income statement accounts (sometimes called *temporary* or *nominal* accounts) to the owner's equity (or equivalent) on the balance sheet. These accounts "reopen," to begin accumulating year-to-date balances once again, on the first day of the new financial year.

6. Post-closing trial balance

   As needed, you can generate a post-closing trial balance—which, at this point, will consist of balance sheet accounts only, because you've closed the income statements in the equity account(s). Again, with Accounting 2007, "out-of-balance" scenarios won't happen, so your primary focus with this statement is to ascertain that all values look correct and properly classified.

Ongoing Requirements for Your Business

Your small business has many reporting and tax responsibilities that Accounting 2007 can help you to meet and maintain. In addition to the financial reports mentioned earlier in this chapter, you will want to maintain many other operational reports, reports that support the completion of tax forms, and a tax filing calendar. The Web sites for the Internal Revenue Service and for the tax authority of the state(s) within which you operate your business provide a great deal of material on tax reporting requirements, specifically regarding income and employment/payroll-related taxes.

Meeting these requirements in an accurate, complete, and timely fashion is critical to avoiding the myriad compliance issues that plague less organized businesses. Moreover, your ability to run both regular financial statements and detailed operational reports will help you to comply with reporting requirements, while making it easy to generate reports that focus upon operational details that will make you a master of your business. Accounting 2007 is a powerful tool in growing and operating a successful business.

Key Points

- With Accounting 2007, you can record, analyze, and report on your company's income, assets, and expenses. It frees you from the tedium of debits and credits in your daily recording activities to focus on operating your business.

- Practical accounting is the process of recording, classifying, summarizing, reporting, and assessing a company's business transactions. By recording transactions accurately, you can analyze your company's performance, plan future endeavors, and fulfill your tax filing and payment obligations, among many other functions.

- Understanding fundamental concepts is vital to your effective use of any accounting system, particularly one as powerful and flexible as Accounting 2007, which can form a complete record of all the activities of your business. Your end rewards include a comprehensive view that contains every aspect of your business. This business intelligence supports your analysis of business trends and enables you to insightfully identify future prospects and opportunities.

- You can learn a lot about your company from these three reports: the balance sheet, the profit and loss statement, and the cash flow statement. Accounting 2007 can produce these and many other reports for you at any time.

- Sound business and accounting policies are vital to surviving in the business environment in which you will find yourself these days. Your accounting policies should include specific rules or guidelines that you consider as you record your company's transactions and present them, as a part of your accounting cycle, within the financial reports of the business and elsewhere.

- Understanding the general steps of accounting for your business cycle, and your overall accounting cycle, together with an appreciation for the importance of accounting policies within your business, can help you maintain consistency in recording and reporting your company's transactions.

Chapter at a Glance

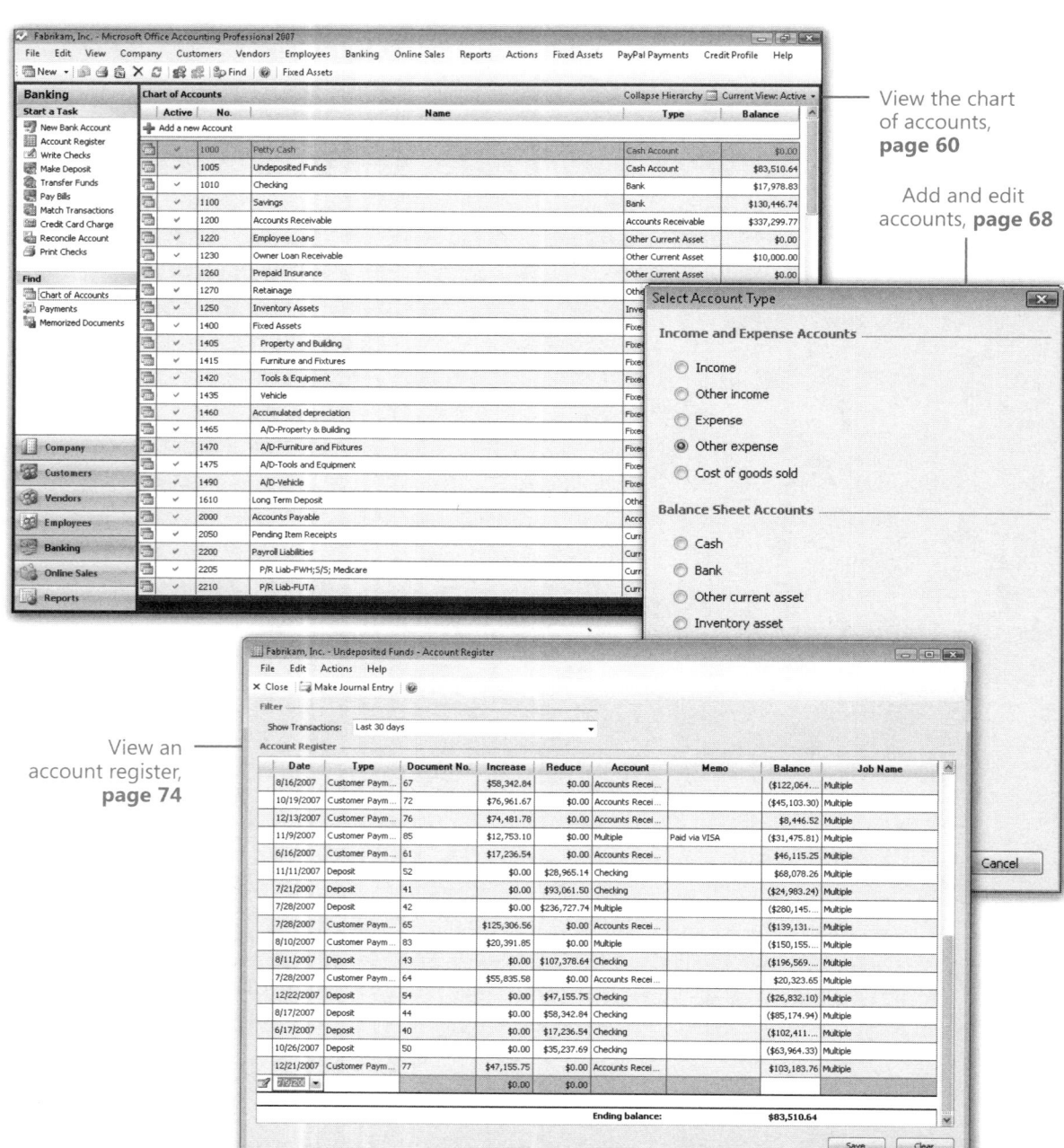

View the chart of accounts, **page 60**

Add and edit accounts, **page 68**

View an account register, **page 74**

4 Managing the Chart of Accounts

In this chapter, you will learn to:

- ✔ View the chart of accounts.
- ✔ Add and edit accounts.
- ✔ Merge accounts.
- ✔ View an account register.
- ✔ Manage journal entries.

Accurate accounting requires attention to many details. The framework that supports detailed recordkeeping about each of a business's transactions—whether income or expense, *asset* or *liability*—is a *chart of accounts* that reflects the company's operations. Building a chart of accounts is one of the tasks you perform when you set up a company in Microsoft Office Accounting 2007. You can have Accounting 2007 create a basic chart of accounts designed for your type of business when you work through the Startup Wizard, and add accounts to the basic set later, or you can create a chart of accounts on your own.

In this chapter, you'll learn how to view the chart of accounts and create and edit accounts. You'll also learn how to work with journal entries. You use journal entries to record transactions such as the opening balance of an account, depreciation charges, the sale of an asset, or accounting adjustments.

> **Troubleshooting** Graphics and operating system–related instructions in this book reflect the Windows Vista user interface. If your computer is running Windows XP and you experience trouble following the instructions as written, please refer to the "Information for Readers Running Windows XP" section at the beginning of this book.

Viewing the Chart of Accounts

A company's chart of accounts lists the individual accounts that together show the company's financial picture. The chart of accounts is made up of different kinds of accounts: *balance sheet* accounts for assets and liabilities, income and expense accounts that reflect day-to-day activities of a business, and system accounts such as *accounts receivable*, *accounts payable*, or discounts.

> **Note** Accounting 2007 creates required system accounts when you set up your company.

The chart of accounts lists asset accounts first, followed by liability accounts, equity accounts, and then income and expense accounts. If you selected Use Account Numbers in Company Preferences, the account number determines the account's position within its grouping in the chart of accounts.

The following list describes the types of accounts you'll use in Accounting 2007:

● **Asset accounts.** Accounts numbered 1000 through 1999. These accounts include bank accounts, cash accounts (such as funds you haven't deposited or petty cash), inventory, and accounts receivable. Asset accounts also include a category called *Other Current Assets*, for items such as a short-term note receivable, a rent deposit, or another asset that you expect to convert to cash within one year. Fixed assets include land and other real estate, machinery, equipment, furniture, and fixtures. Fixed assets have a life greater than one year, and the cost of fixed assets is expensed over time through *depreciation*. Other assets might include a long-term note receivable or a certificate of deposit whose term exceeds 12 months.

> **Note** The balance of an inventory asset account shows the value of the goods or supplies a company has on hand at a specific point in time. In Accounting 2007, an inventory asset account summarizes all the inventory item records that are linked to the account. To set the opening balance for an inventory asset account, you need to create an inventory item and then enter the balance for that item.

See Also For more information about adding items to inventory, see Chapter 5, "Managing Products and Services."

- **Liability accounts.** Accounts numbered 2000 through 2999. Liabilities include amounts payable to vendors and suppliers (the Accounts Payable account), loans you are paying back, tax liabilities, credit card purchases, and other debts. Liabilities such as sales tax and payroll taxes due, accrued salaries and wages, and short-term loans are considered current liabilities. Current liabilities are scheduled to be paid within one year, and long-term liabilities such as a mortgage are scheduled to be paid over a longer period of time.

- **Equity accounts.** Accounts numbered 3000 through 3999. These accounts show a company's net worth, which is calculated by subtracting liabilities from assets. (In accounting, assets equal liabilities plus equity.)

- **Income and expense accounts.** The accounts you work with most frequently from day to day. These accounts are included in an Income And Expense statement that shows business activity for a month, a quarter, or a fiscal year. Income accounts show revenue from sales of goods and services. A chart of accounts might also include an income account for the interest that an investment or a savings account earns. Expense accounts record amounts a company spends on insurance, phone, rent, and other products and services related to its operations. Interest payments are also recorded in an expense account. The account Cost of Goods Sold is the account that shows the cost of products and services that are entered into inventory and then sold.

- **System accounts.** Accounts (including the asset account named Accounts Receivable and the liability account named Accounts Payable) set up by Accounting 2007. You cannot delete a system account, but you can edit the account information. You can view a list of system accounts by choosing Preferences from the Company menu and then clicking the System Accounts tab.

See Also For more information about editing accounts, see "Adding and Editing Accounts" later in this chapter.

> **Tip** You can use the lists on the System Accounts tab of the Company Preferences dialog box to select a different account to act as a system account. For example, for the system account Sales Tax Payable, you could use an account that you create named *Sales Tax Due*.
>
> If you have selected Use Account Numbers as a company preference and then select a different account as a system account, the new account number will change the account's position within the chart of accounts.

- **Opening Balances.** Accounts showing the account balance as of the start date for a company. This account should usually have a zero balance if assets equal liabilities plus equity.

- **Accounts Receivable.** Amounts that customers owe your company from the sales of goods and services are totaled in Accounts Receivable. You cannot post transactions directly to the Accounts Receivable account.

- **Accounts Payable.** Amounts your company owes to vendors and suppliers are reflected in Accounts Payable. You cannot post transactions directly to the Accounts Payable account.

- **Sales Tax Payable.** Accounts representing current liabilities (due in less than one year). It records the amount of sales taxes a company owes.

- **Cash Discount Given.** Accounts recording the amount of cash discounts (if any) you provide to customers based on terms of payment. (For example, some companies provide a discount if a customer pays a bill within 10 days or purchases a high volume of your goods or services.) The amount in this account offsets entries to your income account.

- **Cash Discount Taken.** Shows the amount of cash discounts you take on payments to vendors or suppliers when a discount applies. The amount offsets the expense account Cost of Goods Sold.

- **Undeposited Funds.** A cash account used to record amounts you've received but have not recorded in any other account.

- **Bank Charge.** An expense account used to record the amounts a company pays to its bank for charges such as account fees or transfer charges.

- **Retained Earnings.** An equity account that shows the balances from income and expense accounts at the end of a company's fiscal year. When a company's books are closed at the end of a fiscal year, balances from the income and expense accounts are moved to the Retained Earnings account.

- **Pending Item Receipts.** A current liability that reflects amounts a company owes for goods or services that the company has received but has not yet been billed for.

- **Write Off Account.** An account in which you record reductions to income for amounts that you deduct from the amounts owed to you. For example, you would use the Write Off Account to record the amount a customer's obligation is reduced as part of a payment plan.

> **Tip** You can print the chart of accounts from Accounting 2007 by clicking Chart Of Accounts in the Navigation Pane, and then clicking Print on the toolbar.

In this exercise, you will view and print the chart of accounts for a company.

> **BE SURE TO** start Accounting 2007 if it is not already running.
>
> **OPEN** the Fabrikam sample company file.

1. In the **Navigation Pane**, click **Banking**.

2. Under **Find**, click **Chart of Accounts**.

   A chart of accounts you can scroll through appears.

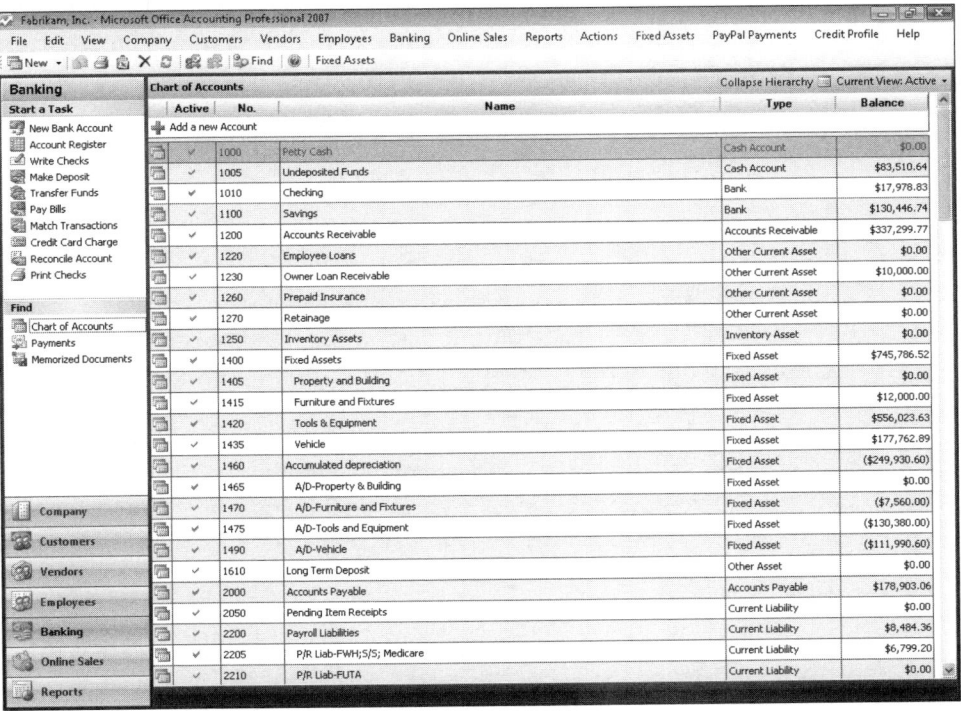

Print

3. On the toolbar of the **Chart of Accounts** window, click the **Print** button.

4. Click **OK** to print the **Chart of Accounts** to the default printer, or click **Cancel** to avoid printing the **Chart of Accounts**.

Create Accounts That Match Your Business

As part of setting up your company in Accounting 2007, you will build a new chart of accounts. After you tell the Startup Wizard the type of business you have, Accounting Professional 2007 proposes a template chart based on that business type. As you'll read in the "Adding and Editing Accounts" section later in this chapter, you can then add accounts to, or remove them from, the template chart to accommodate your specific requirements. As an example, you might establish separate accounts for different revenue streams identified and grown by your business.

Different types of businesses will obviously have different charts of accounts. As an illustration, a retail business will have an account or accounts for recording purchases of its resale inventory, whereas a manufacturing operation will have accounts in its chart for various manufacturing costs. To establish ease of comparison between organizations within a given industry, many industry associations publish recommended charts of accounts for their members to promote consistency. In fact, the predefined, industry-specific charts of accounts offered in many accounting software applications are typically based upon these recommended charts.

Regardless of whether one of the template selections approaches your business needs, it pays to take the time to customize your new chart to closely align it with your operation. Starting with as small a number of accounts as possible means easy setup and overall operating simplicity. You can break large accounts into smaller subaccounts as the need arises to report upon growing balances and their constituent parts. (Be sure to keep in mind the need to provide historical comparability.) Sometimes you need to add accounts, or account groupings, to support specific tax reporting requirements. (An example would be the IRS requirement to break out travel, advertising, business entertainment, and other types of expenses.) Moreover, in virtually any business, separate accounts are appropriate for individual bank accounts, customers, vendors and the like, which belong to a larger "rollup" balance (such as cash, accounts receivable, and accounts payable, respectively).

A Logical Level of Subdivision

Accounting 2007 offers you the flexibility of creating your chart of accounts from scratch. By contrast, you can also begin with the template chart created by the Startup Wizard. With the second method, which is a great way to get up and running quickly, you can easily modify the template, adding specific accounts you need at a couple of levels. After you determine your general ledger accounts—the primary chart of accounts with which you intend to summarize and categorize your transactions for financial reporting (as in the income statement and balance sheet) and analysis—you can add to this chart to customize it to your business. For example, you might add another revenue account, to allow you to separately track a couple of different revenue streams instead of combining them into a single account, or a special inventory account (such as Work In Process or Finished Goods For Resale), to reflect unique aspects of your manufacturing process.

In addition to these primary accounts, you can add accounts that subdivide general ledger accounts. To do this, you go through the standard steps of account creation and then designate the account as a subaccount. You specify a parent account—an account to which the subaccount will "roll up," and which must be of the same type as the new subaccount. For example, an expense subaccount must have a parent account whose type is *expense*, as well.

To illustrate, you might set up an account called *Other Current Assets* as a part of creating your chart of accounts via the Startup Wizard. You might see over time that Other Current Assets frequently contains such items as short-term notes receivable, rent deposits, and other assets that you expect to convert to cash within one year. Because you sense the value of being able to see these detailed components underneath the Other Current Assets total in your reports, you might set up a subaccount for short-term notes receivable, rent deposits, and the like, to allow you to subanalyze these items, and to "break them out" in your reports. (You can always merge accounts if you find the level of subdivision to be unnecessary at a later date.)

When you put subaccounts to work in the right places in your chart of accounts, you give Accounting 2007 the structure it needs to support flexible business intelligence. Your new accounting system will afford you the capability to analyze and subanalyze various revenues and expenses, for example, to determine the individual contributions of underlying subaccounts to their parent general ledger accounts. You can drill down on totals to see their composition, as well as to identify problems and opportunities at a more detailed level than the overall revenue or expense total.

Fixed-Asset and Contra-Asset Accounts

Fixed assets are typically assets that you employ in your business, which usually have a life of more than one year. You commonly expense fixed assets over time, through the process of depreciation. In general, to track and report the total net book value (the historical cost less the accumulated depreciation) of your fixed assets, you need the following three components in place:

- **A general ledger fixed-asset account.** A balance sheet account that you debit for the actual cost of each asset added.

- **An accumulated depreciation account.** A "contra-asset," balance sheet account, which you credit with the amount of each periodic depreciation entry.
- **A depreciation expense account.** An income statement account which, like all other expense accounts, is increased via a debit.

Your debit to the depreciation expense account, together with the corresponding credit you make to the accumulated depreciation account, forms the recurring depreciation entry. (The asset account is debited only for the purchase of the asset(s) it contains.) In the simplest scenario, adequate for many businesses, the depreciation entry can be calculated outside the accounting system (using, for example, Microsoft Office Excel 2007), and posted by creating a journal entry against the corresponding depreciation expense (a debit) and accumulated depreciation accounts (a credit). The result is a net book value when the asset and contra-asset accounts are combined, or "netted together."

If you wish to maintain accumulated depreciation at the individual asset level, Accounting Professional 2007 offers this option through the use of subaccounts. (You can always maintain detailed depreciation schedules outside the system, of course, and post aggregates to the books in unified entries, if this more closely meets the needs of your business.) If you want to maintain accumulated depreciation at the asset level inside Accounting 2007, you set up each asset as a subaccount, and designate a fixed-asset general ledger account as the parent account. You set up a contra-asset account to accumulate depreciation for each asset, as well. You have an option of creating depreciation expense subaccounts for each asset, too, to be consistent in providing access to the same level of detail in the income statement and balance sheet accounts. You will want to carefully consider analysis and reporting needs when deciding how to best go about the setup of fixed assets in your Accounting 2007 books.

Although the mechanics underlying depreciation are virtually identical, Accounting Professional provides, via its Fixed Asset Manager, a built-in way to compute and post depreciation entries directly to the books. When you click any of the various Post Depreciation links, buttons, or Action menu command, the Depreciation Run Wizard comes to your assistance. This wizard enables you to review new assets since your last depreciation run, provides the opportunity to edit the depreciation journal entry if needed, and then enables you to post the entry to your clients' books. Even if you choose this approach, you (or your accountant) should always perform a periodic review of your depreciation entries to ensure that the system making those entries is as expected.

Beginning Balances and Valuation

The Accounting Professional Startup Wizard walks you through the process of creating financial accounts and entering beginning balances. After you choose the accounts that populate your chart, you are ready to enter opening balances for each account. Your account balances, by and large, will usually need to be calculated as of close of business on the last day of a fiscal period (and always at a specific point in time), although this may vary, depending on several factors. It is important to get the valuations correct—particularly if you are converting from another accounting system, so that ending balances in the previous system agree with the beginning balances in the new system.

If you are starting out fresh, and have not used an accounting system to capture the details of the business before implementing Accounting 2007, you will likely find yourself with zero balances in all financial accounts, with balances then being generated by the entry of transactions. (This is common if the business is brand new, and you begin business using Accounting 2007 from the start.) In contrast, your situation may be different: you may have been doing business for one or more years and have not kept adequate records. In cases like this, you can resort to using your tax records; you can reassemble values from purchase invoices/other bills (as in the case of fixed assets, which you will want to record at actual cost); or you might perform other methods of valuation (as an example, an appraisal on a piece of manufacturing equipment). Whatever the approach, you will want your beginning balances to be as accurate and complete as possible, conservatively stating value when uncertainty of sources, volatility of markets, and other such factors are involved.

Classification

Within the Company Preferences dialog box of Accounting Professional, you have the option of specifying that the system use classes. You enable classes so that you can record categories, such as a department or a purpose, for the financial transactions that you post. When classes are turned on, they show up for selection in almost all document forms, as well as in the account registers.

A range of financial reports will also display class information. Additionally, the Profit And Loss By Class report becomes available. Classes, like jobs, can extend the business intelligence provided by Accounting 2007 significantly. As an example of the many possible options for using classes, you can put this categorization technique to work in evaluating performance across various operating units of your company. You might also use classes to track expenses of a specific type in a way that your chart of accounts does not accommodate.

Because classes represent an added capability to categorize—outside, and independently of, the chart of accounts—they can be cumbersome to use if you don't have a handle on the core system components and capabilities first. For the same reason, classes can also be used in reports in a manner that might be confusing to readers, or lead them to draw erroneous conclusions. A well-designed chart of accounts, coupled with the appropriate account forms and documents, might well accomplish classification without the introduction of classes into your accounting model. Use them judiciously, and only after you understand the more skeletal components of Accounting Professional.

Adding and Editing Accounts

You can add accounts for assets, liabilities, income, and expenses to the basic chart of accounts that is created when you set up a company with the Startup Wizard. You can also build a chart of accounts from scratch if you did not select a standard chart of accounts in the Startup Wizard. When you create an account, you provide an account name and number and an opening balance. For credit card accounts, you also enter information such as the credit limit, bank name, and the last four digits of the card number.

When you add an account, you have the option of designating it a subaccount. A subaccount must be the same type of account as its parent account. For example, under an expense account named Advertising And Promotion, you could create a subaccount for expenses related to ads you place in printed material and a subaccount for ads you place on Web sites. By using subaccounts, you keep entries for related items under a single account.

In this exercise, you will add an expense account to the chart of accounts for Fabrikam and then edit information for a different account. The account you add will be a subaccount of the Insurance account and will be used to record expenses for vehicle insurance.

> **OPEN** the Fabrikam sample company file.

1. On the **Company** menu, click **New Account**.

The Select Account Type dialog box opens.

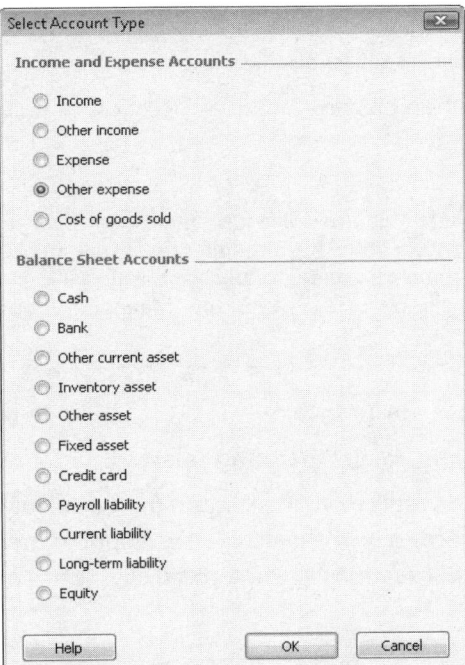

2. In the **Select Account Type** dialog box, , click **Expense**, and then click **OK**.

The title bar of the account form that opens shows the type of account you select.

> **Important** You cannot change the type of account after you add an account.

3. In the account form, type 6176 in the **Account no.** box.

The Account No. box is displayed only if you have Use Account Numbers selected as a company preference. You must include an account number if you are using them. Be sure to use a number related to the type of account so that the new account fits the organization of the chart of account and accounts of the same type are listed together. You can change an account number later if necessary by editing the account.

4. In the **Account name** box, type Ins – Supplemental Liability.

When creating an account, be sure to provide a descriptive name.

5. Keep the **Opening Balance** box set to **$0.00**.

The opening balance will often be zero for a new account, or it could reflect past transactions.

> **Note** You can enter a balance for a new account only in the fiscal year in which you set up a company in Accounting 2007. After the first fiscal year, the balance field is read-only. You will need to enter an opening balance through a journal entry. For more information about making journal entries, see "Managing Journal Entries" later in this chapter.

6. In the **Subaccount of** list, click **Insurance**.

7. In the **Cash Flow Category** list, keep **Operating** selected.

You can select Operating, Investing, or Financing in the Cash Flow Category list. The selection you make specifies how the account will appear on cash flow statements, which summarizes transactions in these three categories of your business activities.

> **Tip** If you are uncertain about which cash flow category to use, open an account from the chart of accounts that is the same type and verify how that account is categorized.

8. In the **1099 Category** list, make no selection for this account.

The 1099 Category list reflects categories on 1099-MISC tax forms that you send to vendors who are 1099 vendors. The categories listed in Accounting 2007 relate to forms in the tax year 2004. You should verify whether these categories have changed for the next year. If the categories have changed, you need to edit the category list in the Modify 1099 Categories dialog box. You can then edit the chart of accounts for the changes.

9. In the **Comments** box, type Use this account to record insurance for delivery trucks and company cars.

You can use the Comments box to provide information about how to use an account.

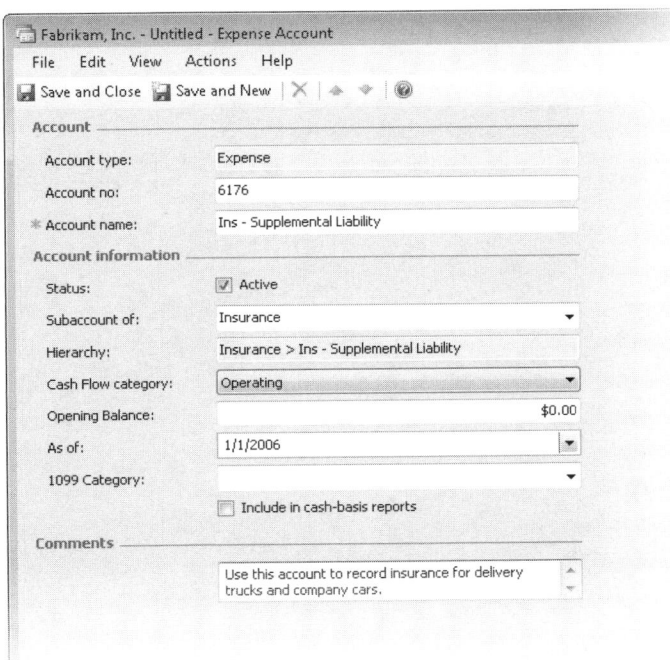

10. Click **Save and Close** to finish creating the account. (If you are adding a series of accounts, click **Save and New**.)

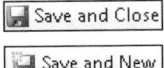

11. In the **Chart of Accounts**, double-click the account **Prepaid Insurance (no. 1260)**, which is an Other Current Asset account.

The Account Register appears.

12. On the **Actions** menu, click **Open Account Details**.

An Account form opens.

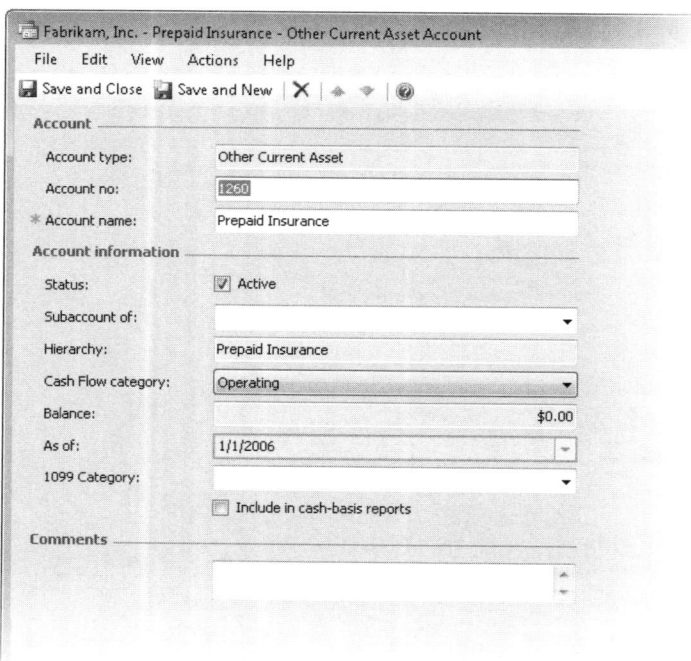

13. Under **Account Information**, next to **Status**, clear the **Active** check box.

14. In the **Comments** box, type No prepaid expenses for this company at this time.

15. On the toolbar, click **Save and Close**.

> **Tip** As the number of accounts in the chart of accounts grows, you can quickly locate an account by using the Find tool. With the chart of accounts displayed, click Find on the toolbar. In the Look For box, type a keyword related to the account. In the Search Under box, select the heading for the column you want to search. Click Find. The chart of accounts now shows only the accounts that meet the criteria you provided. To show the full chart of accounts again, click Clear. The Find operation works for only those accounts currently displayed in the chart of accounts.

Merging Accounts

After working with transactions in your chart of accounts for a period of time, you might see that similar information is recorded in two accounts. To get a better perspective on the activity in these accounts, it would be good to see the information combined when you view financial statements. By using the Merge Financial Accounts dialog box, you can merge two accounts. After you merge two accounts, you cannot separate them again. Also, the accounts you merge must be the same type of account. (For example, you cannot merge an income account with an expense account.) You cannot merge bank and credit card accounts.

In this exercise, you'll merge two accounts from the Fabrikam chart of accounts.

OPEN the Fabrikam sample company file.

1. On the **Company** menu, point to **Merge Accounts**, and then click **Merge Financial Accounts**.

   The Merge Financial Accounts dialog box opens.

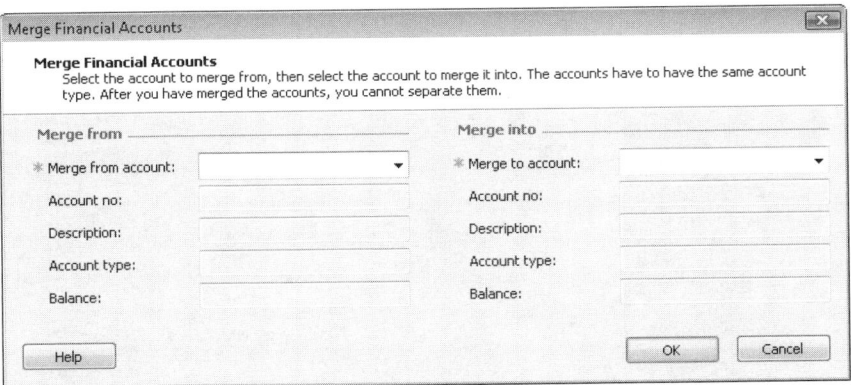

2. Under **Merge from**, in the **Merge from account** list, click the account you want to merge from.

   The account number (if you are using account numbers), description, type, and balance are displayed and cannot be edited.

3. Under **Merge into**, in the **Merge to account** list, click the account into which you will incorporate the records.

   Accounting 2007 combines the two accounts into a single account.

4. Click **OK**.

Viewing an Account Register

The account register displays each transaction for an account, showing the date and number for each journal entry, a memo that describes the entry, the other account or accounts affected by the transaction, the amount of the reduction or increase, and the account balance. With the account register for an account open, you can also make a new journal entry related to the account.

In this exercise, you will view the account register for an account and change the appearance of the account register.

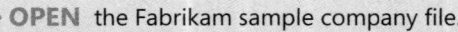

OPEN the Fabrikam sample company file.

1. In the **Navigation Pane**, click **Banking**.
2. Under **Find**, click **Chart of Accounts**.
3. In the chart of accounts, double-click the **Undeposited Funds** account.

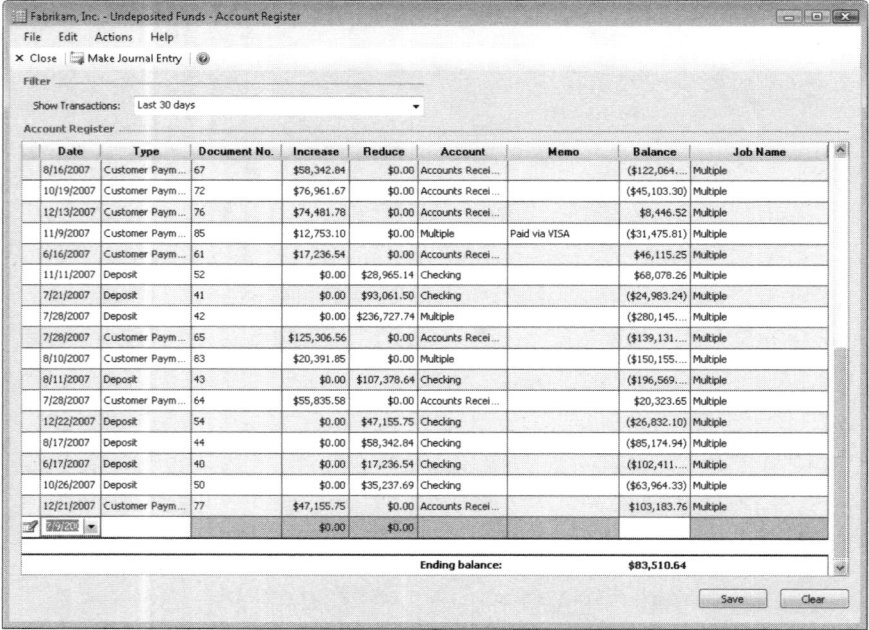

4. To initiate a journal entry from the account register, click **New Journal Entry** in the lower-left corner of the **Account Register** window.

5. To edit information for the account, click **Open Accounts Details** on the **Actions** menu.

6. To sort the list of transactions in ascending or descending order, click a column title.

   The arrow beside the column name indicates the sort order.

> **Note** If you sort the account register by a column other than the Date column, the amounts shown in the Balance column change, but the ending balance does not.

7. To change the width of a column, drag the column divider that is next to the column heading.

8. To change the order of the columns, select a column heading and drag it to the location where you want the column to appear.

9. To close the account register, click **Close** on the toolbar.

Close

Managing Journal Entries

You might use a journal entry to record any business transaction, although Accounting 2007 will largely predefine the entries it uses to record your recurring, day-to-day input. You typically use journal entries to make changes in the accounting system for the purpose of reclassifying items, correcting errors, or recording adjusting transactions. Journal entries are the primary document used by accountants to make adjustments at the end of the month or year.

Among the accounting best practices that surround journal entries, you will want to consider consistency a key concept. Using a consistent format in the entries themselves—for example, with debits first and credits next—tends to make your entries more readable to reviewers in general, your accountant, and other interested users. When you insert a concise, meaningful memo within the journal entry, you perform another best practice. You ensure that the memo line of the account register makes sense, and that readers understand the entry as a whole.

Journal Entries Illustrated

When you create and post a journal entry, you record activity in at least two accounts. As discussed in Chapter 3, "Accounting: A Quick Overview," in double-entry bookkeeping, every transaction affects two areas of the accounting system, and consists of at least one debit and credit, which are contained within the accounting entry. Each entry must balance, meaning that total debits must equal total credits.

A journal entry takes a format similar to that shown in the following table.

Date	Account	Debit	Credit
MM–DD–YYYY	Account to be Debited	x,xxx.xx	
	Account to be Credited		x,xxx.xx
	Memo: A short description of the transaction		

This table comprises a simple journal entry that represents a single transaction. Some systems do not include the memo notation, whereas others contain one or more reference numbers for tracking and other purposes. The table contains the nuts and bolts, however, in that it contains a date, the accounts involved, and the debit and credit amounts, clearly broken out in their placement relative to one another.

You use a compound journal entry to post to more than two accounts. Although the general format is the same, and the entry is still required to balance, the format is slightly different, and takes a format similar to that depicted in the following table.

Date	Account	Debit	Credit
MM–DD–YYYY	Account to be Debited	x,xxx.xx	
	Account to be Credited		x,xxx.xx
	Account to be Credited		x,xxx.xx
	Memo: A short description of the transaction		

An entry like the one in this table would be appropriate in a situation like the example presented in Chapter 3: Your business has purchased a custom printing/collating machine for $18,000 (comprising a payment of $2,500 cash, as required by the manufacturer to begin building the machine, together with a loan from the manufacturer, who finances large purchases for creditworthy customers for $15,500). You would debit a fixed asset account (a balance sheet account where you capture the cost of the asset), for your total purchase price of $18,000. You would credit the cash account with the $2,500 portion of the total submitted with the purchase order, and credit the Equipment Loans (or some similarly named) account with the remainder of the purchase price, $15,500.

In large part, Accounting 2007 applies the rules for you in making most entries to the books, because it performs double-entry bookkeeping every time you input transactions. This enables you to move beyond the mechanics involved in recording exercises to focus on which accounts to use as you categorize your transactions. After you tell Accounting 2007 what transaction occurred, the company account to which it occurred, the value of the transaction, and perhaps other details you wish to capture, the system handles the tedium of the vast majority of postings, summarizations, and so forth. The preceding discussion is simply to remind you of the rules for those "manual journals" that will come along, occasionally, as you or your accountant make adjustments to existing accounts (for, say, accruals or other year-end events). You can use them, as well, to capture unusual, infrequent transactions for which a system journal entry does not exist (for example, when you start a petty cash fund for the first time).

Viewing the Journal Entry List

As with invoices, sales, and purchase orders, with Accounting 2007, you can manage your journal entries by using a list. You can use the controls in the Journal Entry List to view your journal entries. You can use the Journal Entry List controls to sort and filter the entries to focus on just those entries you want to evaluate.

In this exercise, you will view the Journal Entry List.

OPEN the Fabrikam sample company file.

1. On the **Company** menu, point to **Company Lists**, and then click **Journal Entries**. The Journal Entry List appears.

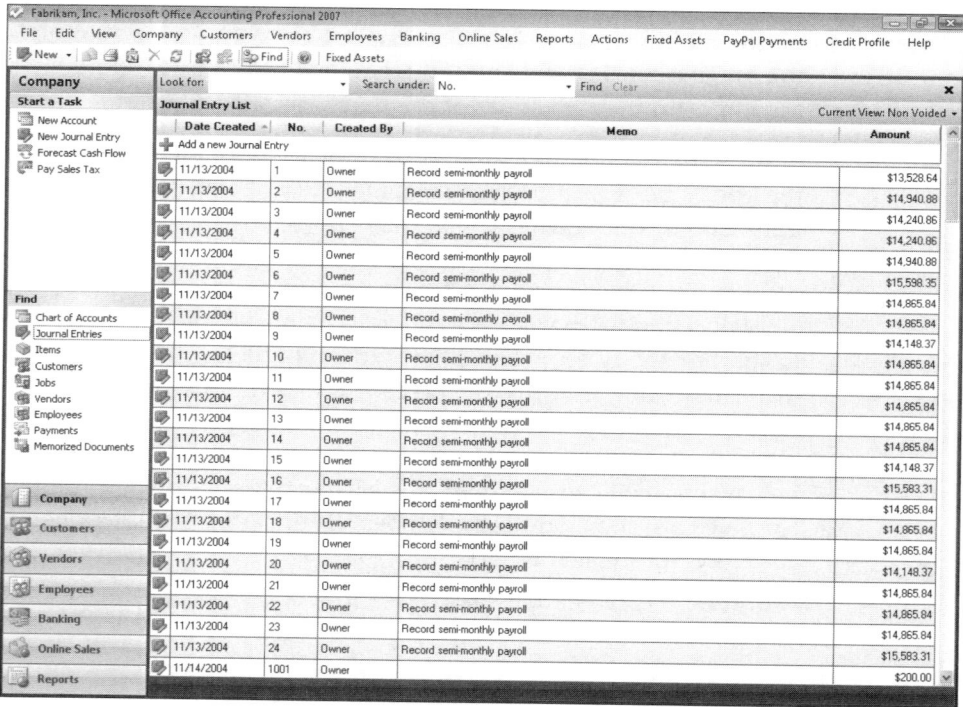

2. Click the **Amount** column header.

   Accounting 2007 sorts the Journal Entry List so that the smallest transactions are at the top of the list.

3. Click the **Amount** column header.

   Accounting 2007 sorts the Journal Entry List so that the largest transactions are at the top of the list.

4. Click the **Amount** column header.

   Accounting 2007 returns the Journal Entry List to its original sorted order.

Making a Journal Entry

With each journal entry, you record activity in at least two different accounts. You debit one account by entering a positive amount, and you credit a second account by entering a negative amount. How the debit and credit entries affect your bottom line depends on the type of account the entries are applied to. A debit increases an asset or expense account and decreases a liability, equity, or income account. A credit increases a liability, equity, or income account and decreases an asset or expense account.

See Also For more information about double-entry bookkeeping, refer to Chapter 3, "Accounting: A Quick Overview."

Note After you add a transaction, you cannot delete it. If an entry is incorrect or invalid, you can edit the entry or mark it void.

In this exercise, you will open a journal entry form and create a journal entry.

OPEN the Fabrikam sample company file.

1. On the **Company** menu, click **New Journal Entry**.

   The Journal Entry window opens.

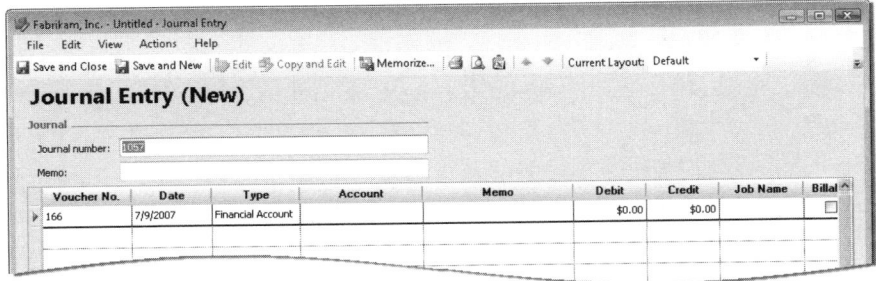

By default, the date shown is the current date. You can change the journal entry date by typing a date or by clicking the arrow to open the calendar and then selecting a date.

Accounting 2007 creates the journal number. The number is incremented from the previous number recorded in this field. It is good practice not to change this number. The total of the debits and credits you enter in a journal entry is calculated in the Balance box. You cannot post the journal entry if the balance is not zero.

2. In the **Memo** box, type Sale of asset.

   You use the Memo box to describe the purpose of the journal entry.

3. In the **Voucher No.** box, keep the present value.

   You use the voucher number to identify the entry. (The voucher number is not the same as the journal number.) Accounting 2007 displays the same number on the next row when you go to that row. Accounting 2007 changes the voucher number when a journal entry is in balance.

   > **Tip** If you are simply adjusting financial accounts, you can record multiple transactions (which have different voucher numbers) in a single journal entry. However, you should change the number when you start a new entry so that each entry can be easily identified.

4. In the **Type** column, select **Financial Account**.

   The selection you make from this list specifies which accounts are displayed in the Account column:

   - **Financial Account.** The Account list shows all financial accounts from the chart of accounts. Select Financial Account for transactions such as adjusting bookkeeping errors or sales of assets.

   - **Vendor.** The Account list shows the list of vendors you've set up in Accounting 2007. Select Vendor to make changes for transactions related to discounts or payments, for example, or to correct an error. A debit reduces a vendor payable, and a credit increases a vendor payable. You can make only one vendor entry for each journal entry. The balancing account line must be an entry for a financial account.

   See Also For more information about creating and working with vendors, see Chapter 13, "Purchasing from Vendors."

   - **Customer.** The Account list includes the list of customers you've set up in Accounting 2007. Use Customer to modify receivable balances for discounts or payments or to correct errors. As with a vendor entry, the balancing account line must be an entry for a financial account, and you can make only one customer entry for a journal entry.

See Also For more information about creating and working with customers, see Chapter 6, "Managing Customers."

- **Tax Code.** The Account list shows all tax agencies. Use this option to make adjustments to sales tax balances due as a result of discounts, payments, or errors. The balancing line must be a Financial Account.

5. In the **Account** column, click **Property and Building** (account number 1405).

> **Tip** You can add a new account while making journal entries by clicking Add A New Account at the top of the Account list.

6. In the **Credit** column, type 65000. Remember that a credit entry decreases the amount of an asset account.

7. Press the Tab key until you create a new entry row in the journal.

   Accounting 2007 creates the balancing entry for you, adding a debit in the same amount as the credit entry made in step 6.

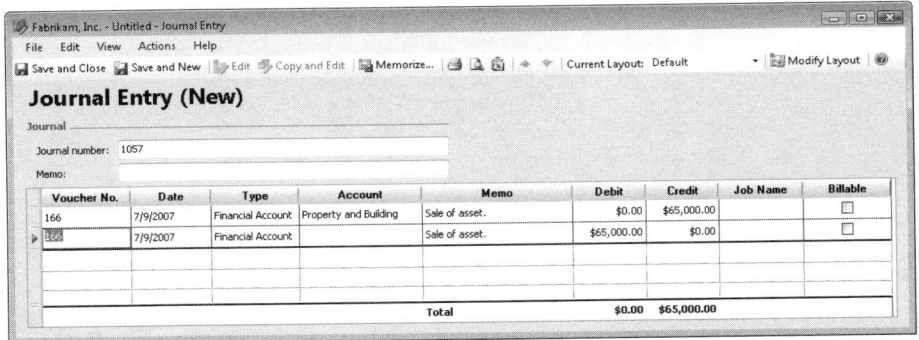

8. In the **Account** list in the second row, select **Savings**.

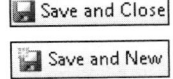

9. On the toolbar, click **Save and Close**. (To save the entry and make another, click **Save and New**.)

> **Note** Additional columns appear on the journal entry form if you select specific company preferences. For example, if you select Use Class on the Company tab of the Company Preferences dialog box, the journal entry form includes the Class column (as do other forms related to income and expense records). Classes let you classify income and expenses in categories such as sales region. The Job Name column appears in the journal entry form if you have selected Use Job to track expenses by job. If you select Use Job, a journal entry form also includes a Billable column. Select the check box in this column to indicate that an expense can be billed to a customer.

Editing and Voiding Journal Entries

After you create a journal entry, you cannot delete it. If you could delete a journal entry, the transaction history of your company would be vulnerable to tampering and your financial records too easily put out of balance.

You can, however, void a journal entry if the entry is no longer applicable. Also, you can make adjustments to the details of a transaction by editing a journal entry.

> **Note** If you attempt to edit a journal entry that appears on a bank statement you have reconciled or that is part of a fiscal year you archived using the compression facility mentioned in the "Archiving Transactions from Past Fiscal Years" section in Chapter 2, you might see a dialog box with the message "You are modifying a transaction that is part of a reconciled bank statement. If you modify this transaction, the reconciliation might no longer be valid. Do you want to continue?" If you do want to continue, click Yes, but be sure that the edited journal entry correctly reflects the state of your account. (In other words, that the original entry was in error.)

In this exercise, you will edit a journal entry and mark a journal entry void.

> **OPEN** the Fabrikam sample company file.

1. On the **Company** menu, point to **Company Lists**, and then click **Journal Entries**.

   The Journal Entry List appears.

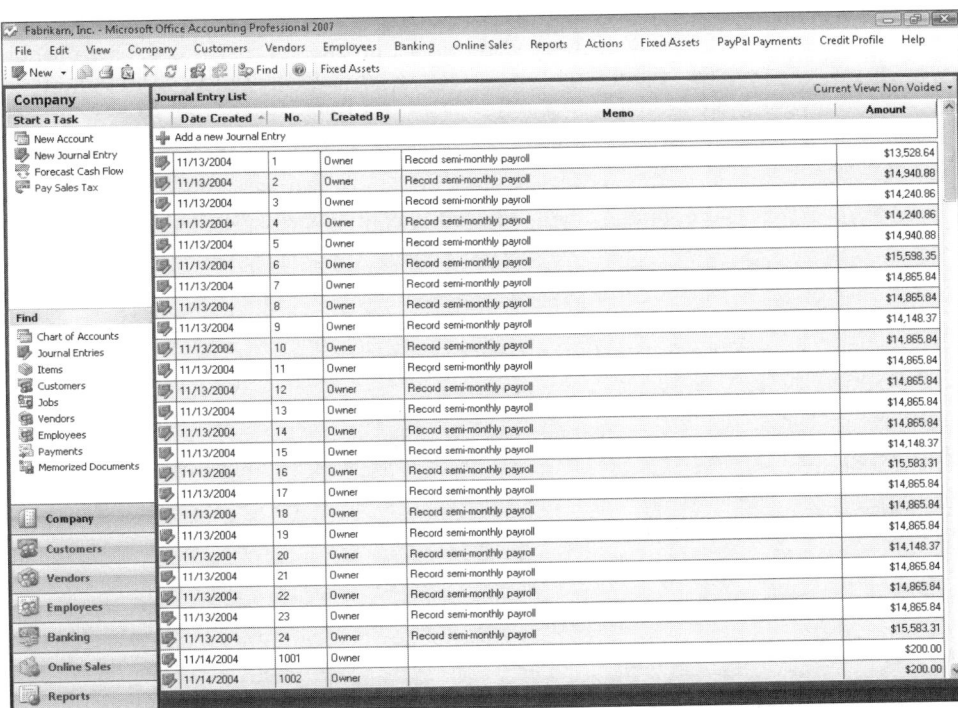

2. Double-click the journal entry you want to edit.

   The journal entry appears.

  3. On the toolbar, click **Edit**.

   The journal entry opens for editing.

4. Change the information on the journal entry form. Be sure that any dates you enter are in the current fiscal year.

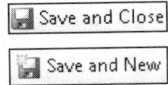 5. On the toolbar, click **Save and Close**. (To save your changes and create another journal entry, click **Save and New**.)

6. In the list of journal entries, double-click the journal entry that you need to void.

   The journal entry appears.

> **Note** If you attempt to void a journal entry that appears on a bank statement you have reconciled or that is part of a fiscal year you archived using the compression facility mentioned in the "Archiving Transactions from Past Fiscal Years" section in Chapter 2, "Setting Up a New Company," you might see a dialog box with the message "You are modifying a transaction that is part of a reconciled bank statement. If you modify this transaction, the reconciliation might no longer be valid. Do you want to continue?" If you do want to continue, click Yes, but be sure that the edited journal entry correctly reflects the state of your account. (In other words, that the original entry was in error.)

7. On the **Actions** menu, click **Void**.

A watermark reading VOID appears across the entry.

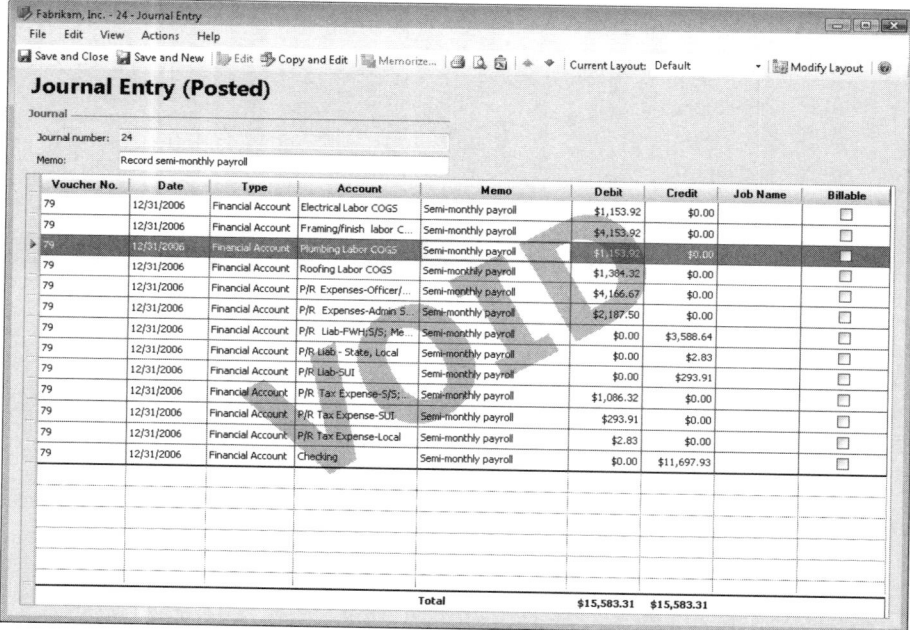

8. To confirm that you want to void the entry, click **Yes**.

The voided journal entry appears.

9. Click **Save and Close**.

CLOSE the Fabrikam sample company file, and if you are not continuing on to the next chapter, quit Accounting 2007.

Tip You can filter the list of journal entries by clicking Voided, Nonvoided, or All in the Current View list. You can change the order of the columns in the list of journal entries, or add or remove columns from the list, by clicking Add/Remove Content on the View menu.

Tip If Excel is installed on the computer on which you are running Accounting 2007, you can export the list of journal entries to Excel. In the Navigation Pane, click Company, and then click Journal Entries under Find. On the toolbar, click Export To Excel. Save the file in Excel if you want to refer to it again for analysis.

Key Points

- The chart of accounts represents the categories of a business's operations.
- You can select a default set of accounts when you set up Accounting 2007. Later, you can add accounts and edit account information.
- The journal is the history of each transaction you record. For each journal entry, the amount of the debits and credits must be equal.
- You cannot delete a journal entry. You can, however, edit a journal entry to correct the entry or mark a journal entry void.

Chapter at a Glance

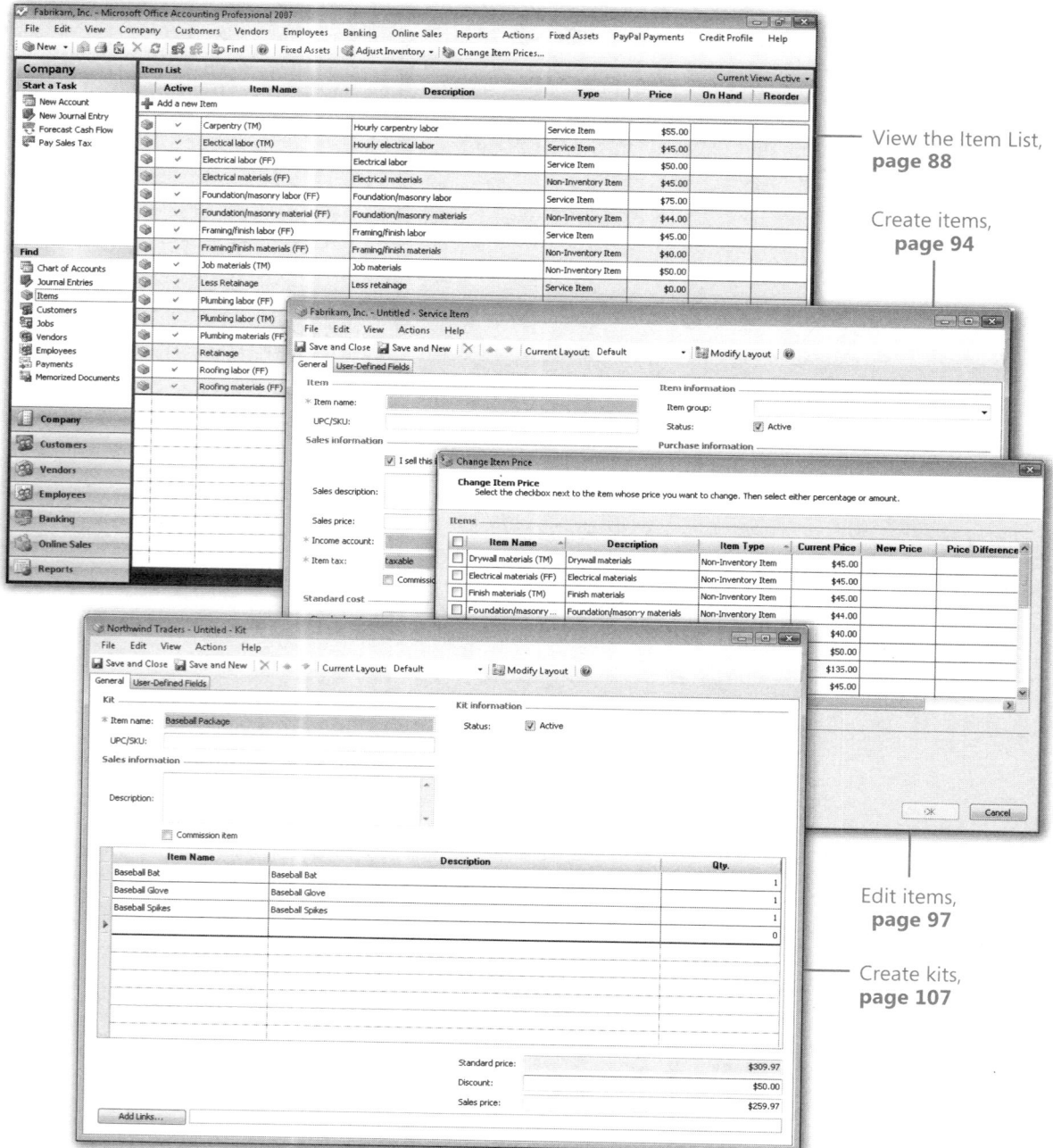

View the Item List,
page 88

Create items,
page 94

Edit items,
page 97

Create kits,
page 107

5 Managing Products and Services

In this chapter, you will learn to:

✔ View the Item List.
✔ Understand division and classification of items.
✔ Create and edit items.
✔ Create kits.
✔ Understand reporting considerations for products and services.

Your business makes money by selling two things: what you have and what you know. Microsoft Office Accounting 2007 classifies a product or service you have for sale as an item; the program maintains a master list of all of your items, whether they are currently for sale or not, and enables you to modify their entries as needed to reflect price changes, inventory results, and other factors.

In this chapter, you will learn how to view the Item List; use available item types; create and edit items; and change item prices, quantities, and values.

> **Troubleshooting** Graphics and operating system–related instructions in this book reflect the Windows Vista user interface. If your computer is running Windows XP and you experience trouble following the instructions as written, please refer to the "Information for Readers Running Windows XP" section at the beginning of this book.

Viewing the Item List

Every business, whether a consultancy or a manufacturer, makes money by selling products and services. Accounting 2007 represents the things you sell, such as an hour of consulting or a steel ball bearing, as an *item*. To display the Item List of all of the items your company sells, on the Customers home page, in the Find section, click Items.

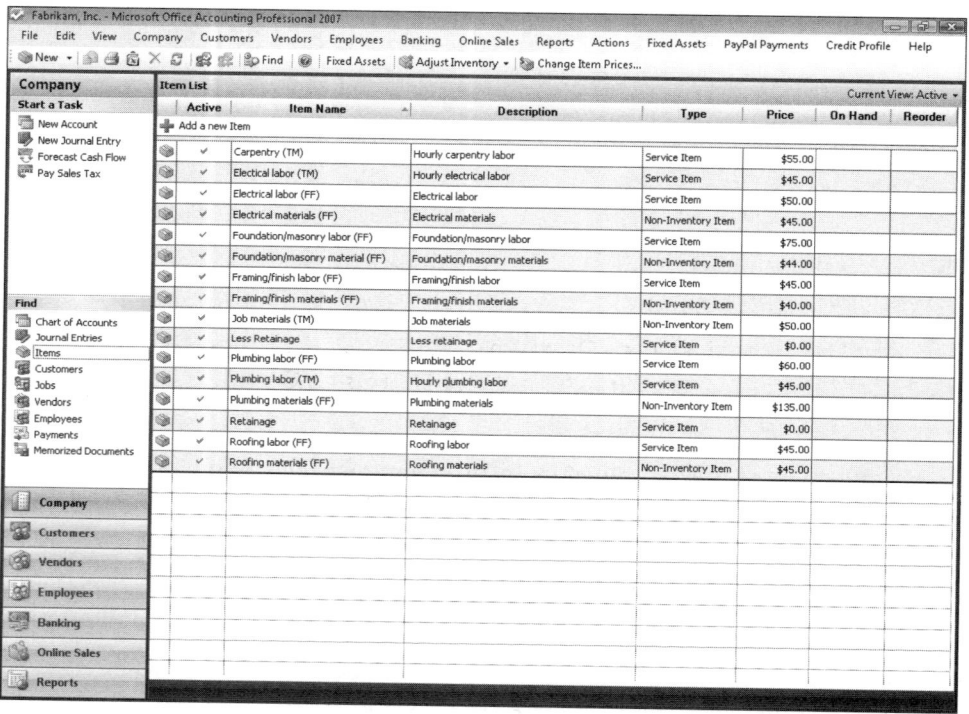

The Item List contains an entry for each item your company sells, although it can also display items that are not currently available for sale. Items that are available for sale are called *active items*, and they have a check mark in the Active column. Items that are not available for sale are *inactive items*. By default, the Item List displays only active items, but you can display both active and inactive items by clicking All in the Current View list.

At the top of each column is a header that describes the data stored in the column. You can sort the contents of the Item List alphabetically based on a column's contents by clicking the column's header. For example, clicking the Item Name header in the Fabrikam sample file's item list would result in the Item List arrangement sorted alphabetically by item name.

Clicking a column header once sorts the Item List in ascending order based on the column's value; clicking the column header again sorts the Item List in descending order.

If your business sells many different items, they might not all fit on one screen. With Accounting 2007, you can limit the items that appear in the Item List by creating a filter. To create a filter, follow these steps.

1. On the **Actions** menu, click **Find** (or press Ctrl+F) to display the **Find** toolbar.

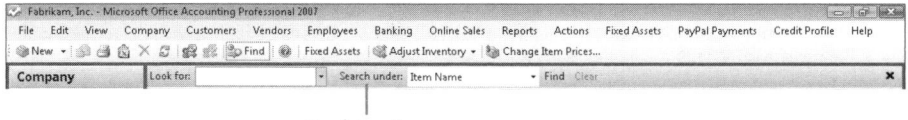

Find toolbar

2. On the **Find** toolbar, type the terms you want to find into the **Look For** field.

3. Select the column in which you want to find the terms by clicking the **Search Under** arrow.

To remove the filter, click Clear. When you're done using the Find toolbar, you can close it by clicking Find on the Actions menu or pressing Ctrl+F.

> **Note** Accounting filters the active list as you type a value into the Look For field.

In this exercise, you will view, filter, and sort the Item List.

> **OPEN** the Fabrikam sample file if you have closed it.

1. On the **Company** menu, point to **Company Lists**, and then click **Items**.

   The Item List appears.

2. Click the **Current View** arrow, and then in the list, click **Inactive**.

   Accounting displays items Fabrikam no longer offers for sale.

3. In the **Current View** list, click **Active**.

   Accounting displays items Fabrikam offers for sale.

4. Click the **Type** column header.

   Accounting sorts the Item List by item type.

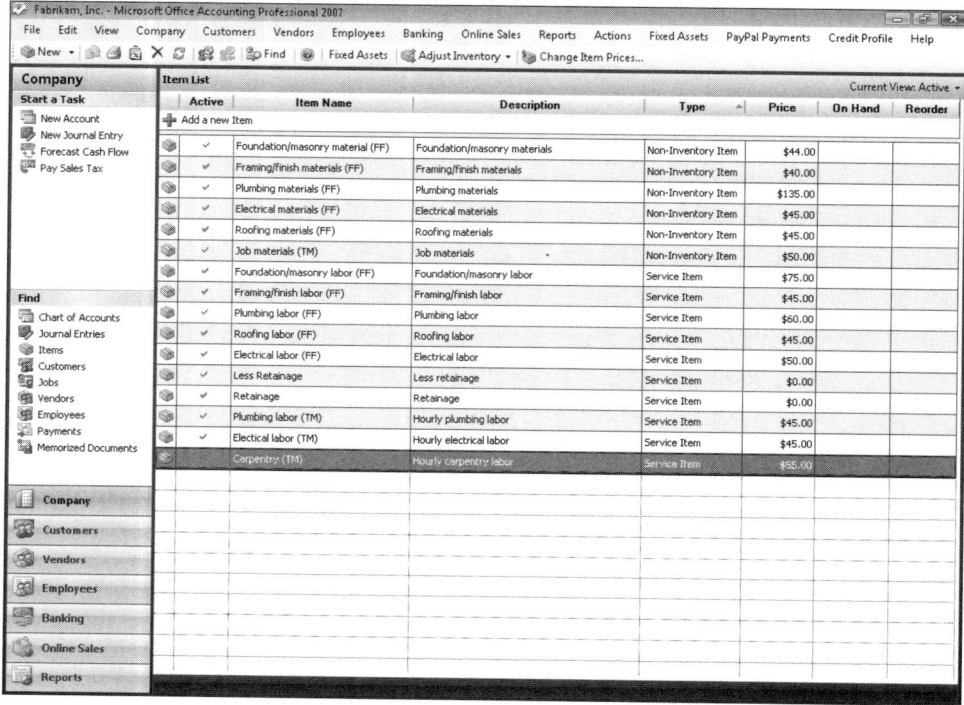

5. Click the **Item Name** column header.

   Accounting sorts the Item List by item name.

6. On the **Actions** menu, click **Find**.

   The Find toolbar appears.

7. In the **Look for** field, type framing.

8. Verify that *Item Name* appears in the **Search under** field.

9. Click **Find**.

   The Item List displays Framing/Finish Materials (FF) and Framing/Finish Labor (FF), the two items that contain the word *framing* in their Item Description field.

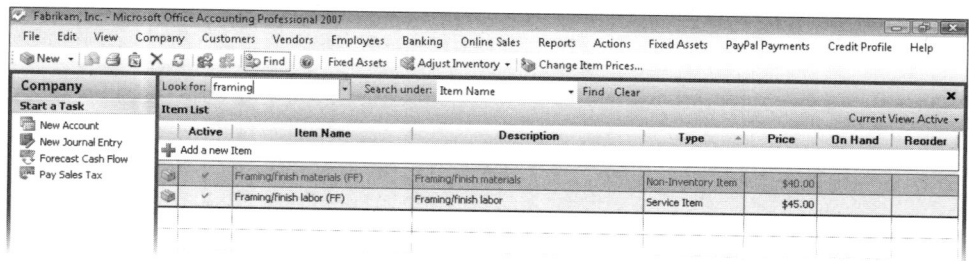

10. Click **Clear**.

The filter deactivates, and the Item List displays all of Fabrikam's items.

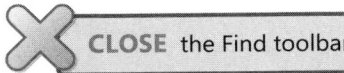 **CLOSE** the Find toolbar.

What Is Your Business?

Because Accounting 2007 is designed to support businesses that sell products or services, you have a great deal of flexibility in setting up items to represent your lines of business. Although this can lead to a temptation to class all possible sale activities into a single company, you should consider isolating a company to a specific business line for clearer analysis and reporting, as well as for other general business considerations. This is particularly true when you expand into other lines that differ significantly from your original core business.

Say you create a consulting service company. You offer office automation support for small and medium-sized clients who have a need to outfit their businesses with computers for staff, as well as to design and create a support structure to maintain their technology investments in house. Having led many such implementations with clients, you find yourself being asked to bundle and sell the computers and other network equipment directly to many clients, rather than simply assisting them in completing their orders to manufacturers. In short, you find yourself faced with the opportunities and challenges of a different sort of business that you want to be able to closely watch over time to determine viability and returns.

You could simply set up product items along with the service items that you currently maintain within your Accounting 2007 company, but you might consider the potential value in setting up a separate company in your accounting system to handle product sales, for several reasons. Potential considerations include ease of analysis and reporting upon the separate business lines without any confusion between them, but other possible advantages may come to light. You might, for example, want to reflect the legal structures of the two operations, which, after the new line of business is identified as being significant, you determine to be better off separately incorporated in a different state for various tax, liability, and other purposes.

You might also want to break out the inventory items into a separate business, after your sales revenues increase significantly relative to your once-dominant services revenues, so as to secure partnerships with manufacturers for the new company while maintaining independence with regard to consulting with competitor products within the original services business. Another reason you might want to move the product sales operation into a separate company might arise when you determine that the product sales business might benefit by adopting different accounting rules—perhaps even a different fiscal year, due to seasonality considerations within the sales cycles. Whatever the considerations, when you experience growth within new products or services offerings, you should always weigh whether to simply continue managing the new revenue streams with existing items in the same set of books, or to separate the businesses into two or more independent companies, each with its own customized chart of accounts.

A Logical Level of Subdivision

In a manner similar to the way you can set up accounts and subaccounts, (see Chapter 4, "Managing the Chart of Accounts"), you can create your item list to support richer analysis and subanalysis by using forethought in the setup process. Moreover, good planning with regard to alignment of the various service and product items your business sells and the accounts (or subaccounts) to which they are pointed can mean dramatically enhanced business intelligence to support your overall success.

Another way you can extend your analysis and reporting capabilities with Accounting 2007 is to use custom item groups. This feature makes it easy to group your items with related items into an appropriate line item within a report. You can then create custom reports that present the groups as line items so as to generate the precise information picture that is useful to you in determining profitability, activity, quantities on hand, and a host of other information about your product and services offerings and the transactions that surround them.

It is critical to think through to the reports you intend to produce as you set up the items of your company. In the forms that you complete as you create the items that you sell, focus upon pointing each to the appropriate income (and other) accounts/subaccounts, as required, as well as attaching each to the best custom item group to meet your reporting needs. As circumstances change, you can modify these pointers, in most cases, in a way to keep your analytical and reporting capabilities in tip-top shape.

Proper Classification of Products and Services

Although your business might simply sell either products or services, it has become quite common to see small businesses that derive revenues both. In some cases, businesses start out deriving income from one of these two general sources, only to discover opportunities in the other from which material revenue results. Classification, then, of the new revenue components may become a consideration. The good news is that Accounting 2007 offers unprecedented flexibility in supporting these changes to your chart of accounts.

Let's study the following example: Suppose you begin business by selling computers and networking gear to small businesses. Your entire revenue account structure consists of a primary Product Sales Revenue account with a handful of subaccounts that break out the general hardware type. (As an illustration, you might have Computer Hardware, Networking Hardware, Other Hardware And Software as these subaccounts, all of which roll up to the Product Sales Revenue account.) Moreover, you have another primary account, Miscellaneous Revenue, which you have used to record minor revenues you have received for providing installation support for customers in emergency situations (where, as an illustration, they needed to be up and running quickly, but still hadn't completely hired adequate support staff to meet immediate requirements).

You find yourself being called upon, more and more, to offer setup services of this sort. Because the sale itself, in many cases, is contingent upon providing this kind of help, you have dedicated a couple of full time staff to handling these requirements when they arise. Moreover, you've hired a network specialist for the same reason, and are excited to find that she is also an expert in the related field of security implementations (focusing upon Active Directory directory service planning and implementation, among other things). You appreciate the fact that this is an expertise area within which many customers have requested support in the past on a "one-off" basis. (They need the skills to support their implementations, but after they're up and running, they can't economically justify hiring a person with these costly credentials as a permanent staff member.)

You see the opportunity to accept more of the service-related work, which will not only help you to fully absorb the cost of the dedicated staff members, but also to enhance significantly your overall bottom line. At this point, you will want to consider reclassifying, perhaps, the associated components of Miscellaneous Revenue with a new Service Sales Revenue primary account (with related subaccounts for, say, System Installation, System Maintenance (including upgrades), Network Installation, Network Maintenance (including upgrades), Security Design And Implementation, and so on). You might even consider, after you have set up these subaccounts, moving affected transactions in the Miscellaneous Revenues account to their new homes in the respective service types they represent, to provide a clean classification back to the beginning, for example, of the year in which you made the chart of accounts changes.

When you properly classify your material revenue streams, you make analysis and reporting far more meaningful. The business intelligence that you obtain from properly classified and aggregated transactions can not only help you to determine optimal product/service mixes to offer, but can offer you insight into new areas to consider adding to your business offerings. The ease with which you can map your Accounting 2007 system to your company's operations means nimble and flexible support that grows with your business.

Creating Items

Some businesses can thrive without offering more than a core set of products and services, but the vast majority of companies need to update their offerings to retain current customers and attract new ones. Whenever your company offers a new product or service for sale, you create a new item in your company file.

When you want to add a new item, click New Item on the New menu to display the Select Item Type dialog box. You can then choose from the following four item types:

- **Service** includes labor or consulting provided to the customer.
- **Inventory** includes items your company keeps in stock.
- **Non-Inventory Item** includes items your company needs to order before you can provide them to your customers.
- **Kit** is a collection of items sold as a group.

Selecting Service, Inventory, or Non-Inventory Item displays a form you can use to fill in details about the item, such as its name, price, and description. However, if you select the Kit option, Accounting displays a form for creating a kit.

See Also For more information about creating a kit in Accounting Professional 2007, see "Creating Kits" later in this chapter.

When you select Service, Inventory, or Non-Inventory Item, you can use the same form to enter items you purchase from vendors as well as items you sell. Accounting 2007 distinguishes between the two types of items and allows you to designate an item as both types.

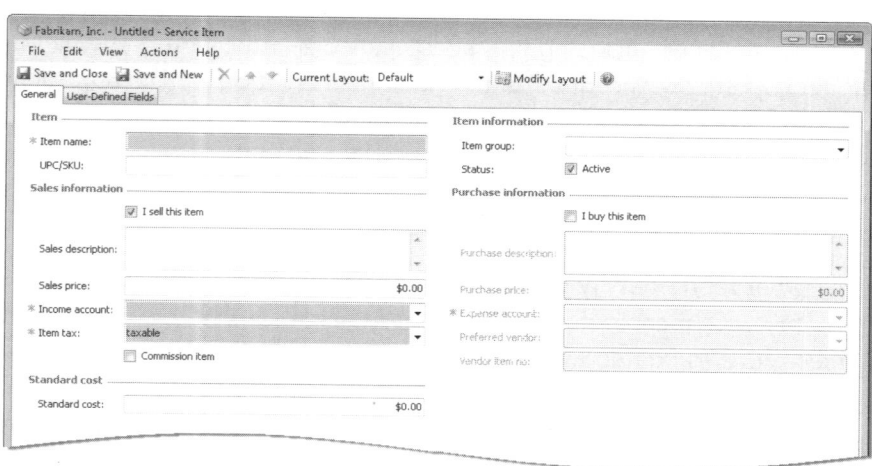

In the form for the new item, you can select the I Sell This Item check box to indicate that you provide the product to your customers. If you select the I Buy This Item check box, you indicate that you purchase the product or service from a vendor. And, yes, you can select both check boxes. If you purchase building supplies for use on your projects and to sell in your showroom, you would select both the I Buy This Item and the I Sell This Item check boxes and fill in the item's information in both areas.

If you find that you want to add information about an item that doesn't fit in the standard form fields, you can create a custom field to hold that information.

To create a custom field for an item, follow these steps.

1. Display the item, and click the **User-Defined Fields** tab.

2. In the lower-left corner of the item window, click the **New Fields** button.

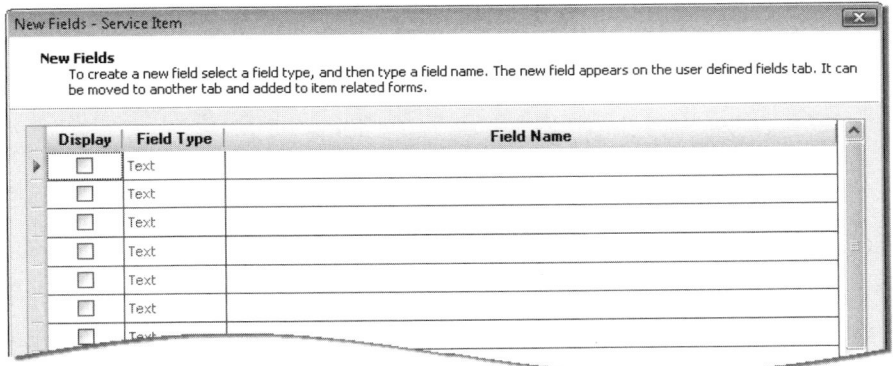

3. In the **New Fields** dialog box, select the check box next to the type of field you want to create (text, date, number, or check box).

4. Type a name for the field in the **Field Name** column, and then click **OK**.

In this exercise, you will create a new item.

OPEN the Fabrikam sample company file.

1. In the **Navigation Pane**, click **Customers**.

2. In the **More Tasks** section of the **Customers** home page, click **New Item**.

   The Select Item Type dialog box opens.

3. Click **Service**, and then click **OK**.

A blank Service Item form appears.

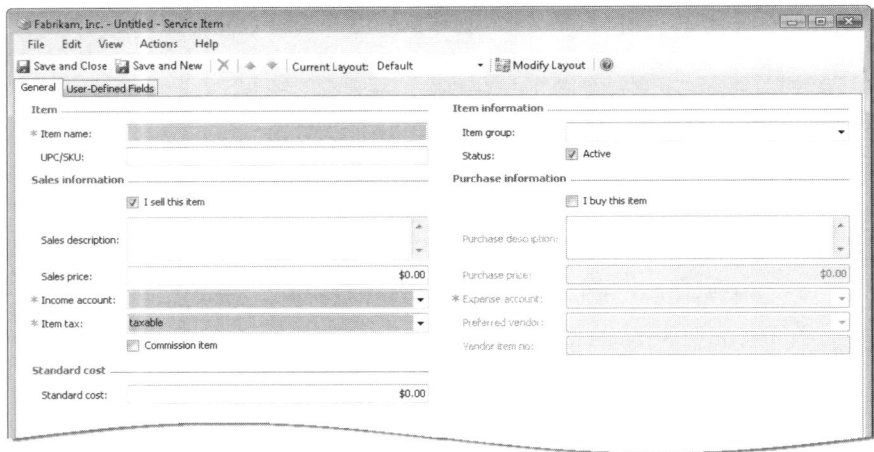

4. In the **Item Name** box, type Landscaping Labor.

5. Verify that the **I Sell this item** check box is selected.

6. In the **Sales Price** box, type 40.

7. In the **Income Account** list, click **4026 Service**.

> **Tip** If you're asked whether you would like to assign this account as the default Income account for service items, click No. Clicking No retains the built-in account mapping. If you do want to assign this account as service items' default Income account, click Yes.

Accounting 2007 assigns the item's income to the Service account.

> **Note** Other labor items, such as Electrical Services and Foundation/Masonry Services, have their own income account. If you wanted to create a new account to track landscaping labor income, you could follow the steps found in the "Adding and Editing Accounts" section of Chapter 4, "Managing the Chart of Accounts."

8. In the **Sales Description** box, type Hourly landscaping labor.

9. Verify that *taxable* appears in the **Item tax** box.

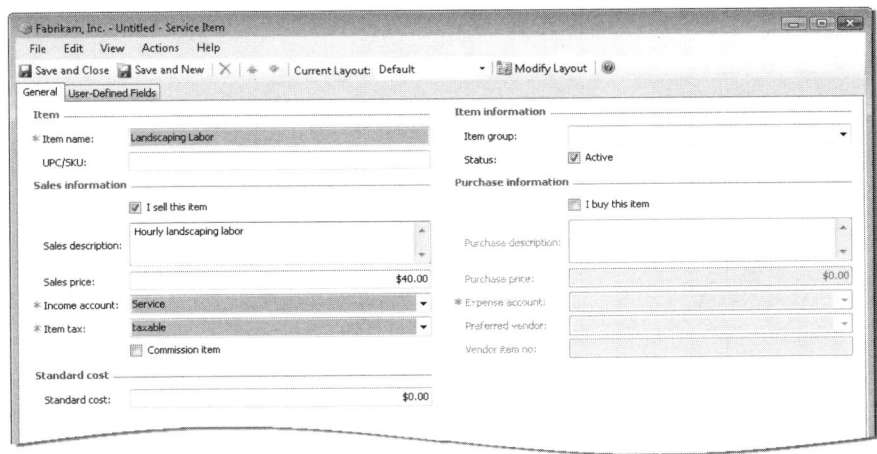

10. On the **Service Item** form's toolbar, click **Save and Close**.

Accounting 2007 saves your new item and closes the Service Item form.

Editing Items

One of the imperatives of running a successful business is maintaining accurate and current information regarding all of your products and processes. Whenever you decide to change anything about a product, such as whether to no longer offer it for sale, change its name, or change its price, you should edit your Accounting 2007 records immediately. This section shows you how to make the most common changes to your items.

Changing Item Prices

Prices change all the time due to inflation, resource scarcity, responses to competitor pricing, and the perceived value of collectible goods. For example, Fabrikam might use a certain type of steel support in their construction projects and bill customers for those materials. If your supplier charges more for those supports, you will need to pass that increase on to your customers.

In this exercise, you will change an item's price.

OPEN the Fabrikam sample company file.

1. In the **Navigation Pane**, click **Customers**.
2. In the **Find** area of the **Customers** home page, click **Items**.

The Item List appears.

3. Double-click the **Carpentry (TM)** item.

The Carpentry (TM) – Service Item form appears.

4. In the **Sales Price** box, change the value to 60.

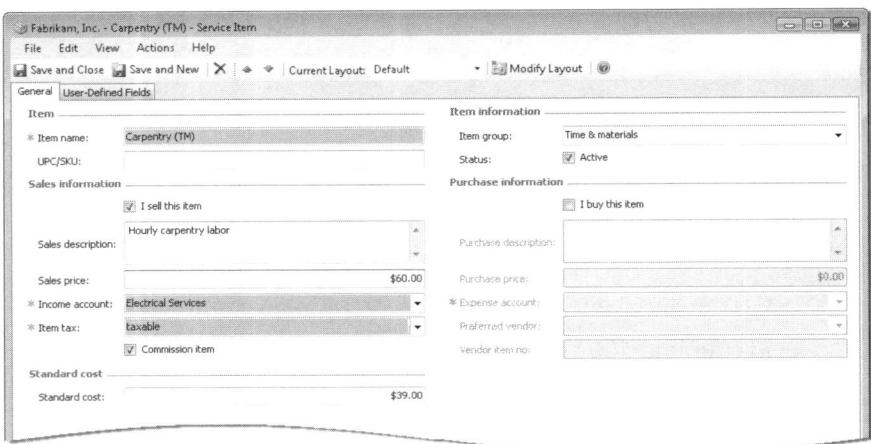

5. Click **Save and Close**.

The Service Item form closes, and the item's price changes to $60.00.

Changing Multiple Price Levels (Professional Only)

One of the benefits of using Accounting Professional is that you can change multiple items' prices from within the Change Item Price dialog box.

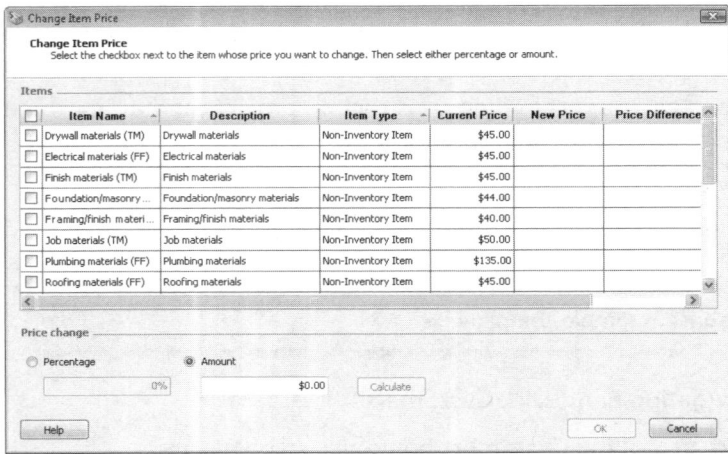

To edit items' prices, in the Change Item Price dialog box, select the check box next to each item and then, under Price Change, click Percentage to change the prices using a percentage of the items' current price, or click Amount to change the prices by a particular dollar amount. Type the percent or amount by which you want to change the prices (positive values increase a price, negative values decrease it) in the box that corresponds to the option you selected.

> **Tip** To select every item in the list, select the check box to the left of the Item Name header in the Items grid. Clearing the check box on the list's header row clears every item's check box.

To see how your increase or decrease affects the items' prices, click Calculate. Accounting Professional displays the new prices in the New Price column of the Items grid and each price's change in the Price Difference column. To accept the new values, click OK. If you'd like to edit an individual item's price, clear every other item's check box, and then use the controls in the Price Change section of the dialog box to set the new price.

In this exercise, you will change the price of an item and then calculate it to see its effect.

> **OPEN** the Fabrikam sample company file.

1. In the **Navigation Pane**, click **Customers**.
2. In the **Find** area of the **Customers** home page, click **Items**.

   The Item List appears.
3. On the **Item List** toolbar, click **Change Item Prices**.

   The Change Item Price dialog box opens.
4. Select the **Drywall Materials (TM)** check box.
5. Select the **Job Materials (TM)** check box.
6. Under **Price Change**, verify that **Amount** is selected, and type 5 in the rightmost text box.

7. Click **Calculate**.

The new values appear in the New Price column.

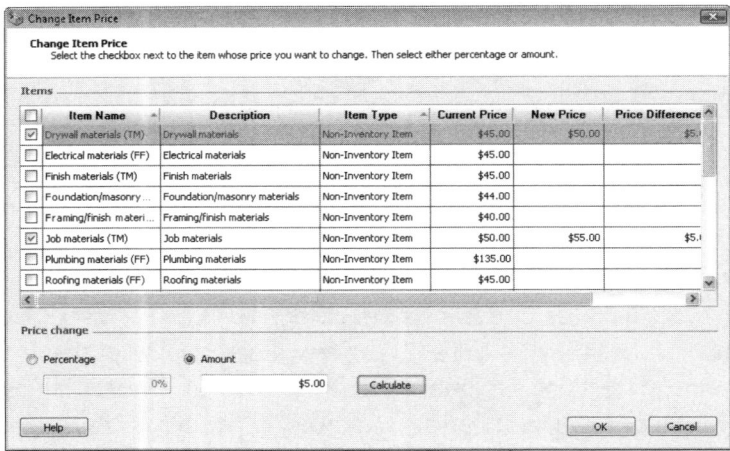

8. Click **OK**.

The Change Item Price dialog box closes, and the new prices appear in the Item List.

CLOSE the Fabrikam sample company file.

Changing Quantity (Professional Only)

Maintaining a physical inventory isn't always a simple task. Items break, get misplaced, or just go missing. It's rarer to find that you have an unexpectedly large quantity of an item in stock, but it happens. When you do need to adjust the quantity of your inventory items, you can do so by using the Adjust Inventory Quantity dialog box.

After you select the account to which you'll ascribe the loss or gain of value, you can set your items' new quantities.

In this exercise, you will change the quantity of several items listed in the Northwind Traders database.

> **Note** The Northwind Traders sample company file is included only with Accounting Professional 2007. The file name is sampleproductcompany.sbc; you can open it using its file name or by clicking Open A Sample Company in the Start dialog box and then clicking Product Based Sample Company.

> **OPEN** the Northwind Traders sample company file.

1. In the **Navigation Pane**, click **Customers**.

2. In the **Find** area of the **Customers** home page, click **Items**.

   The Item List appears.

3. On the **Item List** toolbar, click **Adjust Inventory**, and then click **Adjust Quantity**.

   The Adjust Inventory Quantity dialog box opens.

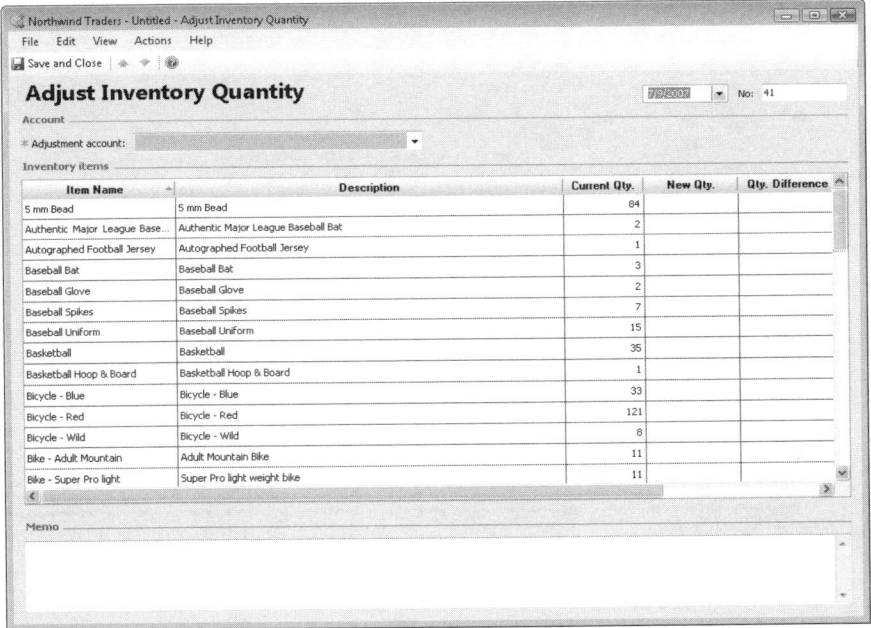

4. In the **Adjust Account** box list, click **6760 Other Expenses**.

5. In the **New Qty.** column of the **5 mm Bead** item, type 82, and then press the Tab key.

   The value *-2* appears in the Qty. Difference column.

6. In the **New Qty.** column of the **Bicycle – Blue** item, type 32.

The value *-1* appears in the Qty. Difference column.

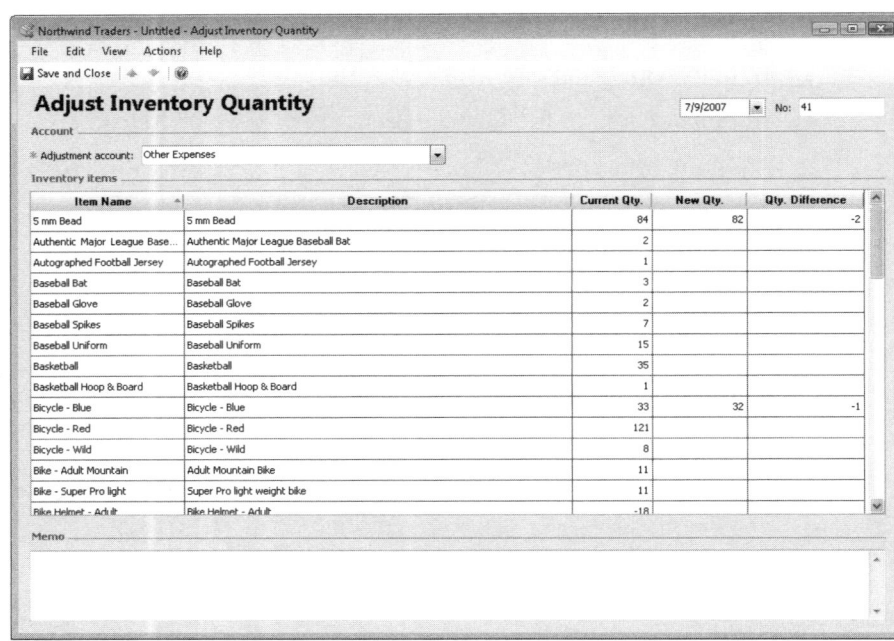

7. Click **Save and Close**.

The Adjust Inventory Quantity form closes, and Accounting Professional updates your item quantities.

 **CLOSE** the Northwind Traders sample company file.

The Need for Periodic Inventory Counts and Adjustments (Professional Only)

Although Accounting Professional 2007 can track and report upon your inventory in real time (this is called *perpetual inventory accounting*), you cannot rely solely on the system to keep your inventory updated and in order. You will also need to perform periodic inventory counts to keep data in the system reconciled to reality. This typically means you make annual counts of all inventory, (although cyclical counts of smaller inventory groups are becoming common as a way to manage the "big count" using bite-sized pieces), as well as to focus recurring counts upon products of high-dollar value, products subject to more-than-average breakage or pilferage, and the like.

After you perform your count(s), and identify differences, you make adjustments to Accounting Professional as appropriate. Because you will likely be decreasing inventory balances in the system for broken or missing items (as well as for other reasons), it's often a good idea to book the other side of the adjustment to an account you set up just for this purpose (you tell Accounting Professional which account this is when you adjust your inventory via the Adjust Inventory Quantity form). Having a special expense account—or perhaps even multiple subaccounts based upon your inventory groups and the like—in place for this purpose can help you to identify trends (such as increasing pilferage or breakage) in time to take effective remedial action.

You can also perform spot checks of inventory and possibly come to conclusions based upon the results. These checks should be performed at least quarterly, in many cases, and perhaps more frequently as an "early warning" procedure within high-risk inventory groups. In addition to these more frequent counts, you would still perform a full inventory with full results reporting once a year. You may also consider hiring outside contractors, your accountant, or other agencies to perform a periodic audit of your inventory to augment your own efforts in performing the counts themselves, or to provide an independent set of results to compare to your own findings. Some small businesses look to their resellers, vendors, and even manufacturers for various types of assistance with this process. However you accomplish them, periodic inventory counts provide great snapshots of your overall inventory management, and contribute significantly to your operational business intelligence.

Optimal Inventory Reorder Levels

To optimize your management of inventory, you must focus upon numerous uncertainties, constraints, and other considerations. Depending upon the complexity of your supply chain (for example, whether you purchase from international suppliers), these considerations can become numerous and complicated. Inventory forecasting, including the setting of inventory targets (including how much of each item you keep on hand) can become key to optimization of your inventory operation, and can mean savings in backordering and holding costs. These considerations tend to increase in importance as your business grows larger, and a greater number of customers need to be kept happy.

Your focus becomes optimal order fulfillment (and hence minimization of lost sales), with a simultaneous decrease in on-hand inventory (to minimize holding costs, risk of obsolescence or softening markets, and so on). This common business need has resulted in the derivation of the highly regarded Economic Order Quantity (or EOQ) model. The primary EOQ model defines the optimal quantity to order that minimizes total variable costs required to order and hold inventory.

Although your business may be somewhat simple, and your knowledge of your customer base and their needs quite comprehensive, you would do well to consider both the EOQ model and some of the several extensions that have been made to it, including provision for backordering costs and multiple items. Also, be aware that the economic order interval can be determined from the EOQ, and that the economic production quantity model (which determines the optimal production quantity) can be determined in a similar fashion.

The EOQ model can seem complex to a small-business owner and may be overkill anyway. But you should be aware of these concepts, and examine the various sites on the Web, as well as some of the many books on the subject, that show how to use the basic model and its extensions. You might find it to be a highly valuable tool as business grows and you develop a more acute need to optimize your management of inventory.

Inventory Write-Ups and Write-Downs

Sometimes it becomes necessary for you to adjust the value of your inventory. The idea, at these times, is to adjust the value of the inventory as of the day you recognize—and can reasonably quantify—the amount of the adjustment. You (or your accountant) make the adjustments to the books via a journal entry, with the amount of the adjustment typically being posted to an extraordinary loss or gain account within your income statement accounts.

Adjustments can occur for several reasons. As examples, you might make write-down adjustments for the following reasons:

- Inventory has been determined to be obsolete, and to have lost market value (based upon age, new innovations that have emerged in the markets, and so on).
- Inventory has not turned over for some time, and/or has become otherwise devalued.
- To correct mistakes that led to overvaluation in previous accounting periods.
- General revaluations are mandated based upon market conditions.
- Market pricing for new items is less than the amounts you paid for identical, older items that you hold in inventory, due to innovations in manufacturing that have come along since you bought the items.

Moreover, you might make write-up adjustments for reasons that include the following examples:

- To adjust inventory items upward for insurance purposes. (The classic examples are works of art.)

● To correct mistakes that led to undervaluation in previous accounting periods.

● General revaluations are mandated based upon market conditions.

Changing Quantity and Value (Professional Only)

You can change the quantity and value of inventory items from within the Item List by clicking Adjust Inventory, clicking Adjust Quantity And Value, and then using the controls in the Adjust Inventory Quantity And Value dialog box to enter the new data.

If you need to change an item's inventory level but don't have the Item List open, you can point to Adjust Inventory on the Vendors menu, and then click Adjust Quantity And Value to open the same dialog box.

In this exercise, you will change the quantity and value of an inventory item.

> **OPEN** the Northwind Traders sample file.

1. On the **Vendors** menu, point to **Adjust Inventory**, and then click **Adjust Quantity and Value**.

   The Adjust Inventory Quantity And Value dialog box opens.

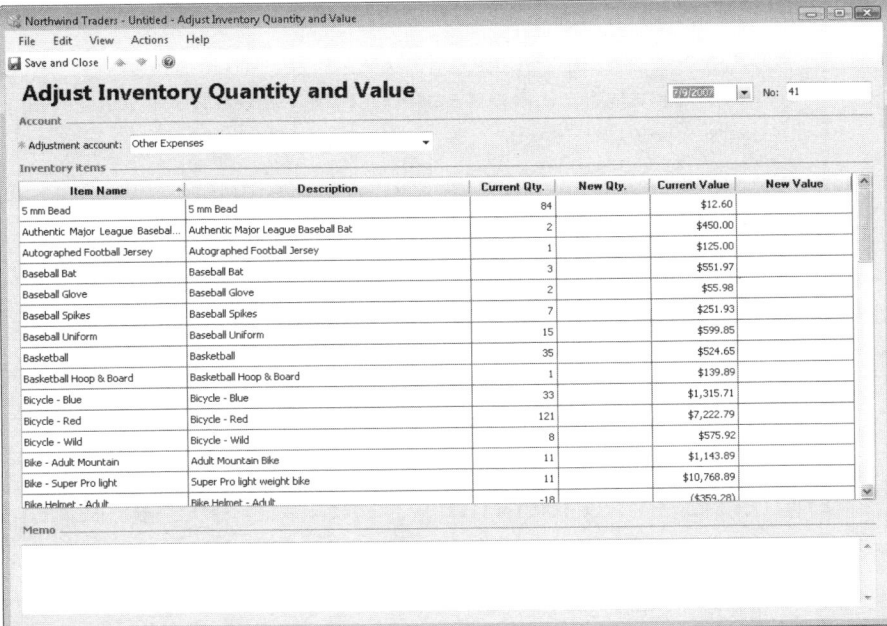

2. Click the **Adjustment Account** arrow, and then click **4510 Cost of Goods – Materials**.

3. In the **Inventory Items** list, in the **Autographed Football Jersey** row, click in the **New Quantity** field, and then type 3.

4. In the same row, click in the **New Value** field, type 250, and then press Enter .

   Accounting Professional updates the current value of your inventory.

5. Click **Save and Close**.

 CLOSE the Northwind Traders sample company file.

Avoiding Negative Inventory

One of the problems faced by businesses of all sizes, but particularly by small businesses, is keeping popular products in stock. It can be tempting to take all of your customers' orders without regard to whether you have the stock on hand to fill the order, but you should look very carefully at your sales orders to ensure there are no items on back order. You should also communicate very clearly to your customers that they will not receive their entire order at one time, and give them the option to change their order.

You can also have Accounting 2007 warn you whenever you create an order that would require more units of a product than you have in stock (that is, create a negative inventory level).

To have Accounting 2007 warn you whenever an order would result in negative inventory, follow these steps.

1. On the **Company** menu, click **Preferences**.

2. In the **Company Preferences** dialog box, click the **Vendors** tab.

3. Select the **Check for item quantity on hand** check box, and then click **OK**.

Understanding Inventory Valuation (Professional Only)

If your business is like most non-service organizations, inventory probably represents a large part of your assets. Whatever the nature of your business, if inventory comprises a significant portion of your balance sheet, it is important to understand how that inventory is valued. The accounting method that a company decides to use to determine the costs of inventory can directly impact the balance sheet, income statement and statement of cash flow. There are three inventory-costing methods that are widely used by both public and private companies, although there are variations and hybrids surrounding each. These are known as the First-In, First-Out (FIFO) method, the Last-In, First-Out (LIFO) method, and the Average Cost method.

Accounting Professional 2007 uses the First-In, First-Out (FIFO) method of inventory valuation. This method assumes that the first unit making its way into your inventory is the first unit sold, and is a very common approach to valuation. For example, let's say that a clothing retailer purchases 100 pairs of a popular line of pants on June 4 at a cost of $27.00 each, and 150 more on June 13 at $27.75 each.

The FIFO method dictates that if the clothier sold 150 pairs of pants on June 6, the Cost Of Goods Sold (the expense component of the sale) is $4,087.50 (100 pairs x $27.00 per pair plus 50 pairs x $27.75 per pair). Cost Of Goods Sold in this example comprises the cumulative cost of the first pairs of pants to enter the inventory account. The remaining inventory on June 30, assuming no more pants were purchased and added to inventory or sold from the same line before that date, would be valued at $2,775.00 (100 pairs x $27.75 per pair). The $27.75 pairs of pants would be allocated to ending inventory (an asset value that would appear on the balance sheet).

The FIFO inventory valuation method gives you a better indication of the value of ending inventory (on the balance sheet), because the units of inventory you have on hand are valued at their most recent costs. To some extent, FIFO can increase net income because inventory that might be several years old is used to value the cost of goods sold. While increasing measured net income would seem to be a great problem to have, the potentially higher taxes and other considerations lead some companies to use LIFO, Weighted Average, or a hybrid approach to valuation. Accounting Professional makes inventory tracking and valuation easy for a small business by handling most of the valuation mechanics in the background. If you have more complicated needs, you should discuss them with an accounting professional, and perhaps consider a more personalized approach, after you set up Accounting Professional 2007.

Creating Kits (Professional Only)

After you've been in business for a while, you'll most likely discover sets of goods and services that customers tend to order together. For example, most new bicycle riders need to purchase a helmet and other accessories in addition to the bicycle, so you should consider grouping those items into a kit. A kit is a collection of two or more items that you offer for sale as a unit, often at a discounted price as compared to the cost of the items if purchased separately.

After you create a kit, you can edit or delete it like any other item.

Note Deleting a kit does not delete any of the items that comprise the kit.

In this exercise, you will define a kit for a commonly requested sports equipment package.

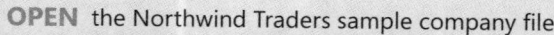 **OPEN** the Northwind Traders sample company file.

1. In the **Navigation Pane**, click **Customers**.
2. In the **More Tasks** section of the **Customers** home page, click **New Item**.

   The Select Item Type dialog box opens.
3. Click **Kit**, and then click **OK**.

   An untitled Kit form appears.

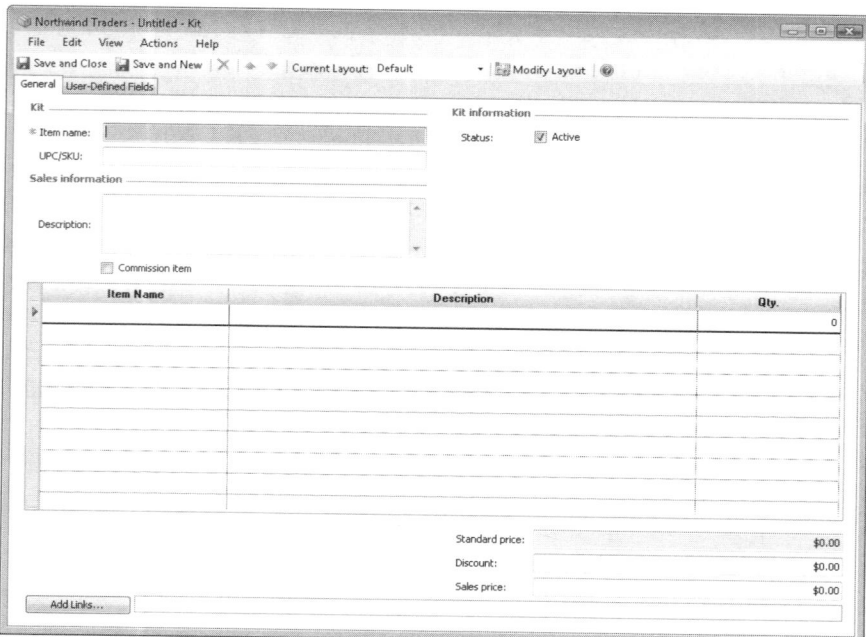

4. In the **Item name** box, type Baseball Package.

5. In the grid, click in the first **Item Name** field, click the arrow that appears, and then click **Baseball Bat**. In the **Qty.** column, type 1.

6. In the grid, click in the second **Item Name** field, click the arrow that appears, and then click **Baseball Glove**. In the **Qty.** column, type 1.

7. In the grid, click in the third **Item Name** field, click the arrow that appears, and then click **Baseball Spikes**. In the **Qty.** column, type 1.

8. In the **Discount** box, type 50.

   The value in the Sales Price box changes to $259.97.

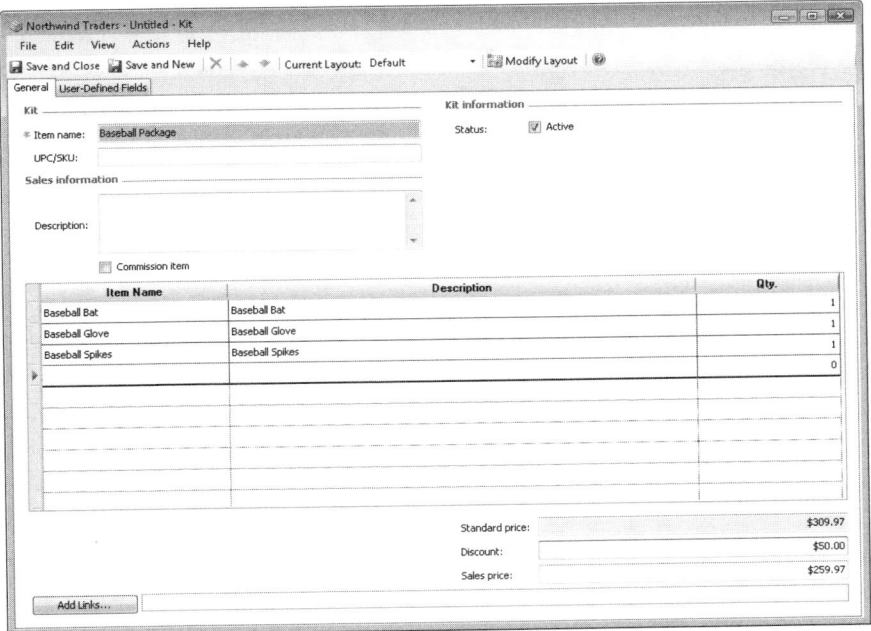

9. Click **Save and Close**.

   The Kit form closes and Accounting Professional adds your kit to the Item List.

CLOSE the Northwind Traders sample company file, and if you are not continuing on to the next chapter, quit Accounting 2007.

Reporting Considerations for Products and Services

The products and services area of your business offers rich reporting opportunities and a wide range of business intelligence. Reports that you base upon products and/or services, and the sales activity they reflect, will focus not only upon the products you have sold, but to whom (your customers) you have sold them. When you look at what you have sold, you can also examine your margins on each of those items, with an objective of increasing margins through pricing, purchasing and marketing strategies while continuously improving your product/service mixes to optimize profits.

Analysis and reporting of inventory can lead to a wealth of information about turnover, waste, obsolescence, and a host of other factors that will also help you to run your business optimally. Knowing not only what you sold, but the rate at which you are selling it and related considerations can mean even finer tuning of your inventory management structure. This, in turn, means having popular products and services in stock and available to meet customer demand without delays—while minimizing the costs that come with holding slow-moving items. (For that matter, slow selling items can be easily identified with regular examination of reports created for this purpose, and action can be taken to relieve your inventory of these items quickly.) Trending reports within this area are particularly important, because they can help you identify diminishing returns, slowdowns in movement, and other conditions, so that you can act upon these scenarios before they become problems.

Typical "views" by which you might arrange product and services information include products/services sold, breakouts of products and services by types, combinations of the items you have sold (via kits or in other groups), and the like. You might also find helpful views that present product and services sold, information by the customers to whom you have made the sales, timing of sales, and associated details.

Key Points

- You can find all of your items on the Item List, which you can search and sort to make it easier to manage your items.
- If your company offers a new product or service for sale, you can add a new item to the item list.
- Be sure to update your items' information whenever it changes.
- With Accounting Professional, you can change multiple item prices from within a single dialog box.
- With Accounting Professional, you can change item inventory quantities and values for product-based companies.
- If your customers frequently purchase several products at the same time, consider grouping those items into a kit and offering a discount to encourage sales.

Chapter at a Glance

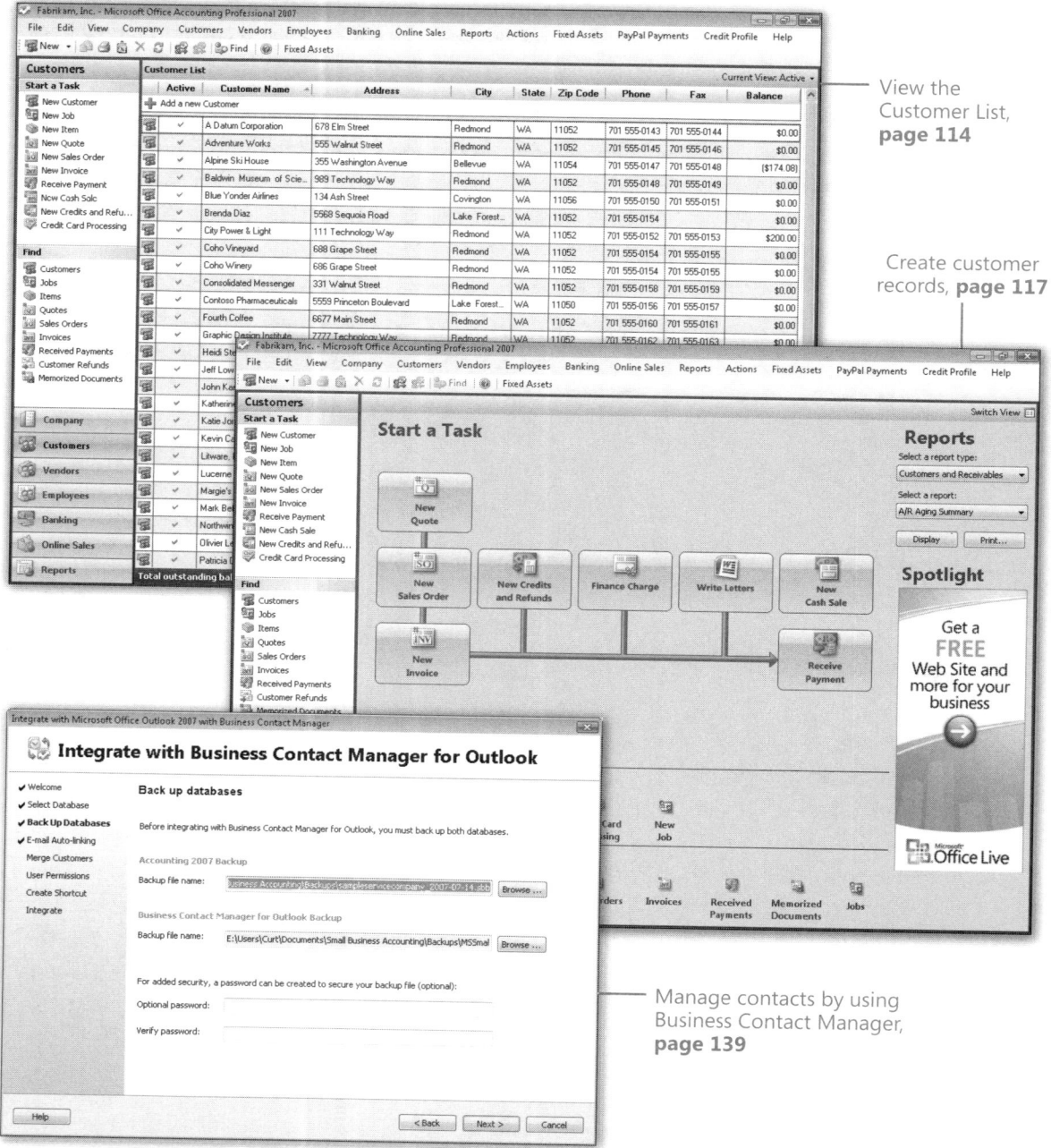

View the Customer List, **page 114**

Create customer records, **page 117**

Manage contacts by using Business Contact Manager, **page 139**

6 Managing Customers

In this chapter, you will learn to:

- ✔ View the Customer List.
- ✔ Create customer records and groups.
- ✔ Create price levels, credit ratings, and payment terms.
- ✔ Define shipping terms and methods.
- ✔ Set up sales tax agencies and sales tax codes.
- ✔ Create sales tax groups.
- ✔ Manage contacts by using Business Contact Manager.

Much of the work involved in operating a small business relates to managing customers. Two key elements of a detailed and informative accounting system are the facts and the figures it stores about a business's customers, including up-to-date contact information and a history of financial transactions. You work with customer records to maintain an accurate list of contact information; documents such as invoices, quotes, and payments make up the breadth and depth of a customer's financial history.

In addition to maintaining customer contact information such as names, addresses, and phone numbers, you need information about the details required to administer a customer's account. For example, you need to know if a discount is applied to the orders a customer makes, and you need to specify a customer's credit rating and tax status, and the payment terms by which a customer is expected to pay. You can also integrate your customer information with Microsoft Office Outlook 2007 with Business Contact Manager, which means that you can enter a customer's contact information into either program and use the information in both programs.

In Microsoft Office Accounting 2007, you initiate your work with customer information on the Customers home page. The home page provides links to your Customer List and to tasks such as creating a customer record, preparing an estimate, issuing an invoice, and viewing reports that summarize information about customer payments.

In this chapter, you will be introduced to the Customers home page and learn how to create and work with customer data in Accounting 2007. You'll learn how to create a customer record, how to view and sort the Customer List, and how to define the discounts, payment terms, pricing levels, and the tax group that you apply to a customer account. You'll also learn how to integrate your customer data with Outlook with Business Contact Manager and, if desired, reverse that integration.

> **Troubleshooting** Graphics and operating system–related instructions in this book reflect the Windows Vista user interface. If your computer is running Windows XP and you experience trouble following the instructions as written, please refer to the "Information for Readers Running Windows XP" section at the beginning of this book.

Viewing the Customer List

The Customer List in Accounting 2007 displays key customer contact information and the amount of the customer's balance. You can use the Customer List as the departure point for working on the information about a particular customer in more detail. For example, you can update contact information, add contact details, view financial status, and enter account details such as credit limits or similar information.

You can also sort the Customer List to group customers. For example, you can group customers by city or sort the Customer List to see customer balances in ascending or descending order.

> **Tip** By default, the Customer List displays only active customers. You can display all customers or only inactive customers by using the Current View list in the upper-right corner of the Customer List.

By default, customers are listed in alphabetical order by customer name. You can click a column heading to sort the list by different criteria. Sorting by city, for example, lets you group customers into geographic areas. By clicking the Balance column heading, you can see which customers owe you the most money and which owe you the least.

You can delete a customer record if you have not recorded any transactions for that customer and the customer has no financial history. If you have recorded transactions for a customer record, you can mark the record inactive but you cannot delete it. A customer record that is marked inactive is not displayed in the Customer List in dialog boxes or forms. To delete a customer record from the Customer List, right-click the customer in the list, and then click Delete.

To make a customer record inactive, right-click the customer record in the Customer List, and then click Make Inactive. You can change an inactive customer's status back to active by selecting the customer record in the Customer List and then clicking Make Active on the Edit menu.

In this exercise, you'll learn how to view and sort the Customer List in Accounting 2007 and how to organize the columns of information that the Customer List displays.

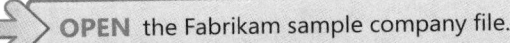 **OPEN** the Fabrikam sample company file.

1. In the **Navigation Pane**, click the **Customers** button.

   The Customers home page appears.

2. In the **Find** area of the **Customers** home page, click **Customers**.

   The Customer List appears.

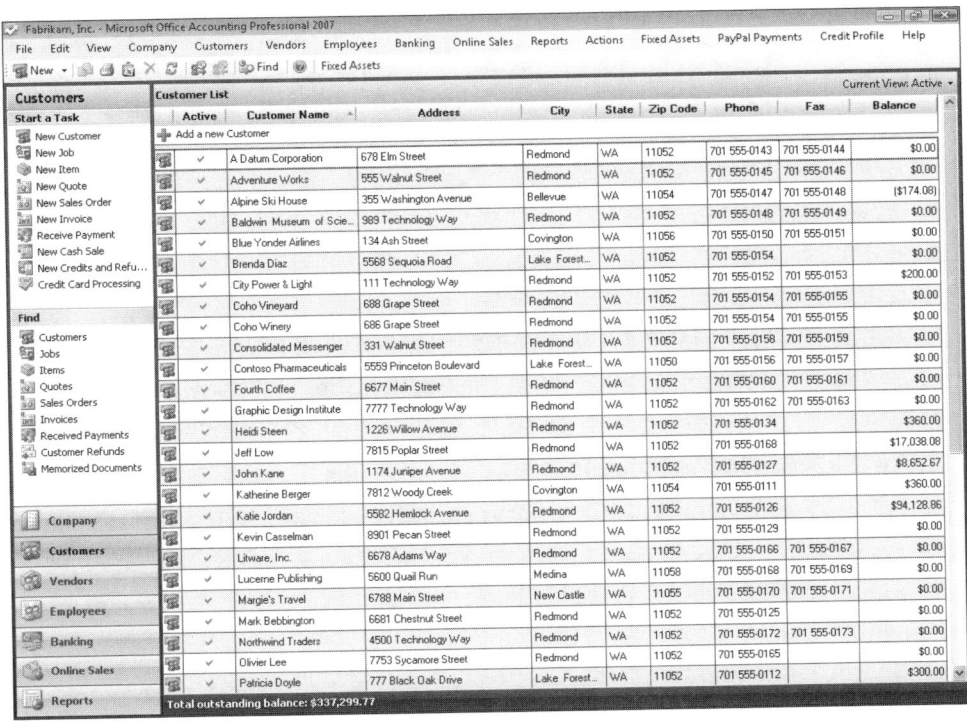

3. At the top of the **Customer List**, click the **City** column heading.

Accounting sorts the Customer List alphabetically by city, in ascending order.

Active	Customer Name	Address	City	State	Zip Code	Phone	Fax	Balance
✓	PayPal Customer							$0.00
✓	Alpine Ski House	355 Washington Avenue	Bellevue	WA	11054	701 555-0147	701 555-0148	($174.08)
✓	Southridge Video	4444 Washington Avenue	Bellevue	WA	11054	701 555-0177	701 555-0177	$0.00
✓	Tailspin Toys	8898 Washington Avenue	Bellevue	WA	11054	701 555-0178	701 555-0179	$0.00
✓	Wingtip Toys	9989 Washington Avenue	Bellevue	WA	11054	701 555-0188	701 555-0188	$136,549.88
✓	Russell King	4447 Cedar Street	Bellevue	WA	11054	701 555-0128		$0.00
✓	Blue Yonder Airlines	134 Ash Street	Covington	WA	11056	701 555-0150	701 555-0151	$0.00
✓	Katherine Berger	7812 Woody Creek	Covington	WA	11054	701 555-0111		$360.00
✓	Shaun Beasley	334 Cherry Street	Covington	WA	11056	701 555-0124		$0.00
✓	Contoso Pharmaceuticals	5559 Princeton Boulevard	Lake Forest...	WA	11050	701 555-0156	701 555-0157	$0.00
✓	Patricia Doyle	777 Black Oak Drive	Lake Forest...	WA	11052	701 555-0112		$300.00
✓	Brenda Diaz	5568 Sequoia Road	Lake Forest...	WA	11052	701 555-0154		$0.00
✓	Lucerne Publishing	5600 Quail Run	Medina	WA	11058	701 555-0168	701 555-0169	$0.00
✓	Margie's Travel	6788 Main Street	New Castle	WA	11055	701 555-0170	701 555-0171	$0.00
	A Datum Corporation	678 Elm Street	Redmond	WA	11052	701 555-0143	701 555-0144	$0.00
✓	Adventure Works	555 Walnut Street	Redmond	WA	11052	701 555-0145	701 555-0146	$0.00
✓	Baldwin Museum of Scie...	989 Technology Way	Redmond	WA	11052	701 555-0148	701 555-0149	$0.00
✓	City Power & Light	111 Technology Way	Redmond	WA	11052	701 555-0152	701 555-0153	$200.00
✓	Coho Vineyard	688 Grape Street	Redmond	WA	11052	701 555-0154	701 555-0155	$0.00
✓	Coho Winery	686 Grape Street	Redmond	WA	11052	701 555-0154	701 555-0155	$0.00
✓	Consolidated Messenger	331 Walnut Street	Redmond	WA	11052	701 555-0158	701 555-0159	$0.00
✓	Fourth Coffee	6677 Main Street	Redmond	WA	11052	701 555-0160	701 555-0161	$0.00
✓	Graphic Design Institute	7777 Technology Way	Redmond	WA	11052	701 555-0162	701 555-0163	$0.00
✓	Litware, Inc.	6678 Adams Way	Redmond	WA	11052	701 555-0166	701 555-0167	$0.00
✓	Northwind Traders	4500 Technology Way	Redmond	WA	11052	701 555-0172	701 555-0173	$0.00
✓	Proseware, Inc.	5579 Evergreen Parkway	Redmond	WA	11052	701 555-0173	701 555-0174	$0.00

Total outstanding balance: $337,299.77

4. On the form toolbar, click the **Find** button.

The Find toolbar appears.

5. In the **Look for** box of the Find toolbar, type Bellevue.

Accounting 2007 filters the list, but does so by searching for Bellevue in the Customer Name field. The result is that no customers appear in the Customer List.

6. In the **Search under** list, click **City**.

Accounting 2007 displays customers located in the city of Bellevue.

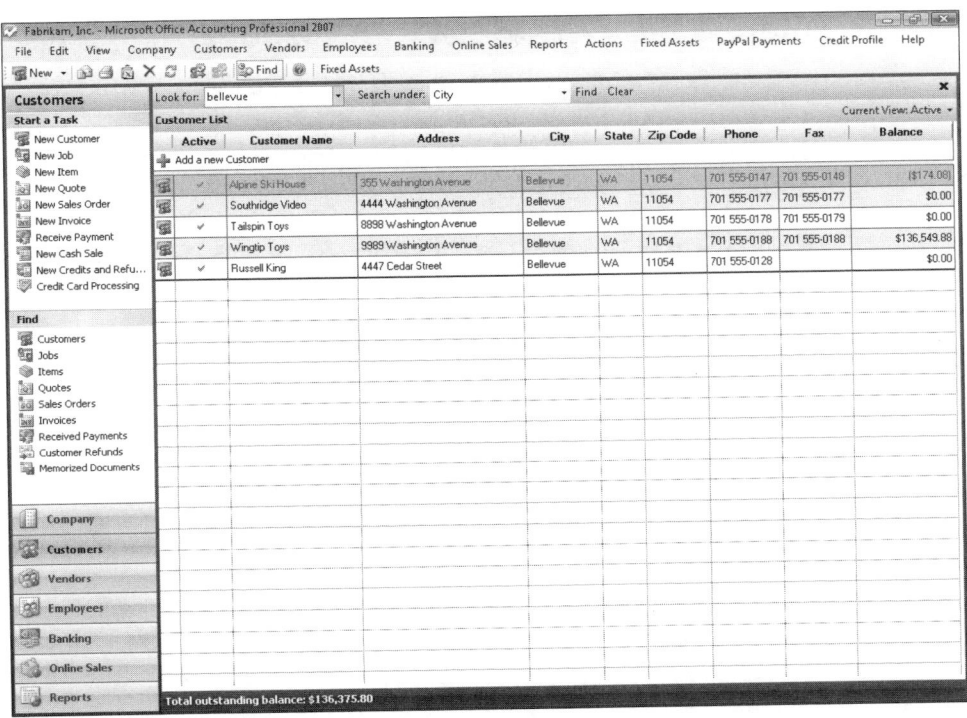

7. To display the complete **Customer List** again, click the **Clear** button on the **Find** toolbar.

The unfiltered Customer List appears.

> **Tip** When you are working with the Customer List, you can send an e-mail message to a customer by clicking the customer entry in the list and then clicking the E-mail button on the toolbar.

Creating Customer Records

In Accounting 2007, you use customer records to store basic contact information such as a customer's name, street and e-mail addresses, phone numbers, and Web site. After you've built a history with a customer, customer records also provide a quick view of a customer's financial picture—information such as the current balance, year-to-date sales, payment history, and a transaction summary.

Entering Basic Customer Information

The Customers home page is a centralized workspace from which you can manage customer information, initiate documents such as quotes and invoices, process payments, view customer reports, and find links to articles and other information that can help you manage your small business.

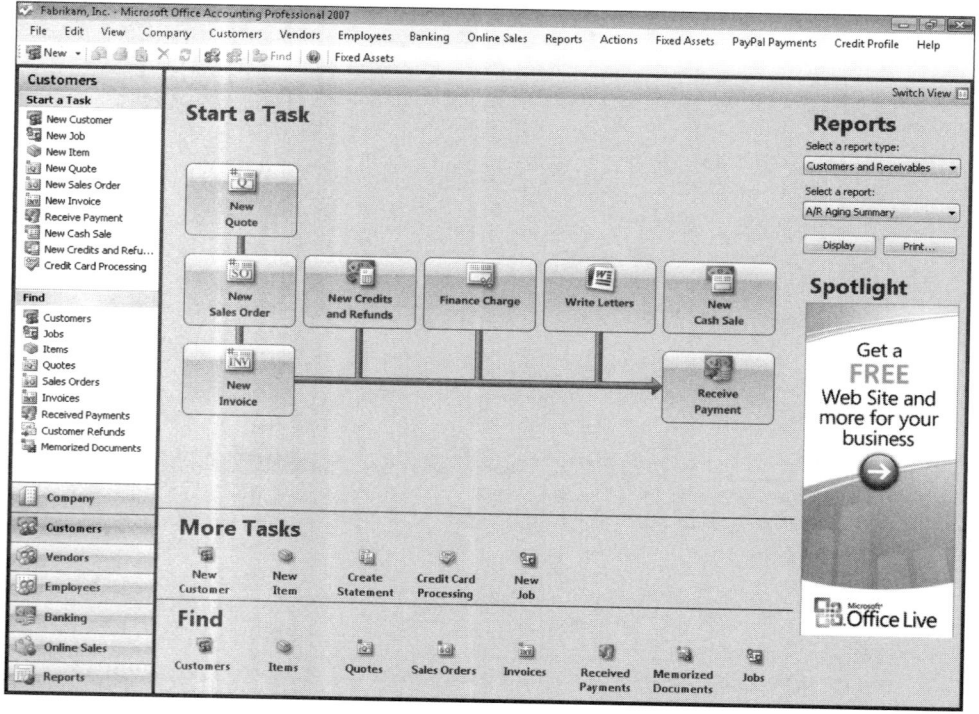

> **Note** The Spotlight section on the Customers home page includes links to information related to small-business services, accounting, and customers. Many of the links take you to Web pages that are part of the Microsoft Small Business Center (*www.microsoft.com/smallbusiness/*). The links in the Spotlight section are updated regularly.

> **Tip** You can view the Customers home page in the task flow view or in list view. To change the view, click Switch View in the upper-right corner of the home page.

From the Customers home page, you can access customer records. Each customer record displays one address, phone number, and fax number at a time; however, you can put in several different entries for each field. For example, in addition to a business phone number, you can enter numbers for a mobile phone and home phone, the phone number for a customer's assistant, and another phone number of your choice.

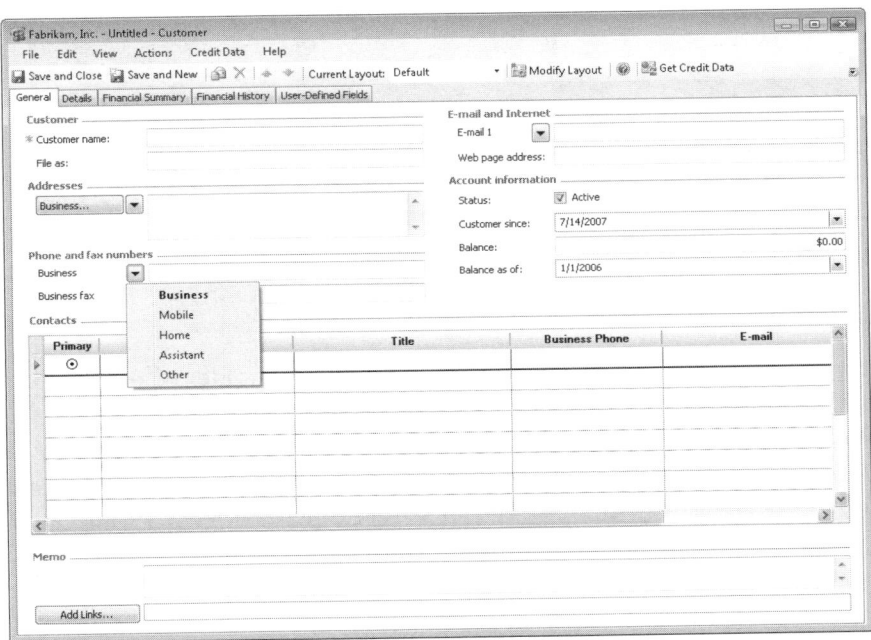

You can also enter up to three fax numbers—business, home, and other. To select which address, phone number, or fax number you want to enter, click the arrow next to the field.

Linking to Existing Files

In some cases, you might have had contact with a customer before you entered that customer's information into a customer record. For example, a customer might have sent you an e-mail message that you saved as a Microsoft Office Word file. If you'd like to link to those documents, click Add Links on the customer record form to display the Select File To Link To dialog box.

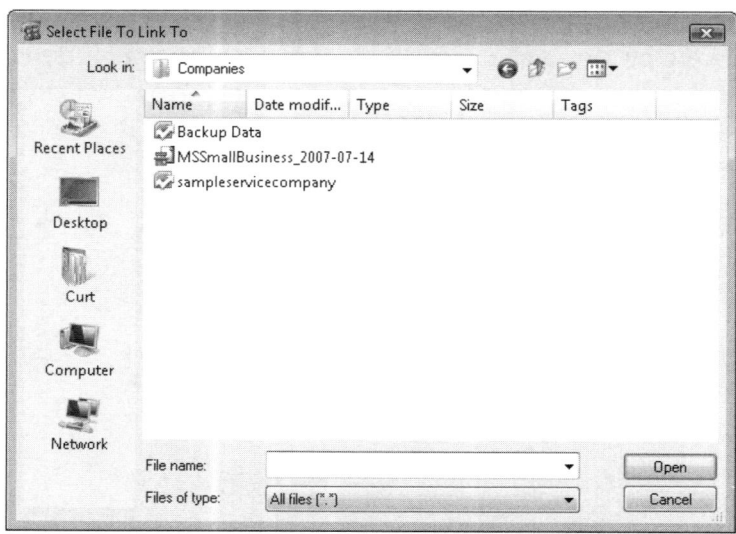

In the Select File To Link To dialog box, browse to the folder where your customer documents are stored and then select a document or documents related to this customer. You can link more than one document to the customer's record, which means that by using the Add Links button on the form, you can build the customer's record over time so that it provides a location from which you can easily access a wide range of documents and information related to the customer.

Viewing a Customer's Financial History

As you enter and process transactions for a customer, the fields on the Financial History and Financial Summary tabs on the customer record form are filled in. You can then use the customer record to gain quick access to financial information about a customer. The Financial History tab displays customer payments, invoices, and quotes. To open a specific item listed on the Financial History tab, double-click the item. The Financial Summary tab displays information such as whether the customer has payments that are past due, their total outstanding balance, and their purchases for the current month, the current year, the last year, and over the customer's lifetime.

See Also For more information about working with payments, see Chapter 12, "Handling Customer Payments." For more information about invoices, see Chapter 11, "Managing Invoices." For more information about quotes, see Chapter 8, "Generating and Managing Quotes."

In this exercise, you will create a customer record. The exercise focuses on entering contact information for a customer. You'll also see what kind of financial information you can view in a customer record and learn how to create a custom field that you can use to add to the information you store on the customer record form. In exercises later in the chapter, you'll learn how to create customer account tools such as price levels, discounts, and customer groups, and how to add these details to a customer record.

> **OPEN** the Fabrikam sample company file.

1. In the **Navigation Pane**, click the **Customers** button.

   The Customers home page appears.

2. Under **More Tasks** on the **Customers** home page, click **New Customer**.

   A blank Customer form opens. This form contains five tabs that you use to enter and view information.

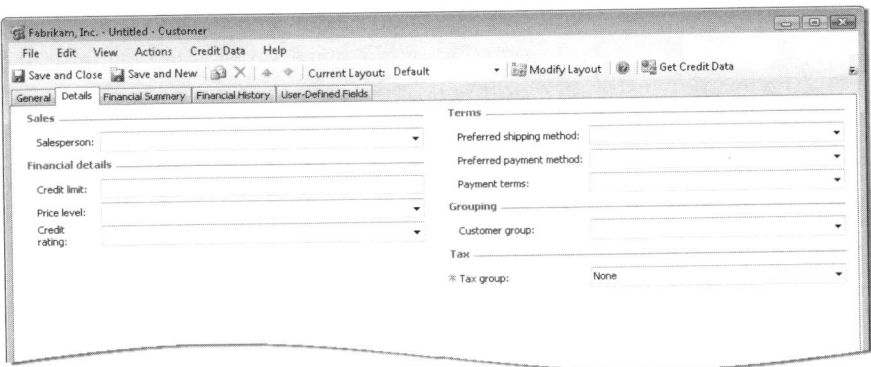

3. In the **Customer name** box on the **General** tab, type Kim Ralls.

4. If necessary, click the **Addresses** arrow, and then click **Business**.

   The address identifier changes to Business.

5. In the **Address** box, type P.O. Box 1001, Redmond, WA, 22841.

6. In the **Addresses** list, click **Ship To**, and then type 456 Water St., Redmond, WA 22841.

7. Under **Phone and fax numbers**, in the **Business** field, type (425) 555-0101.

8. In the **Business fax** field, type (425) 555-0102.

9. In the **Account information** area, keep the **Active** check box selected.

10. In the **Customer since** field, change the date to 6/12/2005.

11. Ensure the entry in the **Balance** field is $0.00.

Assigning a Customer Credit Limit

If you enforce the credit limits you assign your customers, you protect yourself by limiting losses that come when overextended customers default. You can always increase the limit for specific customers after they develop a good payment history, you review their credit reports, and other steps. You should monitor customer balances and heed warnings when credit limits are reached. For orders that will cause customer balances to exceed their assigned limits, you should have policies in place that such orders be approved only if paid in advance or as COD—or that the company is to decline over-limit orders altogether.

Credit Limit Maintenance

Accounting 2007 provides you a couple of ways to manage customer credit. First, you can use the Credit Limit setting to set the maximum credit balance you wish to allow for a given customer. (Leaving it blank simply means that you are not limiting the level of customer credit.) Additionally, you can use the Credit Rating setting to rank and group customers according to credit worthiness.

To effectively use credit limits, you will want to assign thresholds that will represent a balance between the encouragement of sales and the protection of your business. You will then want to review and enforce those limits consistently.

Aging and Credit Balance History as an Analysis and "Early Warning" Tool

When you regularly age and review your accounts receivable, you can gain early warning of liquidity issues. Combining your aging review with analysis of credit balances in general can often arm you with a considerable amount of insight into your customers and their general business practices, as well as into various aspects of their financial health. With this insight, you can monitor and act upon delinquencies (or even losses) before they get out of control. It will also support you in raising limits for creditworthy customers who, for example, may run high balances, but whose balances are paid regularly (leaving the ongoing large balances in acceptable age ranges).

You can gain substantial business intelligence in addition to these early warnings. Regular aging analysis, in conjunction with industry standards, helps you to manage the credit policies of your business. Your regular review of aged accounts receivable, coupled with your analysis of customer balances over time provides you with timely, actionable information.

> **Note** After you save a customer record in which you've entered an opening balance, the Balance box is no longer displayed on the customer record form. The balance information appears in the Balance Due area of the Financial Summary tab.

12. Under **Contacts**, in the **Contact name** field, type Gabriele Cannata, press `Tab` twice, and then type (425) 555-0101 in the **Business phone** field.

> **Note** You can enter more than one contact, but only one contact can be selected as the primary contact.

`Save and Close` **13.** Click the **Save and Close** button.

The Customer form closes.

Creating Customer Groups

Support lists in Accounting 2007 help you organize entities such as customers and vendors and define bookkeeping items such as payment terms and discounts. With customer groups, you might organize customers by city or state or by the volume of business they do. After you have assigned customers to the groups you create, you can view reports based on the groups and examine the similarities and differences in the buying habits of the customers you've grouped together. By analyzing the common details provided by customer groups, you can see trends more quickly and then plan any actions that you need to take.

In this exercise, you'll create two customer groups for the Fabrikam sample company. One group is for customers who are individuals (for example, sole proprietors), and the second group is for customers who are companies.

> **OPEN** the Fabrikam sample company file.

1. On the **Company** menu, point to **Manage Support Lists**, and then click **Customer Group List**.

The Manage Customer Group dialog box opens.

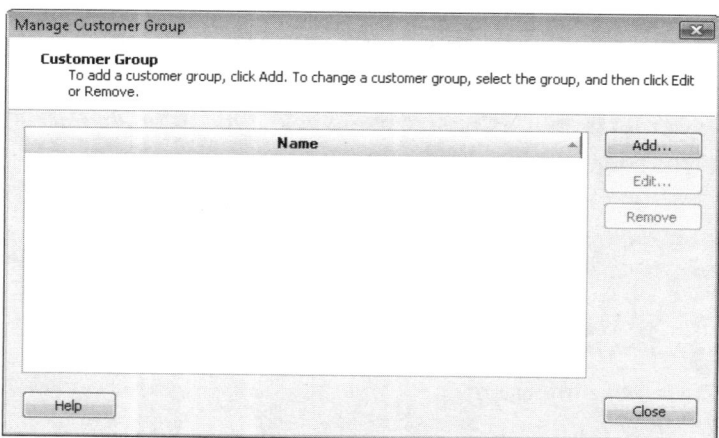

2. In the **Manage Customer Group** dialog box, click **Add**.

The Customer Group dialog box opens.

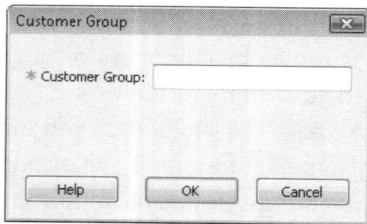

3. In the **Customer Group** dialog box, type Individual, and then click **OK**.

The Customer Group dialog box closes.

4. In the **Manage Customer Group** dialog box, click **Add**.

The Customer Group dialog box opens.

5. Type Company in the **Customer Group** dialog box, and then click **OK**.

6. Click **Close** in the **Manage Customer Group** dialog box.

> **Tip** You can change the name of a customer group by selecting the group in the Manage Customer Group dialog box and then clicking Edit. To delete a customer group, select the group and then click Remove. You cannot remove a customer group to which you've assigned a customer unless you remove all customers from the group first.

Customer Groups Can Be Powerful Business Intelligence Enhancers

Customer management occupies much of your focus in operating a business, no matter what line(s) of business you have chosen. Accounting 2007 offers support lists to help you to manage your customers, just as it provides similar support for vendors and numerous other items. Support lists offer you the capability to enhance business intelligence about your company well beyond standard reports, and nowhere is this more true than with customer groups.

With customer groups, you can organize your customers by using any criteria that is useful to you. Examples include grouping by the following:

- Geography (such as city, state, and zip code).
- General type of services/products provided the customer. (In, for example, a heating and air conditioning business, you might group by types such as New Construction, Renovation, and Do-It-Yourselfers.
- Volume (and other characteristics of) the business they do with you.
- General customer types with which you do business (such as retail or wholesale).
- Source of customer, as a means of tracking the effectiveness of various methods of obtaining customers (such as direct marketing, advertisements, referrals from other customers, customers who found you via your Web site or Web search tools, and many other possibilities).
- Anniversary dates (especially good if you provide professional services such as accounting, where client year ends and the like drive the services you sell them. The concept can even be extended to sending out mailers for events such as client birthdays or anniversaries —a practice that is becoming quite common these days).
- Other customer details (upon which reports can be based, showing customers who have specific attributes, for closer analysis and tracking).

You can use customer groups to sort and organize your customers for analysis and reporting, and even to trigger transactions and other events. The idea is, of course, to use them in a way that matches the manner in which you wish to separate your customers within your reports. You'll find that this highly flexible way of enhancing business intelligence translates to myriad benefits, including the identification of ways to increase business while making you more efficient at keeping your existing Customer List happy and profitable.

Creating Price Levels, Credit Ratings, and Payment Terms

In addition to using support lists to group customers, as you learned in the previous exercise, you can use support lists to define pricing, credit, and payment information that you apply to customer accounts.

> **Note** You can edit or remove a price level, credit rating, or payment term to change the definition of the item or to delete it from your company's lists. However, you cannot remove an item if it is assigned to one or more customers.

Defining New Price Levels

A *price level* is an adjustment to the standard price you charge for the goods and services you sell. For example, for any customer that exceeds a certain volume of sales, you might provide a price level that decreases standard prices by 10 percent. You might also create a list of long-term preferred customers and establish a level that is 15 percent less than standard prices. After you assign a price level to a customer, the prices shown when you create a sales order for that customer reflect the adjustment associated with that level.

You define new price levels in the Add Or Edit Price Level dialog box. By default, the Decrease Price Level By This Percentage option is selected. If you want prices to increase by the percentage you've specified, select the Increase Price Level By This Percentage option. In most cases, the price levels you create for customers decrease prices as an incentive to the customer or as a reward for that customer's loyalty. In cases in which a customer orders products infrequently or orders only products that cost you more to manufacture or import, for example, you might apply a price level that increases standard prices.

Defining New Credit Ratings and Payment Terms

Credit ratings are categories that you set up to rank the credit worthiness of customers. You can make up the credit ratings you want to use (something simple like Excellent, Good, Average, and Poor), or you can use or adapt a standard rating scheme. In the Standard & Poor's system, a rating of AAA is given to companies with the highest credit quality. A credit rating of D indicates that a customer has defaulted on a payment.

For a customer that has a specific credit rating or buys a high volume of goods or services, you might provide special payment terms. For example, you might offer a 2 percent reduction if a customer pays within 10 days of receiving a bill. For customers that have fallen behind in their payments, you might insist on payment terms of cash on delivery. Payment terms are assigned to a customer on the Details tab of the customer record form. The payment term that you enter in a customer record appears on all sales records for that customer.

> **Note** Accounting 2007 does not require you to assign specific payment terms to a customer. For example, you can select the payment terms you want to use when you create an invoice for each customer. If you do specify payment terms for a customer, those terms are displayed by default when you create an invoice. You can change the payment terms for a specific invoice before sending it.

Accounting 2007 provides a default set of payment terms, including a 1 percent discount if a payment is made within 10 days, a 2 percent discount with the same terms, Net 15, and Net 30.

> **Note** The Payment Terms List also includes items for taxes that are due monthly, quarterly, and annually.

In this exercise, you'll create support lists of price levels, credit ratings, and payment terms that you can apply to customer accounts.

OPEN the Fabrikam sample company file.

1. On the **Company** menu, point to **Manage Support Lists**, and then click **Price Level List**.

   The Manage Price Level dialog box opens.

2. In the **Manage Price Level** dialog box, click **Add**.

   The Price Level dialog box opens.

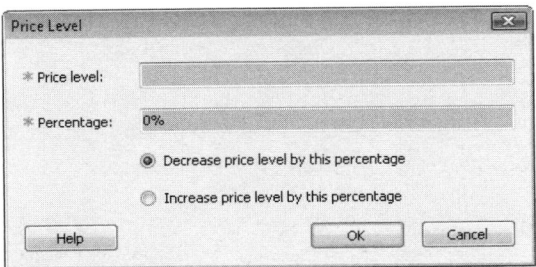

3. In the **Price level** field of the **Price Level** dialog box, type High-volume customer.

4. In the **Percentage** field, type 10 to adjust these customers' prices by 10 percent.

5. Verify that the **Decrease price level by this percentage** option is selected.

6. Click **OK**, and then click **Close** in the **Manage Price Level** dialog box.

7. On the **Company** menu, point to **Manage Support Lists**, and then click **Credit Rating List**.

   The Manage Credit Rating dialog box opens.

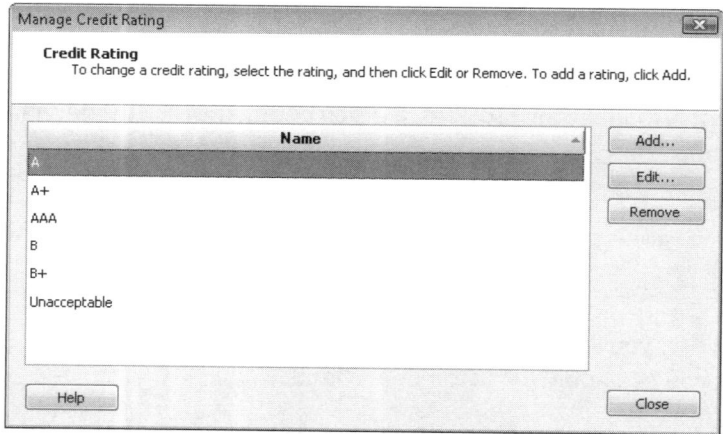

8. In the **Manage Credit Rating** dialog box, click **Add**.

   The Credit Rating dialog box opens.

9. In the **Credit Rating** dialog box, type Excellent.

10. Click **OK** in the **Credit Rating** dialog box, and then click **Close** in the **Manage Credit Rating** dialog box.

11. On the **Company** menu, point to **Manage Support Lists**, and then click **Payment Terms List**.

    The Manage Payment Term dialog box opens.

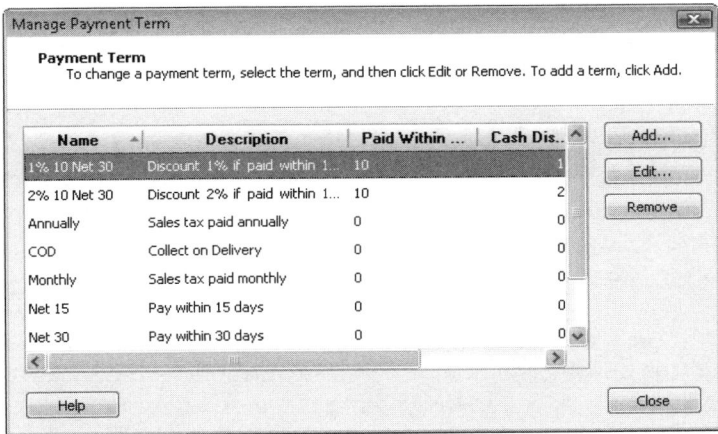

12. In the **Manage Payment Term** dialog box, click **Add**.

The Payment Term dialog box opens.

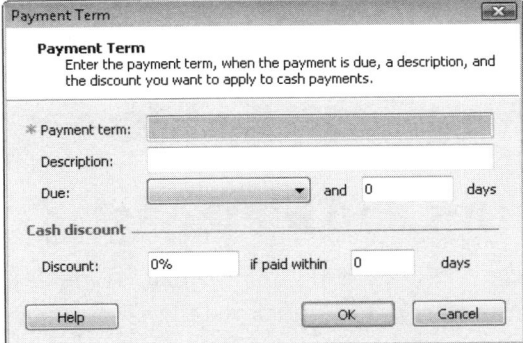

13. In the **Payment Term** box of the **Payment Term** dialog box, type Net 60, and in the **Description** box, type Pay within 60 days.

14. In the right-most of the **Due** box, type 60 for the number of days.

15. Under **Cash Discount**, leave the discount set to 0% and the days set to 0.

> **Note** If you are creating a payment term that provides an incentive for early payment, enter the discount amount and the incentive period in this section of the dialog box.

16. In the **Payment Term** dialog box, click **OK**, and then click **Close** in the **Manage Payment Term** dialog box.

Does It Make Sense to Use Payment Terms as a Cash Flow Enhancement Tool?

With Accounting 2007, you can, on the Details tab of the Customer form, establish payment terms for your customers. It provides a default set of payment terms, including a 1 percent or 2 percent discount for payments made within 10 days, Net 15, and Net 30. You can, of course, offer any terms you like to encourage faster payment by your customers, but consider the true cost of doing so before you make it a consistent practice.

You can often benefit significantly by taking advantage of discounts offered by your vendors for cash or early-payment purchases. But offering discounts to your customers in like manner results in a far less happy outcome: you place yourself into the position of a "borrower" at what can turn out to be very high interest rates. Let's consider a simple example: You offer a customer a 3 percent discount if he pays you in 10 days (the customer's normal payment terms are "within 30 days"). Assuming the customer takes advantage of the discount, this means you are paying around 3 percent interest for what amounts to a 20-day loan. This translates to an annual interest rate of greater than 66 percent!

Defining Shipping Terms and Methods

In addition to payment terms and price levels, many small businesses, especially small manufacturing or retail companies, need to track the shipping method and shipping terms of customer orders. A shipping method might be *Via U.S. Post* or *Via Express*. A shipping term describes the agreement you reach with a customer for payment of shipping and handling charges. For example, you might pay for shipping for preferred customers. For first-time customers, you might require shipping charges to be paid cash on delivery.

If you need to define shipping methods and shipping terms for the company you are setting up in Accounting, point to Manage Support Lists on the Company menu, and then click the Shipping Method or Shipping Term command to open the dialog box you need. The steps for creating a shipping method or shipping term are very similar to those described in the previous exercise for creating payment terms.

Setting Up Sales Tax Agencies and Sales Tax Codes

Most of the goods and services that a small business sells are subject to sales tax, and it's likely that most of the customers that a business sells its products and services to are required to pay sales tax. You need to follow several steps to set up Accounting so that you collect the taxes you need to pay to relevant tax agencies, charge sales tax on the correct items, and charge sales tax to the right customers.

One of the first steps you take is to define the state and local tax agencies to which you need to remit sales taxes. For example, if you do business in a state with a sales tax, you need to set up the state tax authority as a tax agency. In addition, if the county and city in which you do business charge sales tax, you need to set up the city and county as tax agencies. You might also need to set up a neighboring county or city as a separate tax agency if your business delivers products to customers in those locations.

You define a new tax agency by pointing to Sales Tax on the Company menu, and then clicking New Tax Agency to display the Tax Agency dialog box. The fields on the Tax Agency dialog box are organized on three tabs. The General tab contains defining information about the tax agency. You need to fill in only the Tax Agency, Payment Term, and Liability Account fields to set up a tax agency. You can also enter contact information such as an address, phone numbers, or a Web site for the agency.

The Financial History tab displays a list of tax transactions with the agency. On the Custom Fields tab, you can define a field you want to use to store additional information about this tax agency.

After you define the agencies to which you pay sales tax, you create a sales tax code that specifies the name of the sales tax and the amount, which is generally a percentage of the price you charge for the items you sell.

> **Tip** Tax rates change from time to time as states and cities adjust them. If you know the tax rate will increase or decrease on a given date in the future, update the rate for the tax code ahead of time and enter the effective date of the rate change. That way, when you generate invoices and sales orders later, the correct tax rate will be applied to those transactions.

In this exercise, you'll enter information for a tax agency and then create a sales tax code associated with the agency. The form you use to create a tax agency is similar to the customer record form. You enter the agency's name, address, and other contact information and details about the tax account.

> OPEN the Fabrikam sample company file.

1. On the **Company** menu, point to **Sales Tax**, and then click **New Tax Agency**.
   A blank Tax Agency form opens.

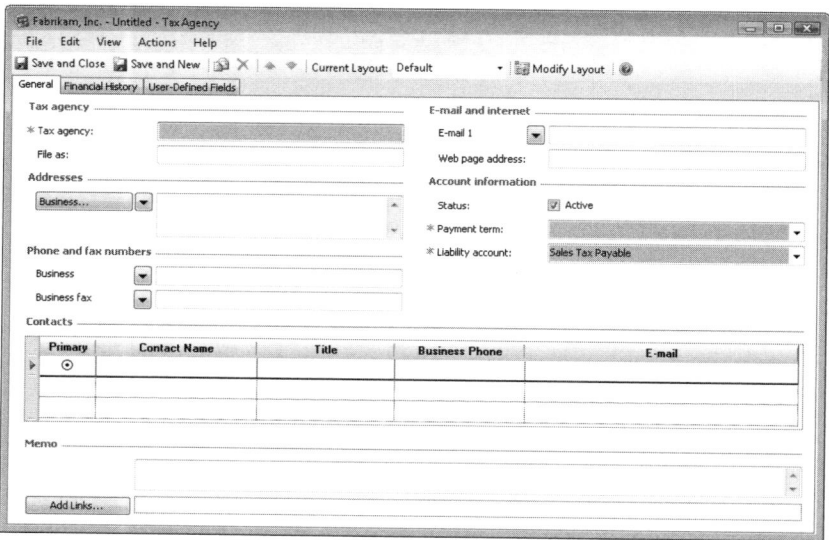

2. In the **Tax agency** box, type Washington State.
3. Under **Account information**, in the **Payment term** list, click **Quarterly**.
4. In the **Liability account** list, click **Sales Tax Payable**.

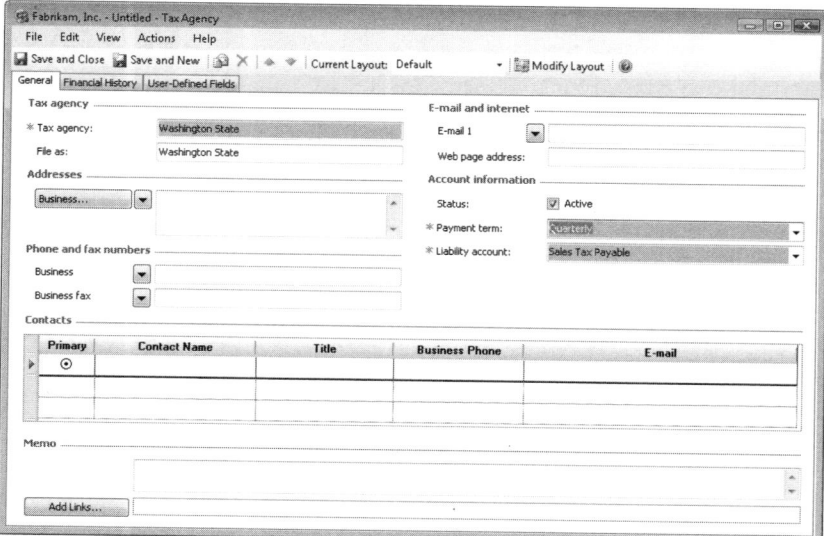

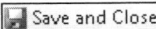 **5.** Complete the contact information you want to enter for the tax agency, and then on the form toolbar, click the **Save and Close** button.

The Tax Agency form closes.

6. On the **Company** menu, point to **Sales Tax**, and then click **Manage Sales Tax Codes**.

The Manage Tax Codes dialog box opens.

7. In the **Manage Tax Codes** dialog box, click **Add**.

The Add Or Edit Tax Code dialog box opens.

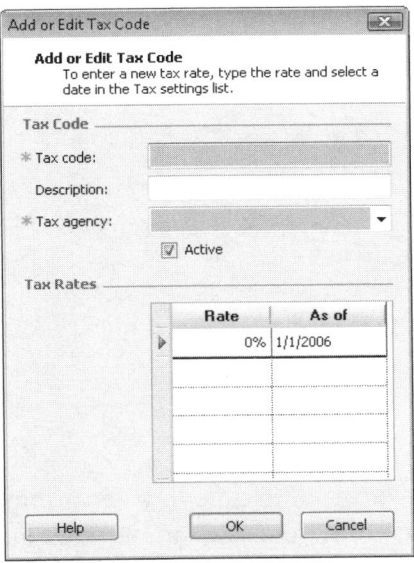

8. In the **Tax code** box of the **Add or Edit Tax Code** dialog box, type King County.

9. In the **Tax agency** list, click **Washington State Dept. of Revenue**.

10. In the **Tax Rates** grid, in the first row of the **Rate** column, type 3.2. Then, in the first row of the **As of** column, type 7/1/2008.

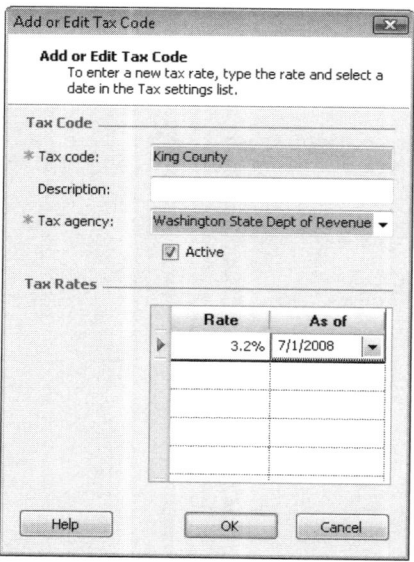

11. Click **OK** in the **Add or Edit Tax Code** dialog box, and then click **Close** in the **Manage Tax Codes** dialog box.

Tax Exempt Sales and Customers

Some products or services you sell (for example, items your customer purchases for resale, in most cases) may be exempt from sales or use taxes. In these cases, although you may not be required to report or collect the tax, you may be required to obtain a copy of the purchaser's certificate of tax exemption (or similar document or number) from the state involved.

In addition to the most common type of sales tax exemption, situations where items are purchased in order to be resold later (and for which it is assumed that the tax will be collected upon ultimate resale to end consumers), you may also encounter tax-exempt customers in the form of non-profits. Although it might be argued that you have a responsibility to ascertain that the purchases are qualified and appropriate (that is, they have been made for the use of the non-profit organization, and not for personal use by individuals within the organization), you can generally assume that an organization that can document its classification as tax exempt within a given state is entitled to exemption from sales taxes on its purchases from you.

Creating Sales Tax Groups

As part of creating a customer record, you assign a sales tax group to a customer. A sales tax group is made up of one or more sales tax codes. For example, a sales tax group might include the sales tax codes for a state taxing agency, the county tax assessor, and a city tax agency.

You need to set up a sales tax group to account for the tax status of different types of customers. For example, some customers might be exempt from paying taxes because the customer is a not-for-profit organization. Determining the tax group to which you assign a customer is based on factors such as the customer's location and whether the customer purchases items on-site at your store or warehouse or whether you deliver purchased goods to the customer.

In this exercise, you'll learn how to create a sales tax group. Each sales tax group is named and then defined by adding the sales tax codes that apply.

OPEN the Fabrikam sample company file.

1. On the **Company** menu, point to **Sales Tax**, and then click **Manage Sales Tax Groups**.

   The Manage Sales Tax Group dialog box opens.

2. In the **Manage Sales Tax Group** dialog box, click **Add**.

   The Tax Group dialog box opens.

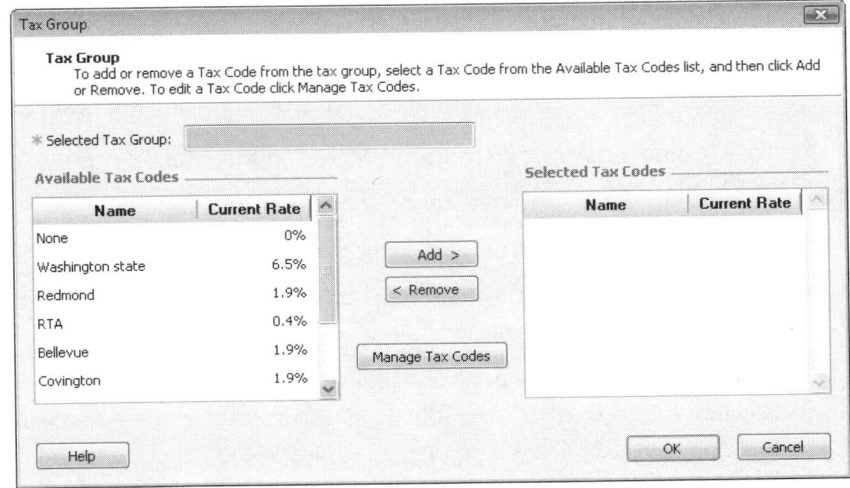

Considerations Surrounding Sales and Use Tax Classifications

You are probably already aware of the fact that sales and use taxes vary widely between states, municipalities, counties, and other jurisdictions. To add to the complication, other special use taxes can come into play for counties and cities. Numerous steps are involved in setting up sales tax handling in your Accounting 2007 company. It is very important that you take the time to not only follow these steps precisely (to ensure, primarily, that you collect the taxes you need to pay the relevant tax agencies, charge the correct sales taxes on the products and services you offer, and charge sales tax to the appropriate customers), but you also need to perform the appropriate registrations with the relevant state and other agencies.

In general, any individual, partnership or corporation (C-corp or S-corp) that engages in business in a given state is required to obtain a certificate of registration for business locations it has within the state. There are, of course, exceptions (if, for example, the business is involved in providing products or services that are not subject to sales tax), but in general the registration needs to be made and the associated fees submitted. Sales tax is due upon qualifying sales you make within the state. Use taxes, designed to cover qualifying items that are brought into the state to be consumed, distributed, leased or rented, stored for use or consumption, or with perhaps other motivations, are charged at similar rates as the sales taxes. Both taxes and the rates involved need to be understood and put into place within your accounting system to help you to comply with the associated laws and regulations.

You might be relieved to know that, most of the time, you won't be required to collect sales tax for every location to which you deliver. The "location" consideration that lies at the heart of all this is known as *nexus*, which refers to a physical presence. While the states also differ in their definition of nexus, you can generally assume that you have nexus in a state if any of the following conditions exist:

- Your business has one or more stores within that state.
- Your business has employees working within that state.
- Your business maintains an office location or other property within that state.
- You, or an employee or other agent of your business, visit a customer within that state at some point within a given fiscal year.
- Your business employs an individual, at any given point within a given fiscal year, to work within that state to solicit sales in some capacity—an example might be that they set up a kiosk at a professional seminar or convention.

You may have established nexus if your business meets these or similar criteria. Although some of these scenarios (such as having stores in the state) are fairly universally accepted as meeting the definition of nexus, other conditions (such as presence at seminars and conventions) may mean different things in different states. These are simply guidelines to consider.

The rules you need to follow for remitting the sales taxes you have collected to the intended agencies vary from state to state. They typically dictate either monthly (by a specific deadline date) or quarterly (particularly when the amount of the payment is low) filing and payment, but you'll need to examine each scenario for each agency involved to get Accounting 2007 fully set up to manage this maze of rules for you behind the scenes.

You should consider taking the following actions in working through setup of sales tax in Accounting 2007:

- List any states within which you suspect you have nexus.
- Contact each of these states to ascertain you actually have nexus within its own definitions.
  - A great place to start is the state's Department of Revenue or similar agency.
  - Other good sources for agency information can be found on small-business sites and other sites on the Web. (A primary source of information on this and related topics exists at the Federation of Tax Administrators site at *www.taxadmin.org*).
- For any state within which you determine you have nexus, do the following:
  - Obtain the sales/use tax rates.
  - Determine the appropriate collection rules.
  - Obtain the requirements (timing and method, and other requirements) for remitting the taxes.
  - Register with the state, and obtain a license/certificate, as required.

After you obtain the above information, proceed with setup in Accounting 2007, as directed within this chapter.

3. In the **Selected Tax Group** box, type King County Businesses.

4. In the **Available Tax Codes** list, click **King County**, and then click **Add**. If more than one new tax applies to the group, you can repeat this step to add any other applicable tax codes.

   Your changes appear in the Tax Group dialog box.

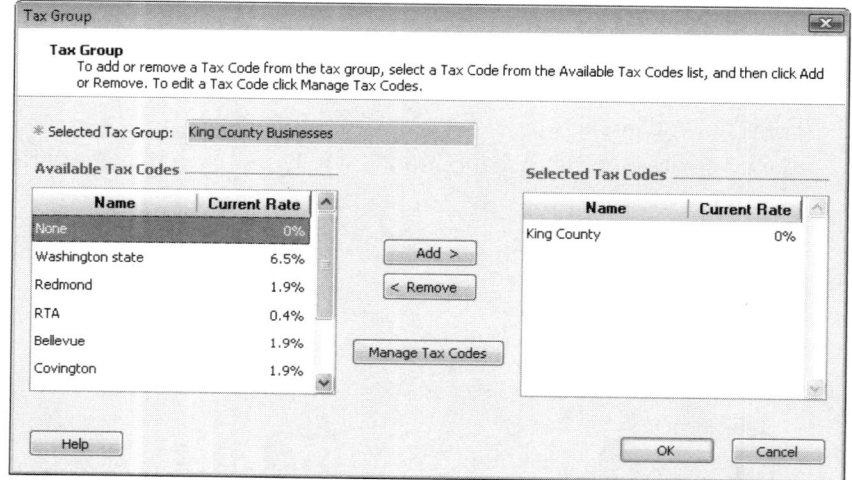

> **Tip** If you need to edit a tax code—for example, update the tax percentage—while you are working in the Tax Group dialog box, click Manage Tax Codes.

5. Click **OK**, and then click **Close** in the **Manage Sales Tax Group** dialog box.

Managing Contacts by Using Business Contact Manager

Outlook 2007 with Business Contact Manager provides powerful and versatile contact management tools you can use to create a professional marketing campaign, save time, and track sales leads and opportunities. Combining those capabilities with the reporting and customer management tools of Accounting 2007 creates a powerful tool you can use to enhance your business opportunities.

Integrating Accounting 2007 with Business Contact Manager

Accounting 2007 provides a wizard that walks you through the process of integrating your Business Contact Manager database with the database of your Accounting 2007 company file. To launch the wizard, on the Company menu, click Integrate With Business Contact Manager. Follow the wizard's steps, which include selecting the Business Contact Manager database you want to use and where to back up the Business Contact Manager and Accounting files, and Accounting will do the technical work for you.

In this exercise, you will integrate Accounting 2007 and Outlook 2007 with Business Contact Manager.

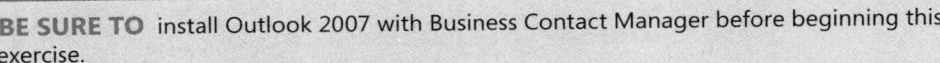

BE SURE TO install Outlook 2007 with Business Contact Manager before beginning this exercise.

OPEN the Fabrikam sample company file.

1. On the **Company** menu, click **Integrate with Business Contact Manager**.

   The Integrate With Microsoft Office Outlook 2007 With Business Contact Manager wizard starts.

2. On the first page of the wizard, click **Next** to display the next page.

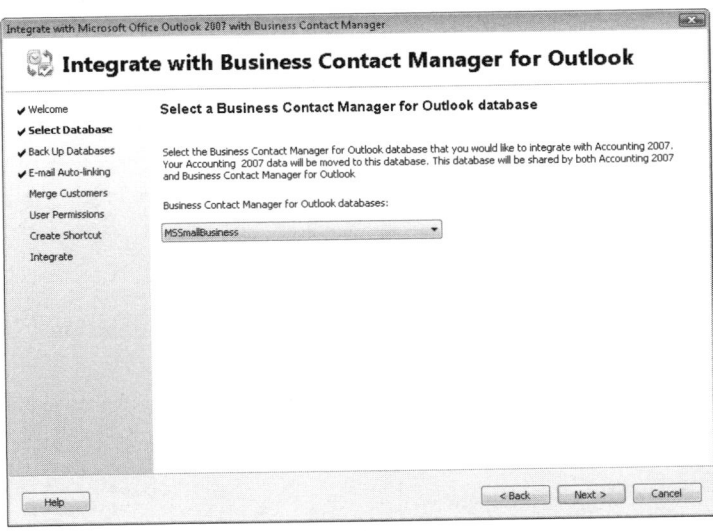

3. If necessary, click the **Business Contact Manager for Outlook Databases** arrow, and then in the list, select the Business Contact Manager database to which you want to connect.

4. Click **Next** to display the next page of the wizard.

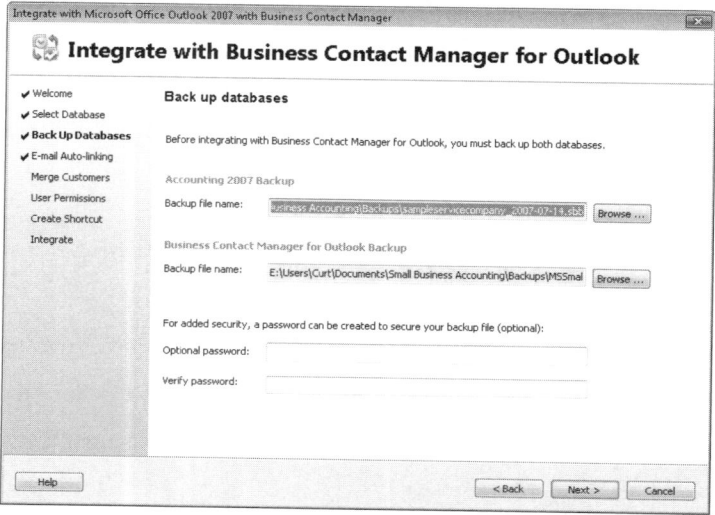

5. Verify that the wizard will back up your Accounting 2007 and Business Contact Manager files, and then click **Next**.

6. Verify that **Keep Current Business Contact Manager for Outlook E-mail Auto-Linking Settings** is selected, and then click **Next** to display the next page of the wizard.

7. Verify that **Merge Duplicate Accounts and Customers** is selected, and then click **Next**.

   The next wizard page appears.

8. Review the list of users that have permission to use the Business Contact Manager data in Accounting, and then click **Next**.

9. Verify that the new company file's shortcut appears in the **Shortcut Name** box, and then click **Next**.

10. Click **Integrate**.

    Accounting 2007 integrates your Business Contact Manager database into your company database.

11. Click **Finish** to complete the wizard.

Disabling Business Contact Manager Integration

Should you decide that having your Accounting 2007 and Business Contact Manager databases integrated no longer suits your needs, you can disable the integration by using another wizard. As before, you can find the proper command, Disable Business Contact Manager For Outlook Integration, on the Company menu.

In this exercise, you will disable the integration of Accounting 2007 and Business Contact Manager.

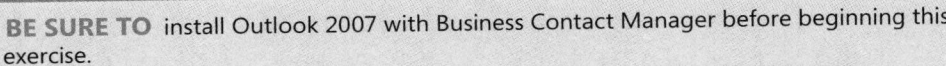

BE SURE TO install Outlook 2007 with Business Contact Manager before beginning this exercise.

OPEN the Fabrikam sample company file.

1. On the **Company** menu, click **Disable Business Contact Manager for Outlook Integration**.

The Disable Business Contact Manager For Outlook Integration dialog box opens.

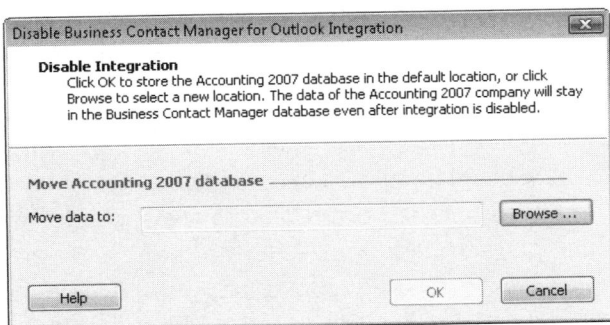

2. In the **Disable Business Contact Manager for Outlook Integration** dialog box, click **Browse**.

The Moving Microsoft Office Accounting Data To dialog box opens.

3. In the **File name** box, type Backup Data.

4. Click **Save**.

The Moving Microsoft Office Accounting Data To dialog box closes.

5. Click **OK**.

The Disable Integration dialog box, which contains a progress indicator, opens. After the integration is disabled, a message box appears.

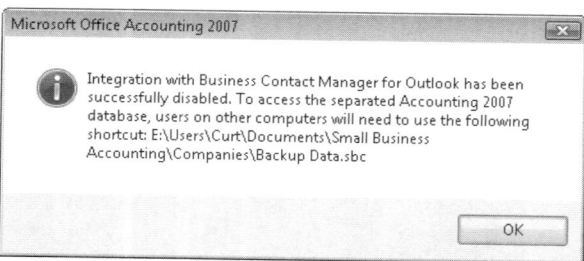

6. Click **OK** to close the message box.

CLOSE the Fabrikam sample company file, and if you are not continuing on to the next chapter, quit Accounting 2007.

Reporting Considerations: Customers

Within the context of this chapter, you should be aware of the potential for reports surrounding customers in general, including various settings made within their records.

An example of this would be a report listing customers alongside their credit limits and credit ratings. This example might be extended, in conjunction with the balances on the customer accounts as a given date, to present such data as remaining credit on the account, percent utilization of allowed credit, and other data. These details might also fit well into trending reports that showed the metrics over time (for example, over the months of a rolling year). Combination of this information with aging accounts receivable and other accounts receivable ratios (some of which are discussed in detail in Chapter 12, "Handling Customer Payments") could help to pinpoint potential problems with customers whose condition has deteriorated, along with other "early warning" benefits.

Finally, you could monitor payment terms (if you choose to offer them) in a basic report. A possible extension in concept might be a report to track the degree of customer participation in the discount scheme. Other possible "views" of your business might focus upon the true cost of extending the terms to your customers, and other considerations.

Key Points

- The Customers home page is a centralized location from which you can work with customer records and customer transactions.

- Customer records store contact information in addition to account details, and provide a view of a customer's financial history.

- You can sort the Customer List by fields such as City and Balance.

- Support lists let you create and define administrative tools such as company groups, credit ratings, payment terms, pricing levels, and tax groups.

Chapter at a Glance

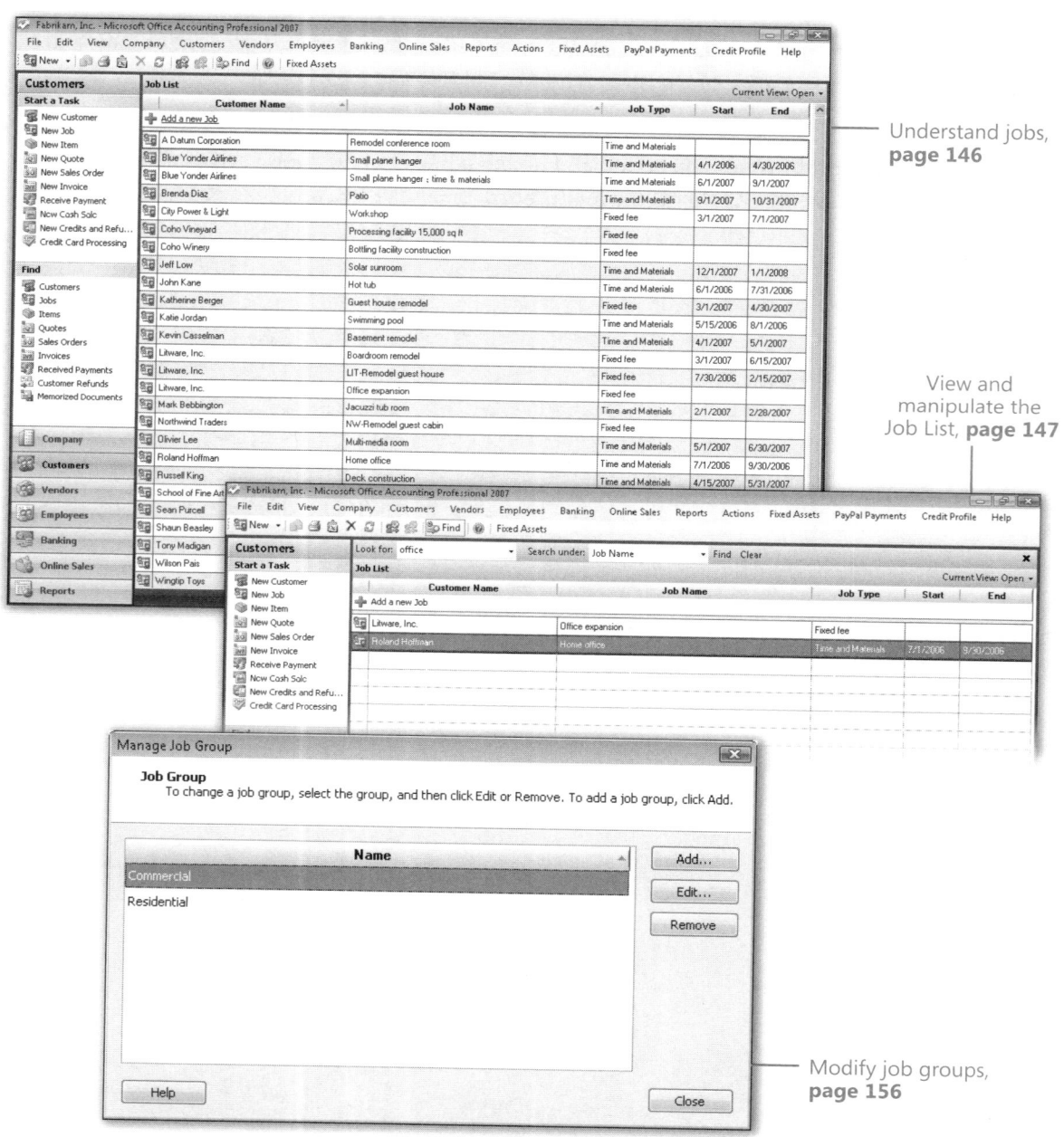

Understand jobs, **page 146**

View and manipulate the Job List, **page 147**

Modify job groups, **page 156**

7 Managing Jobs

In this chapter, you will learn to:

- ✔ Understand jobs.
- ✔ View and manipulate the Job List.
- ✔ View job details.
- ✔ Create, edit, and delete jobs.
- ✔ Modify job groups.
- ✔ Assign cash sales to jobs.
- ✔ Analyze job histories.
- ✔ Understand job group profitability and best practices for jobs.

Retail stores sell items, but when your company builds houses, repairs cars, or builds information systems, you need a way to track every payment and expenditure related to the project. In Microsoft Office Accounting Professional 2007, you can create a single entity enabling you to record everything related to your project. That entity, called a *job*, provides places to enter information about the customer, the job's start and end dates, and the transactions related to the job.

In this chapter, you will learn how to define a job, view and manipulate the Job List, create a new job, edit information about existing jobs, and assign cash transactions to existing jobs.

> **Important** The information in this chapter applies to Microsoft Office Accounting Professional 2007 only.

> **Troubleshooting** Graphics and operating system–related instructions in this book reflect the Windows Vista user interface. If your computer is running Windows XP and you experience trouble following the instructions as written, please refer to the "Information for Readers Running Windows XP" section at the beginning of this book.

What Is a Job? (Professional Only)

In Accounting Professional 2007, a job represents a multi-part project made up of products and services that you deliver over time. For example, if a ski resort's general manager asked Fabrikam to build a ski waxing and maintenance facility at their trail base, Fabrikam would create a job for the ski resort in its Accounting file and then respond with a quote that would be linked to that job.

See Also   For more information about creating a job based on an existing quote, see Chapter 8, "Generating and Managing Quotes."

Enabling Jobs in Accounting Professional 2007

To use jobs in Accounting Professional, the Use Jobs check box must be selected in your company preferences. If you aren't sure whether you enabled jobs in your company's file, click Preferences on the Company menu, and on the Company tab of the Company Preferences dialog box, ensure the Use Jobs check box is selected. When this check box is not selected, the Jobs option does not appear in the Find area at the bottom of the Customers home page.

Types of Jobs

Accounting Professional 2007 offers two types of jobs: *fixed-fee* and *time-and-materials*. A fixed-fee job is just what the name implies: a job your company agrees to complete for a set price. The other job type, the time-and-materials job, charges the customer for the labor and supplies used to complete the project, plus a markup for your profit. In either case, you will usually prepare a quote for the customer; if the customer accepts your quote and you both sign a contract, you can then start work. After you begin work on a job, you can track the time it takes and expenditures you incur to complete the job. For example, if Fabrikam purchases lumber with which to build a shed, the company can link those purchases to the job. Whenever you create a purchase order; buy an item by using cash, check, or charge; or subcontract service items to another provider, you can assign the cost to the job for which you're making the purchase. You can assign service items, including time spent by your employees working on the job, by clicking the Job Name arrow in the appropriate window and selecting the job to which you want to assign the costs.

Viewing and Manipulating the Job List (Professional Only)

Accounting Professional 2007 stores all of your jobs in one list, the *Job List*. To display the Job List, click the Customers button in the Navigation Pane and then, in the Find section of the Customers home page, click Jobs.

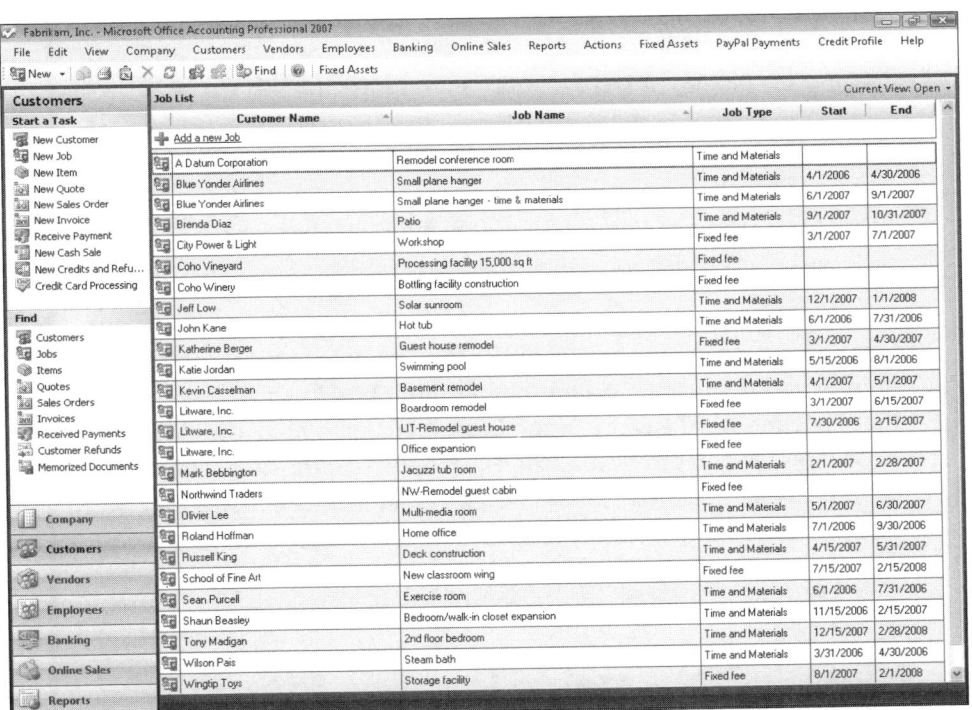

Sorting and Filtering the Job List

If you've been in business for a while, it's very likely that your Job List contains numerous entries. With Accounting Professional, you can rearrange and limit the data that appears in the Job List, making it easier for you to find the job entry you're looking for.

Each Job List column header includes the following three sorting options:

- **Unsorted.** Displays the jobs in the order in which they were entered into the program.

- **Sorted In Ascending Order.** Sorts the list by placing the jobs with the lowest values in the selected field at the beginning of the list. For example, sorting the Start field in ascending order would put a job with a start date of 2/9/2008 before a job with a start date of 8/2/2008.

- **Sorted In Descending Order.** Sorts the list by placing the jobs with the highest values in the selected field at the beginning of the list. For example, sorting the Start field in descending order would put a job with a start date of 8/2/2008 before a job with a start date of 2/9/2008.

Clicking the header of an unsorted column sorts the Job List in ascending order based on the contents of that column; clicking the header again sorts the Job List in descending order; and clicking the header a third time restores the column and the Job List to their original order. If you'd like to sort the list based on the values in more than one column, such as by Customer Name first and then by Job Name, hold down the Ctrl key, and then click the column headers in the order by which you would like the list to be sorted.

If you're having trouble finding a job you want to view, you can locate just those jobs that contain a specific value in either the Customer Name, Job Name, or Job Type column. For example, if you want to filter the Job List so that it contains only those jobs that have the word *Litware* in the Customer Name field, click the Find button on the Accounting toolbar to display the Find toolbar. In the Look For field, type the value you want to search for. Then, in the Search Under list, click the field in which you want to search. Accounting Professional 2007 filters the Job List to reflect your criteria.

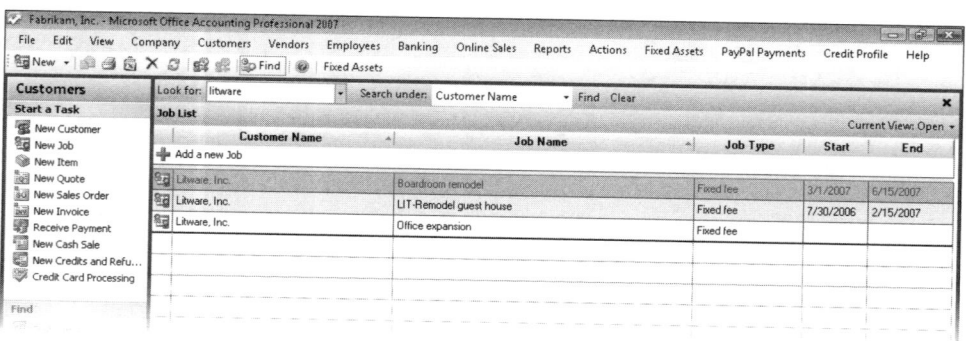

Clicking the Find button again removes the active filter and closes the Find toolbar. If you'd rather remove the current filter but keep the Find toolbar open, click the Clear button.

In this exercise, you will manipulate the Job List to display only the jobs you want to view.

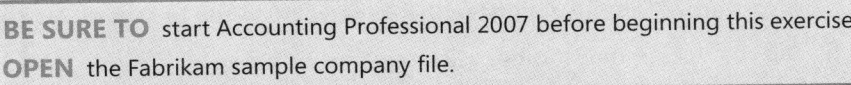

BE SURE TO start Accounting Professional 2007 before beginning this exercise.
OPEN the Fabrikam sample company file.

1. In the **Navigation Pane**, click the **Customers** button.

   The Customers home page appears.

2. In the **Find** section of the **Customers** home page, click **Jobs**.

   The Job List appears.

3. In the **Job List**, click the **Customer Name** column header.

   Accounting sorts the Fabrikam Job List in ascending order by using the values in the Customer Name column.

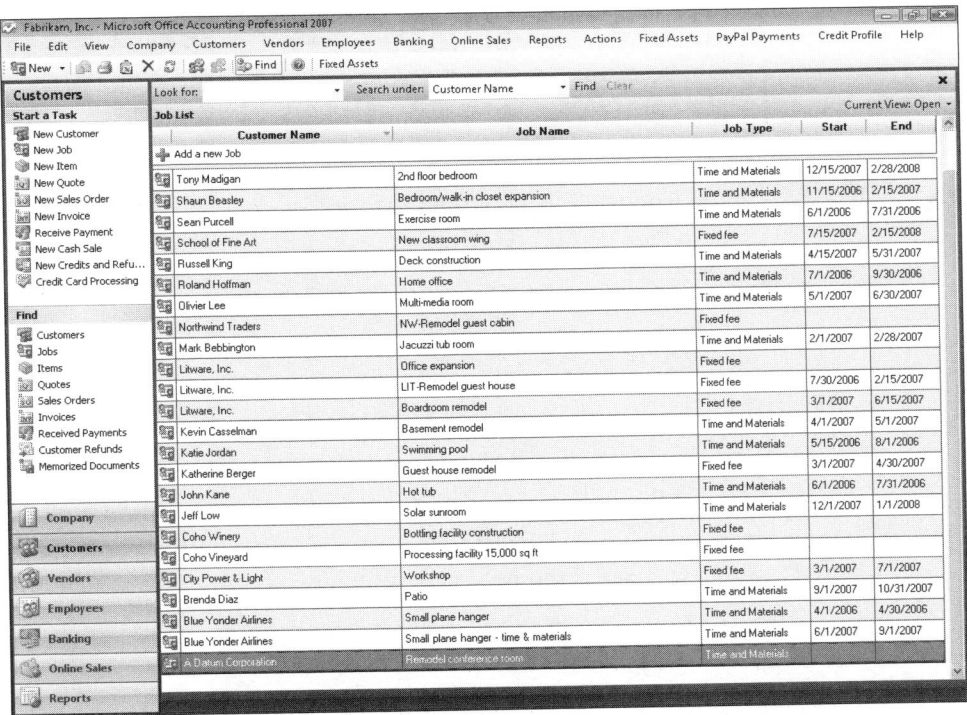

4. Hold down the ⌈Ctrl⌉ key and click the **Customer Name** and **Job Name** column headers, in that order, to select both columns.

Accounting sorts the Job List by using the values in the Customer Name column as its primary sorting criteria, using the values in the Job Name column to determine a sort order for jobs that have the same value in the Customer Name column.

5. On the Accounting toolbar, click the **Find** button.

The Find toolbar appears above the Job List.

6. In the **Look for** field of the **Find** toolbar, type office.

7. Click the **Search under** arrow, and then in the list, click **Job Name**.

Accounting displays in the Job Name field the two jobs that contain the term *office*.

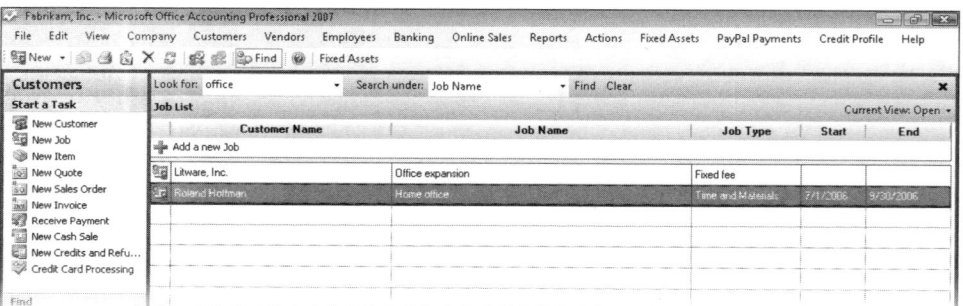

8. On the Find toolbar, click the **Clear** button.

Accounting removes the filter from the Job List.

9. On the Accounting toolbar, click the **Find** button.

The Find toolbar closes.

Viewing the Job List by Job Status

Managing a company requires that you know how your projects are progressing. It's important to know which of your job offers were not accepted, how many projects are in progress for a given client at any one time, and whether you have a lot of projects that are due to start in the near future.

To help you capture that information, Accounting Professional assigns jobs to the following five status categories:

● **Open.** Indicates that a job listing has been created for the project but that the job has not yet been completed or canceled.

● **In Progress.** Indicates that a job has been started but has not been completed.

● **Completed.** Indicates that a job has been started and finished.

- **Not Started.** Indicates that a job has been created but that work has not begun.
- **All.** Lists every job regardless of its status.

In this exercise, you will filter the Job List by job status.

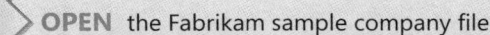
OPEN the Fabrikam sample company file.

1. In the **Navigation Pane**, click the **Customers** button.
2. In the **Find** section of the **Customers** home page, click **Jobs**.
3. In the **Job List**, click the **Current View** arrow, and then in the list, click **In Progress**.

   Accounting filters the Job List so that it shows just those projects that are in progress.

4. On the Accounting toolbar, click the **Find** button.

   The Find toolbar appears above the Job List.
5. In the **Look for** field of the Find toolbar, type remodel.
6. In the **Search under** list, click **Job Name**.

   The Job List displays only those remodeling efforts that are in progress.

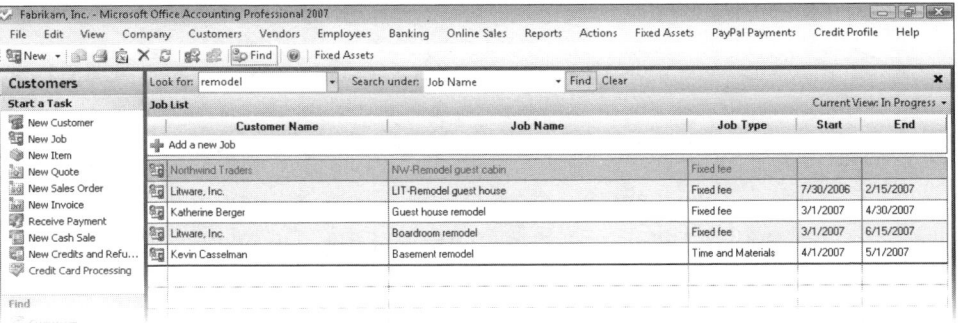

7. On the Accounting toolbar, click the **Find** button.

   The Find toolbar disappears and Accounting removes the filter from the Job List.
8. In the **Current View** list, click **Open**.

   Accounting displays jobs for which a quote has been generated and that have not been completed or canceled.

Viewing Job Details (Professional Only)

If you want to view a job's details, double-click anywhere on the job's row. When you do, a job form opens for the job you double-clicked.

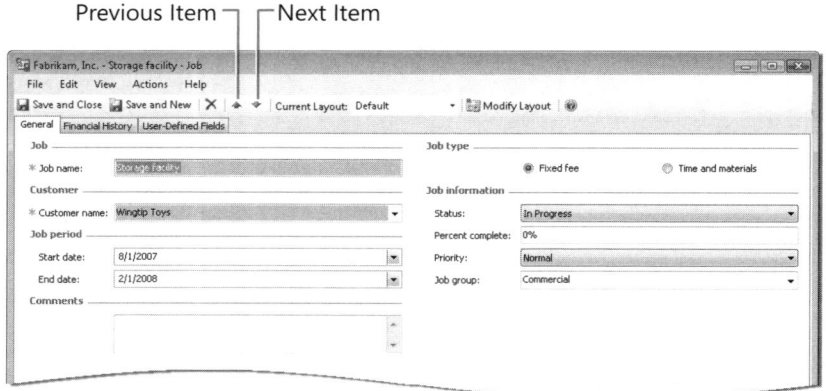

Previous Item ⌐ ⌐Next Item

> **Tip** While you are viewing a job's details, you can display the next job in the Job List by clicking the Next Item button on the Job form toolbar. To display the previous job in the list, click the Previous Item button.

Each job form has three tabs: General, Financial History, and User-Defined Fields. The General tab contains fields such as the job name, customer for whom the job will be performed, whether the job is a fixed-fee or time-and-materials job, and the job's status.

Clicking the Financial History tab displays every transaction related to a job, including the original quote (if any), all purchases made in relation to the project, and all invoices sent to the customer.

See Also For information on creating progress invoices, which are requests for partial payment as a job progresses, see Chapter 11, "Managing Invoices."

In this exercise, you will view a job's details, including its financial history.

> **OPEN** the Fabrikam sample company file.

1. In the **Navigation Pane**, click the **Customers** button.

2. In the **Find** section of the **Customers** home page, click **Jobs**.

3. Scroll through the **Job List**, and then double-click the job for the customer **Wilson Pais**.

   The Steam Bath job form opens.

4. Click the **Financial History** tab.

   The Financial History tab displays the transactions related to Wilson Pais.

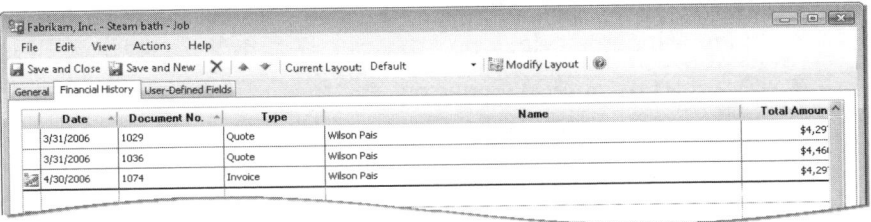

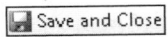

5. On the **Steam Bath - Job** form toolbar, click the **Save and Close** button.

   The Steam Bath - Job form closes.

Creating Jobs (Professional Only)

When you're ready to create a job, you can do so by clicking the Customers button in the Navigation Pane to display the Customers home page. On the Customers home page, you can click the New Job item to open a job form and enter the details of your new job.

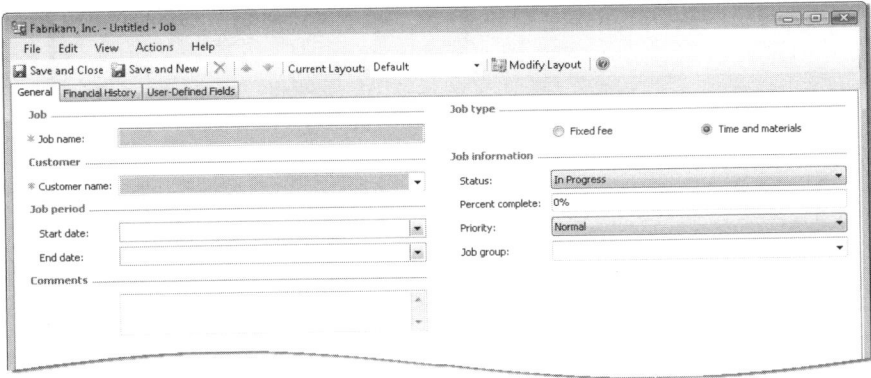

In this exercise, you will create a job.

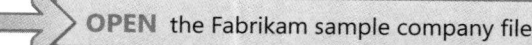

OPEN the Fabrikam sample company file.

1. In the **Navigation Pane**, click the **Customers** button.

2. In the **More Tasks** section of the **Customers** home page, click **New Job**.

   An untitled job form opens.

3. In the **Job name** field, type Adventure Works Wax Shack.

4. Click the **Customer name** arrow, and then click **Adventure Works**.

5. In the **Start date** field, type 5/1/2008.

6. In the **End date** field, type 5/30/2008.

7. Under **Job Type**, click **Fixed Fee**.

8. Leave the **Status**, **Percent complete**, and **Priority** field values at their defaults
   (**In Progress** status, **0%** complete, and **Normal** priority).

9. In the **Job group** list, click **Commercial**.

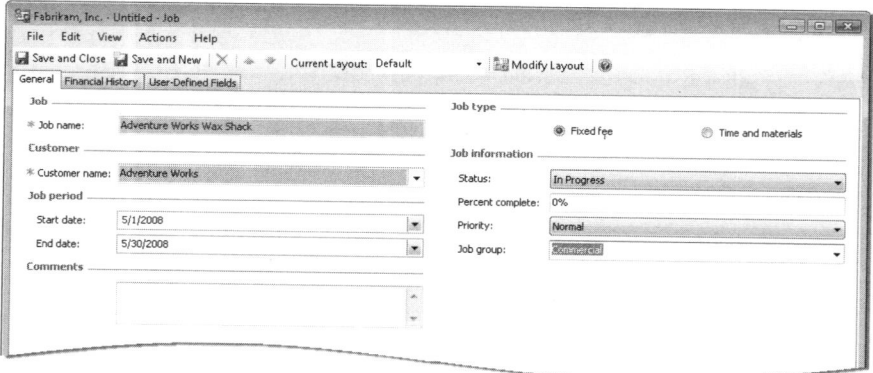

10. On the form toolbar, click the **Save and Close** button.

    The job form closes.

Editing and Deleting Jobs (Professional Only)

Circumstances change in every industry, regardless of whether it's the construction industry (the home industry of our fictitious Fabrikam), automobile sales, or software programming. The bid you submit for a job may or may not be successful. You could enter incorrect information about a job, perhaps assigning it to the wrong customer, and need to fix your listing. Finally, you might hear back from a potential client that they're not going forward with a project, which means that you can safely delete the job you added to your company file.

To change a job's information, just display the job's information on screen and edit the values that need editing. For example, you might change a job's status from Open to In Progress. You could also change the project's start or end date if the client needs you to start or finish the project at a time other than the one you first entered into the job.

Deleting a job is a straightforward but final operation that you should only undertake if there are no other documents related to the job in your company file. You should also consider keeping all of your jobs around. For example, if you maintain a record of unconsummated deals, when a potential client contacts you about possible projects but never follows through with an offer of work, you might consider changing how you handle requests for proposals from that client in the future.

In this exercise, you will modify and then delete a job.

> **OPEN** the Fabrikam sample company file.

1. In the **Navigation Pane**, click **Customers**.
2. In the **Find** area of the **Customers** home page, click **Jobs**.
3. Double-click the job named **Adventure Works Wax Shack**.

   The Adventure Works Wax Shack job form opens.

   > **Important** You created the Adventure Works Wax Shack job in an exercise earlier in this chapter. If you didn't create that job, or if you don't want to edit or delete it, move through this exercise but don't save your changes or delete the job you use.

4. In the **Start date** field, change the date to 6/1/2008.

5. In the **End date** field, change the date to 6/30/2008.

6. Under **Job type**, click **Time and Materials**.

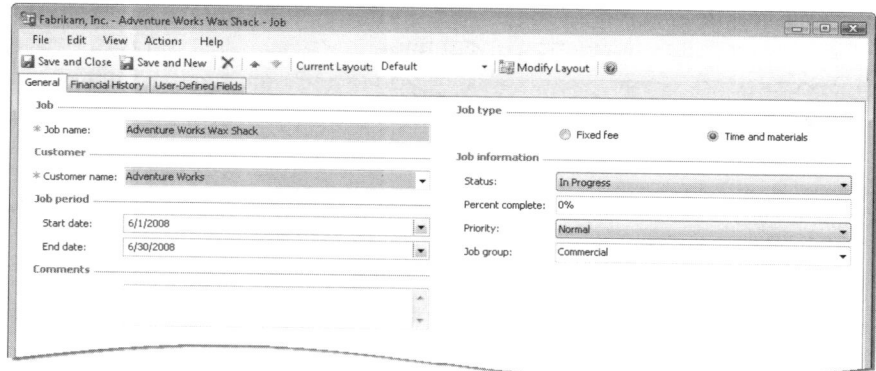

7. On the **File** menu, click **Close**. Click **No** when you're asked if you want to save your changes.

   The job form closes.

Delete

8. On the toolbar, click the **Delete** button.

   A confirmation dialog box opens.

9. In the confirmation box, click **Yes** to confirm that you want to delete the selected job.

Modifying Job Groups (Professional Only)

When you create a company file, Accounting Professional assumes all of your projects should be considered together when you generate reports to analyze your business performance. If you would like to distinguish one set of jobs from the other jobs undertaken by your company, you can do so by creating a new job group. The Fabrikam sample company file, for example, contains two job groups: commercial and residential. By setting up separate groups, you can use the Profitability By Job Summary report to compare Fabrikam's commercial and residential projects.

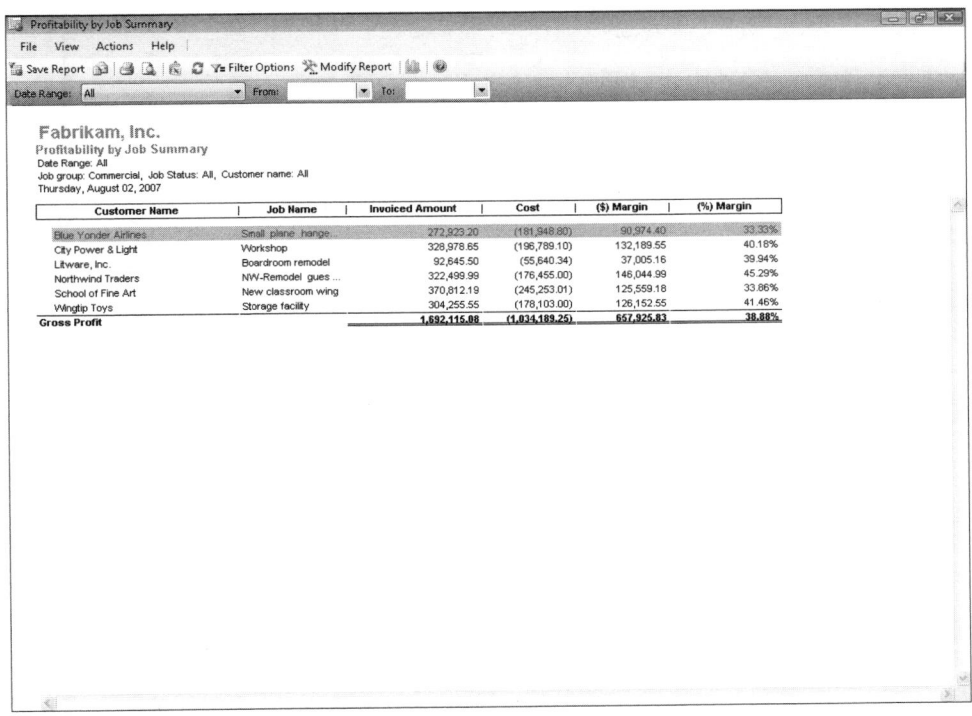

See Also For more information on working with reports, see Chapter 15, "Creating Reports to Manage Your Business," on the CD.

You can create a new job group by pointing to Manage Support Lists on the Company menu, and then clicking Job Group List. When you do, the Manage Job Group dialog box opens.

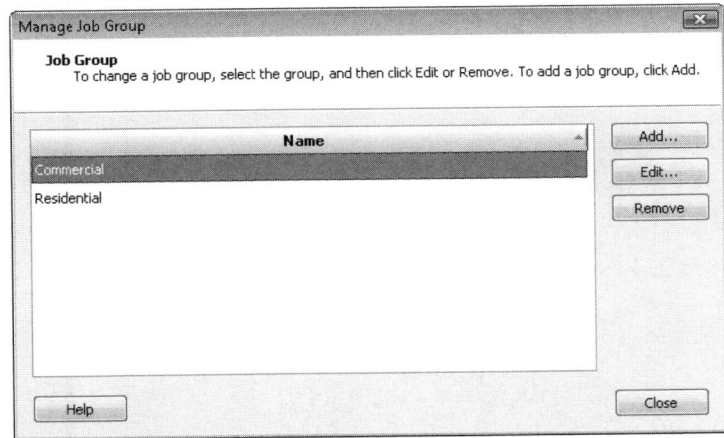

The Name list displays all of the available job group names. You can then click the Add button to create a new group, click the Edit button to change information about an existing group, or click the Remove button to delete a group entirely.

In this exercise, you will create a new group for Fabrikam jobs.

OPEN the Fabrikam sample company file.

1. On the **Company** menu, point to **Manage Support Lists**, and then click **Job Group List**.

   The Manage Job Group dialog box opens.

2. Click **Add**.

   The Job Group dialog box opens.

3. In the **Job Group Name** field, type Aviation.

4. Click **OK**.

   The Job Group dialog box closes, and the Aviation job group appears in the Manage Job Group dialog box.

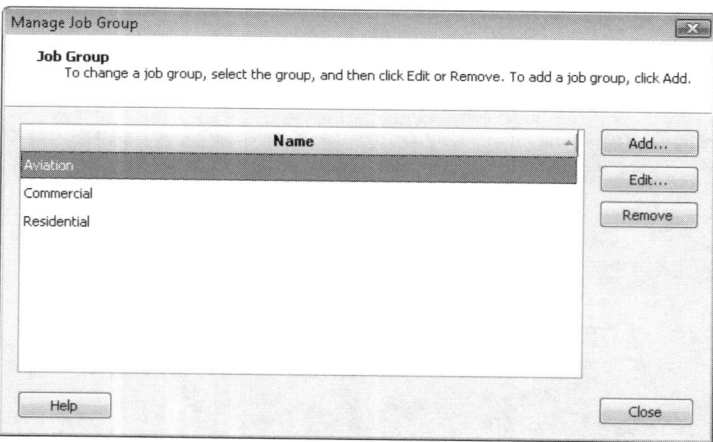

5. Click **Close**.

   The Manage Job Group dialog box closes.

Assigning Cash Sales to Jobs (Professional Only)

Handling cash purchases is difficult for any company. Cash is messy and hard to keep track of, and employees always seem to lose the receipt they need to submit to deduct an expense on your corporate taxes. Those considerations aside, Accounting Professional 2007 attempts to make assigning cash transactions to a particular job as straightforward as possible.

In this exercise, you will assign a cash sale to a job.

OPEN the Fabrikam sample company file.

1. In the **Navigation Pane**, click the **Customers** button.

2. In the **Find** area of the **Customers** home page, click **Jobs**.

3. Click the **Solar sunroom** project for **Jeff Low**.

4. On the **Actions** menu, click **Create Cash Sales**.

   A Cash Sale form opens.

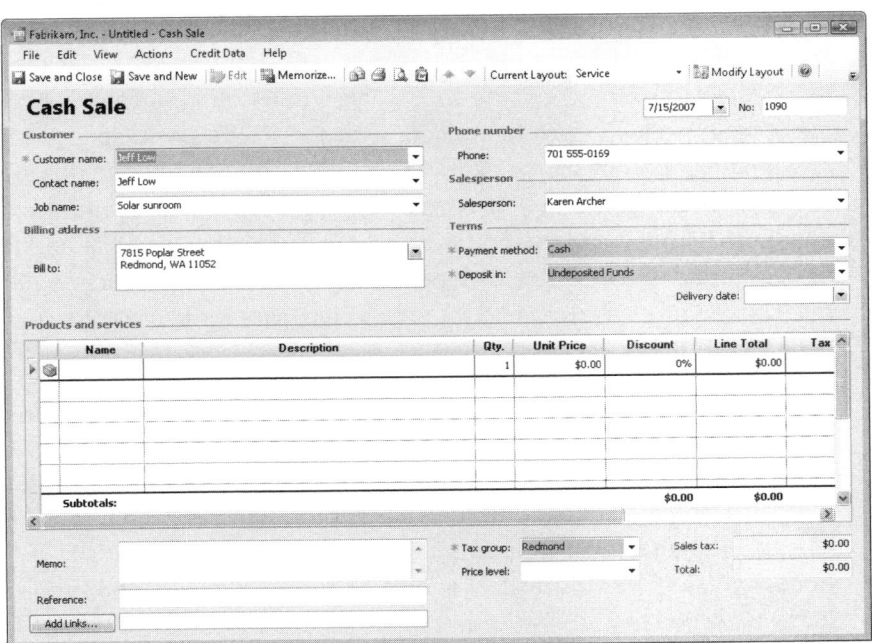

5. In the **Products and Services** grid, click the **Name** field on the active row.

6. Click the **Name** field arrow, and then click **Carpentry (TM)**.

 7. Click the **Save and Close** button on the toolbar.

See Also For information about assigning a purchase order to a job, see Chapter 13, "Purchasing from Vendors."

CLOSE the Fabrikam sample company file. If you are not continuing directly to the next chapter, exit Accounting 2007.

Analyzing Job Histories (Professional Only)

If you rely solely upon your chart of accounts, you will likely find that creating transactional history reports for customers or projects can prove difficult and time-consuming. To create reports of this nature, you have to select only the revenue and expense accounts appropriate to the customer/project, and then have to perform significant filtering to deliver only the appropriate details. By using jobs in Accounting Professional 2007, you can perform the same steps with far less setup and maintenance effort.

Tracking your customers by jobs means easy presentation of the related histories, and efficient analysis of the income and expense transactions involved. Your use of jobs can range from tracking discrete projects, with specific beginning and ending dates, to tracking general jobs that simply describe type of work, and so forth (for example, such types as management consulting, technical consulting, design and implementation, or within an information technologies services organization). You have the added capability of flexibly grouping your jobs (by types or any other characteristics you find useful), which means even more analysis and reporting capability for your business.

In many ways, your jobs resemble subaccounts. They typically provide a subanalysis path for customers, if you choose to use them, and you can put them to work in many different ways. If you are a service organization, you will probably find that setting up at least a "general" job for your customers makes sense, even if you don't feel you need to track jobs initially. With this foresightedness, you have the flexibility of adding more jobs to your customers' accounts later, when you identify needs to begin monitoring "focus" projects with a specific function or scope. This way "non-monitored" transactions remain in a general "bucket" together, while you can class the "focus" items in a job you create for that purpose.

You have probably guessed that you can use jobs within contexts that extend well beyond traditional "customers." In educational/non-profit organizations, for example, a job can be set up for each contract, grant, or the like upon which you might want the capability to individually report for a given donor entity. With jobs, you can obtain important information about the internal workings of your business, even if you don't have an immediate requirement to provide external, job-based reports. Jobs mean the capability to focus upon a discrete group of related revenues and costs, and therefore profitability—just the intelligence you need to make decisions to generate the most income within your business.

Job Group Profitability—How It Works

Depending upon the kind of business you have, you might find it useful to analyze and report not only upon the profitability of individual jobs, but of job groups, as well. As an illustration, say you operate a consulting services business. You might have many customers, and you set up separate jobs for each customer's projects. You might then group these projects by the following types: Design, Implementation, Upgrade, and System Support. These job groups will allow you to track the profits and losses for each general type of project as a whole, providing you important business intelligence with which you can compare project types with regard to your returns on each, as well as other key metrics.

The information you obtain will help you to determine the types of projects that deliver the greatest overall returns, among other considerations. This can translate to better deployment of staff and resources. When you analyze and report upon your jobs, and particularly upon your job groups, you can often obtain information you need to optimize your business.

Jobs—A Few Best Practices

Because a job in Accounting Professional 2007 can represent a multi-part project made up of products or services (or even both) that you deliver over time, you can use this feature in several flexible ways to generate detailed business intelligence about your operation. To make the most of jobs, you can do the following:

- Select the job type (fixed-fee or time-and-materials, for instance) that best matches the nature of the respective project.

- Use the arrangements and filters in the Job List to easily navigate between job entries in the system.

- Use the job status categories (Open, In Progress, Completed, Not Started) by assigning and updating statuses as required. (This allows for filtering the Job List by job status, and, once again, easy navigation between job entries.)

- Fully use the job form to view job details, including general information, financial history of the job, and custom fields.

- Exploit custom fields to track job information specific to your individual business practices and customer needs.

- Edit (including job status) and delete jobs as necessary to keep your system updated and free of clutter.

- Maintain jobs for projects for which you have bid, or otherwise made proposals, and which turn out to be unconsummated. This tracks prospect behavior, and might serve as an indicator to consider—especially when the same prospect makes future requests for proposals.

- Use job groups to enable you to analyze and report upon one or more sets of jobs, in addition to individual jobs. This allows, for example, grouped profitability summaries, with which you can compare revenues, expenses, and overall profits between multiple types of jobs.

- Set up a "general" job, even for customers for whom you may not think you initially need jobs. You can then add jobs as required, to address needs that arise to monitor specific projects, later.

Jobs in Accounting Professional 2007 offer you a flexible extension to your chart of accounts in reporting and analyzing the projects you undertake. You will find the capability to group the transactions within a given project, as well as the capability to group projects themselves for summarized reporting by type, among other features, to provide powerful analysis and reporting support.

> ### Reporting Considerations: Jobs
>
> Reports that you base upon jobs, and the revenue and expense activity they reflect, will focus upon the customers to whom you have sold products or services and the dates of the transactions, expenses and the dates they are incurred, customer receipts and respective dates, and other information. Typical "views" by which such information is arranged include jobs (in many cases, a given report will be related to one job upon which you wish to perform review and analysis), job groups, customers, products/services sold, timing of sales, and associated job details. Job reporting and analysis provides you with business intelligence surrounding job profitability, the time and costs recorded on individual jobs or groups of jobs, and actual versus estimated values for any of these measures.

Key Points

- By creating jobs, you can store all products and services related to a project in one entity.
- You can sort and filter the Job List to make it easier to find the jobs you are looking for.
- The job form has a Financial History tab, on which you can find every transaction related to the job.
- You can assign your jobs to a job group, which enables you to create reports for each job group (for example, all commercial construction jobs as compared to all residential construction jobs).

Chapter at a Glance

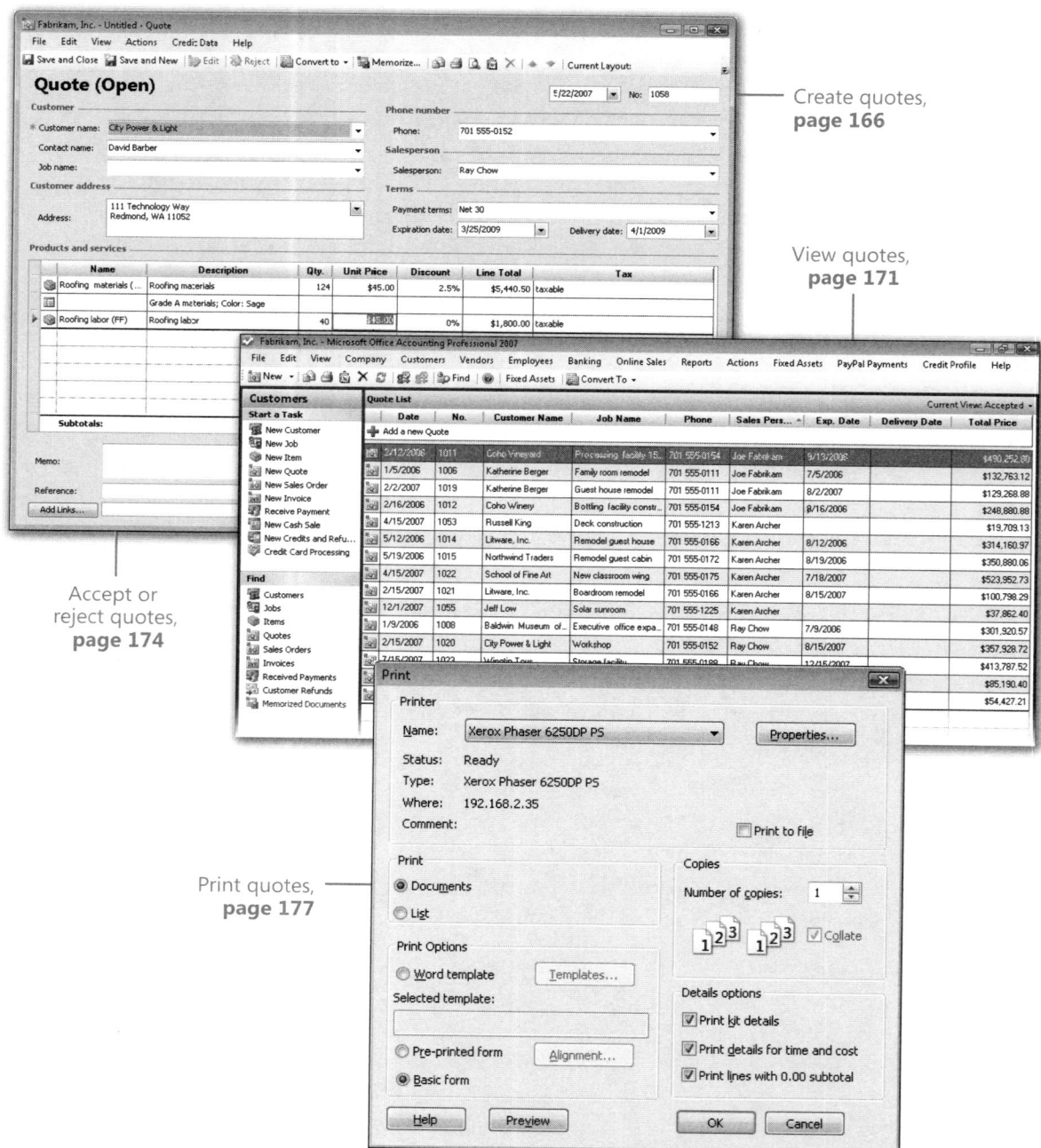

Create quotes, **page 166**

View quotes, **page 171**

Accept or reject quotes, **page 174**

Print quotes, **page 177**

8 Generating and Managing Quotes

In this chapter, you will learn to:

- ✔ Create quotes.
- ✔ View quotes.
- ✔ Accept or reject quotes.
- ✔ Print quotes.

In a small business such as an engineering or architectural firm, a general contractor, or a small manufacturer, customers often require that the company provide an estimate of the costs of products and services before the customer commits to a purchase. Likewise, a small business needs to be clear about the products and services it agrees to provide, what it will charge for those items, and when the work is due.

In Microsoft Office Accounting Professional 2007, a *quote* specifies the products and services you agree to sell or provide to a customer, what those items will cost, and the delivery date of a proposed transaction. In addition to price information, a quote specifies discounts, shipping information, and *payment terms*. A quote also specifies its expiration date to define the time period for which the terms of the quote are valid.

You build a quote in Accounting Professional from the list of products and services set up for your company as items. For example, a quote might list all the plumbing parts you need for a job plus the labor required to complete the work. Or a quote might list a series of tasks for a landscaping job with the hourly rates and time required to complete each task. A quote can also be associated with a job that you define in Accounting Professional. For complex jobs, you might provide a quote for different phases of the job.

When you create a quote, the status of the quote is open. The customer that receives the quote can then notify you whether it is accepted or rejected, or the quote can simply expire if the expiration date passes without the customer taking action. A quote that a customer accepts serves as the basis for an invoice or a sales order for the goods and services described in the quote. A quote that a customer rejects might represent a lost business opportunity, but you might be able to revise a rejected quote based on feedback you solicit from the customer and submit the quote again.

In this chapter, you will learn how to create, manage, and print a quote. You will also learn how to view the list of quotes and gain some helpful insights about your business by creating reports based on your quotes.

> **Troubleshooting** Graphics and operating system–related instructions in this book reflect the Windows Vista user interface. If your computer is running Windows XP and you experience trouble following the instructions as written, please refer to the "Information for Readers Running Windows XP" section at the beginning of this book.

Creating Quotes

Preparing a quote is part business operation and part customer relationship. For example, quotes have expiration dates. In setting the expiration date for a quote, you might need to take several factors into account, such as cost of goods you are reselling or using for manufacturing for a customer. If your supplier can guarantee a price for 30 days, a quote based on this price should expire in an equivalent period of time; otherwise, you risk losing part of your profit.

In addition, although not all prospective business transactions require that you provide a quote, many small businesses operate in competitive environments, and their customers request proposals from more than one company before deciding which company to use. A quote that details the financial terms of a business transaction might be part of a larger presentation prepared in response to a formal Request For Proposal (RFP). At other times, it is simply good practice to create a quote so that you as the seller and the customer as the buyer agree to the terms of a sale before the deal is closed.

Initiating a Quote

When you initiate a quote by filling out a quote form, the quote's status is Open. The status is displayed beside the main label at the top of the form. Accounting 2007 fills in the current date and assigns a number to the quote, but both can be modified. For example, you can change the date to reflect the date on which you submit the quote (assuming you work on the quote for more than one day) or to reflect the date of a meeting you have with the customer. You can change the quote number to conform to a numbering system you've set up for your company.

The upper half of the quote form displays contact information for the customer and the payment terms, expiration date, and delivery date. You use the Products And Services area of the form to specify each line item included in the quote. Each line item includes the name and a description of the item, the quantity, the price, and other details.

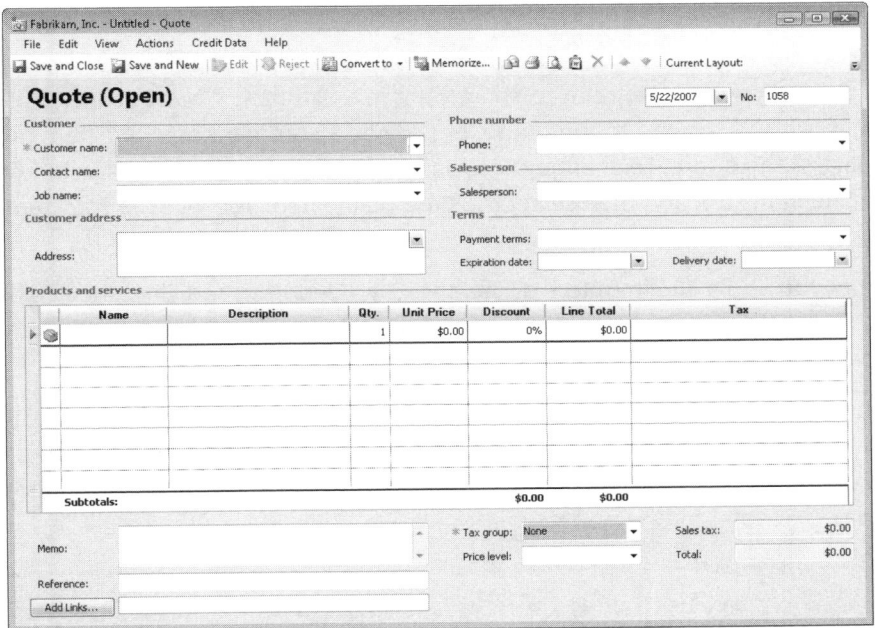

When you select the customer's name from the Customer Name list, other contact fields are filled in based on the customer's record. These fields include the principal contact person for this customer, the business address and phone number, and the salesperson assigned to the customer's account. If the customer's record specifies default payment terms, the Payment Terms field is filled in. You can change the payment terms for this particular quote if you need to.

At the bottom of the quote form, the Tax Group that this customer belongs to is displayed. (If a customer has not been assigned to a tax group, the field is blank.) As the quote is built, the sales tax rates are applied to the price of line items. These rates are defined in the tax codes that are included in the tax group.

> **Note** If you select the Use Jobs option in the Company Preferences dialog box, the quote form includes the Job Name field. You can create a quote for a fixed fee or a time and materials job. If you select the Use Class option as a company preference, the quote form includes the Class field. You can use this field to include which class a quote belongs to. For example, if you have set up sales regions as classes, you can designate the region in the quote.

Adding Line Items to a Quote

The products and services listed are mostly those you have set up as *items*. The description of the item comes from the item's record. If you type a name of an item that is not included in the list of products and services, Accounting 2007 prompts you to add it to the list before you continue creating the quote.

Most of the line items in a quote are products and services defined in a company's item list. A line item can also refer to an account in a company's chart of accounts, indicate a sales tax that applies to the quote, or provide a comment on a line item or another aspect of the quote. To change the type of a line item, click the icon in the first cell of the line item row, and then select the type of line item you want to use: Item, Comment, Sales Tax, or Account.

When you add a line item to a quote, the Qty. (*Quantity*) and Unit Price fields are filled in with the default quantity of one unit and the retail price as noted in the item record. Line Total is calculated as a product of Quantity and Unit Price.

You can change the unit price in the quote to balance your company's profit with the overall cost of the quote to the customer. When you change one of these fields, Accounting 2007 recalculates the values in the others and adjusts the line total, sales tax, and overall total for the quote.

Analyzing Historical Quotes vs. Profitability to Refine Your Quote Process

Analyzing profit margins on completed sales comes naturally to most business owners. Profit margins provide a great overall indication of how much money you are making on the products or services you sell, and provide insight as to your overall efficiency. But if quotes are a regular part of your business, you can take profitability analysis one step further: you can examine the actual margins you obtained on various products and services, in light of your original quotes, to refine your estimates for future sales.

Just as you monitor profit margins for recurring sales of products or services to become aware of opportunities to improve efficiencies, you can analyze margins alongside the corresponding quotes to determine how accurate your estimates really were. If, for example, margins have begun to decline for a given service, analyzing the quotes to discover the profitability of completed sales can help you to drill down into the causes. It's possible that recent estimates haven't accounted for increasing labor charges, overhead expenses, and the like. Regular cost analysis can drive adjustments of the estimates upon which you base your quotes and help you generate the margins you have targeted.

In this exercise, you will create a quote in Accounting 2007 by using one of the customers in the Fabrikam sample company. You will specify line items in the quote by using the list of products and services, and learn how you can adjust prices and discounts while creating a quote. You'll also add a comment to a line item in a quote, and you'll see the steps and calculations that Accounting 2007 performs for you when you prepare a quote.

> **BE SURE TO** start Accounting 2007 before beginning this exercise.
>
> **OPEN** the Fabrikam sample company file.

1. In the **Navigation Pane**, click **Customers**.

   The Customers home page appears.

2. Under **Start a Task**, click **New Quote**.

   A blank quote appears.

3. Click the **Customer name** arrow, and then in the list, click **City Power and Light**.

   Accounting 2007 populates the customer's information into the quote form.

4. In the **Expiration date** field, type 3/25/2009.

5. In the **Delivery date** field, type 4/1/2009.

6. Under **Products and services**, click in the **Name** column, click the arrow that appears, and then click **Roofing materials (FF)**.

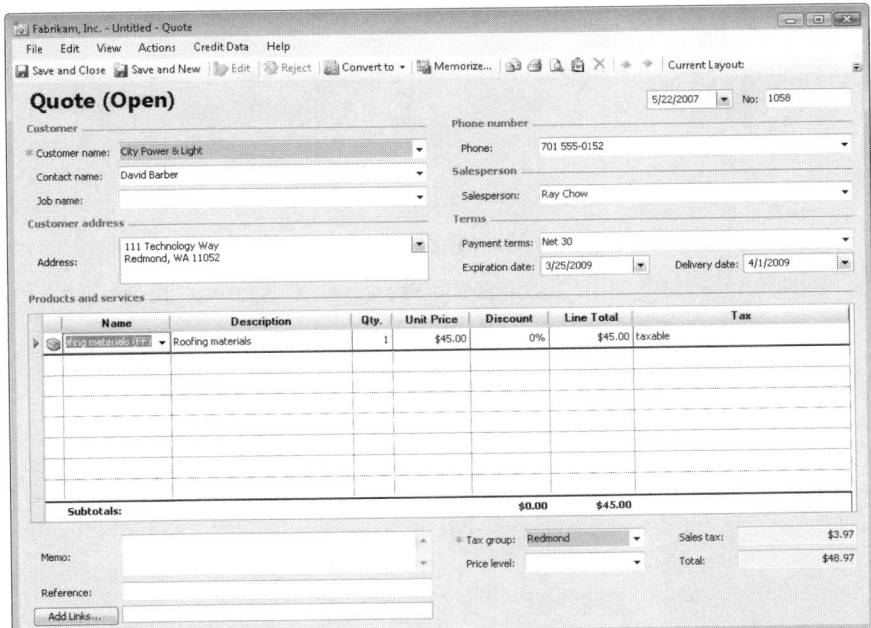

7. In the **Description** field, modify the default description or enter a new one.

8. In the **Qty.** (quantity) field, type 124.

9. In the **Discount** field, type 2.5.

10. Click the **Item** icon at the far left of the second row, and then click **Comment**.

11. In the **Description** field, type Grade A materials; Color: Sage.

12. In the row below the comment you entered, click in the **Name** column, and then click **Roofing labor (FF)**.

13. In the **Qty.** field, type 40 and then press Tab.

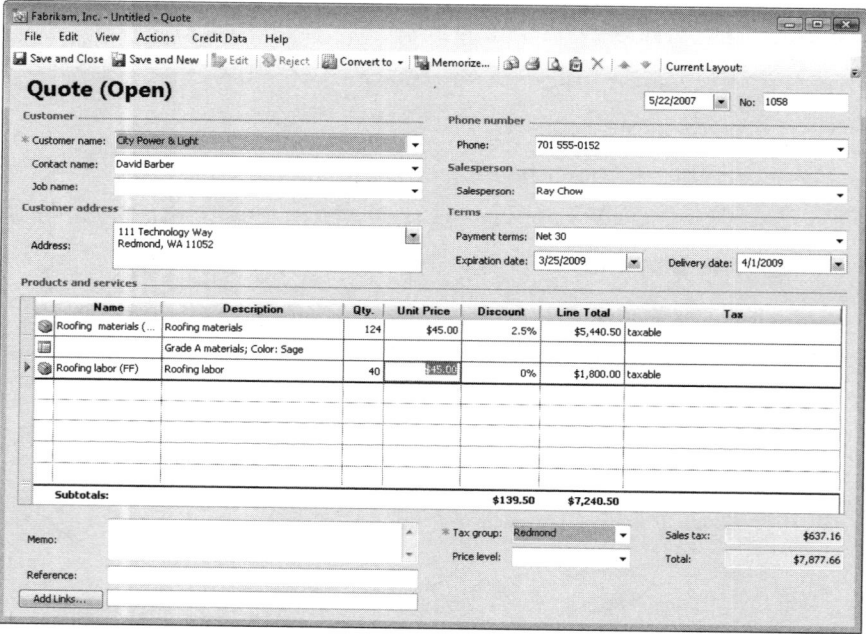

14. In the **Price level** list, click **Preferred Customer**.

Accounting 2007 applies the Preferred Customer discount to the quoted prices.

15. Click **Save and Close**.

Accounting 2007 saves the quote and closes the quote form.

Viewing Quotes

If you use Accounting 2007 to manage a company that provides quotes to customers, you should regularly review the list of quotes. You use the list of quotes to manage the status of the quotes you have provided to customers and to gain information about the quotes the company provides. For example, you can sort the list of quotes by expiration date to see which quotes are due to expire soon. You can then follow up with each customer or with the salesperson assigned to the customer's account to determine whether the customer has made a decision about the quote.

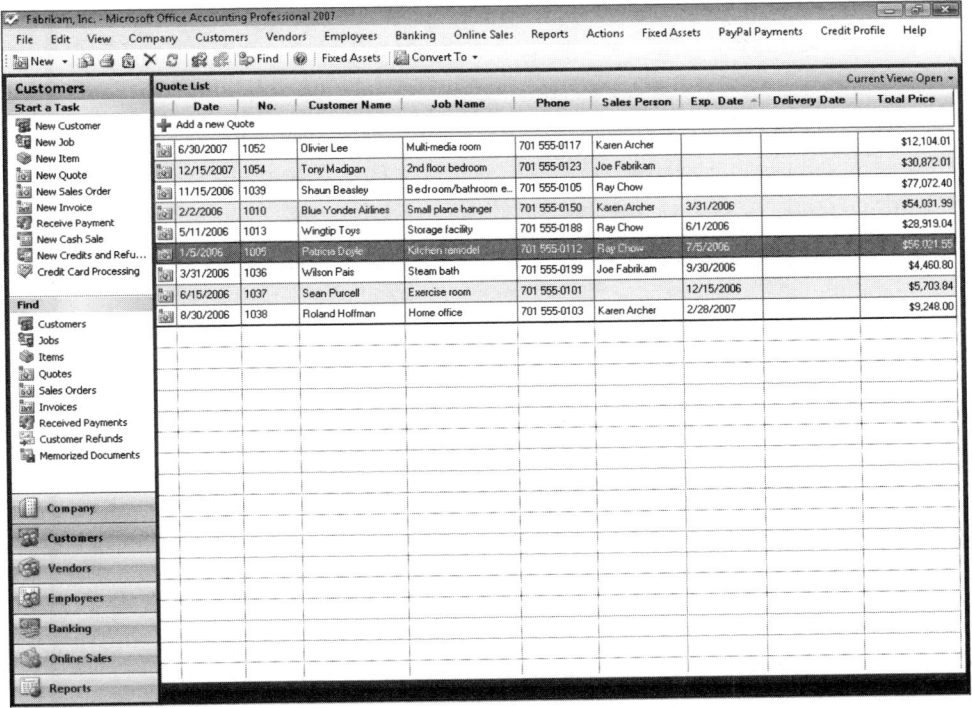

Also, by reviewing the Quote List, you gain information that can provide insights into your business. Viewing the list of quotes that have been rejected, for example, might reveal patterns about why your company wasn't awarded a job or a sale. Does a particular item you sell or service you provide appear frequently on rejected quotes? Does that mean that the price you charge for this item or service is not in line with your competitors' prices? Which of your goods and services are more often included on successful quotes? By sorting the Quote List by salesperson, you can see which of the sales staff have generated more quotes and which of the salespeople have their quotes accepted the majority of the time.

By default, the Quote List displays Open quotes—those quotes that a customer has not yet accepted or rejected. The Quote List displays a summary of information about each quote, including the customer's name and phone number, the related job name, the sales person, the expiration and delivery dates, and the amount of the quote.

In addition to viewing all quotes, you can use the Current View list to filter the list to show quotes that have a particular status—Open, Accepted, Rejected, or Expired. You can also display all quotes by clicking All in the Current View list. Switching the view of the Quote List is a simple way to gather information about possible trends in your business. For example, click Expired in the Current View list to see how many quotes have expired in the past 2 weeks, 30 days, or 6 months. Do the quotes that you provide to a particular customer always expire? If so, should you continue providing quotes to this customer or does this customer need some additional cultivation?

To sort the Quote List, click the header of the column by which you want to sort the list. For example, if you wanted to sort the Fabrikam Quote List by the values in the Total Price column, you would click the Total Price column header.

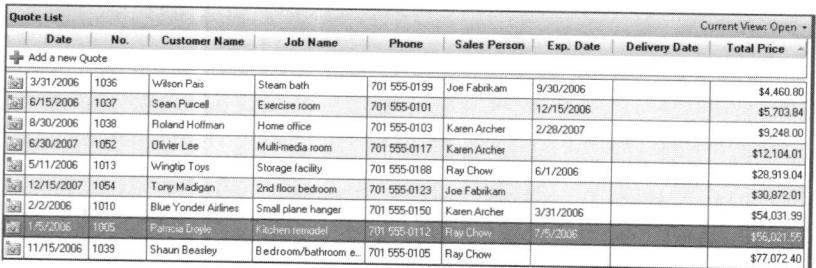

Clicking a column header once sorts the list in ascending order (lowest to highest) based on that column's value; clicking a column header again sorts the list in descending order (highest to lowest) based on that column's values; and clicking a column header once again restores the list to its original order.

> **Note** Column headers display up or down arrows to indicate whether the list is sorted in ascending or descending order based on the values in that column.

In this exercise, you will display the Quote List, change the status of quotes displayed, and sort the Quote List by sales person.

OPEN the Fabrikam sample company file.

1. In the **Navigation Pane**, click **Customers**.

   The Customers home page appears.

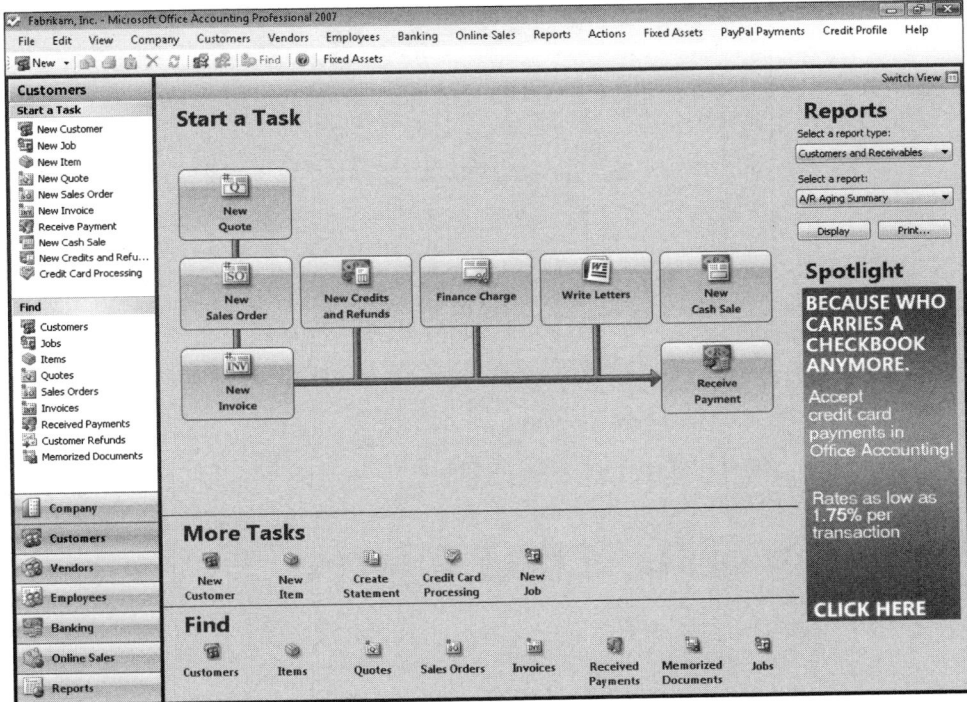

2. Under **Find**, click **Quotes**.

   The Quote List appears.

3. Click the **Current View** arrow, and then in the list, click **Expired**.

   The expired quotes appear in the Quote List.

4. In the **Current View** list, click **Accepted**.

   The accepted quotes appear in the Quote List.

5. Click the **Sales Person** column header.

   Accounting 2007 sorts the quotes in ascending order by sales person.

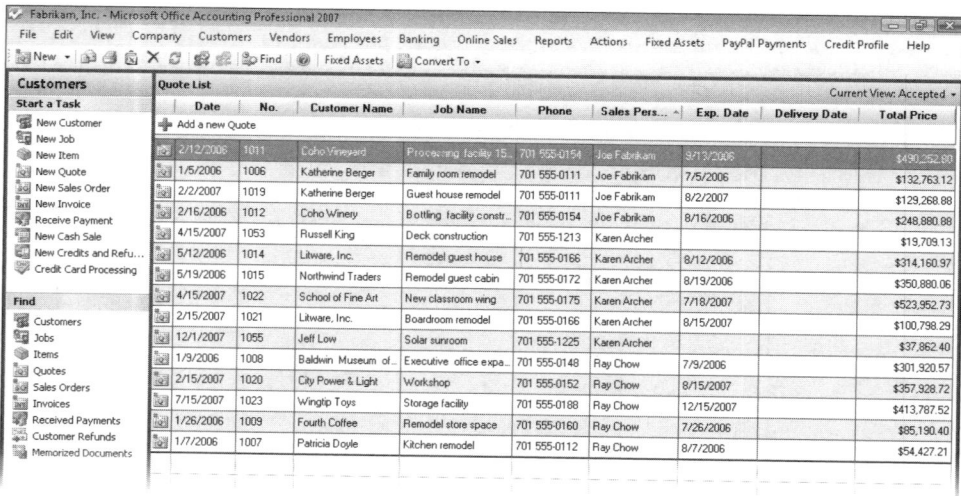

6. Click the **Sales Person** column header again.

   Accounting 2007 sorts the quotes in descending order by sales person.

7. Click the **Sales Person** column header again.

   Accounting 2007 returns the Quote List to its original order.

Accepting or Rejecting Quotes

A quote that you prepare is not a posted transaction. In other words, a quote itself does not become part of your accounting records in the way that a journal entry or an invoice does. However, each quote that you submit to a customer, whether through e-mail, regular mail, or in person, needs to be tracked so that you know when the status of a quote changes and can then take the action required.

A quote that a customer accepts can be converted to an invoice or a sales order so that the transaction becomes an entry in your accounting records. If a customer does not accept a quote, you should change the status of the quote to Rejected and enter a brief memo on the quote form to indicate why the customer didn't accept the quote. You can also edit a quote that a customer rejects and create a new open quote that you present to the customer again. Finally, you can delete a quote that you no longer need for your company's records. For example, you can delete a quote that passes its expiration date without the customer accepting or rejecting the quote.

You might have no other work to do on a quote that has been rejected. The sales opportunity that the quote represents falls through, and you change the status of the quote to Rejected to keep a record of your business activity. However, a customer might reject a quote, offer feedback about why the quote is not acceptable, and give you the opportunity to change the pricing or other terms of the quote so that it better meets the customer's needs.

When you edit a rejected quote, the status of the quote changes to Open. You can then make changes to the list of products and services, discounts, markup, or other terms of the quote and submit the quote to the customer again.

> **Tip** Editing a rejected quote changes the status of the quote and removes it from the list of rejected quotes. If you want to edit the quote and keep a copy of the rejected quote so that you have a full record of your business's activity, open the quote, click Copy And Edit on the File menu, and edit the quote.

When a customer accepts a quote, you don't directly change the status of the quote to Accepted. Instead, you convert the quote to an invoice or a sales order. The act of converting a quote changes the quote's status and creates the new accounting document that is posted to your company's records.

You can convert a quote to an invoice or a sales order only once. A quote that pertains to a job, however, can be converted to a series of progress invoices, each one covering a portion of the work defined by the job. A sales order derived from an accepted quote acts as an agreement between your business and the customer. An invoice (or a progress invoice) relates to work already accomplished or goods delivered to the customer. A sales order can be converted to an invoice at a future date. It is used for back orders of merchandise or as a work order for services.

See Also For more information about creating and working with sales orders, see Chapter 9, "Handling Sales." For more information about working with invoices, see Chapter 11, "Managing Invoices."

In this exercise, you will work with the list of quotes in the Fabrikam sample company to learn about the different actions you can take to manage a quote after a customer accepts or rejects the quote.

OPEN the Fabrikam sample company file.

1. In the **Navigation Pane**, click **Customers**.

   The Customers home page appears.

2. Under **Find**, click **Quotes**.

   The Quote List appears.

3. In the **Current View** list, click **Open**.

   The Quote List displays only open quotes.

4. In the **Quote List**, double-click quote **1037**, for the customer Sean Purcell.

   The quote for Sean Purcell appears in a quote form.

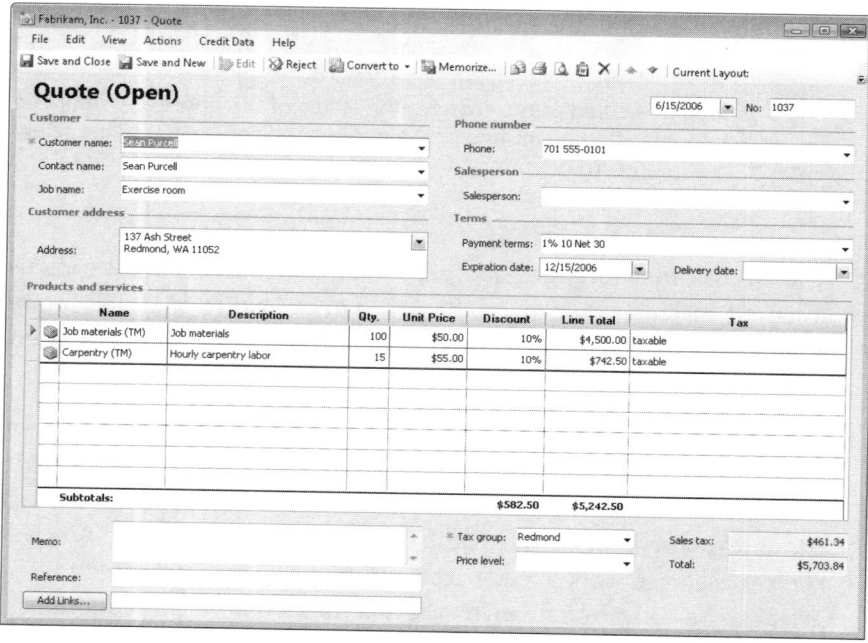

5. In the **Memo** box, type Rejected because prices are too high.

6. On the form toolbar, click **Reject**.

7. On the toolbar, click **Save and Close**.

8. In the **Current View** list, click **Rejected**.

   The Quote List displays only those quotes that have been rejected.

9. In the list of rejected quotes, double-click quote **1037** for Sean Purcell.

   The quote for Sean Purcell appears in a quote form.

10. On the toolbar, click **Edit**.

    The quote opens for editing.

11. In the **Products and Services** list, type 20% in the **Discount** fields for the **Job materials (TM)** and **Carpentry (TM)** items.

    Adding this price level to the quote applies a 20 percent discount to the total amount of the quote.

12. On the toolbar, click **Save and Close**.

13. In the **Current View** list, click **Open**.

The Quote List displays only those quotes that are open.

14. Double-click quote number **1037**, for customer Sean Purcell.

The quote appears.

15. On the toolbar, point to **Convert to**, and then click **Convert to Invoice**.

The status of the quote changes to Accepted, the invoice appears, and both the quote and the invoice now appear on the Financial History tab of the customer record.

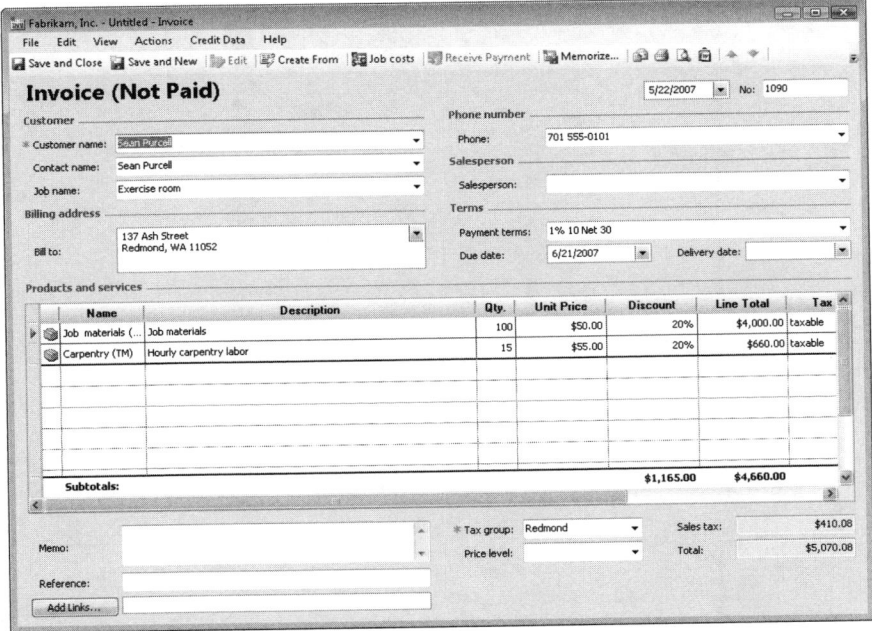

16. To save the invoice, on the toolbar, click **Save and Close**.

After you convert the quote, it no longer appears in the list of open quotes.

Printing Quotes

With Accounting 2007, you can perform all of your important financial recordkeeping tasks electronically, which makes it possible to enter all of your sales, quotes, payroll, and other data directly into your company file. After you enter a quote into your company file, you can view it on screen, display it next to other quotes by using the Quotes List, and print a paper copy of the quote. Even if you do most of your work on the computer, you should still be prepared to print paper copies of your reports in case a customer drops by your office and requests a paper copy for their records, or if a customer asks you to fax a copy of the quote and your recordkeeping process requires that you maintain a paper copy of all outgoing faxes.

When you're ready to print a quote, display the Quote List, select the quote you want to print, open the File menu, and click Print to display the Print dialog box.

> **Tip** To print more than one quote at a time, display the Quote List, hold down the Ctrl key, and click the quotes you want to print.

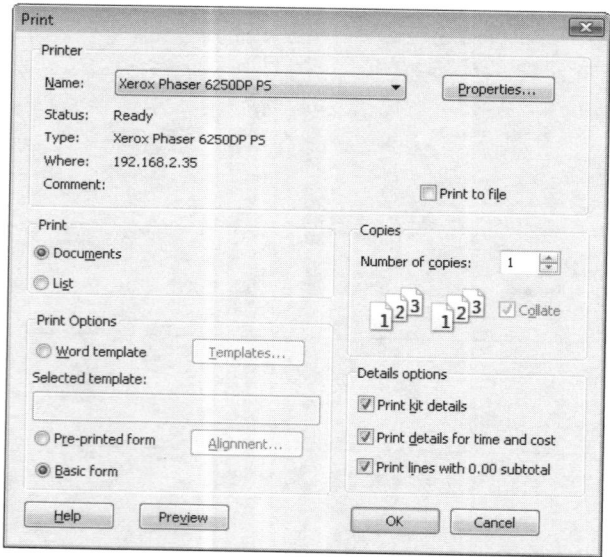

You can use the controls in the Print dialog box to select a printer; specify the number of copies to be printed; choose whether to print the contents of kits, time and cost details, and lines with a $0.00 subtotal; and display a preview of what your quote will look like when printed. To select a printer, click the Name box arrow, and then click the printer to which you want to send your quote. If you want to print more than one copy of your quote, type the desired number of copies in the Number Of Copies box.

When you print a copy of a quote for internal use, you might just need the summary information and total price for a kit, the total hours of labor and its cost, and avoid printing any line items with a total cost of $0.00. If a customer requests a printed copy of a quote, however, you should probably include all of the available details, particularly if a line item has a total cost of $0.00 because a sales representative included a service or product for free as an incentive to buy. To specify which details to print, select or clear the check boxes in the Details Options section of the Print dialog box.

> **Note** The options available in the Print dialog box change to reflect the capabilities of the printer displayed in the Name box.

By default, Accounting Professional prints individual quotes. If you'd rather print a list of the quotes currently displayed in the Quote List, under Print in the Print dialog box, click List. To print individual quotes again, click Documents instead.

When you print an individual quote, Accounting Professional applies the standard quote template. If you'd like to print the quote by using a custom template you created in Microsoft Office Word, Under Print Options, click Word Template, and then click Templates to display the Select Word Templates dialog box.

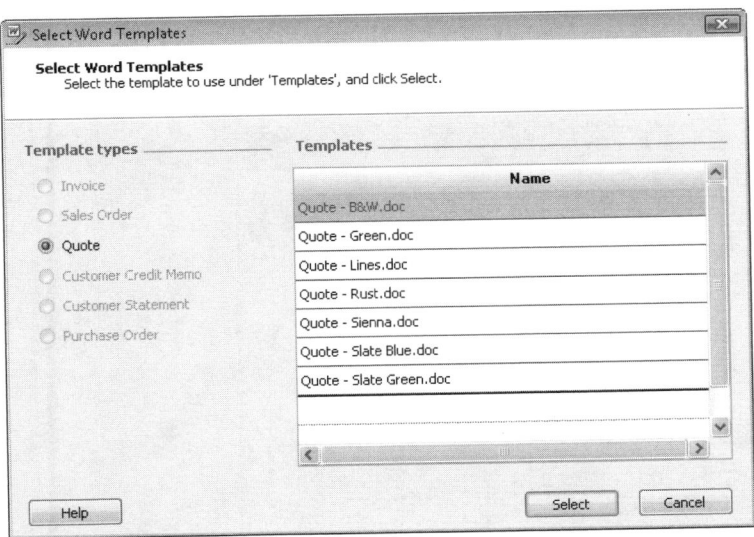

To select a template, click the template you want to use, and then click Select.

See Also For more information about creating or modifying a template, see "Modifying Templates in Word 2007" in Chapter 17, "Interacting with Other 2007 Microsoft Office System Applications," on the CD.

In this exercise, you will print two copies of an individual quote, minus kit details, by using an existing template, preview the list of quotes currently displayed in the Quote List, and then print the Quote List.

> **OPEN** the Fabrikam sample company file.

1. In the **Navigation Pane**, click **Customers**.

2. In the **Find** area of the **Customers** home page, click **Quotes**.

   The Quote List appears.

3. If necessary, in the **Current View** list, click **Accepted**.

   The accepted quotes appear in the Quote List.

4. Click quote number **1023**, for Wingtip Toys.

5. On the **File** menu, click **Print**.

   The Print dialog box opens.

6. In the **Print** dialog box, enter 2 in the **Number of copies** box.

7. Under **Details options**, clear the **Print kit details** check box.

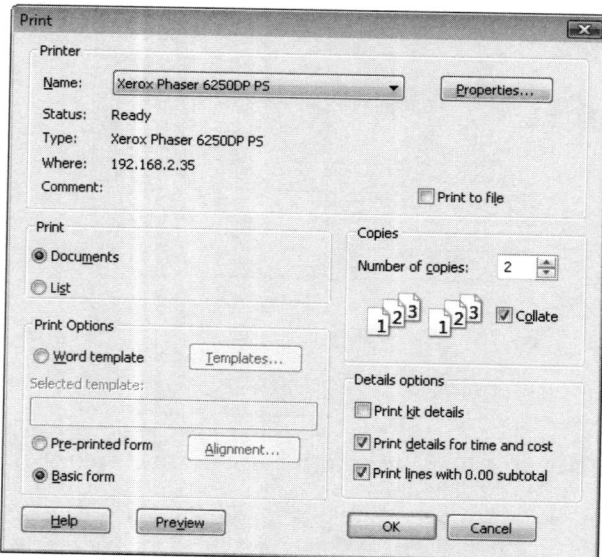

8. Under **Print Options**, click **Word template**, and then click **Templates**.

    The Select Word Template dialog box opens.

9. In the **Templates** panel, click **Quote – Slate Blue.doc**.

10. Click **Select**.

    The Select Word Template dialog box closes, and the Quote – Slate Blue.doc
    template appears in the Selected Template box.

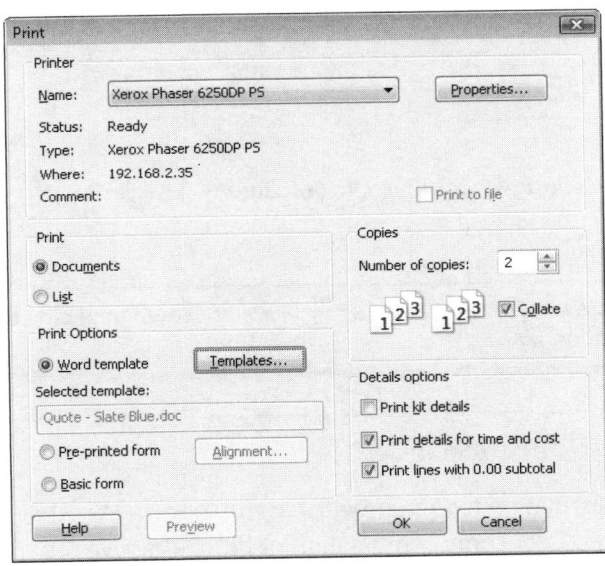

11. Click **OK** to print the quote (or click **Cancel** if your computer is not connected to
    a printer).

    Accounting 2007 prints your quote.

12. On the **File** menu, click **Print**.

    The Print dialog box opens.

13. In the **Print** dialog box, under **Print**, click **List**.

14. Click **Preview**.

    The Preview window opens.

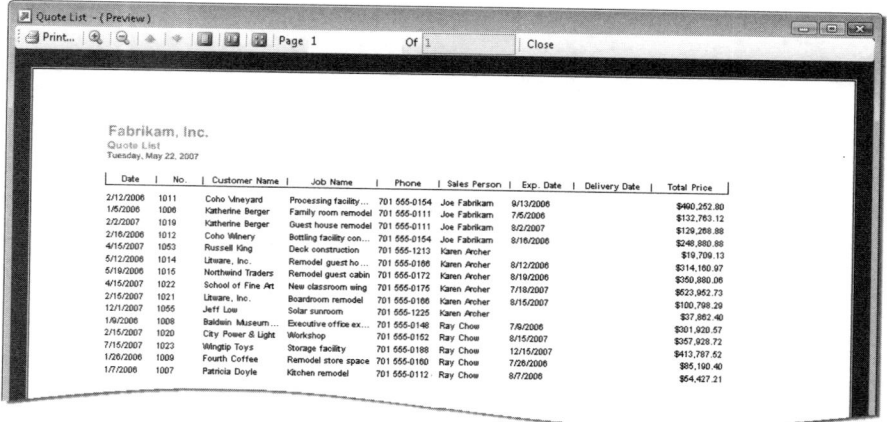

15. On the **Preview** window's toolbar, click **Close**.

The Preview window closes.

CLOSE the Fabrikam sample company file. If you are not continuing directly to the next chapter, exit Accounting 2007.

Reporting Considerations: Quotes

Quotes provide information for a number of useful reports. Whether your company sells products, services, or some combination of both, effective reports focus on the prices at which you have proposed to sell, should the customer accept your terms.

You can discover useful business intelligence by arranging your quotes by customer, sales representative, and items and services sold. Your analytical reports should compare quotes for given items and services to the actual costs you experienced plus the profit you had targeted, both to determine effectiveness of the quote process and to help you refine estimate accuracy going forward.

Key Points

- You build quotes by using the products and services you've defined as items in your company records.

- Modify the discounts and product markups in a quote to balance the need to make the quote competitive with the need to realize a profit.

- Be sure to specify an expiration date for a quote and describe conditions and assumptions you used to prepare the quote.

- A quote that a customer accepts is converted to an invoice or a sales order.

- Be sure to print a copy of a quote when needed, but take the time to set the printing options so you get exactly the output you want.

Chapter at a Glance

Enter a sales order,
page 185

View the Sales Order List,
page 191

Manage back orders,
page 195

Edit sales orders,
page 192

9 Handling Sales

In this chapter, you will learn to:

✔ Enter a sales order.

✔ View the Sales Order List.

✔ Edit sales orders.

✔ Manage back orders.

Sales revenue forms the backbone of any business. Regardless of whether you sell products or services, you need to find customers for your wares. When someone asks to buy one of your products or an hour of your consulting time, you need to create a record of the request in Microsoft Office Accounting 2007. That record is known as a sales order.

In this chapter, you'll learn how to create a sales order, view and manipulate the Sales Order List, create sales order templates, edit existing sales orders, and manage back orders (orders you can't fulfill without receiving additional products into inventory).

> **Troubleshooting** Graphics and operating system–related instructions in this book reflect the Windows Vista user interface. If your computer is running Windows XP and you experience trouble following the instructions as written, please refer to the "Information for Readers Running Windows XP" section at the beginning of this book.

Entering a Sales Order (Professional Only)

A sale is a sale. It's nice to know whether you won a bidding contest or attracted the customer through word-of-mouth advertising, but the sale is the important part of the equation. In Accounting Professional, you represent a customer's intention to buy by using a sales order. You can create a sales order for any customer with active status, although you might need to create a new customer record before you start to create your sales order.

See Also For more information on creating a new customer record, see Chapter 6, "Managing Customers."

The default sales order template depends on the type of company you set up. If you created a service-based company, the Service template appears. If you created a product-based company, the Product template appears. The Product and Service templates are similar, but the Product template contains a Ship To section with information on where to deliver your product.

There are two ways you can create a new sales order: from scratch or by basing the new sales order on an existing quote.

See Also For more information on recording a cash sale, which is possible in Microsoft Office Accounting Express 2007, see Chapter 12, "Handling Customer Payments."

Creating a Sales Order from Scratch

If you get a call from a customer who wants to place an order, you can open a blank sales order form.

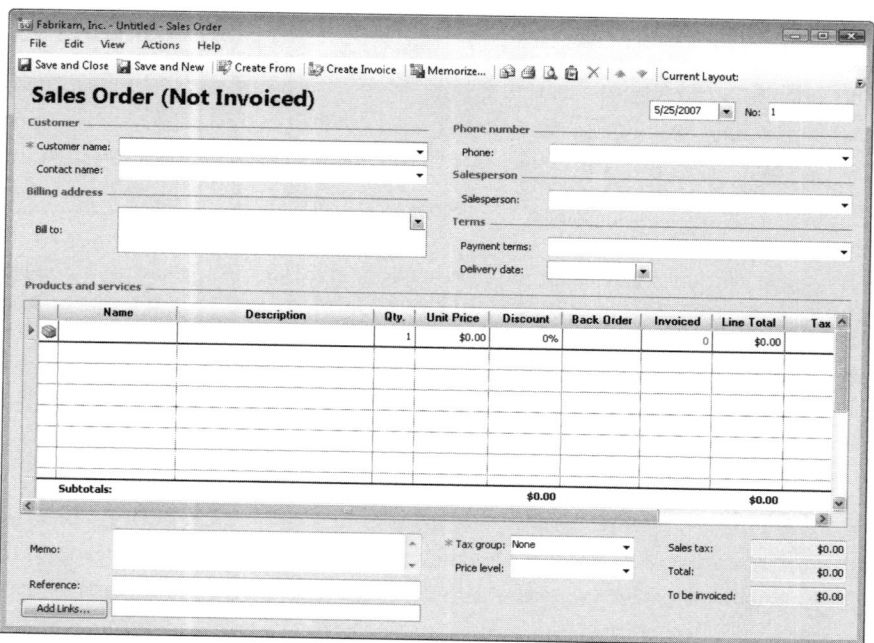

After you display the sales order form, you can fill in the data required to initiate the transaction.

In this exercise, you will create a sales order from scratch.

> **BE SURE TO** start Accounting Professional 2007 before beginning this exercise.
>
> **OPEN** the Fabrikam sample company file.

1. In the **Navigation Pane**, click **Customers**.

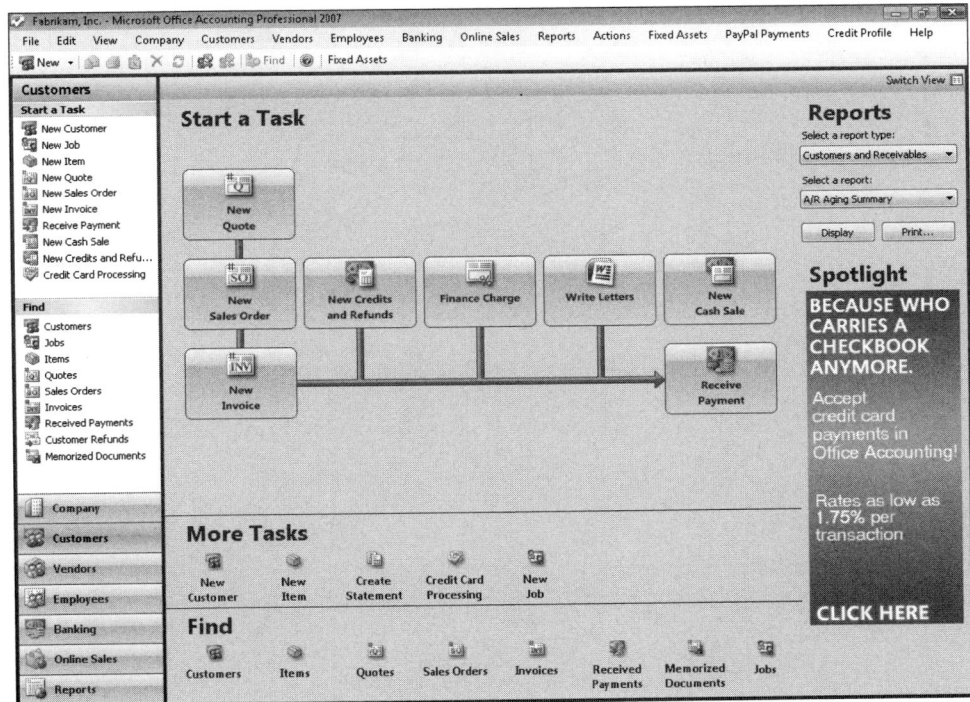

2. In the **Start a Task** section of the **Customers** home page, click **New Sales Order**.

   A new sales order form based on the default template appears.

3. If the sales order form contains a **Shipping Address** section (indicating that it is the **Product** template), on the **Actions** menu, point to **Select Template**, and then click **Service**.

4. In the **Customer Name** list, click **Coho Winery**.

Contact information for Coho Winery appears in the top section of the sales order form.

5. In the **Terms** section of the form, click the **Payment terms** arrow, and then click **1% 10 Net 30**.

6. Click the **Delivery date** arrow.

A calendar control appears.

7. Use the calendar control to select a delivery date within the next month. For this exercise, we selected July 12, 2008.

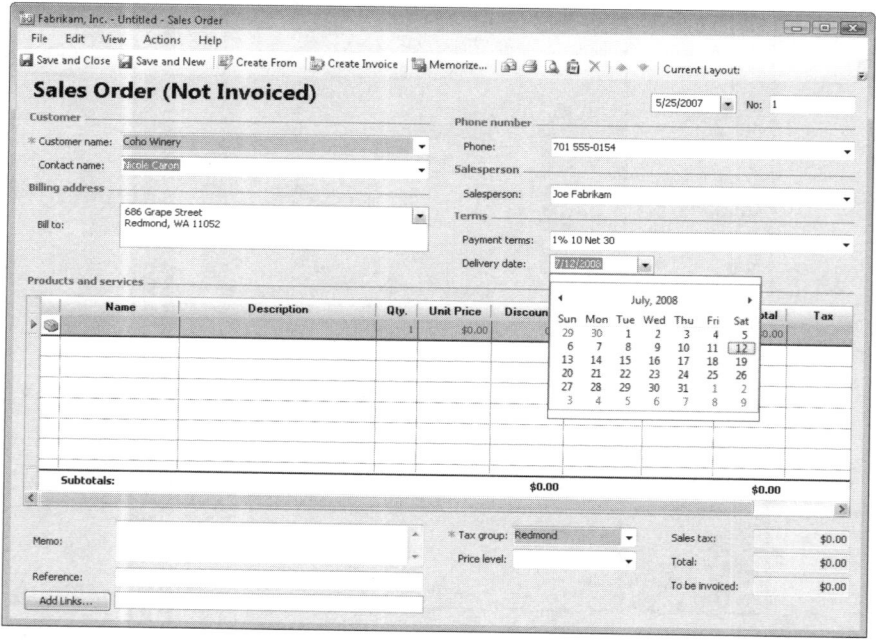

8. In the **Products and services** section of the form, click the first **Name** field, click the arrow that appears, and then click **Plumbing labor (TM)**.

The new item appears in the Products And Services list.

9. In the **Products and services** list, click the **Name** field in the row below the list item you just created.

A new item line appears.

10. Click the new **Name** field, click the arrow that appears, and then click **Plumbing materials (FF)**.

The new item appears in the Products And Services list.

11. Right-click the row header (the gray vertical bar at the left edge of the Products And Services grid) for the **Plumbing labor (FF)** item, and then click **Delete**.

The item disappears from the Products And Services list.

12. In the **Price Level** list, click **Preferred Customer -15%**.

The prices and sales tax displayed in the sales order change to reflect the discount.

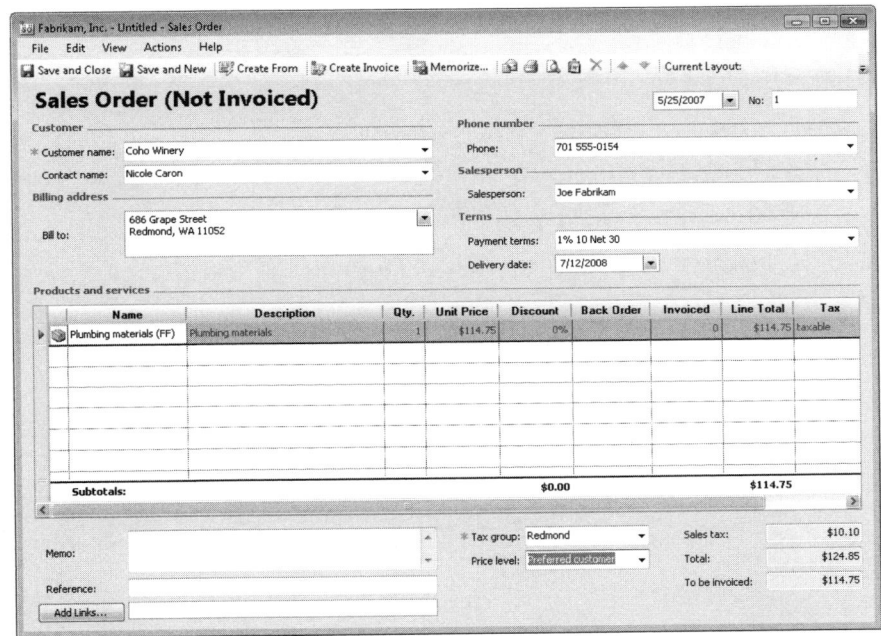

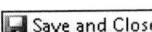 **13.** On the sales order form toolbar, click the **Save and Close** button.

14. If a message box appears asking if you want to save the new payment term information for future sales orders, click **No**.

Accounting Professional saves your sales order and closes the sales order form.

 CLOSE the Fabrikam sample company file.

Creating a Sales Order from a Quote

If you've already generated a quote that's been accepted by a customer, you can base your sales order on the contents of that quote. All you need to do is use the controls on the Customers home page to start a new sales order and then select the quote on which you want to base your sales order.

In this exercise, you will create a sales order from a quote.

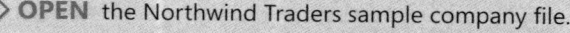

OPEN the Northwind Traders sample company file.

1. In the **Navigation Pane**, click **Customers**.

2. In the **Start a Task** section of the **Customers** home page, click **New Sales Order**.

A new sales order based on the default template appears.

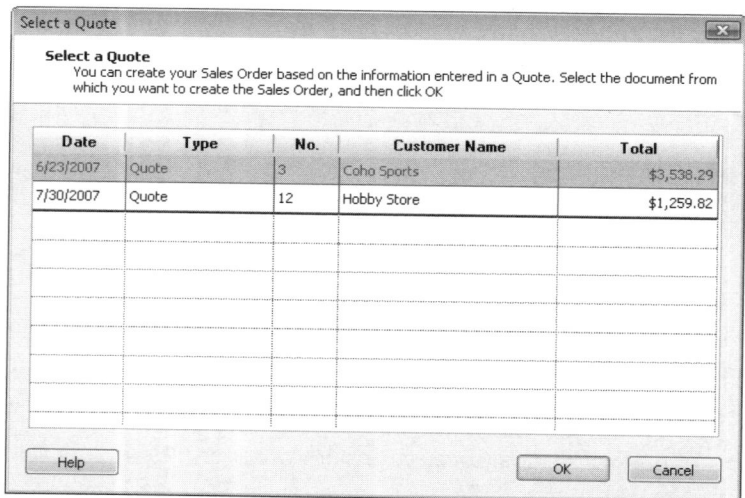

Create From

3. On the toolbar, click the **Create From** button.

The Select A Quote dialog box opens.

Date	Type	No.	Customer Name	Total
6/23/2007	Quote	3	Coho Sports	$3,538.29
7/30/2007	Quote	12	Hobby Store	$1,259.82

4. In the **Select a Quote** dialog box, click the quote for **Coho Sports**.

5. Click **OK**.

The Select A Quote dialog box closes and the sales order form appears, now containing the customer and item information from the quote.

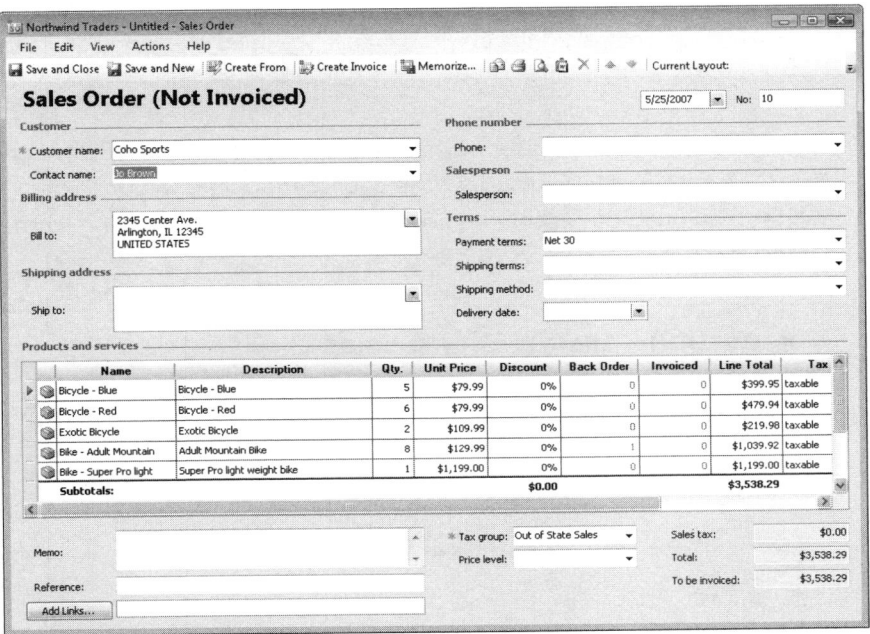

6. Click **Save and Close**.

7. If a message box appears asking if you want to save the changed payment terms information, click **No**.

   Accounting Professional saves your sales order and closes the sales order form.

Viewing the Sales Order List (Professional Only)

Office Accounting stores all of your sales orders in a single list, the Sales Order List. To display the Sales Order List, open the Customers menu, point to Customer Lists, and then click Sales Orders. The Sales Order List from the sample Northwind Traders database contains one sales order.

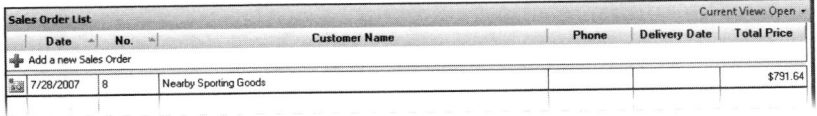

> **Note** If you completed the previous exercise by using an existing quote from the Northwind Traders sample company file, the Sales Order List will contain two sales orders.

If you've been in business for a while, it's very likely that your Sales Order List is fairly long. You can rearrange and limit the data that appears in your Sales Order List by using the list manipulation techniques covered in the section "Viewing Quotes" in Chapter 8, "Generating and Managing Quotes."

> ## Reporting Considerations: Sales
>
> Regardless of whether your company sells products, services, or some combination of both, useful sales reports focus on what you have sold and the customers to whom you have made the sales. Typical views by which sales information is arranged include customer, sales representative, items sold, and timing of sales.

Editing Sales Orders (Professional Only)

You try to keep the mistakes in your business to a minimum, but they always seem to crop up at the worst times. If you run a small business, the person taking phone orders is often performing another task at the same time, such as answering other phone calls, minding a retail counter, or checking stock. Or, if you're the person taking the orders, you might be busy running the business. In other words, it's very easy to make mistakes when you enter sales orders.

Fortunately, you can edit a sales order as long as one of two conditions exists:

- You have not created an invoice based on the sales order.
- You have created only a partial invoice based on the sales order.

If you've created a full invoice based on a sales order, you will need to delete the existing invoice, delete the existing sales order, and then create a new sales order.

When you display the Sales Order List and double-click a sales order, the sales order appears in an editable window. From there, you can change any of the information in the sales order and use it to generate a new invoice.

In this exercise, you will edit the Northwind Traders sample company file's Nearby Sporting Goods sales order to change the number of football spikes requested and to choose a new delivery date.

> **OPEN** the Northwind Traders sample company file.

1. On the **Customers** menu, point to **Customer Lists**, and then click **Sales Orders**.

   The Sales Order List appears.

2. Double-click the **Nearby Sporting Goods** sales order.

   The Nearby Sporting Goods order appears in a new sales order form.

3. In the **Terms** section of the Sales Order form, click in the **Delivery date** field, and edit the date so that it contains a date within the next month. For this exercise, enter 7/14/2008.

4. Click in the **Qty.** field on the third row of the **Products and services** list.

5. Type 6, and then press Tab.

   The Sales Order form updates its calculations to reflect the additional item.

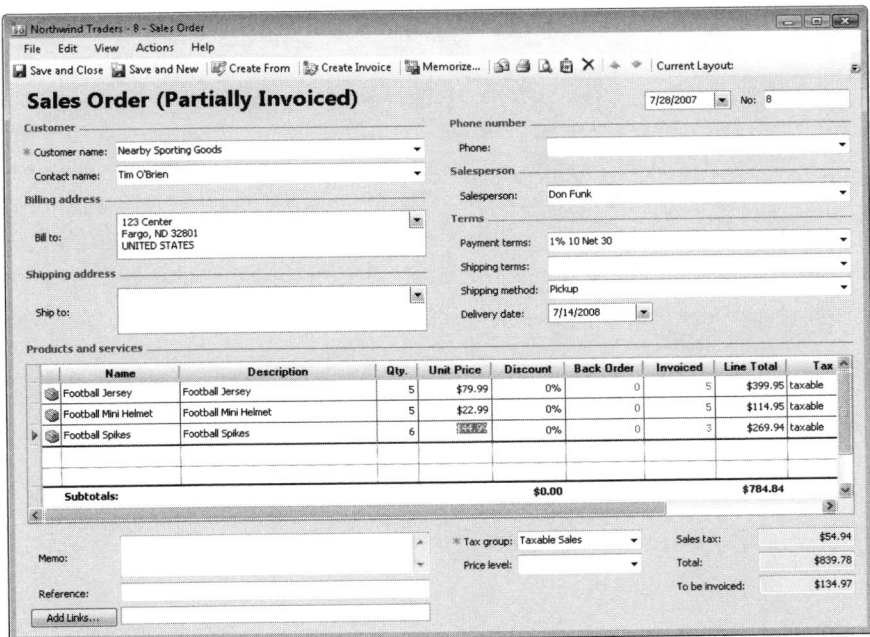

6. Click **Save and Close**.

   Accounting Professional saves your changes and closes the sales order.

Online Sales, and Sales and Use Tax Considerations

"Tax-free" shopping is one of several drivers for the exploding growth of sales on the Internet, and ranks alongside convenience as a motivation for click-and-charge purchasing. It is important to keep in mind, however, that some Internet sales are subject to sales tax, and that the trend toward more focused taxation in this arena will only continue to grow.

A 1992 Supreme Court decision, which held that mail-order merchants did not need to collect sales taxes for sales into states where they did not have a "physical presence," has served as the basis for a general rule of thumb thus far. An online retailer with a physical presence in a particular state (for example, a store, business office, or warehouse) must collect sales tax from customers in that state, plain and simple. If a business does not have a physical presence in a state, it is not required to collect sales tax for sales into that state.

The use of separate legal subsidiaries to handle Internet sales once served as a means of skirting sales taxes for large retailers with local stores, but lawsuits and other actions within several states have largely rendered this practice a thing of the past. When Internet retailers don't collect sales tax in states where it is required, consumers living in those states are technically required to pay it. The term *use tax* refers to scenarios like this, where purchasers are required to pay the tax directly to the state. The distinguishing factor between sales and use taxes is simply the *identity of the taxpayer*—the seller or the buyer, respectively.

Because collecting use taxes (in effect, a backup to ensure the collection of revenue on every taxable item purchase within a given state) on small transactions would require an immense amount of effort, states have historically focused collection efforts on high-value items such as boats and cars, which must be licensed and registered. But tax-hungry states have begun to eye use taxes as a significant source of revenue that can be tapped with less political risk than more visible, politically unpopular tax increases elsewhere. Some states have added line items to income tax returns requiring residents to provide information regarding how much they owe for Internet, mail order, out-of-state, and other purchases, some have begun campaigns to advise taxpayers how to determine the use taxes that they owe, and so forth.

It is only natural to assume that Congress and state legislatures will continue to pursue increased collections. Moreover, the Streamlined Sales & Use Tax Agreement (SSUTA) initiative, wherein member states cooperate to "simplify" their sales tax codes and to make collections more straightforward, and enforceable, continues to gain momentum. Some national retailers have negotiated with participating states to obtain amnesty for past sins in return for future collection of sales tax, and more are expected to follow. This trend, combined with the fact that several states have already begun modifying their tax laws to conform to the SSUTA, sends a clear signal that state sales and use tax rules need to be monitored closely by anyone doing business on the Internet.

Managing Back Orders

When you sell a popular product, you benefit from the profits the sales generate. Unfortunately, you also risk running out of that popular product. Small hardware stores are particularly vulnerable to this phenomenon if they stock an item featured at a home improvement show. When you have only a few units of a suddenly desirable doorknob in stock but anticipate being able to get more units from your supplier, you might need to accept orders from your customers and ship their doorknobs when they arrive. The items you don't have in stock are said to be on *back order*.

The procedure to handle back orders combines the capabilities of sales orders and invoices. Whenever you create a sales order that includes items that must be back ordered, the quantity of items not in stock appears in the Back Order column of the Products And Services section of the Sales Order form.

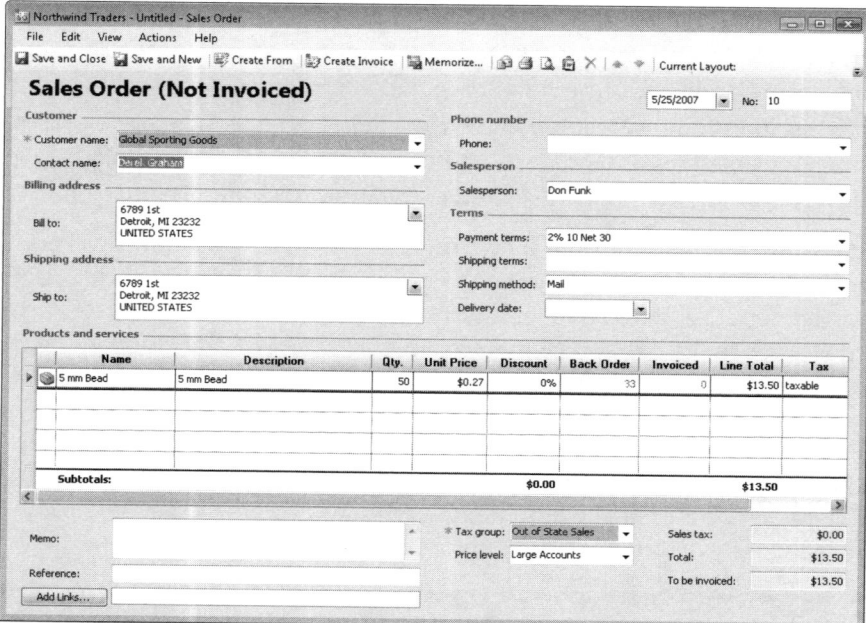

Your next steps are to create a partial invoice that charges the customer for only those items you have in stock, order the items you need, receive the items into inventory, create an invoice for the remaining items, and then ship the order with the invoice.

See Also For more information on creating a partial invoice, see Chapter 11, "Managing Invoices." For more information on ordering and receiving items into inventory, see Chapter 13, "Purchasing from Vendors."

You can choose to have Accounting 2007 remind you of your back orders on the Company home page. In this exercise you will turn on this reminder.

> **OPEN** the Northwind Traders sample company file.

1. Display the **Company** home page.

2. In the lower-right corner of the **Reminders** section, click **Add/Remove**.

   The Add/Remove Reminders dialog box opens.

3. If necessary, in the **Add/Remove Reminders** dialog box, select the **Back Orders** check box.

> **Note** The selected check boxes indicate which reminders will be displayed.

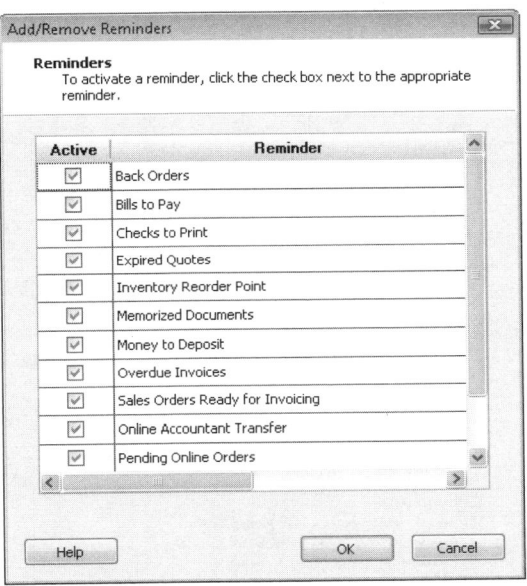

4. Click **OK**.

The Add/Remove Reminders dialog box closes. Accounting 2007 will now inform you when there are items on back order.

CLOSE the Northwind Traders sample company file. If you are not continuing directly to the next chapter, exit Accounting 2007.

Key Points

- You can enter sales orders quickly by using sales order forms.
- Rather than re-type information from a quote, create a sales order based on that quote.
- Pay close attention to tax issues and the collection and reporting burdens that local, state, and federal authorities put on your business.
- Be sure to have Accounting 2007 remind you of any items on back order.

Chapter at a Glance

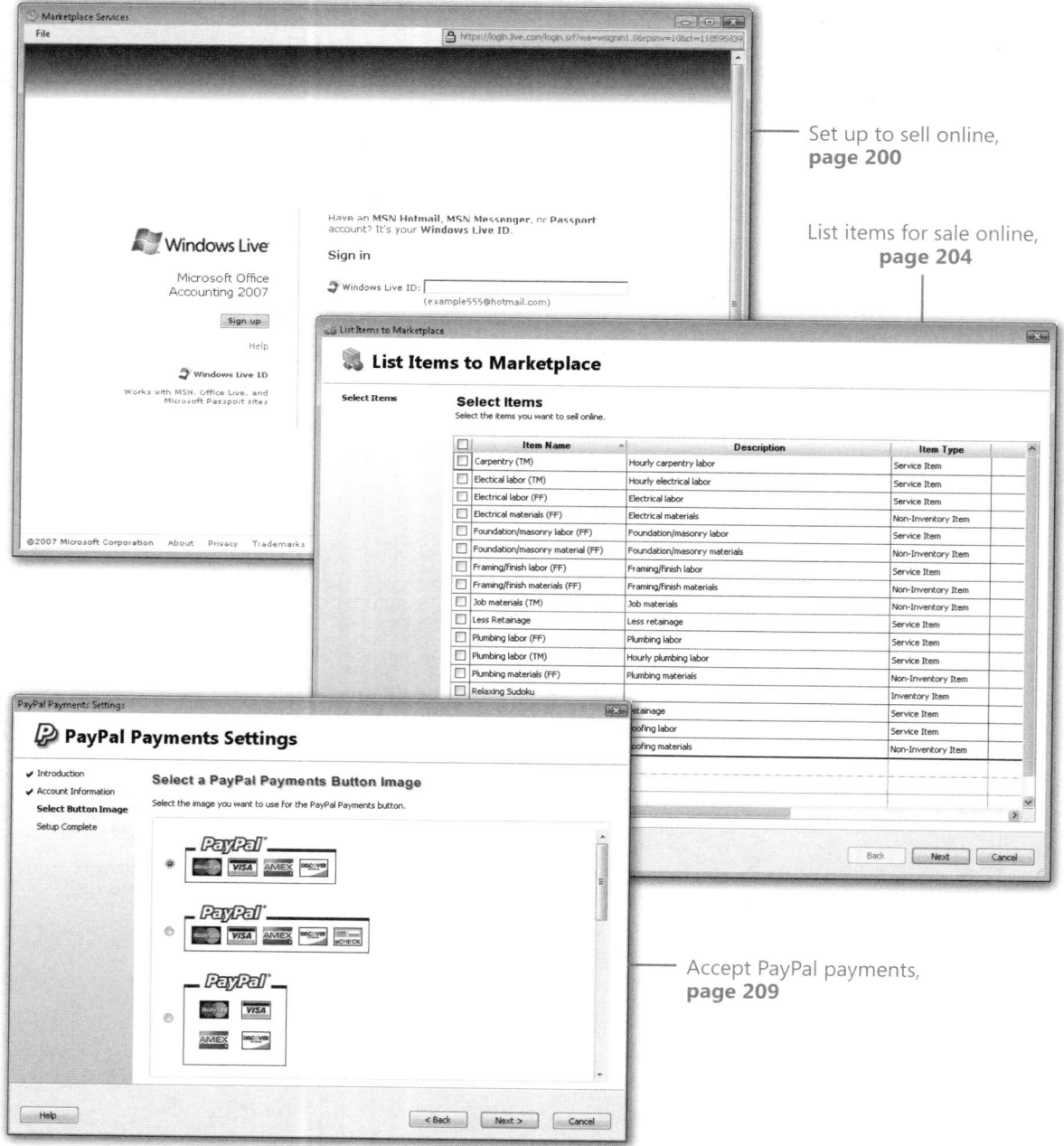

Set up to sell online,
page 200

List items for sale online,
page 204

Accept PayPal payments,
page 209

10 Selling Goods and Services on eBay

In this chapter, you will learn to:

- ✔ Set up to sell online.
- ✔ List items for sale online.
- ✔ Download orders and fees.
- ✔ Accept PayPal payments.

As the online community has expanded, so has electronic commerce. Many businesses make their catalogs available on their Web sites, and most of those companies allow their customers to place orders online and have those purchases delivered. Offering your company's goods and services for sale online doesn't guarantee success, but creating a Web site or selling your products on popular auction sites can help potential customers find your offerings and spread the word about your company. With the integrated online sales support built into Microsoft Office Accounting 2007, you can sell your products and services online without disrupting your normal business practices.

In this chapter, you will learn how to set up Accounting 2007 so that you can sell items online, list items for sale, download orders and fees, and accept payments using PayPal.

> **Troubleshooting** Graphics and operating system–related instructions in this book reflect the Windows Vista user interface. If your computer is running Windows XP and you experience trouble following the instructions as written, please refer to the "Information for Readers Running Windows XP" section at the beginning of this book.

Setting Up to Sell Online

When you're ready to start selling your items online, display the Online Sales home page in Accounting 2007. This home page hosts all of the tools you'll need to start managing the online sales process.

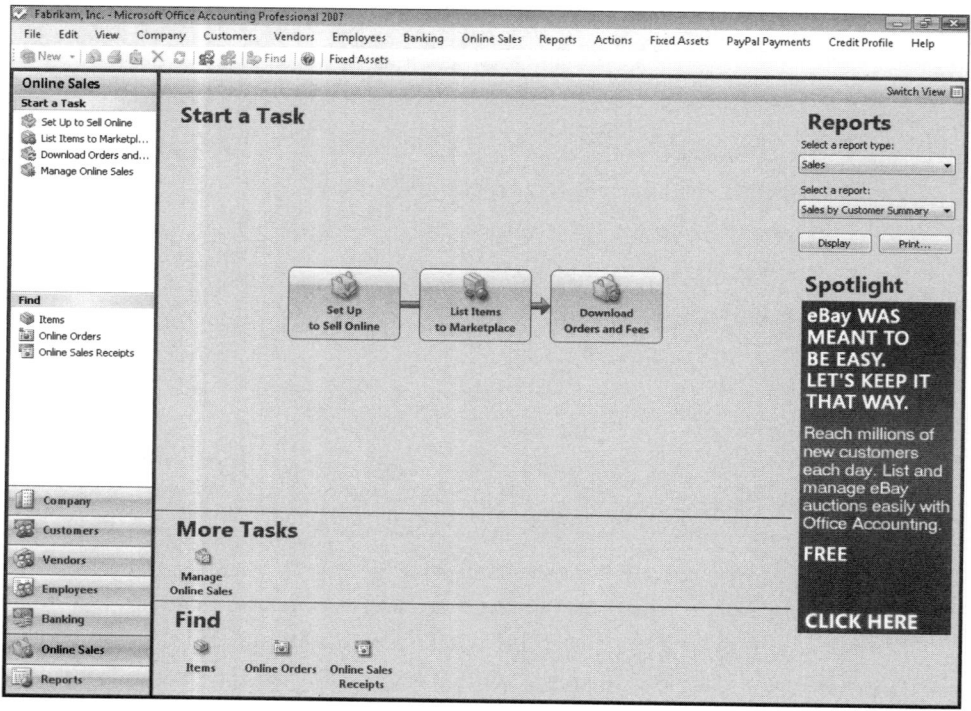

Clicking Set Up To Sell Online starts the Marketplace Services wizard, which walks you through the process of creating your online sales presence. You will need both a Windows Live ID and an active eBay account to sell your items online, but you can sign up for a Windows Live ID when you start the wizard. Similarly, you can create an account from within the eBay Download Options Wizard.

In this exercise, you will establish an online sales account in Accounting 2007.

> **BE SURE TO** start Accounting 2007 before beginning this exercise.
>
> **OPEN** a company file that contains items you want to sell online.

1. In the **Navigation Pane**, click **Online Sales**.

   The Online Sales home page appears.

2. Under **Start a Task**, click **Set Up to Sell Online**.

   The Marketplace Services wizard starts.

3. Click **Next** on the first page of the **Marketplace Services** wizard.

   The Windows Live sign-in page appears.

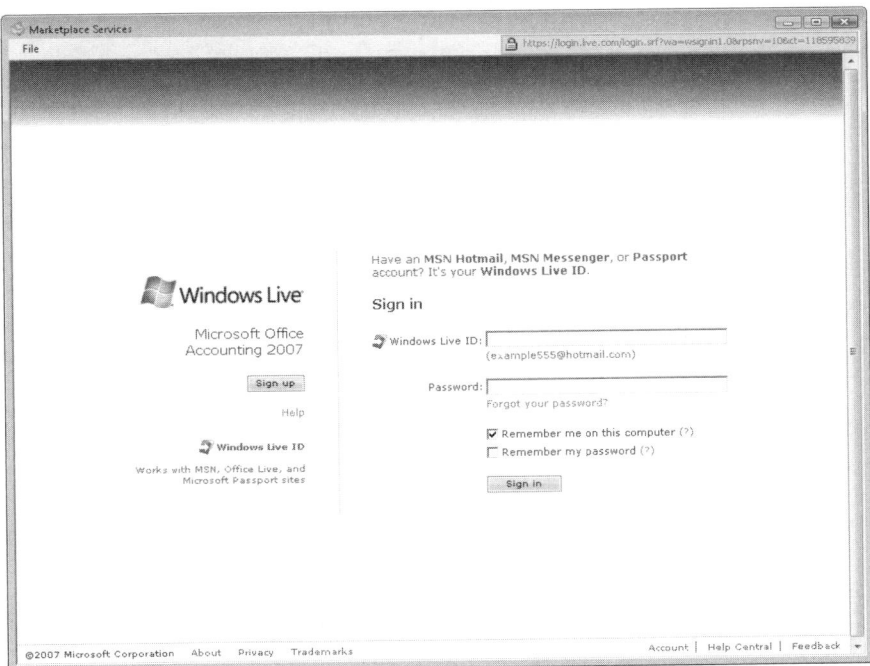

4. Type your Windows Live ID and password in the fields provided, and then click **Sign In**.

   The Select A Service Plan page appears.

5. Select the desired service plan, and then click **Next**.

    The Enter Contact Information page appears.

6. Type your contact information in the fields provided, read the Terms of Service agreement, and then click **I Accept** to accept the terms of service.

    The Next button becomes active.

7. Click **Next**.

    The Enter Payment Information page appears.

8. Type your payment information in the fields provided, and then click **Next**.

    The Set Up Marketplaces wizard starts.

9. Under the eBay logo, click the **Sign Up** button.

    The eBay Download Options page appears.

10. Click **Next**, and then click **Next** again on the **Sign in to eBay** page.

    The eBay sign-in page appears.

11. Type your eBay user ID and password in the fields provided, and then click **Sign In Securely**.

    The Microsoft Corporation Authorization page appears.

12. Click **Agree and Continue**.

    The Account Configured page appears.

13. Click **Close**.

    The Manage Order Downloads page appears.

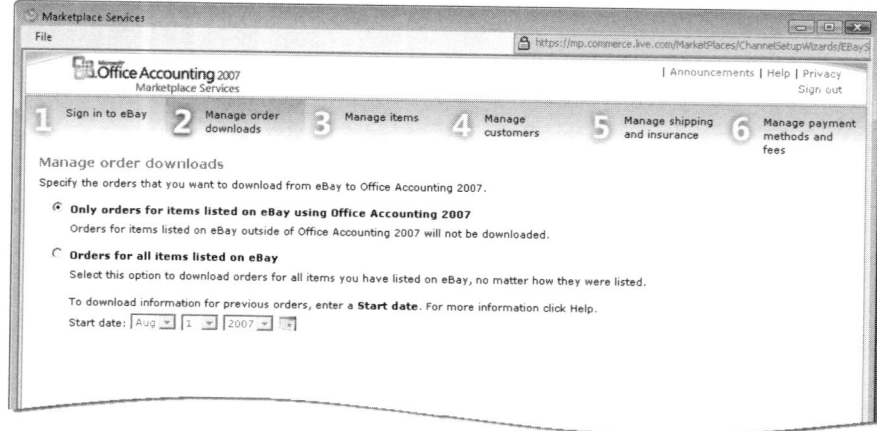

14. Verify that **Only orders for items listed on eBay using Office Accounting 2007** is selected, and then click **Next**.

> **Tip** If you'd like to download every order into Accounting 2007, click Orders For All Items Listed On eBay, and enter the starting date from which you want to download transactions. Be careful not to mix corporate sales and personal sales!

The Manage Items page appears.

15. Click **Track unrecognized items individually**, and then click **Next**.

The Manage Customers page appears.

> **Tip** If you'd like to have Accounting 2007 group all unknown objects into one sales item, click Track Unrecognized Items As One Item, and type a name for the item in the Select Item box.

16. Click **Track individual customers**, and then click **Next**.

The Manage Shipping And Insurance page appears.

> **Note** If you make quite a few sales on eBay, you should consider clicking Do Not Track Individual Customers to consolidate the sales under one record.

17. Click **Next** to accept the suggested accounts for eBay shipping, insurance, and extra charges.

The Manage Payment Methods page appears.

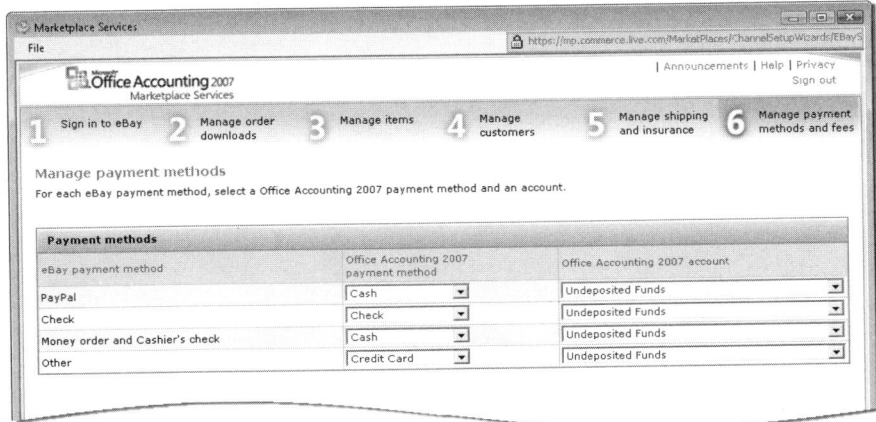

18. Click **Next** to accept the suggested accounts to which you want to assign payments using the listed methods.

    The Fees page appears.

19. Click the **Download eBay fees** and **Download PayPal fees** options to download those fees.

20. Click **Finish** to accept the suggested accounts and starting dates.

    The Setup Complete page appears.

21. Click **Close** to close the wizard.

 CLOSE the open company file.

> **Tip** After you set up your online sales account, you can change your service level, view your listings, add pictures, and change your eBay account settings by using the Manage Online Sales dialog box. To display the Manage Online Sales dialog box, display the Online Sales home page, and then under More Tasks, click Manage Online Sales. Sign in to Windows Live, and then use the tools found in the Manage Online Sales dialog box to control your online selling experience.

Listing Items for Sale Online

In this exercise, you will list items for sale online.

OPEN a company file that contains items you want to sell online.

1. In the **Navigation Pane**, click **Online Sales**.

2. On the **Online Sales** home page, under **Start a Task**, click **List Items to Marketplace**.

    The List Items To Marketplace wizard starts.

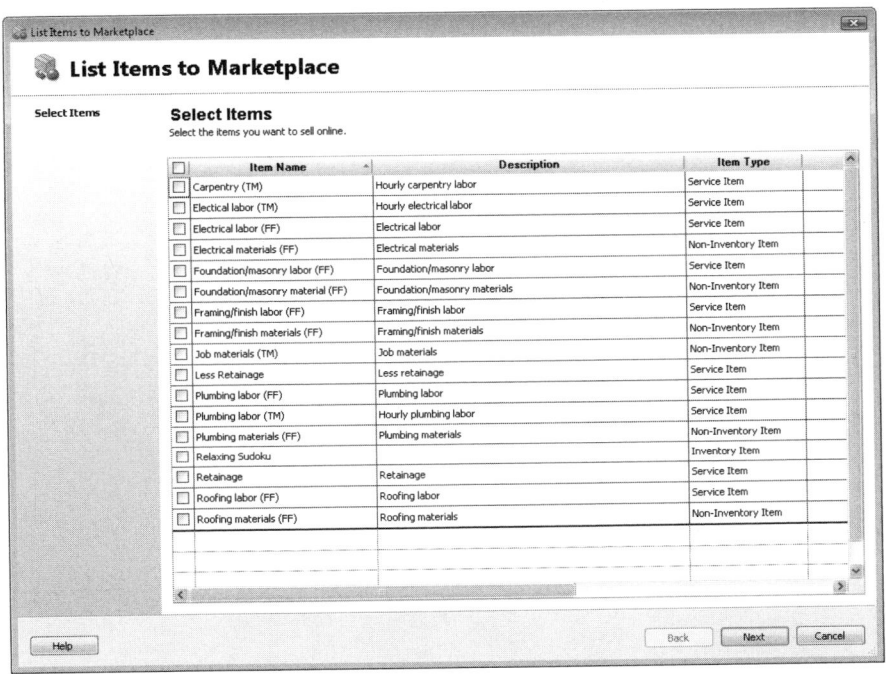

3. On the **Select Items** page, select the check box next to any item you want to sell online, and then click **Next**.

> **Tip** Selecting the check box next to the column headers selects every item in the list.

The Windows Live sign-in dialog box opens.

4. Type your Windows Live ID and password in the fields provided, and then click **Sign In**.

The Windows Live sign-in dialog box closes and the Select A Marketplace page of the Marketplace Services wizard appears.

5. Verify that **eBay** is selected, and then click **Next**.

The Review And List Products On eBay page appears.

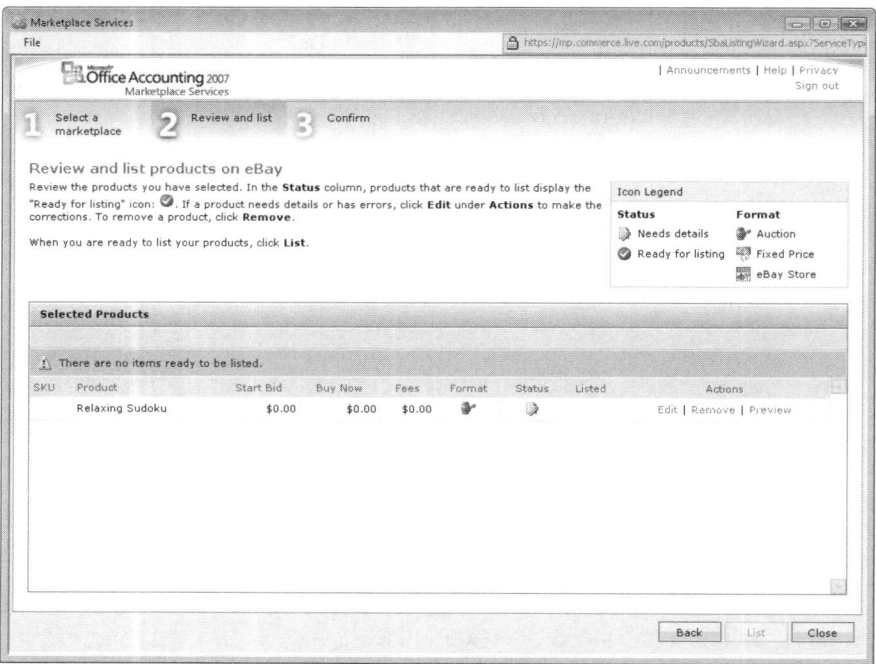

6. In the **Selected Products** pane, click **Edit** next to the item to which you want to add details.

The Edit Product Details page appears.

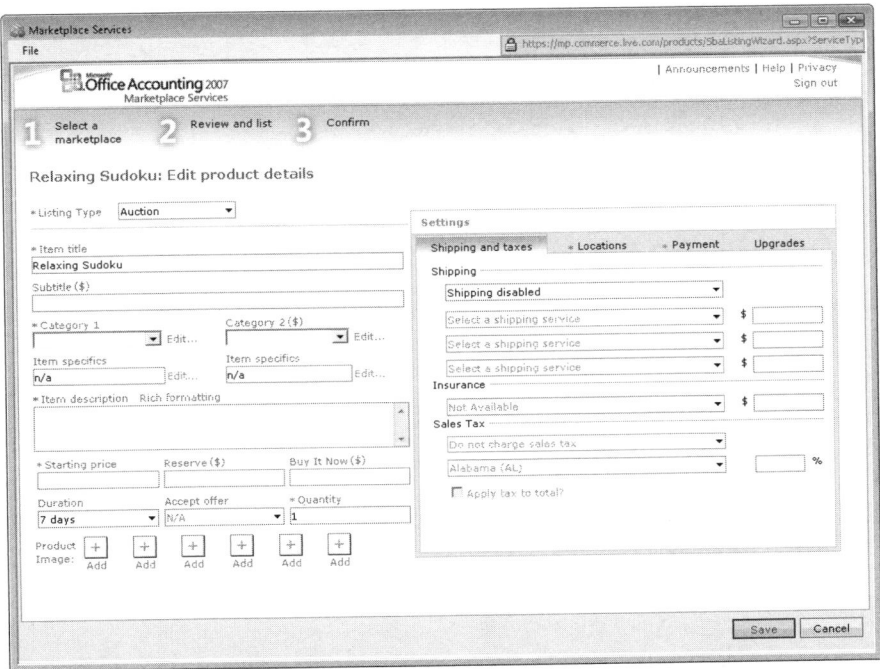

7. Fill in the fields to set the listing type, item title, category, description, starting price, auction duration (if applicable), shipping options, and payment options, and to add images. Click **Save** when you're done.

8. In the **Marketplace Services** wizard, click **List**.

9. On the **Submission Complete** page, click **Close** to close the wizard.

CLOSE the open company file.

Downloading Orders and Fees

After you begin doing business online, those orders and payments are stored online. To bring those records into your Accounting 2007 company file, you need to download the transactions from the sales site. To do that, you click Download Orders And Fees on the Online Sales home page.

> **Important** Be sure to install Microsoft Office Accounting 2007 Service Pack 1 (SP1), which enables you to download online transactions with customer names that include characters such as # and *. Prior to SP1, Accounting 2007 was not able to download those transactions into its company files. You can find more information about Accounting 2007 SP1, including instructions on how to download the file, at *support.microsoft.com/kb/932726/*.

You can have Accounting download just those transactions for items listed on eBay through Accounting 2007, or choose to download orders for all items regardless of how they were listed.

> **Tip** If Accounting 2007 doesn't recognize an item you're selling online as one of your inventory items, perhaps because you sell the item online under a different name than you list it in your Item List, you can match the unrecognized item to the correct entry in your Item List. Download your online sales, and then in the Match Unrecognized Items dialog box, click the unrecognized item. Then, in the Match To Item column, click the arrow to select the corresponding item. If there is no corresponding item in the list, click Add A New Item and create the item you need. When you're done, click Next to continue working with your online orders.

After you download your orders and fees, you can manage your online sales and receipts by using the Online Orders List and Online Sales Receipts list. As with other Accounting 2007 lists, you can sort and filter the list, display specific transactions, and void any transactions where you don't receive payment within a reasonable time.

When a customer pays for an online order, the order's status changes from Pending to Not Converted, which means that you haven't converted the order to an online sales receipt. To convert an online order into an online sales receipt, display the Online Sales home page, and then under Find, click Online Orders to display the Online Orders List. Double-click the order you want to complete, and then click Convert To Online Sales Receipt.

See Also For more information about managing data lists in Accounting 2007, see "Viewing the Item List" in Chapter 5, "Managing Products and Services."

In this exercise, you will download orders and fees related to your online sales.

> **OPEN** a company file for which you have enabled online sales.

1. In the **Navigation Pane**, click **Online Sales**.
2. On the **Online Sales** home page, under **Start a Task**, click **Download Orders and Fees**.
   The Windows Live sign-in dialog box opens.
3. Type your Windows Live ID and password in the spaces provided, and then click **OK**.
   The Windows Live sign-in dialog closes and Accounting downloads your orders and fees.
4. To review errors related to failed order and fee downloads, in the **Download Results** dialog box, click **View Error Details**.
5. Click **Finish**.

Accepting PayPal Payments

PayPal, which was acquired by eBay in 2002, is a service that computer users can use to send funds electronically to other users. eBay integrated PayPal payments into their auction structure after the acquisition, so many eBay customers use PayPal to pay for their online purchases.

If you would like to accept PayPal payments, set up an account by visiting the main PayPal Web site at *www.paypal.com*. After the site opens, click the Sign Up link and fill out the application form.

> **Important** Be sure to read the PayPal terms of service agreement and the files available on the site's Help page, which detail PayPal's policies and procedures, including dispute resolution.

After you establish your PayPal account, start Accounting 2007, and then on the PayPal Payments menu, click PayPal Settings to display the PayPal Payments Settings wizard.

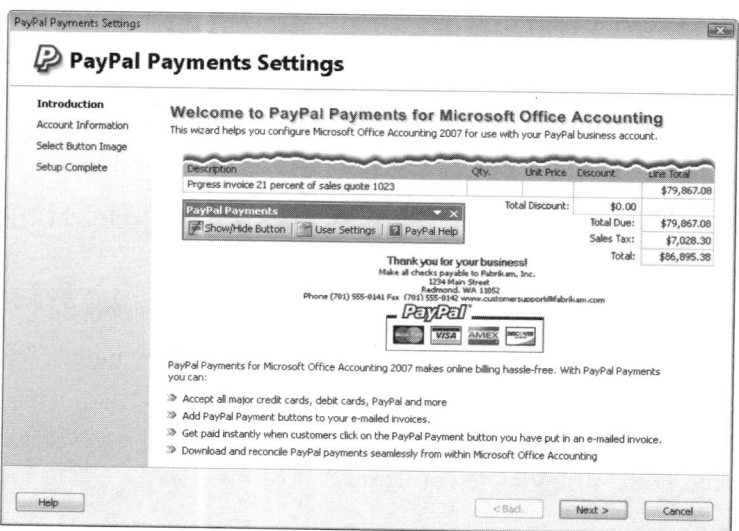

Click Next to move to the next wizard page, which prompts you for your PayPal account information. Type your User ID in the space provided, and then click Next to have Accounting enable you to receive PayPal payments.

In this exercise, you will enable Accounting 2007 to accept PayPal Payments.

OPEN a company file for which you have enabled online sales.

1. On the **PayPal Payments** menu, click **PayPal Settings**.

   The PayPal Payments Settings wizard starts.

2. Read the information on the first page of the wizard, and then click **Next**.

   The Enter PayPal Account Information page appears.

3. Type your PayPal e-mail address in the box provided, and then click **Next**.

   The Select A PayPal Payments Button Image page appears.

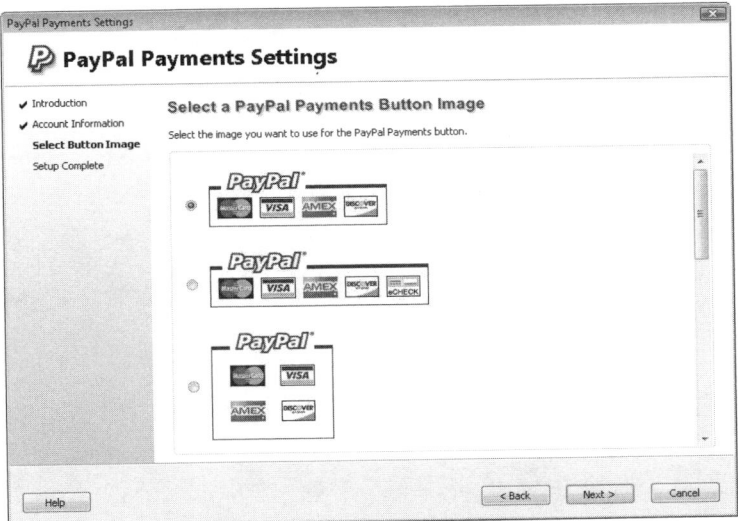

4. Select the button you want, and then click **Next**.

   The PayPal Payments Setup Complete page appears.

5. Click **Finish** to close the wizard and complete your setup.

CLOSE the open company file. If you are not continuing directly to the next chapter, exit Accounting 2007.

Key Points

- Setting up your company to sell online makes it possible to sell to individuals who shop online and might not otherwise have encountered your products.

- Selling on eBay by using Accounting 2007 requires both an active eBay account and a Windows Live ID, but you can sign up for both of those accounts from within Accounting 2007.

- If you want to accept PayPal payments, you can sign up for that service within Accounting 2007.

Chapter at a Glance

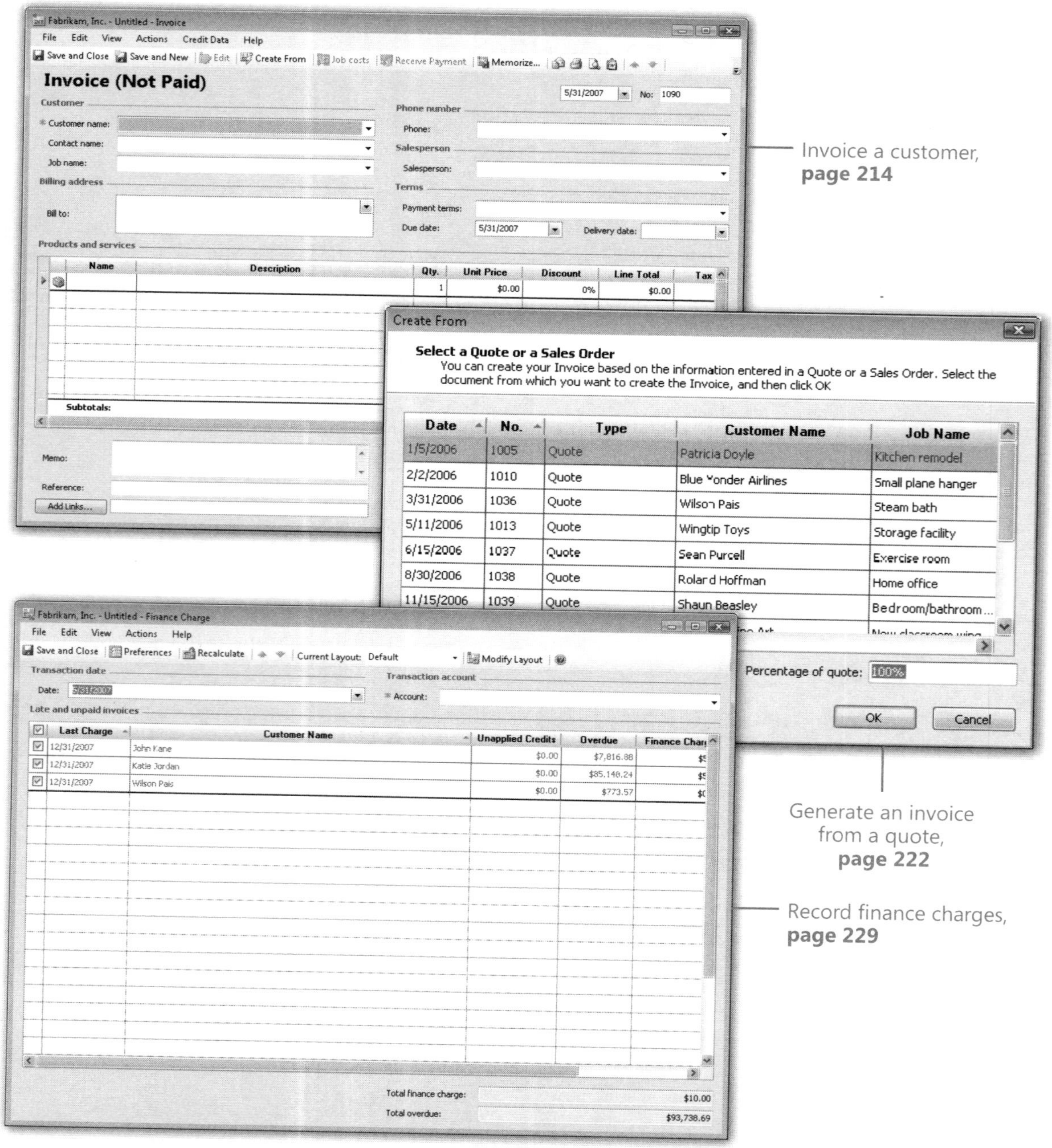

Invoice a customer,
page 214

Generate an invoice
from a quote,
page 222

Record finance charges,
page 229

11 Managing Invoices

In this chapter, you will learn to:

- ✔ Invoice a customer.
- ✔ View the Invoice List.
- ✔ Generate an invoice from a quote.
- ✔ Void and edit invoices.
- ✔ Record finance charges.

An invoice shows the products and services that a customer has purchased, the quantity of each item, the amount of the sale, the date the invoice is due, payment terms, and other details of a sales transaction. The items billed on an invoice can include materials from your inventory, professional services or labor that you provide, or expenses incurred that you pass on to the customer.

Microsoft Office Accounting 2007 provides several ways to create invoices. You can create an invoice from scratch by filling in the invoice form with customer information and the list of products and services you are billing for. You can also create an invoice from a quote (or a sales order) that you have provided to a customer or, if your company is set up to use jobs, you can create an invoice from a job record. For invoices related to jobs, you can create a progress invoice that bills the customer for a percentage of the job amount, or you can itemize the time, expenses, and materials that are associated with the job in Accounting 2007.

In this chapter, you will learn how to create and work with invoices. You'll learn about the different ways to create an invoice. You'll also learn how to handle finance charges for past-due invoices, and how to void and edit an invoice.

> **Troubleshooting** Graphics and operating system–related instructions in this book reflect the Windows Vista user interface. If your computer is running Windows XP and you experience trouble following the instructions as written, please refer to the "Information for Readers Running Windows XP" section at the beginning of this book.

Invoicing a Customer

An *invoice* is a request for payment that you send to a customer. Your invoices contain customer information, a list of products and services you are billing for, and the quantities, prices, discounts, and other details that are part of the sale. When you save an invoice, Accounting 2007 posts it to your company's accounts, and it becomes a permanent part of your records.

> **Important** You cannot delete an invoice after it is posted. The act of posting the invoice generates journal entries that debit (increase) the amount of your accounts receivable and credit other accounts such as labor costs or inventory. You can void an invoice if the invoice is no longer valid or edit an invoice to change or update its details or terms. For information about how to void an invoice, see "Voiding and Editing Invoices" later in this chapter.

To open a blank invoice form, click Customers in the Navigation Pane and then, in the Start A Task section, click New Invoice.

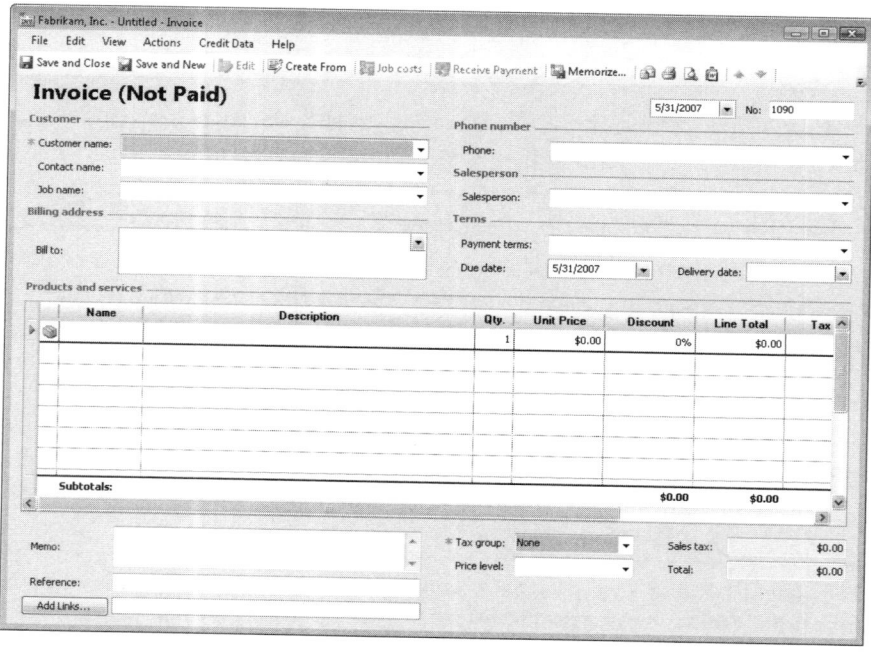

When you create an invoice, the status of the invoice is Not Paid. Accounting 2007 fills in the current date and assigns a number to the invoice, but you can change the invoice number to conform to your company's numbering system, if necessary.

In the top portion of the invoice form, you enter customer information, payment terms, the due date for the invoice, and the delivery date. In the Products And Services area of the invoice form, you list the items the invoice covers. Each line item in an invoice shows the name and a description of the item, the quantity, the unit price, any discount, the line total, and the tax status of the item.

If you assigned a customer to a tax group, you can find that information at the bottom of the form. The sales tax rates defined in the tax codes that are included in the tax group are applied to the price of items as you build the invoice.

See Also For information about creating customer records, see Chapter 6, "Managing Customers."

> **Note** If you select the Use Jobs option in the Company Preferences dialog box, the invoice form includes the Job Name field. Later in this chapter, you'll learn more about creating invoices for jobs. If you select the Use Classes option as a company preference, the invoice form includes the Class field. You can use this field to specify which class a quote belongs to. For example, if you have set up sales regions as classes, you can designate the region in the invoice.

The list of products and services are those you have set up as items. To add an existing item to the Products And Services grid, click the item you want in the Name list; the item description comes from the item record. If the item you want to include in the invoice doesn't appear in the list, you can add the item by clicking Add A New Item in the Name list. Also, if you type a name of an item that is not included in the item list, Accounting 2007 requires that you create a record for the item before you continue creating the invoice.

A line item in an invoice can also refer to an account in a company's chart of accounts, specify a sales tax that applies to the quote, or provide a comment on a line item or another aspect of the quote. To change the type of line item, click the icon in the first cell of the line item row and then select the type of line item you want to use: Item, Comment, Sales Tax, or Account.

> **Tip** To apply a discount to the total amount of the quote rather than to a single line item, add an Account line item to the quote, specify the Discount expense account, and then enter the percentage of the discount in the Unit Price field.

In this exercise, you'll create an invoice from scratch by filling in the fields in the invoice form. (In the exercise that follows, you'll create an invoice from a quote.)

> **BE SURE TO** start Accounting 2007 before beginning this exercise.
>
> **OPEN** the Fabrikam sample company file.

1. In the **Navigation Pane**, click **Customers**; then, in the **Start a Task** section of the **Customers** home page, click **New Invoice**.

   A blank invoice form opens.

2. In the **Customer name** list, click **Brenda Diaz**.

   The appropriate customer information appears in the invoice.

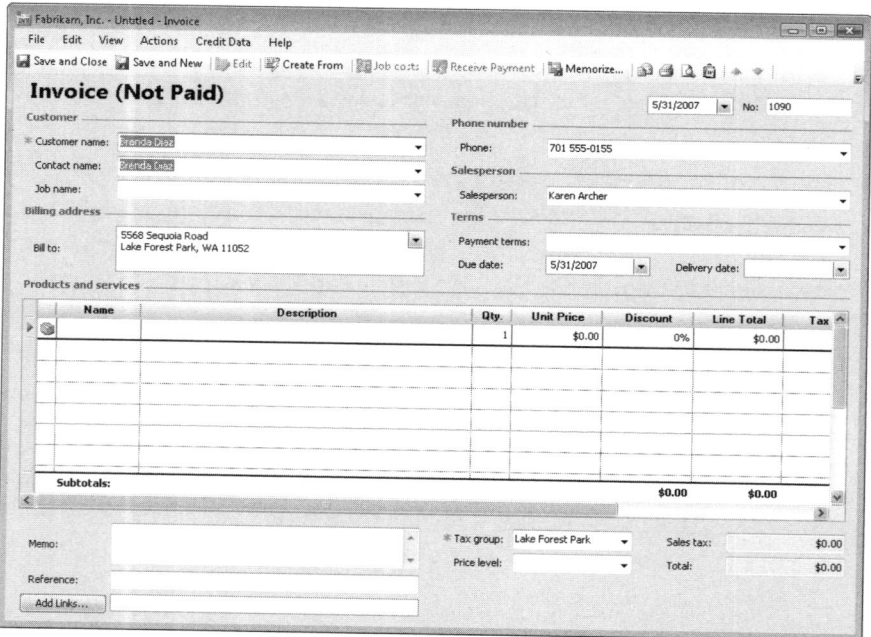

3. In the **Payment terms** field, click **Net 30**.

   The due date changes to reflect the time period of the payment term.

4. In the **Delivery date** field, type a date later than the present date.

5. Under **Products and services**, click in the **Name** column for the first row, click the arrow, and then click **Carpentry (TM)** from the list of products or services.

The Carpentry (TM) item appears in the Products And Services grid.

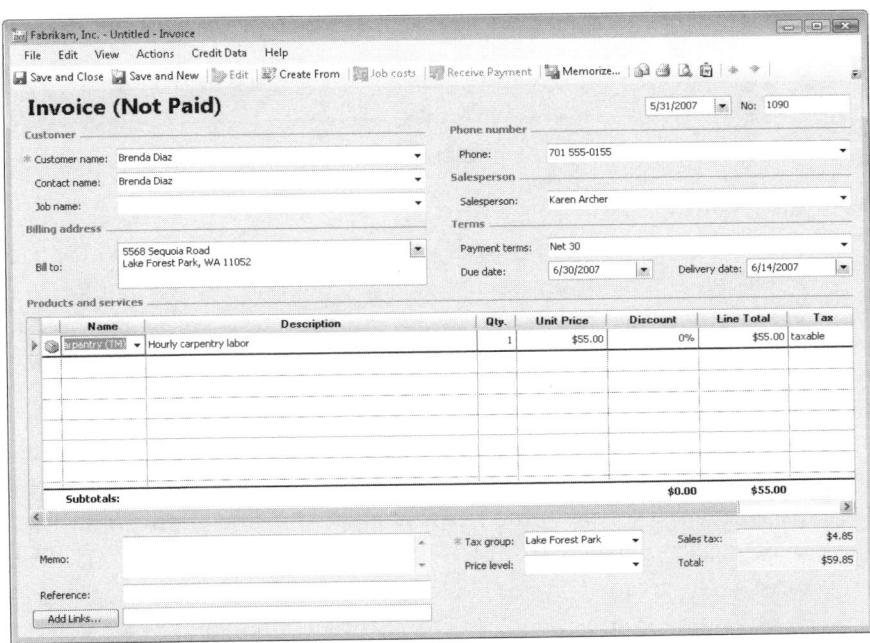

6. In the line item for hourly carpentry labor, in the **Qty.** (quantity) field, type 24.

7. In the **Discount** field, type 5.

The invoice changes to reflect a 5% discount on this line item.

8. Click in the leftmost column of the second row, and then click **Comment**.

9. In the **Description** field, type Framed addition to bedroom.

10. In the row below the comment you entered in step 9, click in the **Name** column, and then select **Framing/finish materials** from the item list.

11. In the **Qty.** field, type 40.

12. In the **Price level** list, click **Preferred Customer**.

See Also For information about defining price levels and assigning a price level to a customer, see Chapter 6, "Managing Customers."

| Save and Close | **13.** Click the **Save and Close** button on the toolbar.

> **Note** If a dialog box appears asking if you want to save the change to Brenda Diaz's payment terms, click No to indicate that the payment terms will be for this invoice only.

Accounting saves your invoice, and the invoice form closes.

Business Intelligence Through Accounts Receivable Aging Analysis

Analyzing components of your current assets can provide you with critical business intelligence. One of several benefits you gain is early warning of liquidity issues. When you regularly age and review your accounts receivable, you acknowledge a proven business principle: the longer your accounts are left unpaid, the more likely they are to become uncollectible.

By developing the habit of reviewing your aged receivables, you can monitor and act upon delinquencies before they get out of control. You age a given receivable based upon the date of the sale that created it, and classify it into an "aging bucket" of days, such as 0-30, 31-60, 61-90, Over 90, and so forth. (You'll probably find it most useful to age by multiples of your sales terms, but this can vary to meet your business needs and cycles.) You can present your aging as a periodic report showing all outstanding receivables balances, broken down by customer and month due. Your aging schedule will help to reveal patterns of late payment, and show you where to concentrate collection efforts. Your regular analysis of aged receivables can help you to prevent losses on future sales, too, because customers with old receivables may find other sources of supply, and leave you with bad debts.

You can gain substantial business intelligence in addition to these early warnings. Regular aging analysis, in conjunction with industry standards, helps you to manage the credit policies of your business. For example, if your accounts receivable tend to become older than the average for your line of business, you become aware that you must put more effort into collecting for products or services you have already sold. If, on the other hand, your accounts receivable agings are substantially below industry averages, you may be able to increase sales by loosening your credit policies.

Your regular review of aged accounts receivable provides you with timely, action-able information. This is especially true when you calculate and review your aging in conjunction with other ratios, such as Days Receivable. These tools can tell you:

- Where collection efforts need to be concentrated.

- How much actual investment your company has in receivables.

- Which of your accounts might need to have product or service sales discontinued (at least until their aging receivables improve).

- Whether the terms you offer attract quality customers and increase sales.

- Other details, such as whether good accounts, paying, for example, in the 10-30 day period, are also taking cash discounts (which might mean you are providing terms of 2/30 versus the Net 60 you intended).

Viewing the Invoice List

Creating an invoice adds an entry to your company's Invoice List.

Triggering Customer Aging Based Upon Invoice Date

When your company maintains accounts receivable, it postpones the collection of cash upon the sale of its goods or services. The existence of receivables on your balance sheet means that your company has invested cash—cash it might otherwise have collected—into what are, in effect, loans to customers. (Trade receivables take the form of invoices rather than promissory notes or other instruments.) It is important to the health of your business to remember that receivables are a use of funds. Receivables represent dollars that cannot be used to pay company debts or to reinvest in inventories and projects.

If you extend, for example, 30-day terms, you should be generally collecting your receivables within 30 days. One method you can use to measure receivable quality is to compare how long it actually takes to collect to the payment terms you are granting. You can derive an actual collection period ratio known as Days Receivable to help you make this comparison. Because accounts receivable is a use of your company's cash, you should review your Days Receivable regularly.

You can compute Days Receivable by using the following formula:

Days Receivable = Average Accounts Receivable / Day's Sales

When you use this formula, the Average Accounts Receivable is the average actual receivables on your balance sheet for the time period you are analyzing. Day's Sales is the sales you recorded in the same time period divided by the number of days in the time period.

If you find that Days Receivable exceeds your sales terms, your first step in analyzing why is to classify your receivables into "buckets" of multiples of your sales terms. As an illustration, if you offer terms of Net 30, (telling your customers to pay invoice totals within 30 days), your "aging buckets" might be 0-30, 31-60, 61-90, and Over 90.

After you classify and total the amount due from each of your customers or clients into an aging schedule, you can more easily identify those whose credit should be suspended (perhaps you should enforce COD terms until their older receivables are paid), those who should be closely monitored because their accounts receivable are increasing in age, and so forth. By comparing your Days Receivable to industry averages, you can obtain other business intelligence, too. As an example, your comparison might make you aware of opportunities to increase sales by loosening your credit policies, should you determine that your Days Receivable metrics are lower than those of businesses similar to your own.

By reviewing the Invoice List, you gain information that can provide insights into your business. Viewing the list of unpaid invoices, for example, should reveal slow-paying customers and how finance charges add to what your customers owe. By default, the Invoice List displays Open invoices—those invoices that a customer has not yet paid. The Invoice List displays a summary of information about each invoice, including the nature of the charge (for example, original invoice or finance charge), the customer's name and phone number, the related job name, the due date, and the amount of the invoice.

In addition to viewing all unpaid invoices, you can use the Current View list to filter the list to show invoices that have a particular status—Open, Overdue, or Voided. You can also display all invoices by clicking All in the Current View list. Switching the view of the Invoice List is a simple way to gather information about possible trends in your business. For example, click Overdue in the Current View list, and you can see how many invoices are past due, and which customers have overdue invoices.

To sort the Invoice List, click the header of the column by which you want to sort the list. For example, if you wanted to sort the Fabrikam Invoice List by the values in the Total Price column, you would click the Total Price column header. Clicking a column header sorts the Invoice List in ascending order, based on the values in that column; clicking the same column header again sorts the Invoice List in descending order, based on the values in that column; and clicking the column header a third time restores the Invoice List to its original order.

In this exercise, you will display and sort the Fabrikam sample company's Invoice List.

> **OPEN** the Fabrikam sample company file.

1. In the **Navigation Pane**, click **Customers**; then, in the **Find** section of the **Customers** home page, click **Invoices**.

   The Invoice List appears.

2. Click the **Current View** button, and then in the list, click **Overdue**.

   The overdue invoices appear in the Invoice List.

3. Click the **Total Price** column header.

Accounting sorts the invoices in ascending order based on total price.

4. Click the **Total Price** column header again.

Accounting sorts the invoices in descending order based on total price.

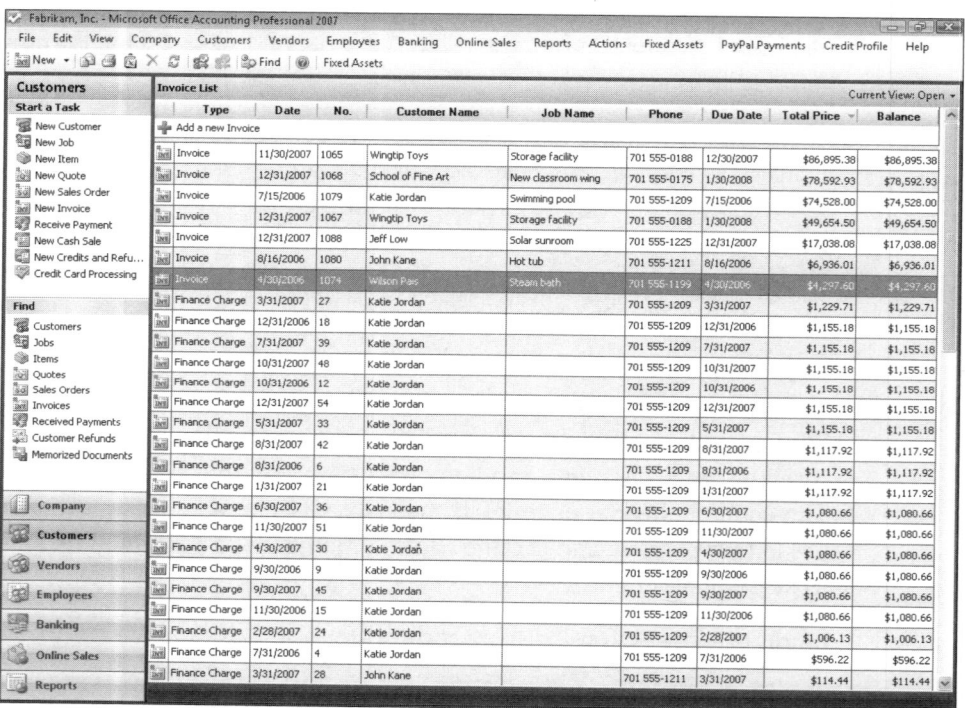

Generating an Invoice from a Quote

In Chapter 8, "Generating and Managing Quotes," you learned that you can convert a quote (or a sales order) to an invoice. Similarly, you can create an invoice from a quote or sales order by clicking Create From on the invoice form toolbar of a new (blank) invoice to display the Create From dialog box.

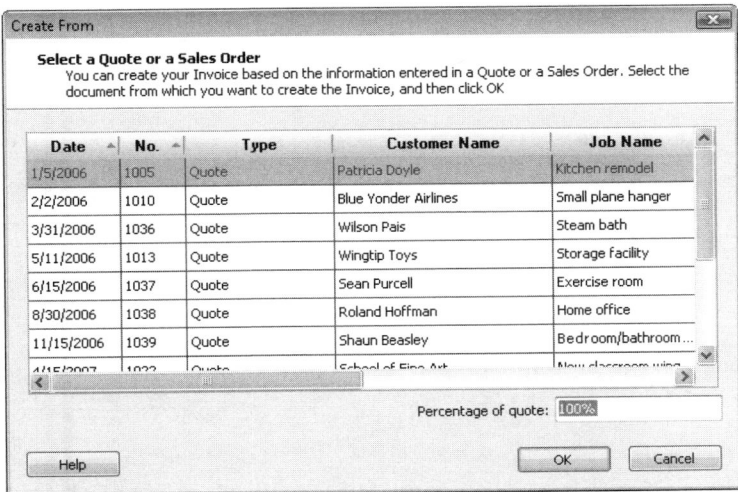

A quote that details the products and services for a job that you have set up in Accounting 2007 can serve as the basis of a progress invoice in which you bill for a specified percentage of a job. You can also itemize job costs on an invoice you create from a quote. To itemize job expenses, display the invoice and then, on the form's toolbar, click the Job Costs button to display the Time And Materials dialog box.

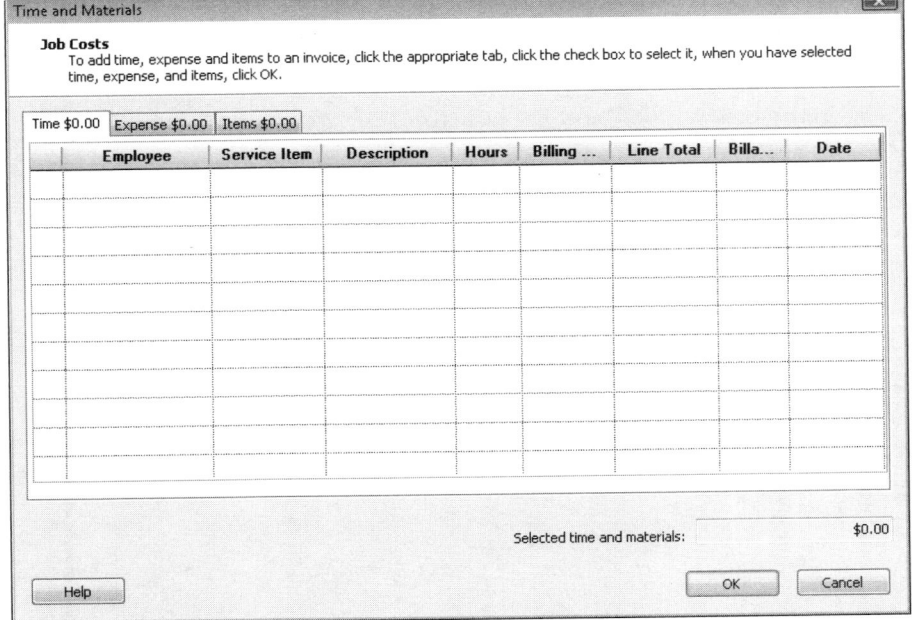

> **Important** Only Accounting Professional 2007 supports jobs; Accounting Express 2007 does not.

You can use the tools in the Time And Materials dialog box to compile an itemized job invoice. The entries on the Items tab originate from a quote that is associated with a job. Entries on the Time tab are created when an employee bills time to a specific job. Entries on the Expense tab are created when you record vendor expenses that relate to a job.

See Also For more information about vendor expenses, see Chapter 13, "Purchasing from Vendors." For more information about billing employee time, see Chapter 16, "Managing Employee Time and Payroll," on the CD.

In addition to generating an invoice from the Customers home page, you can use the job list to create an invoice for a specific job. You can use this approach to create a progress invoice for a fixed-fee job or an itemized invoice for a time and materials job.

See Also For more information about fixed-fee and time and material jobs, see Chapter 7, "Managing Jobs."

In this exercise, you will use quotes from the Fabrikam sample company to create a progress invoice from a quote and add detailed job costs to an invoice.

> **OPEN** the Fabrikam sample company file.

1. In the **Navigation Pane**, click **Customers**; then, in the **Start a Task** section of the **Customers** home page, click **New Invoice**.

   A blank invoice form opens.

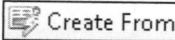

2. On the invoice form toolbar, click **Create From**.

   The Create From dialog box opens.

3. Click quote number **1038** for customer Roland Hoffman.

4. In the **Percentage of Quote** box, type 50.

5. Click **OK**.

   The Create From dialog box closes and Accounting updates the invoice.

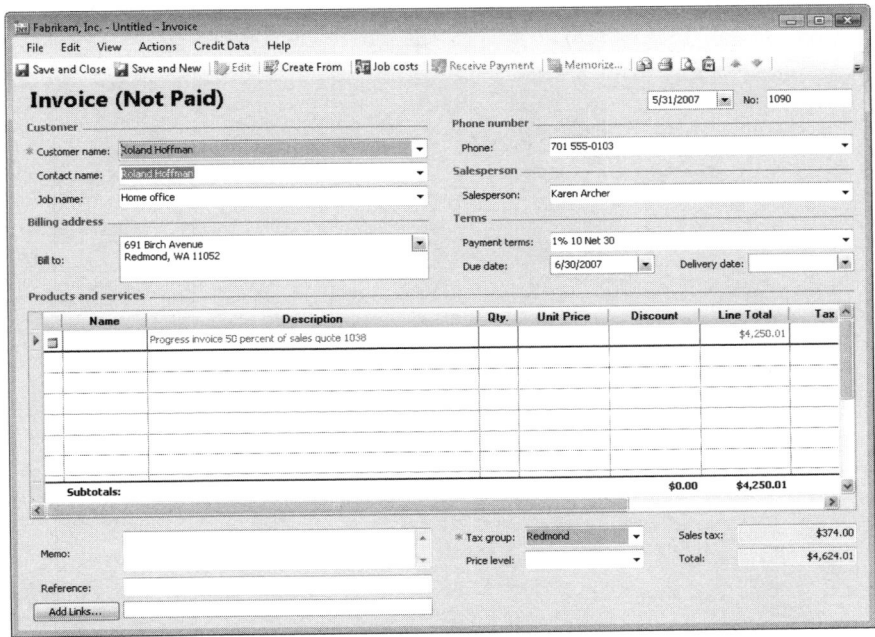

Save and Close **6.** On the invoice form toolbar, click **Save and Close**.

> **Note** If a dialog box appears, asking if you want to use the new Payment Terms setting for Roland Hoffman's future transactions, click No to indicate the change is for this transaction only.

The invoice disappears.

> **Note** The following steps apply only to Accounting Professional 2007.

7. In the **Navigation Pane**, under **Find**, click **Jobs**.

The Job List appears.

8. In the **Job List**, click the **Swimming pool** job for customer Katie Jordan.

9. On the **Actions** menu, click **New Invoice for Job**.

An invoice form opens.

Job costs **10.** On the invoice form toolbar, click **Job Costs**.

The Time And Materials dialog box opens.

11. Click the **Items** tab of the **Time and Materials** dialog box.

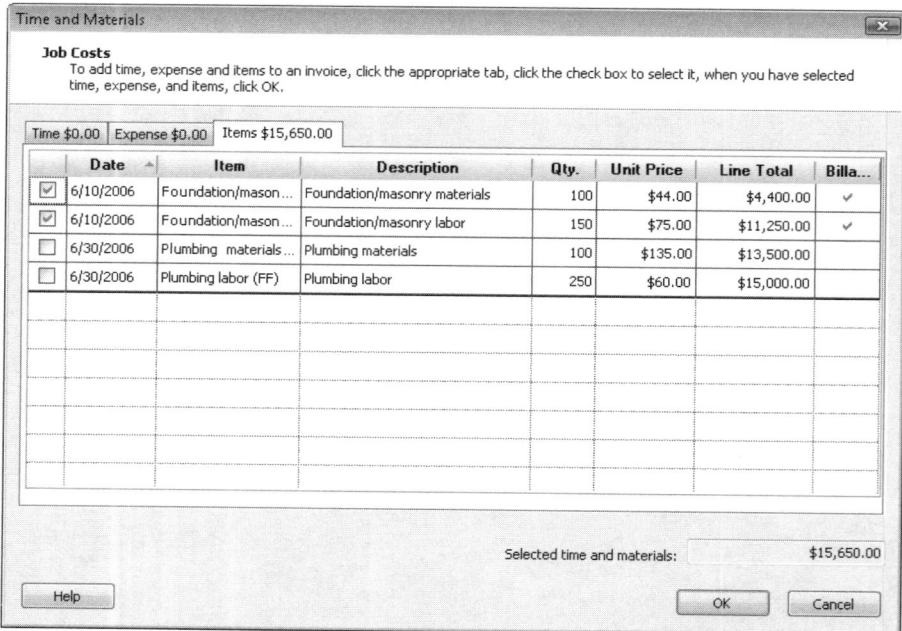

12. Clear the **Foundation/masonry materials** and **Foundation/masonry labor** check boxes, and select the **Plumbing materials** and **Plumbing labor (FF)** check boxes.

13. Click **OK**.

The new invoice appears.

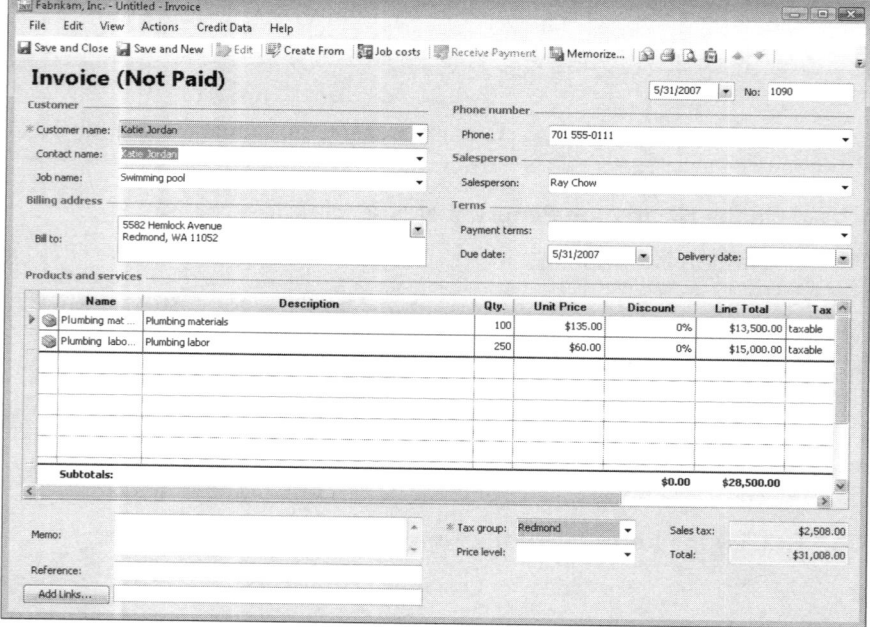

14. Click **Save and Close**.

Accounting saves the invoice.

Voiding and Editing Invoices

When you save an invoice, the invoice is posted to your company's books. You cannot delete an invoice that has been posted, but you can make changes to the invoice or void an invoice that is no longer valid. After you void an invoice, you cannot change the status of the invoice back to Open. If you want to charge your customer for the items listed in the voided invoice, you must create a new invoice.

You can use a voided invoice as the basis for a new invoice. For example, if you need to change the discount terms on an invoice, you can void the invoice and then make a copy of the voided invoice to edit. If you sell the same items to the same customer or want to create an invoice that is similar to an existing one, you can create a new invoice by copying an invoice and editing the copy.

When you void an invoice, Accounting 2007 enters a reverse posting with the same date as the original invoice so that the invoice does not appear in your general ledger but a record of the transaction is retained.

> **Note** When you void an invoice, the label VOID appears on the invoice form. However, the label does not appear when you send a voided invoice as an e-mail message. To avoid confusion about the status of the invoice, you can attach the voided invoice to the e-mail message instead.

In this exercise, you will void an invoice and edit an invoice by using examples from Fabrikam, Inc.

OPEN the Fabrikam sample company file.

1. In the **Navigation Pane**, click **Customers**.

2. In the **Find** section, click **Invoices**.

3. In the invoice list, double-click invoice number **1074** for the customer Wilson Pais.

> **Troubleshooting** If you receive an error message indicating that voiding an invoice would change a transaction in a reconciled account, select an invoice in the current fiscal year to use in this exercise.

4. On the **Actions** menu, click **Void**, and then click **Yes** in the message box. Accounting voids the invoice.

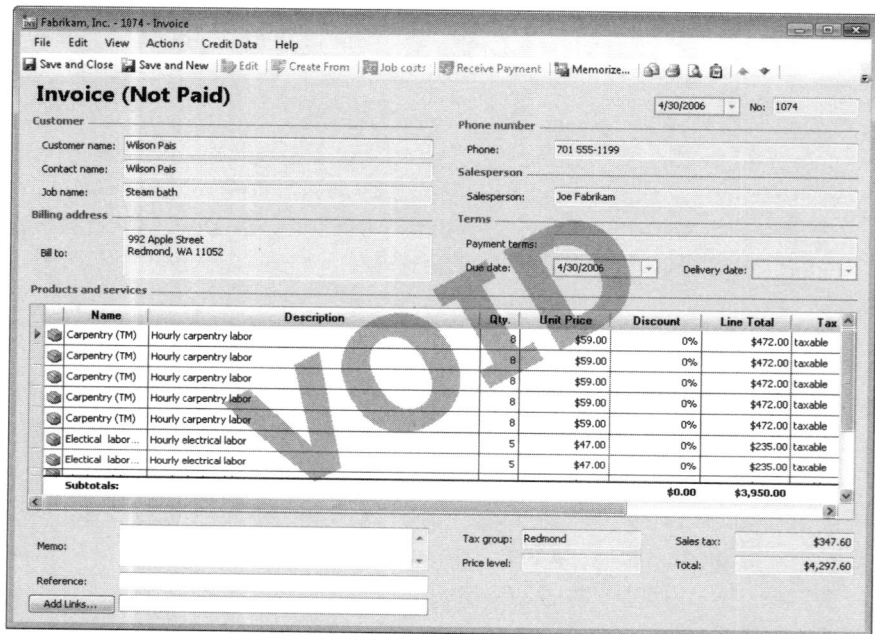

> **Tip** Use the Memo box on the invoice form to enter a brief description for the reason this invoice is no longer valid. To open a voided invoice, select Voided from the Current View list, and then double-click the invoice.

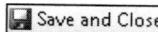

5. On the toolbar, click **Save and Close**.

6. In the **Current View** list, click **Voided**.

7. In the list of voided invoices, double-click invoice **1074**.

8. On the **File** menu, click **Copy and Edit**.

The new invoice appears with the customer information and line items from the original. Accounting 2007 assigns a new number to the invoice and sets the date to the current date. You can now make changes to the details of the invoice. The status of the voided invoice that you used as the basis of the new invoice does not change. The voided invoice is retained in your accounting records.

Recording Finance Charges (Professional Only)

Among the company preferences you can set in Accounting Professional 2007 is the finance charge for unpaid balances on past due invoices. To calculate a finance charge, you specify a default value for the annual interest rate at which the finance charge is assessed, a default minimum charge, the number of grace days, and whether the finance charge is calculated from the invoice due date or the date of the invoice itself.

Each finance charge that is assessed is included in the invoice list. The amount of a finance charge is calculated on the unpaid balance for all open invoices. You should apply any payments and credits to overdue invoices before you apply a finance charge.

In this exercise, you'll review the settings for finance charges in the Company Preferences dialog box and then apply a finance charge to a customer balance.

BE SURE TO start Accounting Professional 2007 before beginning this exercise.
OPEN the Fabrikam sample company file.

1. In the **Navigation Pane**, click **Customers**.

2. In the **Start a Task** section, click **Finance Charge**.

   The Finance Charge form opens.

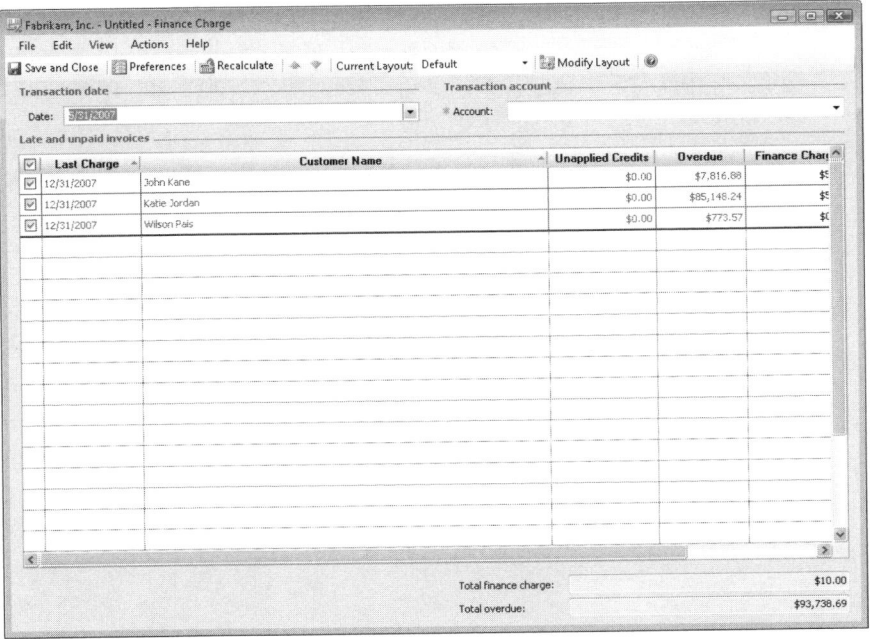

3. Clear the check boxes on the rows for the John Kane and Wilson Pais accounts.

4. In the **Finance Charge** column of the row that contains Katie Jordan's overdue invoice, type 25.

> **Tip** You can change the amount assessed for finance charges by clicking Preferences on the toolbar and then changing the settings on the Customers tab of the Company Preferences dialog box.

5. Click the **Account** arrow, and then in the list, click **9020 – Interest Expense**.

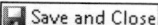 6. On the toolbar, click the **Save and Close** button.

The Finance Charge form closes.

 CLOSE the Fabrikam sample company file. If you are not continuing directly to the next chapter, exit Accounting 2007.

Reporting Considerations: Invoices

Reports that you base upon invoices, and the sales activity they reflect, will focus upon the customers to whom you have made the sales, the terms you have offered, sales and invoice dates, and the like. Typical "views" by which such information is arranged include customers, products/services sold, timing of sales, due dates, and associated details. Invoice details drive collections reports, accounts receivable reports (general listings and agings), Days Receivable and other ratio calculations, and underlying detail reports.

To some extent, you will find it important, from a reporting perspective, to intersect invoice details with payment receipt information. For instance, the way you match customer payments to outstanding invoices will determine the agings of the remaining unpaid balances. If you review these details in conjunction with your agings on a regular basis, you will have overviewed, to some extent, the accuracy and completeness of finance charges. Such information is nice to have handy to support responses to customer inquiries about the charges, as well as balances in general.

Accounting for Finance Charges

To compensate your business for the overhead involved in extending credit, as well as to motivate customers to pay you in a timely manner, you can assess finance charges on your customers' unpaid invoice balances. Accounting Professional does much of the work of generating these charges for you, based upon Company Preferences and other settings that you make within your accounting system. Among the accounting decisions you are asked to make in setup are the annual interest rate, the minimum finance charge, and the number of grace days you want to apply. Another choice you can make is whether to apply finance charges from the invoice date or the due date.

As you prepare to complete the Finance Charge worksheet, where most of your setup choices for finance charges will be made, consider which account you want to use for posting these charges. Unless you are in the business of loaning money, you usually consider finance charges as "other" income. You'll probably want to post them into an account that is separate from your regular business revenues.

Whatever preferences you set within your Finance Charge worksheet, you will still have the ongoing opportunity to edit finance charge invoices, as well as to ignore some finance charges (say in a case where the charge generated is a small amount). This allows you to apply charges in a way that promotes good will with customers, as well as to make other modifications to keep things clean and efficient.

Key Points

- You can create invoices on their own or by using information in a quote, sales order, or job.
- Invoices are posted to your company's accounts. After an invoice is posted, you cannot delete the invoice, but you can void or edit it.
- You can set up finance charges for overdue invoices in the Company Preferences dialog box.
- Pay close attention to your overdue invoices and how you account for any finance charges that accrue.

Chapter at a Glance

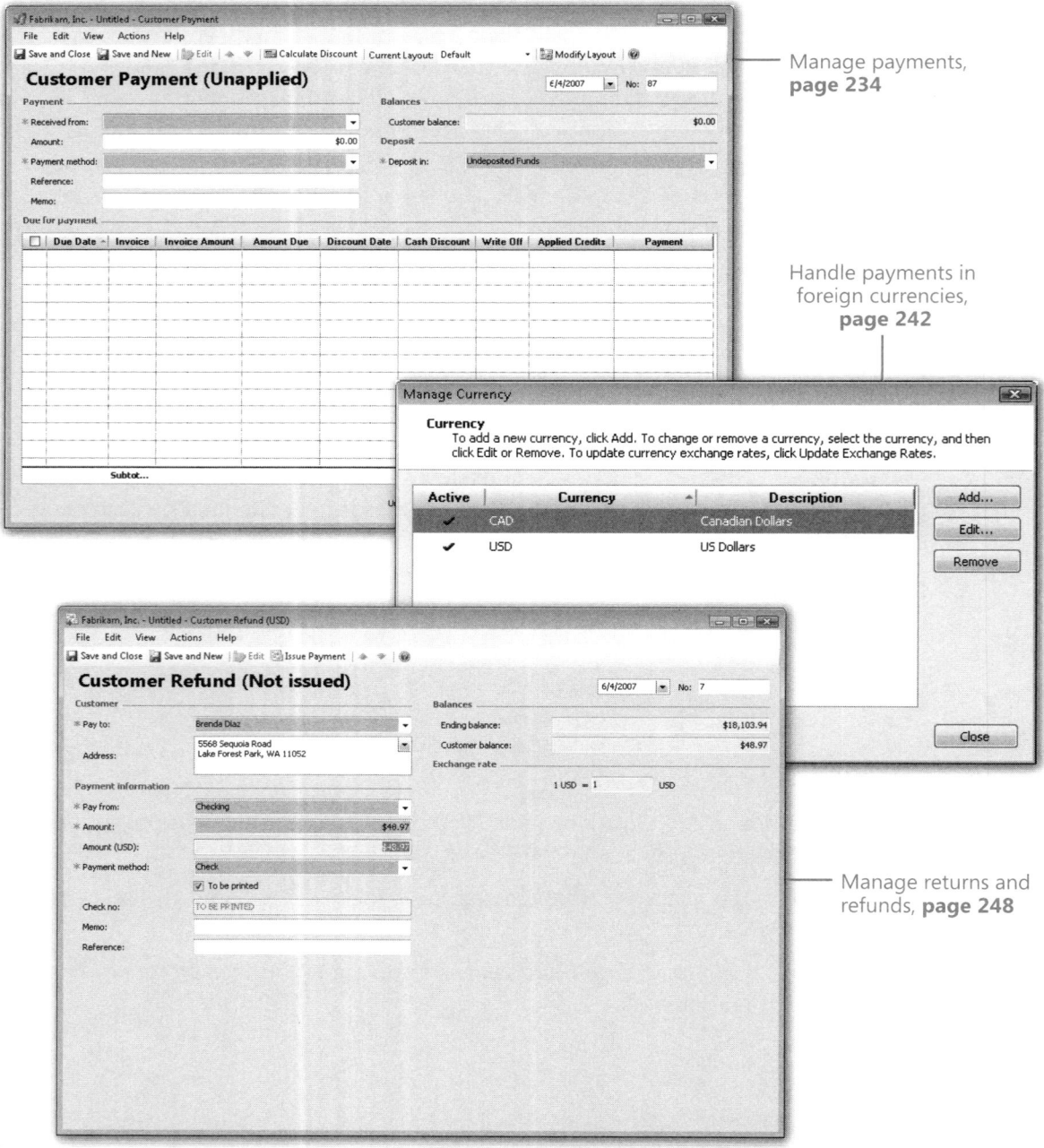

Manage payments, **page 234**

Handle payments in foreign currencies, **page 242**

Manage returns and refunds, **page 248**

12 Handling Customer Payments

In this chapter, you will learn to:

✔ Manage payments.

✔ Handle cash sales.

✔ Set up credit card processing.

✔ Handle payments in foreign currencies.

✔ Manage returns and refunds.

Without income, your company would wither on the vine. But if you don't handle your customers' payments effectively, you won't know how much money you have or who owes you what amount. Microsoft Office Accounting 2007 uses a set of consistently designed forms with which you can track your payments, assign payments to invoices, and even handle customer returns and refunds efficiently.

In this chapter, you will learn how to manage customer payments, handle cash payments, manage refunds, and issue a general credit.

> **Troubleshooting** Graphics and operating system–related instructions in this book reflect the Windows Vista user interface. If your computer is running Windows XP and you experience trouble following the instructions as written, please refer to the "Information for Readers Running Windows XP" section at the beginning of this book.

Managing Payments

You can extend credit to your customers, delivering their goods and services along with an invoice, but eventually you must get paid for your efforts. Managing your payments in Accounting 2007 means that you can be prepared for payment by check, cash, and credit card. You can also be prepared for those unfortunate times when a payment must be reversed, whether that's because a customer's check doesn't clear or there was a problem with a credit card.

Receiving Payments into Accounting 2007

When a customer gives you a credit card, a check, or cash in payment for goods or services, you can enter that payment into Accounting 2007 by using a Customer Payment form.

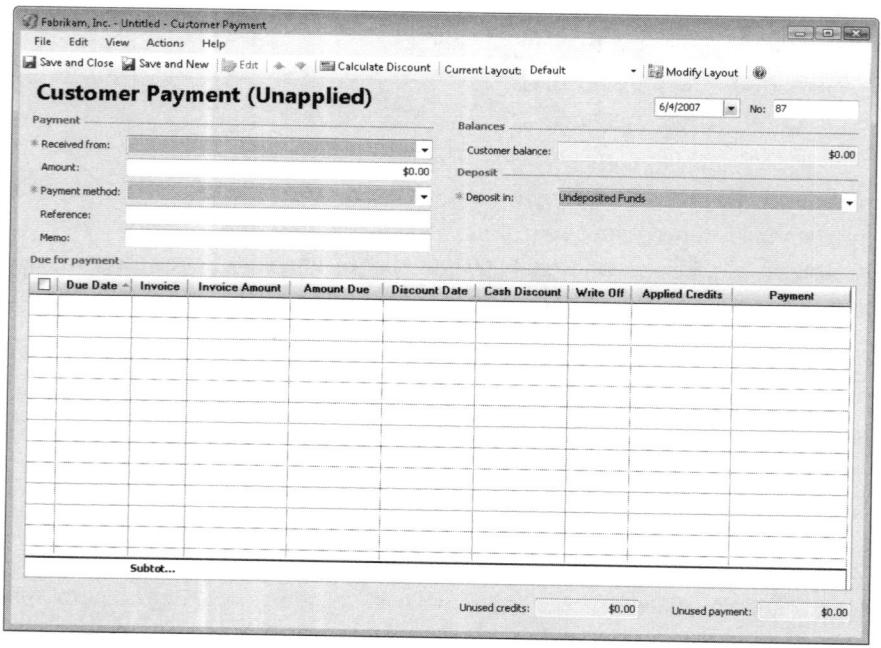

A Customer Payment form is very similar to other Accounting 2007 forms. It contains fields for the customer's name, the amount received, how the customer paid, the customer's remaining balance (if any), and the customer's outstanding invoices. If there is more than one outstanding item in the Due For Payment list, you can decide to which of the items you want to apply the payment.

> **Note** If a customer has more than one outstanding invoice, Accounting 2007 assigns the payment to the oldest invoice by default.

In this exercise, you will receive a payment into Accounting 2007.

> **BE SURE TO** start Accounting 2007 before beginning this exercise.
>
> **OPEN** the Fabrikam sample company file.

1. In the **Navigation** pane, click **Customers**.

2. In the **Start a Task** section of the **Customers** home page, click **Receive Payment**.

   A Customer Payment form opens.

3. If necessary, type the current date in the unnamed date field in the upper-right corner of the **Customer Payment** form.

4. In the **Received from** list, click **Wingtip Toys**.

   The payments due from Wingtip Toys appear in the Due For Payment list.

5. In the **Amount** field, type 86895.38, and then press the Tab key.

   Accounting applies the payment amount to invoice number 1065 in the Due For Payment list and selects that row's Apply check box.

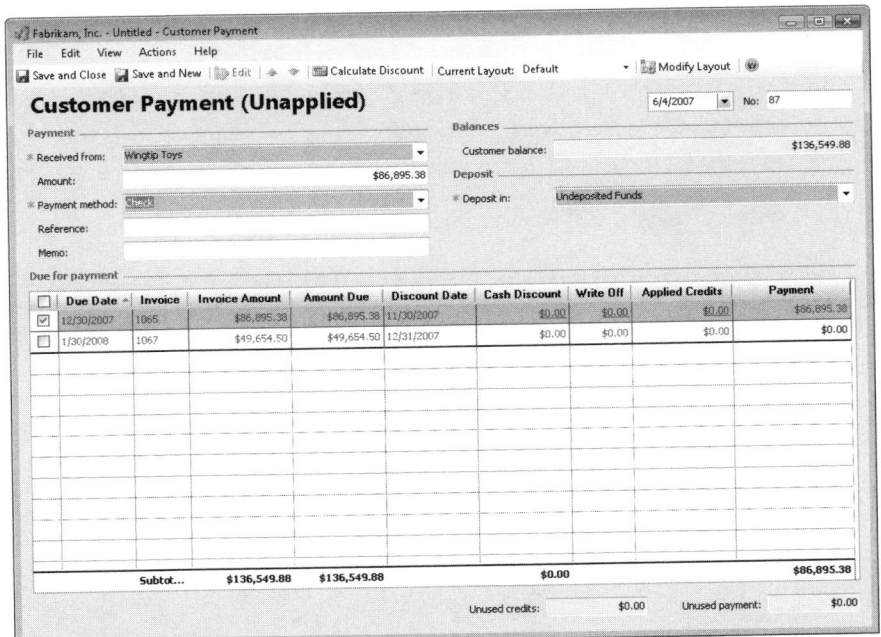

6. In the **Deposit in** list, click **Checking**.

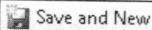 7. On the toolbar, click the **Save and New** button.

Accounting saves the payment and opens a new Customer Payment form.

8. In the **Received from** list, click **Katie Jordan**.

The payments due from Katie Jordan appear in the Due For Payment list.

9. In the **Amount** field, type 100, and then press `Tab`.

Accounting applies the payment amount to invoice number 1079 in the Due For Payment list and selects that row's Apply check box.

10. In the **Deposit in** list, click **Checking**.

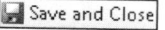 11. On the toolbar, click the **Save and Close** button.

Accounting saves the payment and closes the Customer Payment form.

Voiding a Payment

It's unfortunate, but there will be times when a customer's check is returned for insufficient funds or you run into a problem with the credit card the customer used. One possibility? The card was stolen. When you run into these difficulties, you'll have to correct your accounts to reflect the change. You can't delete payments; they generate accounting records that the program must maintain. You can, however, void a payment so that the monies you thought you had received are removed from your account records.

Voiding a payment is a straightforward process. You need to display the payment, open the Actions menu, click Void, and confirm that you want to void the payment. The original record remains in your company file, but the transaction is correctly identified as voided.

In this exercise, you will void a payment.

> **Important** To complete this exercise as written, you must have created the payment from Wingtip Toys in the previous exercise. If you didn't create that payment, you can void any other payment in the sample file.

OPEN the Fabrikam sample company file.

1. In the **Navigation Pane**, click **Customers**.

2. In the **Find** section of the **Customers** home page, click **Received Payments**.

   The Received Payment List appears.

3. Click the **$86,895.38** payment from Wingtip Toys.

4. On the **Actions** menu, click **Void**.

   A message box appears, asking if you're sure you want to void the transaction.

   > **Tip** You can prevent Accounting 2007 from displaying the verification message box by selecting the In The Future, Do Not Show This Warning check box, but it's a good idea to have the program verify you want to void the payment.

5. Click **Yes**.

   Accounting voids the payment and changes the payment's indicator to reflect its status.

The Importance of Matching Receipts to Receivables

You use the customer payment form to record payments received from customers. An important part of recording these receipts is to settle, or match, them against the invoices that generated them. When you match each payment with the individual invoice(s) that the customer intended to pay, you can easily tell, at any point in time, which invoices have been paid and when, and which invoices remain outstanding. After you fully settle an invoice with a payment, Accounting sets the status of the invoice to Paid. You can also record partial payments effectively, because the system sets the status to Partially Paid in such cases.

Although you might follow the common practice of paying the oldest invoices first with the payments you receive (to help your customers minimize finance charges), you can settle a payment against any invoice you want with Accounting 2007. It is important to match receipts properly to invoices, because the way you do this will determine the agings of the remaining unpaid balances. The age of a receivable can trigger finance charges as well as other collection and customer interaction events, depending upon the policies of your company. If you misallocate payments, finance charges can be overstated, understated, or missed entirely. In addition, you might accidently suspend customer purchases, or perhaps even fail to properly do so, if your agings are based upon misapplied or unapplied payments.

You can also leave customer payments unapplied or partially unapplied. With this procedure, you can book the receipt; for example, to realize the benefit of a cash deposit on your financial statements, even if you have a question about how to apply the payment. You can then return later, when the customer has supplied information you requested about which invoice she intended to pay, and apply the payment properly.

Handling Cash Sales

Many customers prefer to pay with credit cards or debit cards, but if you run a retail store, you must be ready to accept cash payments. Counting and securing cash can be a pain, but recording cash sales in Accounting 2007 follows procedures that are similar to those for other payment forms.

> **Important** Some customers who pay cash do so to protect their privacy by not giving their name and contact information to the seller. You should strongly consider creating a dummy account, perhaps named Cash Customer, with which to associate sales to customers who don't want to release their personally identifiable information.

When a customer pays for an item by using cash, you can record the sale by clicking Customers in the Navigation Pane and then, in the Start A Task section, clicking New Cash Sale. The form that appears has fields to enter the customer's name (if he or she wants to share it), the delivery date, and the products and services purchased. When you're done entering the transaction, you can either click Save And Close to conclude entering sales, or click Save And New to open a blank Cash Sale form.

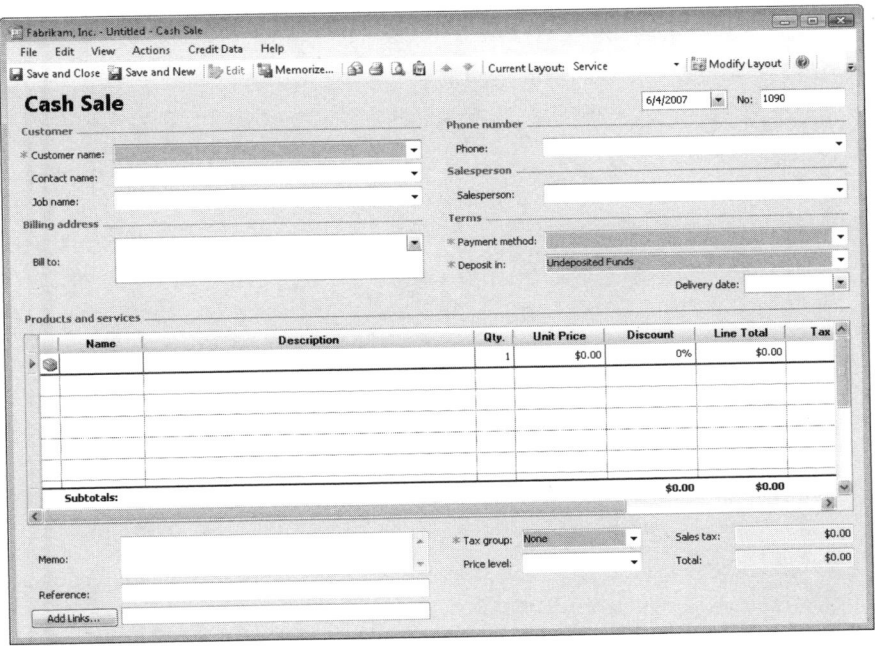

> **Note** Because cash sales generate accounting records, you can't delete cash sales from your company file. To change a cash sale's record, you need to void or edit the transaction. The procedure to void a transaction appears earlier in this chapter.

In this exercise, you will record a cash sale in Accounting 2007.

OPEN the Fabrikam sample company file.

1. In the **Navigation Pane**, click **Customers**.

2. In the **Start a Task** section of the **Customers** home page, click **New Cash Sale**.

   A blank Cash Sale form opens.

3. In the **Customer Name** list, click **Katie Jordan**.

4. In the first row of the **Products and services** grid, click in the **Name** field, click the arrow that appears, and then click **Electrical materials (FF)**.

   Accounting adds the Electrical Materials (FF) item information to the first line of the Products And Services grid.

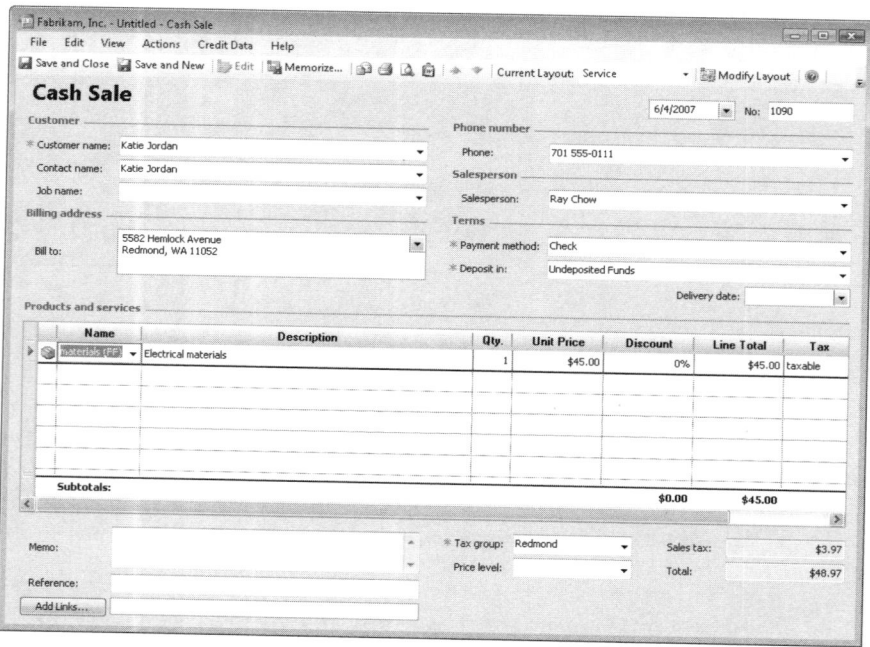

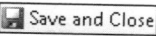 5. Click **Save and Close**.

   Accounting records the cash sale.

Setting Up Credit Card Processing

Cash might still be the backbone of modern commerce, but credit cards make transactions much easier to handle. You can accumulate sales information electronically, you don't have to count a stack of dirty paper, and there's no need for one or two daily trips to the bank. You record credit card payments by using the procedures for receiving payment described earlier in this chapter. If you're already set up with a credit card merchant account, you can enter that information into Accounting 2007. If you don't have a merchant account, you can sign up for one from within the program.

> **Note** The available credit card processing plan details might have changed since this book went to press.

In this exercise, you will run the Credit Card Processing Wizard and set up your credit card processing account.

> **OPEN** the Fabrikam sample company file.

1. In the **Navigation Pane**, click **Customers**.

2. In the **More Tasks** section of the **Customers** home page, click **Credit Card Processing**.

   The Windows Live Sign-in dialog box opens.

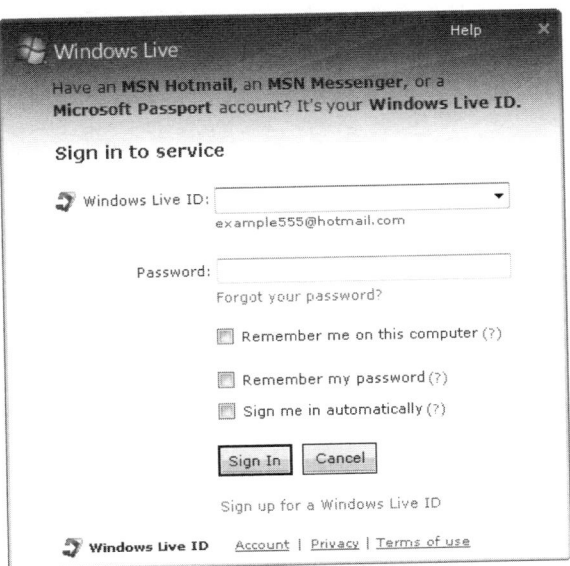

> **Note** If the Welcome To Credit Card Processing screen appears instead of the Windows Live Sign-in dialog box, click Sign Up Now and follow the directions in the wizard.

3. Sign in to the Windows Live service by using your Windows Live ID and password.

Follow the directions in the Credit Card Processing Wizard to establish your account.

> **Important** You can't access the Credit Card Processing Wizard from a sample company file; you must have set up your own company file to start the wizard.

Handling Payments in Foreign Currencies (Professional Only)

Most of your customers will likely pay for their purchases in your local currency. Businesses near borders, however, might choose to accept cash payments in multiple currencies. You could also choose to accept online payments or credit card payments in multiple currencies if your processing agent doesn't automatically convert payments from foreign currencies to your base currency.

You must set your Company Preferences to enable Accounting Professional 2007 to accept payments in foreign currencies. To display the Company Preferences dialog box, click Preferences on the Company menu. Then, in the Company Preferences dialog box, on the Company tab, select the Use Foreign Currencies check box. When you accept the setting, the Accounting 2007 forms and documents change to reflect the possibility that you could enter a transaction amount in a currency other than your base currency.

The following table summarizes the changes that occur when you enable foreign currencies in Accounting Professional.

Customer form	Currency display	Additional fields, columns, or buttons	Notes
Quote	Currency displayed in title after you save document	Exchange Rate field Additional Total field	Selecting the base currency when you add the customer disables the Exchange Rate field. One Total field is in base currency; the other is in foreign currency. All items in customer account currency. Although the Cost and Markup columns are not visible, they are in base currency.
Sales Order	Currency displayed in title after you save document	Exchange Rate field Additional Total field	Selecting the base currency when you add the customer disables the Exchange Rate field. One Total field is in base currency; the other is in account currency. All items in customer account currency.
Invoice	Currency displayed in title after you save document	Exchange Rate field Additional Total field	Selecting the base currency when you add the customer disables the Exchange Rate field. One Total field is in base currency; the other is in account currency. All items in customer account currency.
Cash Sale	Currency displayed in title after you save document	Exchange Rate field Additional Total field	Selecting the base currency when you add the customer disables the Exchange Rate field. One Total field is in base currency; the other is in account currency. All items in customer account currency.
Customer Credit Memo	Currency displayed in title after you save document	Exchange Rate field Additional Total field	Selecting the base currency when you add the customer disables the Exchange Rate field. One Total field is in base currency; the other is in account currency. All items in customer account currency.

Customer form	Currency display	Additional fields, columns, or buttons	Notes
Customer Payment	Currency displayed in title after you save document	Currency displayed in title after you save document	Selecting the base currency when you add the customer disables the Exchange Rate field.
			All table items are in customer account currency.
			One Amount field is in base currency; the other is in customer account currency.
Apply Credits and Payments	No change	None	All line items are in customer account currency.
Finance Charge	No change	Exchange Rate buttons on Actions menu and toolbar	Overdue amounts are listed in both account and base currency.
			Charges are calculated for all currencies at the same time.
			You must set up exchange rates before you calculate finance charges.
Print Customer Statements	No change	Currency filter field	Generating paper copies of the statements.
		Balance columns in both base and customer currency	
Write Off	No change	Currency Code and Exchange Rate fields	The write-off amount is in the account currency.

After you enable foreign currency usage in Accounting Professional, you can change a company's default currency to reflect how the company pays its bills. For example, if A. Datum Corporation were a Canadian company with an office in the United States, you could change its company information to reflect that the company made its payments in Canadian dollars. To do that, you display the company's Customer form, and then in the Currency list, click CAD (which represents Canadian dollars).

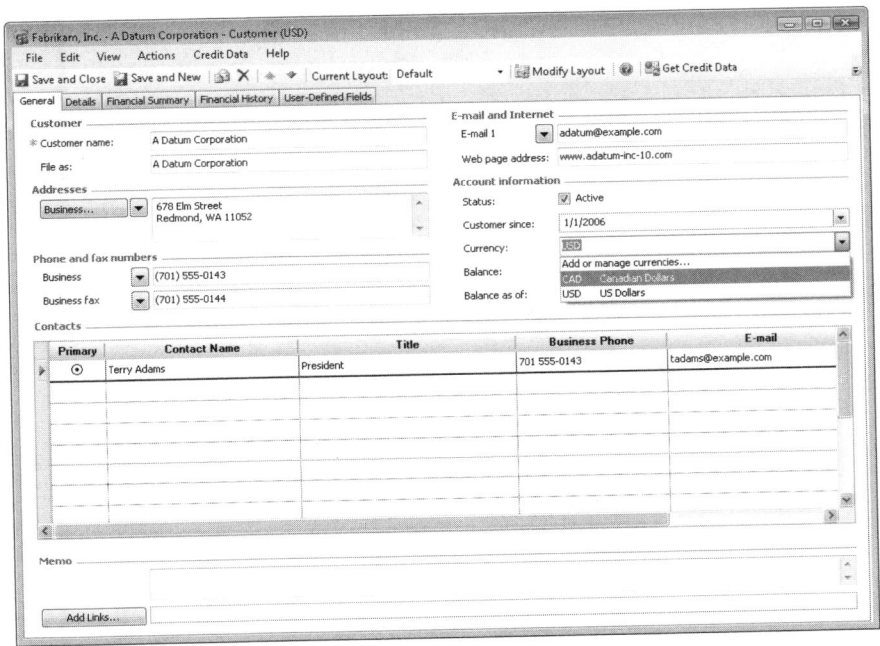

Note A customer's default currency appears in the title bar of every form and dialog box where you can enter monetary amounts.

When you turn on foreign currency handling for the first time, with Accounting Professional, you can denominate transactions in United States dollars and Canadian dollars. If you need to use another currency, such as the euro, you can enable that currency by displaying the Manage Currency dialog box. To do so, open the Company menu, click Foreign Currency, and then click Currency List.

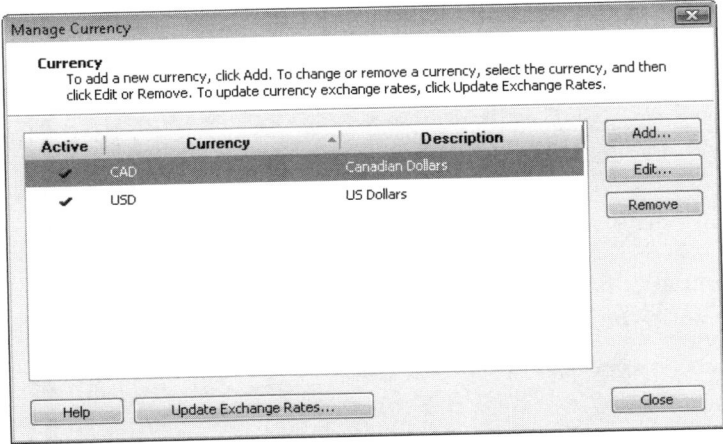

You can use the controls in the Add Or Edit Currency dialog box to add a new currency or to modify an existing currency. When you add a new currency to the list, you should use a standard three-letter currency code for any currencies you add. You can find those codes on sites such as *www.xe.com*.

> **Important** If you use foreign currencies, you should update the exchange rate at least once a week, and preferably every day.

In this exercise, you will enable foreign currency usage in the Fabrikam sample company file, change a company's base currency, and create a quote denominated in that currency.

> **BE SURE TO** start Accounting Professional 2007 before beginning this exercise.
> **OPEN** the Fabrikam sample company file.

1. On the **Company** menu, click **Preferences**.

   The Company Preferences dialog box opens.

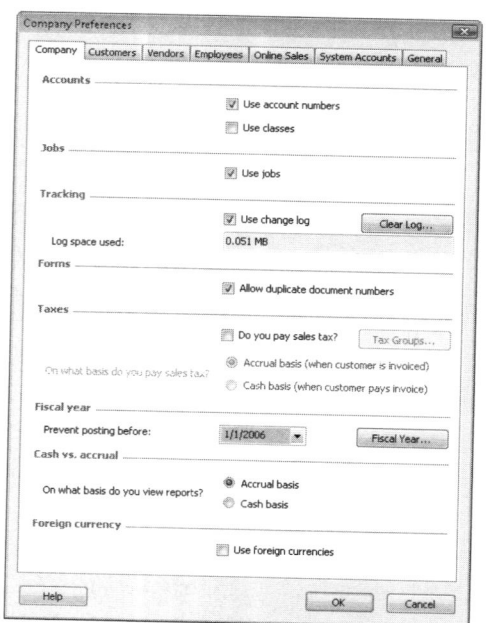

2. On the **Company** tab, in the **Foreign currency** section, select the **Use foreign currencies** check box. Then click **OK**.

   The Company Preferences dialog box closes.

3. In the **Navigation Pane**, click **Customers**.

4. In the **Find** section of the **Customers** home page, click **Customers**.

   The Customer List appears.

5. Double-click **Lucerne Publishing**.

   A Customer form containing information for Lucerne Publishing appears.

6. In the **Accounting Information** section, click the **Currency** arrow, and then in the list, click **CAD Canadian Dollars**.

   The form changes to reflect the company's new base currency.

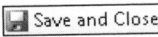

7. Click **Save and Close**.

   The form closes.

8. In the **Navigation Pane**, click **Customers**.

9. In the **Start a Task** section of the **Customers** home page, click **New Quote**.

   A blank Quote form opens.

10. In the **Customer Name** list, click **Lucerne Publishing**.

    The Quote form changes to reflect Lucerne Publishing's information, including that the company's base currency is Canadian dollars.

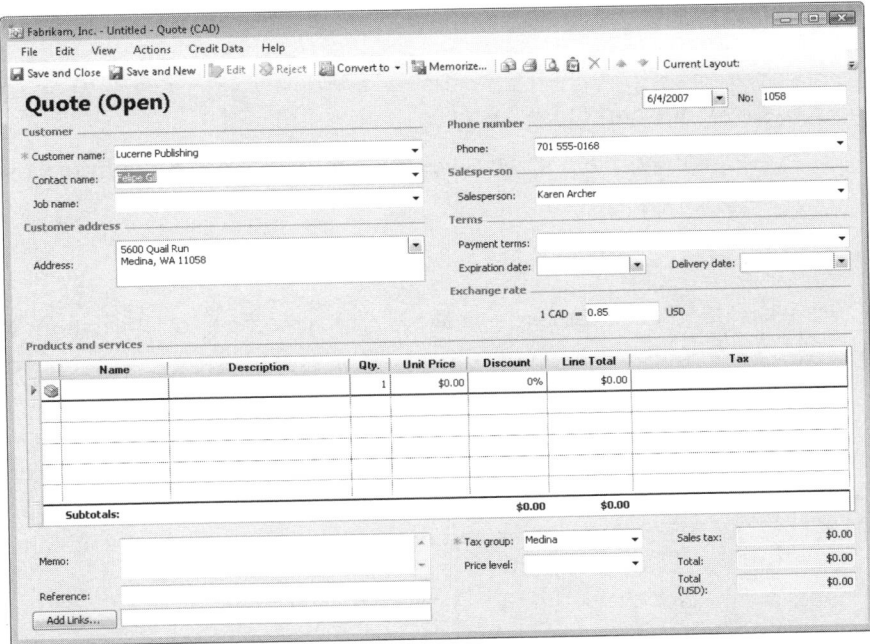

11. In the first row of the **Products and services** grid, click the **Name** arrow, and then click **Foundation/masonry material (FF)**.

   The form updates to reflect the added product, with the cost displayed in Canadian dollars.

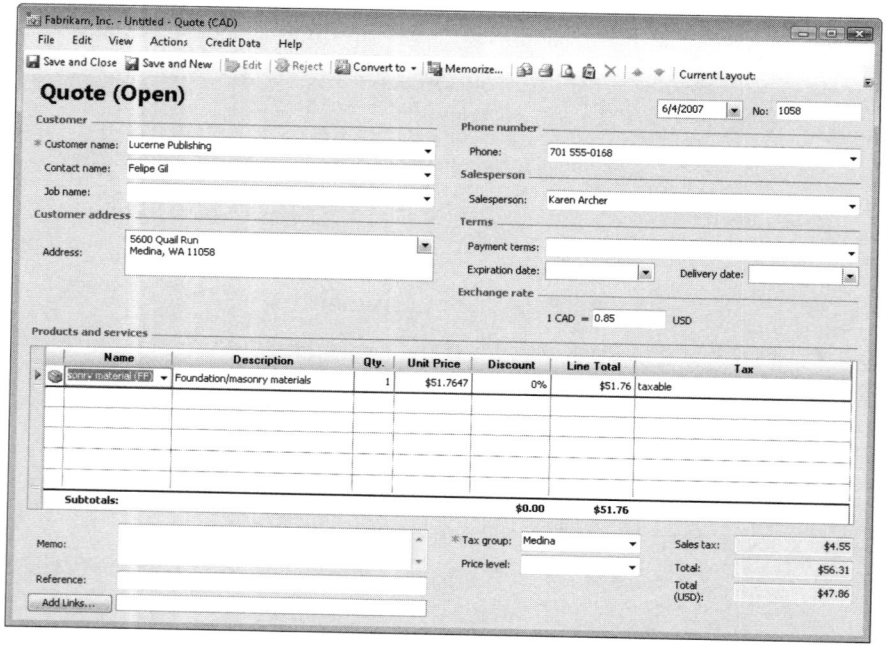

12. Click **Save and Close**.

   Accounting Professional saves the quote and the Quote form closes.

Managing Returns and Refunds

It makes good business sense to allow your customers to return items they have purchased. Sometimes customers leave your store with products that need to be fixed or replaced. In some cases, your customer might have bought a product for a project that didn't materialize, purchased too many units of a product, or simply had a change of mind about a purchase. As a courtesy (or as a matter of law in some jurisdictions), you should accept the return of the unwanted product, provided the customer returns the item within a reasonable time and in a condition that allows the item to be resold.

The basic mechanism for customer refunds is the credit memo, which you can create by displaying the Customers home page and then, in the Start A Task section, clicking New Credits And Refunds. When you do, Accounting displays a blank Customer Credit Memo form.

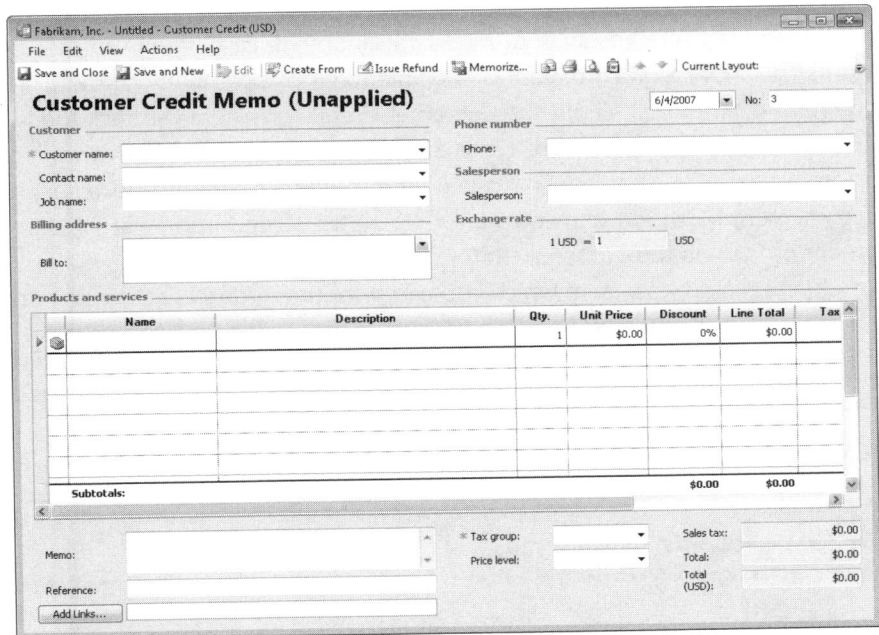

The credit memo you create depends on how you create it. The basic Customer Credit Memo form assumes you will refund money the customer paid for goods or services. However, if you issue a refund for payment based on an invoice or for a job, you can save time by basing the credit memo on the invoice or job information stored in Accounting.

Handling Customer Returns

When you accept a return, you need to place the item back into your inventory. If the item is still in salable condition, you can add it to your inventory; however, if the item is no longer in brand-new condition or is in an open box, you will probably sell the item at a discount. If the item is defective, you will be returning the item to the vendor from which you purchased it.

See Also For more information about adjusting inventory quantities and values, see Chapter 5, "Managing Products and Services." For more information about returning an item to a vendor, see Chapter 13, "Purchasing from Vendors."

Issuing a Refund by Check

When a customer pays for an item with a check or with cash, and in some cases when the customer pays by credit card, you will be able to write a company check for the amount of the refund. After you fill out the Customer Credit form, you can click the Issue Refund button at the top of the form to create a new Customer Refund form. In this form, select the account from which you want to draw the refund, and then, if necessary, click Check in the Payment Method list. If you want to issue the refund immediately, click the Issue Payment button on the Customer Refund form toolbar. Accounting 2007 displays the Print Checks dialog box, from which you can print the refund check. If you don't want to issue the refund immediately, click Save And Close.

See Also For more information about printing checks, see Chapter 14, "Managing Bank Accounts and Transactions."

In this exercise, you will create a check to refund a customer's purchase price.

OPEN the Fabrikam sample company file.

1. In the **Navigation Pane**, click **Customers**.
2. In the **Start a Task** section of the **Customers** home page, click **New Credits and Refunds**.

   A blank Customer Credit Memo form opens.
3. In the **Customer Name** list, click **Brenda Diaz**.
4. In the **Products and services** grid, click in the first **Name** field.
5. Click the arrow in the **Name** field, and then click **Electrical materials (FF)**.
6. On the **File** menu, click **Save**.

   > **Note** You use the Save command on the File menu so that Accounting doesn't close the form or create an unneeded new form.

   Accounting saves your credit memo but leaves the form open.

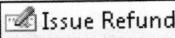 7. On the **Customer Credit Memo** form toolbar, click the **Issue Refund** button.

An untitled Customer Refund form opens.

8. In the **Pay from** list, click **Checking**.

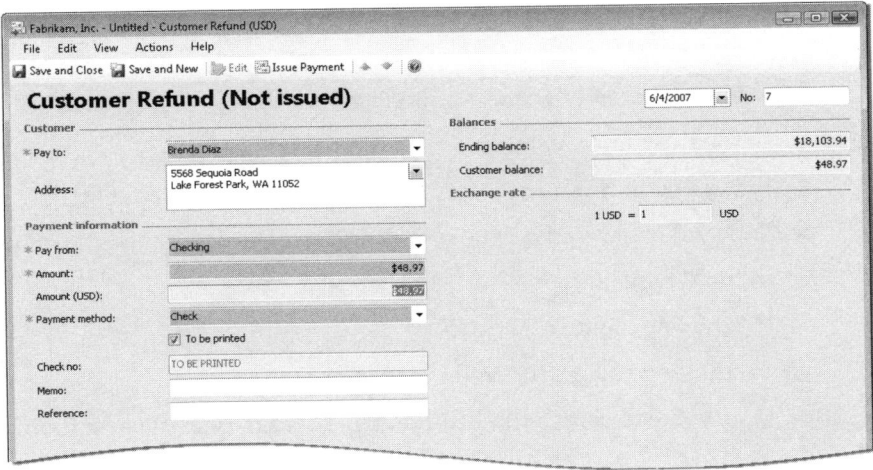

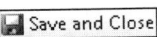 9. Click **Save and Close**.

Issuing a Refund by Credit Card

Because customers might have to pay interest on credit card purchases from the date of the purchase, it's good business practice to offer to transfer the amount of a return to the customer's credit card. The first part of issuing a refund to a customer's credit card is similar to issuing a refund by check, but the last steps depend on your credit card processing plan.

> **Important** You must be signed up for a credit card processing plan to issue refunds to a customer's credit card.

In this exercise, you will refund a customer's money by crediting the amount of the purchase to the customer's credit card.

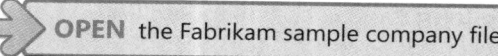

OPEN the Fabrikam sample company file.

1. In the **Navigation Pane**, click **Customers**.

2. In the **Start a Task** pane of the **Customers** home page, click **New Credits and Refunds**.

   A blank Customer Credit Memo form opens.

3. In the **Customer Name** list, click **Alpine Ski House**.

4. In the **Products and services** grid, click in the first **Name** field.

5. Click the arrow in the **Name** field, and then click **Framing/finish materials (FF)**.

6. In the **Qty** field, type 4.

7. On the **File** menu, click **Save**.

   Accounting saves your credit memo.

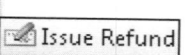

8. On the **Customer Credit Memo** form toolbar, click **Issue Refund**.

   A Customer Refund form opens.

9. In the **Pay from** list, click **Checking**.

10. In the **Payment method** list, click **Credit Card**.

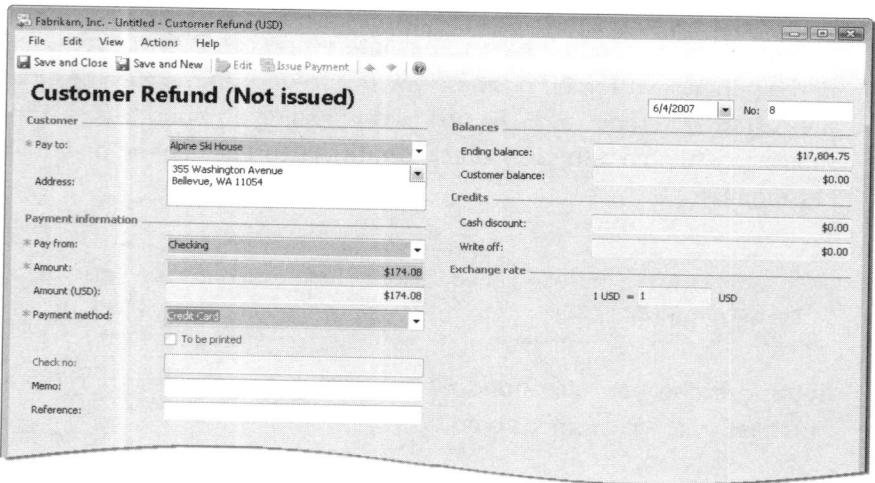

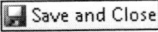 **11.** Click **Save and Close**.

Accounting issues the refund.

> **Note** The instructions you see depend on the credit card processing plan you selected.

Creating a Customer Credit Memo for a Job (Professional Only)

When you work for a service-oriented company, you might be in the unfortunate position of being required to refund a customer's money for a job. If you build a deck that subsequently collapses, or if a customer decides to cancel a contract within the legally allowed time period, you will need to refund the money. Rather than manually create a credit memo that contains the individual line items from the job, you can create the credit memo based on the job itself.

In this exercise, you will create a customer credit memo for a job.

> **OPEN** the Fabrikam sample company file.

1. In the **Navigation Pane**, click **Customers**.
2. In the **Find** section of the **Customers** home page, click **Jobs**.

   The Job List appears.
3. Double-click the **City Power & Light** job.

   The Workshop – Job window opens.
4. On the **Actions** menu, click **New Credit Memo for This Job**.

   A Customer Credit Memo form opens.

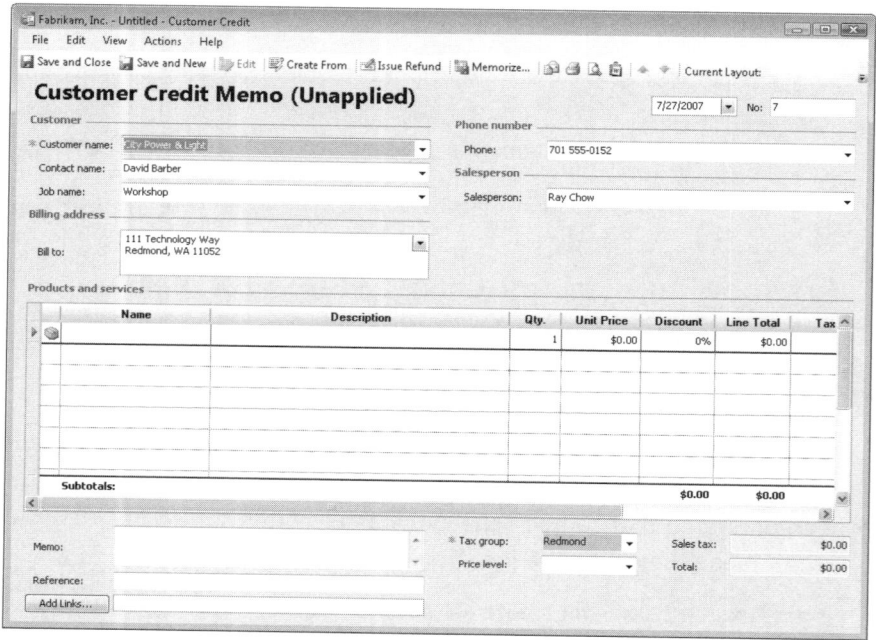

5. In the first row of the **Products and services** grid, click in the **Name** field.

6. Click the arrow in the **Name** field, and then click **Framing/finish materials (FF)**.

7. In the **Qty** field, type 3.

8. Click **Save and Close**.

Accounting saves your credit memo.

Creating a Customer Credit Memo from an Invoice

Just as you can create a credit memo based on a job's details, you can create a credit memo from an invoice. The process is quite similar; the only difference is that you display the Invoice List and then click Create Credit Memo on the Actions menu.

In this exercise, you will create a credit memo based on an invoice.

OPEN the Fabrikam sample company file.

1. In the **Navigation Pane**, click **Customers**.

2. In the **Find** section of the **Customers** home page, click **Invoices**.

   The Invoice List appears.

3. Click invoice **1088**, the invoice for Jeff Low's solar sunroom.

4. On the **Actions** menu, click **Create Credit Memo**.

   A Customer Credit Memo based on the selected invoice appears.

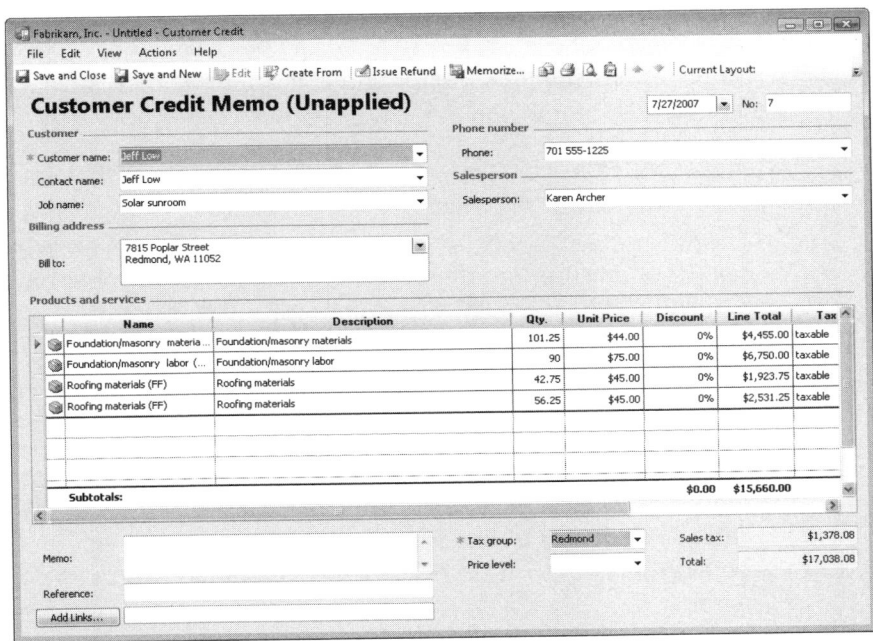

5. Click in the first row of the **Products and services** grid, right-click anywhere in the selected row, and then click **Delete**.

   The Foundation/Masonry Materials item disappears.

6. Click anywhere in the **Foundation/masonry labor** item's row, right-click the row, and then click **Delete**.

7. Right-click the first **Roofing materials (FF)** item, and then click **Delete**.

8. In the remaining row's **Qty** field, type 5.

 9. Click **Save and Close**.

   Accounting saves your credit memo.

✕ **CLOSE** the Fabrikam sample company file. If you are not continuing directly to the next chapter, exit Accounting 2007.

Reporting Considerations: Customers and Receipts

Reports that you base upon customers and receipts will focus on the customers to whom you have made the sales, the payments you have received from those customers, dates of those receipts, and the invoices to which the payments are applicable. "Views" by which you might arrange such information include customers, receipt dates, due dates, and associated details. In conjunction with invoice details, receipt details play a role in your collections reports, accounts receivable reports (general listings and agings), Days Receivable and other ratio calculations, and underlying detail reports.

Other possible reports include an unapplied cash report that you can regularly review to highlight receipts that have been booked, but which you need to allocate to the appropriate accounts receivable invoices. This is but one tool you can use to ensure that the process of matching customer payments to outstanding invoices—which determines the agings of the remaining unpaid balances—is taking place accurately and completely. You might learn, through such a report, that the inability to match received payments is increasingly becoming an issue.

Don't forget that, if you review receipts and matching details in conjunction with your agings on a regular basis, you will have overviewed, to an extent, the accuracy and completeness of finance charges. Such information is nice to have handy to support responses to customer inquiries about the charges, as well as balances in general.

Key Points

- With Accounting 2007, you can receive payments made by check, cash, or credit card.
- You can't delete a payment after you have received it—you can only void the payment.
- Managing refunds is vital to maintaining good customer relations. Learn how to handle refunds smoothly!
- If you have Accounting Professional 2007, you can accommodate customers that need their transactions denominated in foreign currencies.

Chapter at a Glance

Create a vendor record,
page 260

Receive purchased items,
page 271

Pay vendor bills,
page 274

13 Purchasing from Vendors

In this chapter, you will learn to:

- ✔ Create a vendor record.
- ✔ View the vendor list.
- ✔ Create a purchase order.
- ✔ Receive purchased items.
- ✔ Pay vendor bills.
- ✔ Prepare 1099 forms for vendors.

Vendors are the companies and individuals from whom you purchase goods and services. Legal advice, office supplies, contract labor, and inventory items are all examples of the kinds of services and materials you buy from vendors. Transactions with vendors affect the balances of the Accounts Payable account, your inventory account (if your business holds inventory), and expense accounts.

In Microsoft Office Accounting Professional 2007, you often initiate a transaction with a vendor by creating a purchase order that specifies the items you are purchasing and the prices, discounts (if any), and payment terms that apply. As part of managing vendor transactions, you can enter a transaction that records your receipt of the goods and services you have purchased, and you can also set up vendor bills to pay when you receive related invoices.

In certain cases, you need to report the amounts you pay to a vendor for tax purposes. Many of these cases affect only specific types of businesses. For example, you need to report royalty payments as well as proceeds from the operation of a fishing boat. However, the compensation you pay to an individual who is not an employee—a graphic designer, a freelance marketer, or a carpenter, for example—also falls into this category, and many businesses have expenses such as these.

In this chapter, you'll first learn how to set up vendor records and work with the vendor list. You'll then learn how to create and manage purchase orders, item receipts, and vendor bills, and how to compile the information you will need to prepare tax forms for vendors.

> **Troubleshooting** Graphics and operating system–related instructions in this book reflect the Windows Vista user interface. If your computer is running Windows XP and you experience trouble following the instructions as written, please refer to the "Information for Readers Running Windows XP" section at the beginning of this book.

Creating a Vendor Record

A vendor record contains contact information and details about the vendor's account. For example, in a vendor record you can specify the method the vendor uses most often to ship goods to you, the payment terms you have set up with the vendor, and the discount you typically receive on goods you purchase. In addition to the General tab on which you enter contact information, and the Details tab on which you enter account details, the vendor record form includes Financial Summary and Financial History tabs. As you enter and process purchase orders and vendor bills, these tabs provide an overview of the status of the vendor's account. You can also use the entries on these tabs for quick access to vendor transactions.

From the Vendors home page, you can manage vendor information, initiate purchase orders, receive items into inventory, and enter and pay vendor bills. The Vendors home page also includes a Spotlight section that provides links to Web sites and online resources with information related to managing a small business.

When you want to purchase an item from a new vendor, you need to add that vendor's information to the vendor list. To add a vendor to your company file, click Vendors in the Navigation Pane to display the Vendors home page. Then, in the More Tasks section of the home page, click New Vendor. A blank Vendor form opens.

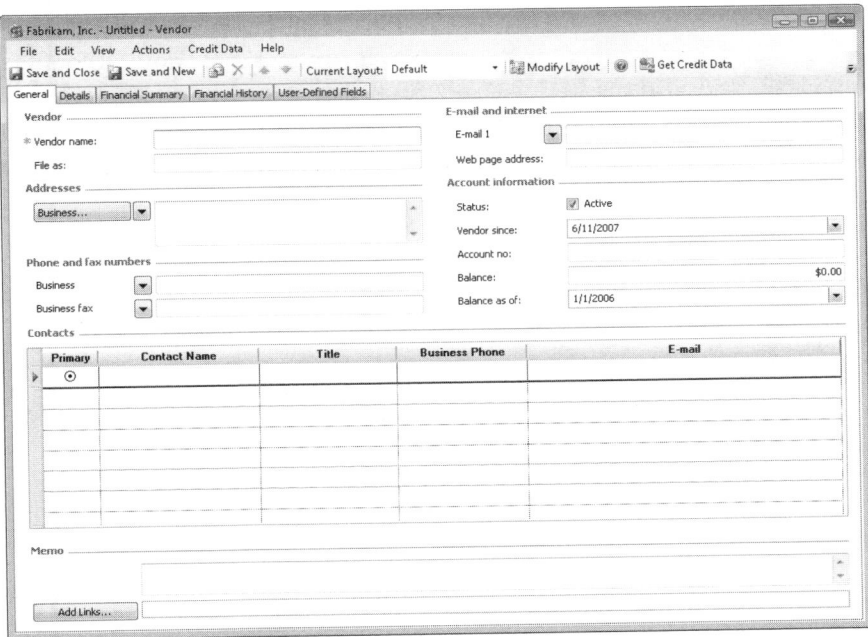

The Vendor form includes five tabs. When you first create a vendor record, you work mainly with the fields on the General and the Details tabs. From the User-Defined Fields tab, you can define your own fields in which to store vendor information. You can create text, date, number, and check box fields. The fields you create are not unique to a specific vendor—they appear on every vendor record.

Most of the form fields are self-evident, but the fields in the Addresses, Phone And Fax Numbers, and E-mail And Internet sections require some explanation because you can add more than one street address, phone number, fax number, and e-mail address to each vendor's record. When you click the arrow to the left of the phone number box in the Phone And Fax Numbers section of the form, for example, Accounting displays a list that contains the items Business, Mobile, Home, Assistant, and Other. If you click Mobile, the Business label changes to Mobile, the saved Business number (if any) disappears, and you get a blank space into which you can type the vendor point-of-contact's mobile phone number.

If the vendor you're recording has an opening balance, such as a credit for signing up or an outstanding charge not transferred over from your previous accounting package, you type that value in the Balance field. After you save a vendor record in which you've entered an opening balance, the Balance field is no longer displayed on the vendor record form. The balance information appears in the Total Balance area of the Financial Summary tab.

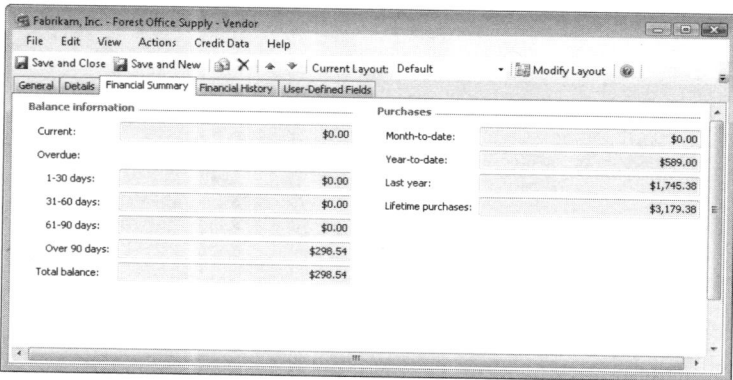

You can organize the vendors you work with into groups. Vendor groups let you review vendor transactions in more detail, which helps you analyze your business more effectively. You can create a group for "Preferred" vendors, for example, and add to this group those vendors from whom you receive volume discounts. To create a vendor group, point to Manage Support Lists on the Company menu, and then click Vendor Group List. You can then use the controls in the Modify Vendor Group dialog box to add, edit, or remove vendor groups.

In this exercise, you'll create a record for a vendor, set up a vendor group, and specify account details for a vendor.

BE SURE TO start Accounting 2007 before beginning this exercise.

OPEN the Fabrikam sample company file.

1. In the **Navigation Pane**, click **Vendors**.

   The Vendors home page appears.

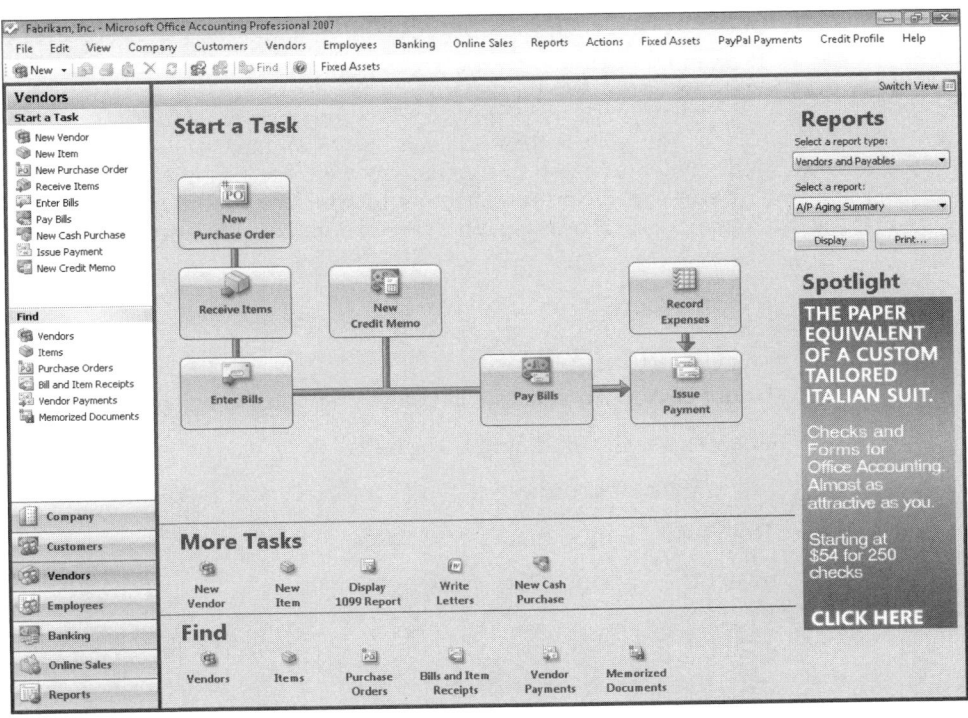

2. On the **Vendors** home page, under **More Tasks**, click **New Vendor**.

   A blank Vendor form opens.

   See Also For detailed information about creating custom fields, see "Creating Customer Records" in Chapter 6, "Managing Customers."

3. In the **Vendor name** box, type David Jaffe.

4. Under **Addresses**, click **Business**.

5. In the **Address** box, type 345 Elm St. in the **Street** box, Aberdeen in the **City** box, WA in the **State/Province** box, and 22841 in the **Zip/Postal code** box.

6. Under **Phone and Fax Numbers**, in the **Business** field, type (425) 555-0134.

   > **Tip** You can enter the phone number by typing only the numbers 4255550134; Accounting will apply the phone number format to your entry.

7. Under **Account Information**, with the **Active** check box selected, type 3/14/2007 in the **Vendor since** box.

   By default, the vendor list displays only active vendors.

8. Under **Contacts**, in the **Contact Name** field, type David Jaffe, and press the ⌨Tab key. Then in the **Title** field, type Sole Proprietor.

> **Tip** You can use the Add Links button on the General tab to assemble links to documents related to a vendor account. For example, you can create a link to a credit application you filled out to establish an account with a vendor, or a link to a proposal or budget that the vendor has submitted to you.

9. Click the **Details** tab.

10. Under **Terms**, in the **Credit limit** field, type 10000.

11. Under **Grouping and tax**, in the **Vendor group** list, click **Add a new Vendor Group**.

   The Vendor Group dialog box opens.

12. In the **Vendor group** field, type Preferred, and then click **OK**.

   The Vendor Group dialog box closes.

13. Select the **Vendor 1099** check box.

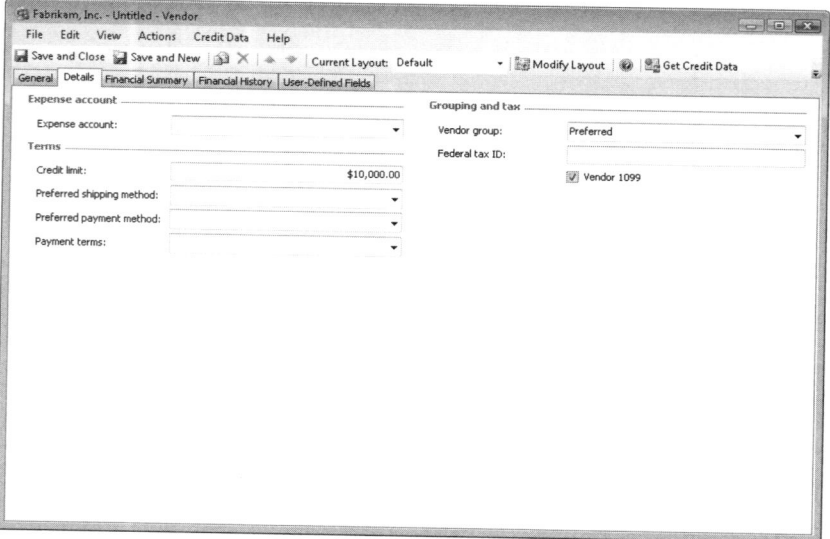

 14. On the **Vendor** form toolbar, click the **Save and Close** button.

> **See Also** For more information about 1099 tax forms, see "Preparing 1099 Forms for Vendors," later in this chapter. For information about the categories of vendor payments that affect 1099 tax reporting, point to Manage Support Lists on the Company menu, and then click 1099 Category List.

The Vendor form closes.

Tip You can delete a vendor record if you have not recorded any transactions for that vendor and the vendor has no financial history in Accounting. If you have recorded transactions for a vendor, you can mark the vendor record inactive, but you cannot delete the record. A vendor record that is marked inactive is not displayed in vendor lists in dialog boxes or forms. To delete a vendor record from the vendor list, select the record, and then click Delete on the toolbar. To make a vendor record inactive, select the record in the vendor list, and then click Make Inactive on the Edit menu. You can change an inactive vendor's status back to active by selecting the vendor record in the vendor list, and then clicking Make Active on the Edit menu.

Viewing the Vendor List

The Vendor List provides a summary of contact information and shows the balance you owe to vendors. You can sort and filter the list to view a group of vendors or to see the record of a specific vendor. To display the Vendor List, click Vendors in the Navigation Pane to display the Vendors home page. Then, in the Find section of the home page, click Vendors.

See Also For more information about sorting and filtering lists, see "Viewing Quotes" in Chapter 8, "Generating and Managing Quotes."

Creating a Purchase Order (Professional Only)

You can use a purchase order to initiate and document a vendor transaction in which you buy inventory items or services that you need to run your business. You can send a purchase order to a vendor or simply use a purchase order as part of your company's internal accounting controls so that you can keep track of what and how much you have ordered.

A purchase order often serves as an authorization to place an order. For example, in addition to listing the items you are ordering and the price for each item, a purchase order specifies details such as payment terms, shipping terms, shipping methods, and delivery date.

To create a new purchase order, click Vendors in the Navigation Pane to display the Vendors home page. Then, in the Start A Task section of the home page, click New Purchase Order. A new Purchase Order form opens.

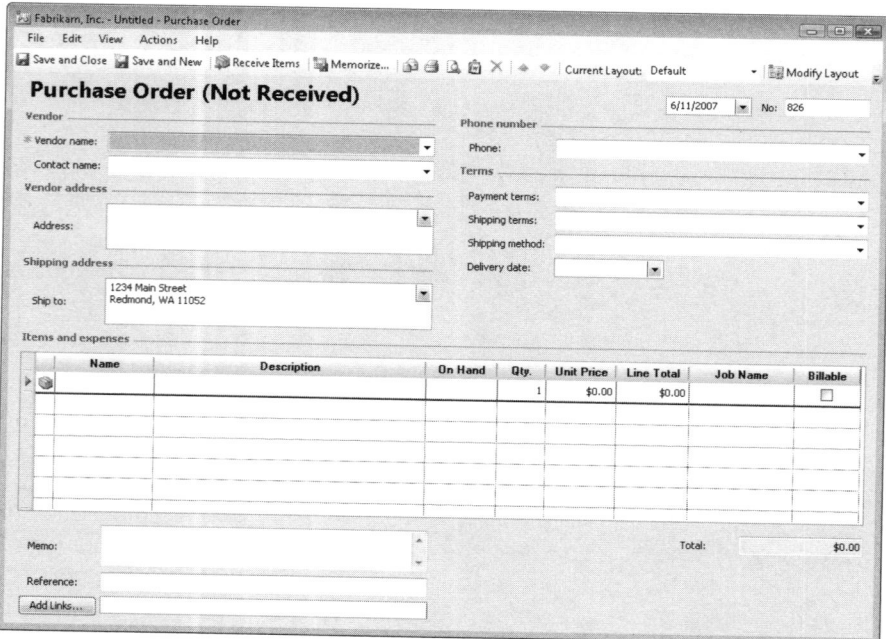

When you first create a purchase order, the status of the order is Not Received. Accounting Professional 2007 fills in the current date and assigns a number to the purchase order. The program also fills in the Ship To address. You can modify the date and the purchase order number if you need to. For example, you can change the number to conform to a purchase order numbering system that you have set up for your company or that matches the numbering system for a vendor.

On the top portion of the purchase order form, you enter vendor contact information and specify the terms of the purchase order: when payment is due, whether you or the vendor pays for shipping, how the order should be shipped, and when the order is due.

In the Items And Expenses area of the form, you create the list of items the purchase order covers. Each line item shows the name and a description of the item, the quantity, unit price, and the line total. To add an item to a purchase order, click in a blank row's Name field, click the arrow that appears, and then click the item you want to add to the purchase order. You can also create a new item by clicking Add A New Item, the first entry on the list that appears when you click the arrow.

If your company preferences are set up to use jobs or classes, each line item includes a field for selecting a job or class name and a field for specifying whether an item you are ordering is billable. If an item is billable, you can bill a customer for the cost of this item later when you create an invoice.

When you have completed the list of line items for a purchase order, you can use the Memo box to provide a brief annotation about the order. You can use the Reference box to indicate an internal reference for your company or to add a reference number provided by the vendor. To link to a document that is related to this purchase order, click Add Links, and then select the document in the Select File To Link To dialog box.

In this exercise, you will create a purchase order for one of the vendors set up in the Fabrikam sample company.

> **Note** This exercise illustrates a purchase order for office supplies, which are most often accounted for in an expense account. You can also create a purchase order for inventory items or for services.

> **OPEN** the Fabrikam sample company file.

1. In the **Navigation Pane**, click **Vendors**.
2. In the **Start a Task** section of the **Vendors** home page, click **New Purchase Order**. A blank Purchase Order form opens.
3. In the **Vendor name** list, click **Mountain Lumber Supply**.
4. In the **Payment terms** list, click **1% 10 Net 30**.
5. In the **Shipping method** list, click **Local Delivery**.
6. In the **Delivery date** field, enter or select tomorrow's date..

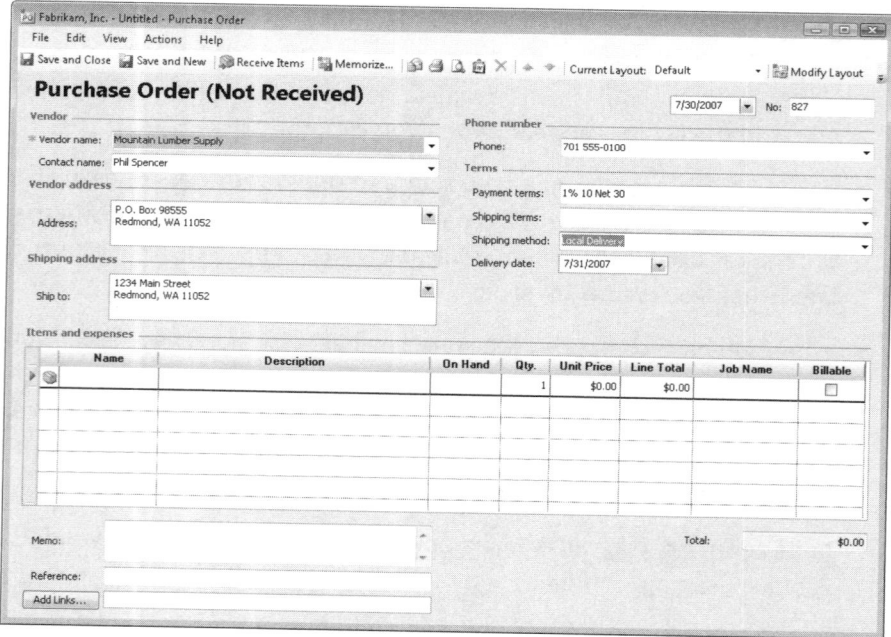

Note Shipping terms specify who will bear the cost for transporting an order. The cost of shipping is not a vital component of every purchase you place, but for orders that come from overseas or from other states or regions, whether you or the vendor is paying for shipping the goods makes a big difference. You might be responsible for paying freight charges before delivery or at the time of delivery, or the vendor will agree to pay the shipping costs. You compile the list of available shipping terms by creating a support list in Accounting. To view the list and create a new shipping term, point to Manage Support Lists on the Company menu, and then click Shipping Term List.

7. In the **Name** column, select **Framing/finish materials**.

8. In the **Description** box, replace the existing text with Cherry wood.

9. In the **Qty.** (quantity) field, type 15, and then press the ⟮Tab⟯ key.

   When you change the value in the Qty field, Accounting recalculates the dollar value of the Line Total by multiplying Unit Price by Qty.

10. Repeat steps 7 through 9 to add a line item for **Job materials (TM)** to the purchase order. In the **Qty.** field, type 20, and then press the ⟮Tab⟯ key.

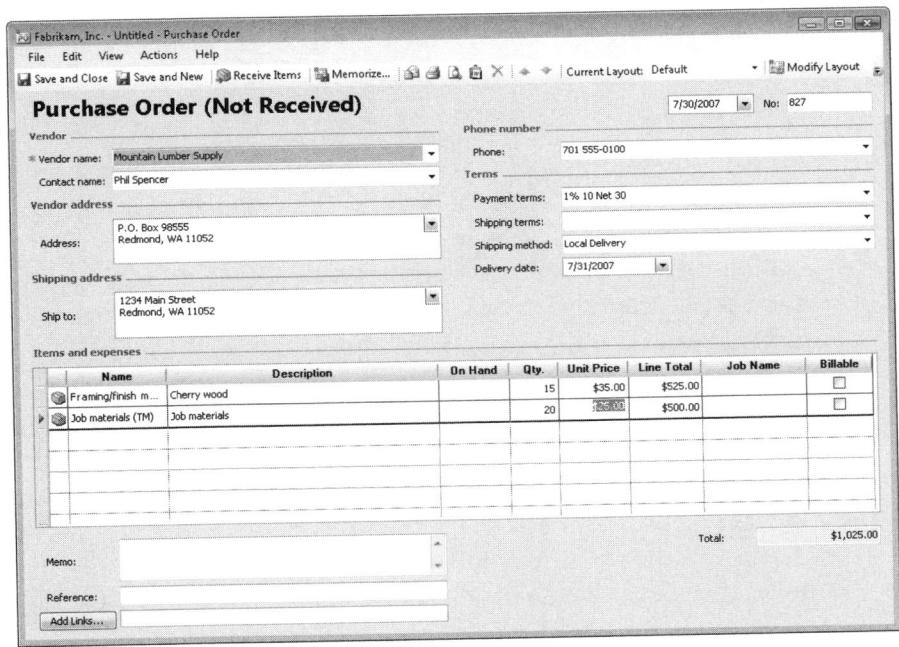

11. On the toolbar, click the **Save and Close** button.

> **Note** If a dialog box appears asking if you want to save the new payment information for future use, click No.

Accounting records the purchase order, and the Purchase Order form closes.

When to Recognize Purchases and Book the Associated Assets

Because you have to value dissimilar items (for example inventory, office furniture, and the company computer) in the same units for a financial statement (more specifically, a balance sheet) to make sense, it's easy to see why those units are best expressed in dollar values. When you convert the various assets you have into their monetary equivalents, you can do arithmetic (such as determine a total value) with them. The action of booking your assets at their money values illustrates yet another traditional accounting principle: the *money measurement* concept. (The money measurement concept actually stipulates that "only those transactions which are capable of being measured in value/monetary terms are to be considered in accounting.")

Because you want to state the values of your assets in money terms, you immediately encounter a couple of deeper considerations. These are 1) how do I value the assets, and 2) as of what date? Because you want the values to be as objective and accurate as possible, you will want to rely upon yet another traditional accounting concept, *historical cost*. Historical costing—pricing your assets at what you actually paid for them—avoids the more subjective process of assigning market value or some other value to your assets. This turns out to be a great way to value assets that are used within the business, to conduct its operations—not assets that the business intends to sell, such as inventory. When valuing an asset for sale, things get a little trickier, but the general rule is "cost adjusted to bring the asset to fair market value"—a concept that allows for adjusting valuation downward for obsolescence and other things that might impair the value of stock on hand. The idea, again, is to keep assets valued conservatively on the balance sheet.

The next question that arises is "As of what date do I value my asset?" Under accrual accounting, you recognize the purchase as of the date that ownership transfers to you, typically upon its receipt. Specific shipping terms (such as of *FOB destination*, where the title to the goods usually passes from the buyer to the seller at the destination) can help you determine exactly when title passes, and therefore when you should book the asset. With cash-basis accounting, you can simply book the asset when you pay for it.

Note You can export a purchase order to Microsoft Office Word and then print the purchase order. In the Word document, you can add your company logo or other information before you print the purchase order. To export a purchase order, display the purchase order, and then, on the Actions menu, click Export To Word. In the Select Word Templates dialog box, select the template you want to use, and then click Select.

You can also create your own template for a purchase order, just as you can for invoices, quotes, and other accounting documents. For detailed instructions for creating a template, see "Modifying Templates in Word 2007" in Chapter 17, "Interacting with Other 2007 Microsoft Office System Applications," on the CD.

Accrual Basis Accounting and the Accounts Payable Method of Bill Payment

When you use accrual basis accounting, you record expenses when they are incurred. (When you use cash basis accounting, as many smaller businesses do, you record expenses when they are paid.) Accrual-basis expense accounting means the existence of accounts payable. (There are, of course, no payables in a cash-basis balance sheet.) Your Accounting 2007 reports display, by default, either a cash-basis view or an accrual-basis view, depending on what you selected in the Preferences section of the Startup Wizard. You can change your selection on the Company tab of the Company Preferences dialog box.

Receiving Purchased Items

The status of a purchase order can help you track the orders you place. For example, you can filter the list of purchase orders to see the orders that you have received and those that are still pending.

Sometimes you receive an order from a vendor before the vendor invoices you for the items you purchased. At other times, a vendor delivers only a portion of an order. In Accounting 2007, you can create an item receipt so that items you receive can be entered into your inventory or recorded as an expense. You can view item receipts on the Bills And Item Receipts list.

You can create an item receipt from scratch or directly from a purchase order. In the item receipt, you can verify that you received the full quantity of the items ordered or update the quantity received in the event a vendor sends a partial shipment.

When you receive items, Accounting posts the item receipt to the Pending Item Receipts account and to the Inventory Asset account or the applicable expense account. When you enter the bill, the item receipt is removed from the Pending Item Receipts account and the Inventory or Expense account, and the bill is posted to Accounts Payable and the Inventory or Expense account.

> **Note** When you save an item receipt, it is posted to your company's accounts. Because an item receipt affects accounting, you cannot delete it. If you need to reissue an item receipt, you can edit it or void it.

By specifying a vendor name on the Item Receipt form before clicking Create From, you can filter the list of purchase orders in the Select A Purchase Order dialog box to show only purchase orders for the vendor you select. If you click Create From before you specify a vendor name, you will see a complete list of open purchase orders.

To help manage your receipt of a partial order, you can create more than one item receipt from a single purchase order. Accounting keeps track of the quantity ordered and the quantity received. When you create an item receipt from this purchase order again, the purchase order would reflect the undelivered items.

For accounting purposes, the expense account is credited with the amount due only for the number of items you receive, not for the entire amount covered by the purchase order.

In this exercise, you will create and post an item receipt.

> **USE** the purchase order you created in the previous exercise.
> **OPEN** the Fabrikam sample company file.

1. In the **Navigation Pane**, click **Vendors**.

2. On the **Vendors** home page, under **Start a Task**, click **Receive Items**.

   A blank Item Receipt form opens.

3. In the **Vendor name** box, click **Mountain Lumber Supply**.

The Select A Purchase Order dialog box opens.

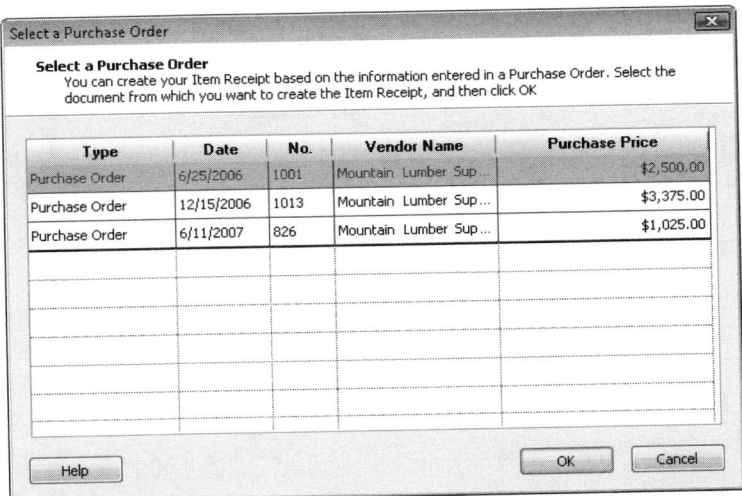

4. Click the purchase order you created in the previous exercise, and then click **OK**.

5. In the **Item Receipt** form, in the line item for framing/finish materials, change the value in the **Qty.** field from 15 to 10.

6. In the **Memo** field, type 5 units on back order.

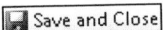

7. On the toolbar, click the **Save and Close** button.

> **Note** If a dialog box appears asking if you want to save the new payment information for future use, click No.

Accounting records the items received into inventory, and the Item Receipt form closes.

> **Note** You can see the need to keep up with your accounting paperwork in the relationship between customer invoices, inventory levels, and purchase orders. When you add a quantity of an item from your inventory to a customer invoice but don't have enough of that item in stock to fill the order, Accounting warns you of the shortage.

Commitments vs. Liabilities

Analyzing your commitments, or obligations, can provide you with useful, predictive business intelligence. While commitments may often seem the same as liabilities, there are some differences. Commitments are obligations you make to employees, outside contractors, or vendors for future expenditures. When you develop the habit of tracking your commitments, you enable your business to forecast its expenditures. This means you can plan cash flow and avoid exceeding budgets, among other desirable actions.

Sometimes you might find commitments and liabilities hard to separate. It is important to understand the difference. To help with this, you can consider a transaction, in general, as occurring in steps similar to the following example.

1. You order a case of trash bags for use within your business. In doing so, you become obligated to pay $136 to the cleaning products vendor that you use for these sorts of purchases.

2. The case of trash bags is delivered to your office.

3. You receive the invoice from the cleaning products vendor.

4. You send a $145 check ($136 plus shipping) to the cleaning products vendor for the bags you have received.

You created a commitment (or obligation) in step 1, when you ordered the bags. With step 2 you could record a liability—but probably won't until step 3. (In either case, you relieve yourself of a commitment, in that you transform it into something you really owe.) When you receive the product and record the liability, the product becomes the property of your company. Step 4, of course, extinguishes the liability, as you record the payment to the vendor.

Paying Vendor Bills

To keep track of the amounts you owe to vendors, you need to enter bills you receive into Accounting. You can enter the details of a bill from scratch by using an invoice or other paperwork the vendor provides, or you can create a bill from a purchase order or an item receipt that you created in Accounting.

The form you use to create a bill resembles the purchase order and item receipt forms you worked with in exercises earlier in this chapter. In filling out the Vendor Bill form, you identify the vendor, specify payment terms, and enter details about the items for which you're billed. When you create a bill from a purchase order or an item receipt, the information in the source document is carried forward into the bill form. You can modify information in the bill (for example, updating payment terms if you are paying the bill early and qualify for a discount) or you can simply save the bill as is and pay it when you process your monthly checks.

If the bill you are preparing relates to a job that you have set up in Accounting, you can enter a job name for the line item and then select the Billable check box. An item that you mark Billable appears in the Time And Materials dialog box. You can then add this item to a customer's invoice.

See Also For more information about preparing invoices for a job, see "Generating an Invoice from a Quote," in Chapter 11, "Managing Invoices."

The Pay From list displays cash accounts, bank accounts, and credit card accounts that are included in your chart of accounts. If you select a credit card account, the amounts of the bills you choose to pay are added to the current liability for that credit card. If you select a cash account or a bank account such as Checking, the amounts of the bills are deducted from the balance of that account when the bills are paid.

The Amount box displays a running total of the amounts of the bills you select to pay. The Balance box initially shows the balance of the account you select in the Pay From list. As you select each bill to pay, the balance of this account changes accordingly.

In this exercise, you will first enter a vendor bill from an item receipt. You will then follow the steps to select which vendor bills to pay.

> **USE** the item receipt you created in the previous exercise.
> **OPEN** the Fabrikam sample company file.

1. In the **Navigation Pane**, click **Vendors**.
2. Under **Start a Task** on the **Vendors** home page, click **Enter Bills**.

    A blank Vendor Bill form opens.

3. In the **Vendor name** box, click **Mountain Lumber Supply**.

   The Select A Purchase Order Or An Item Receipt dialog box opens.

4. In the dialog box, click the item receipt you created in the previous exercise, and then click **OK**.

   The Select A Purchase Order Or An Item Receipt dialog box closes and the vendor bill form opens.

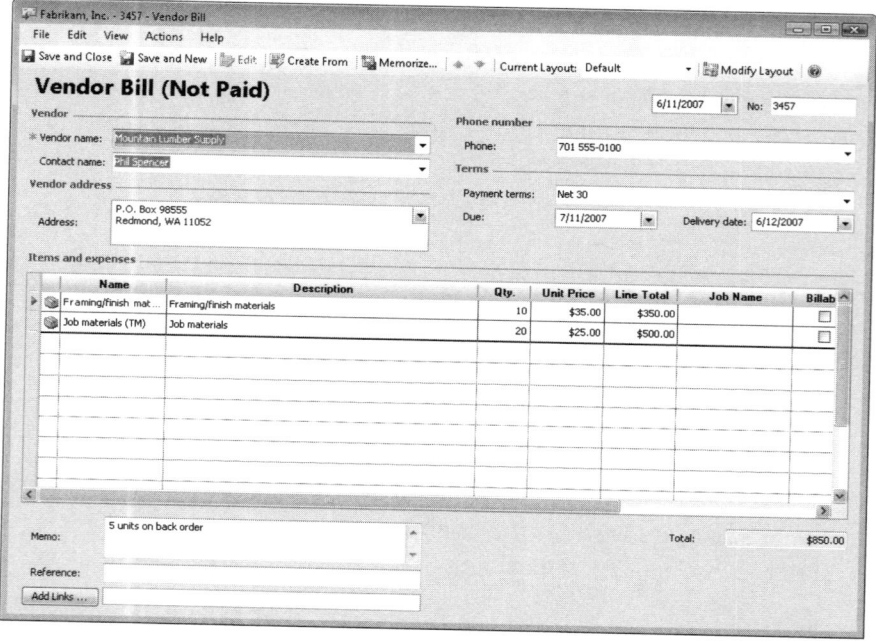

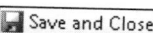 5. On the **Vendor Bill** form toolbar, click the **Save and Close** button.

   The Vendor Bill form closes.

6. On the **Vendors** home page, under **Start a Task**, click **Pay Bills**.

   The Pay Bills form opens.

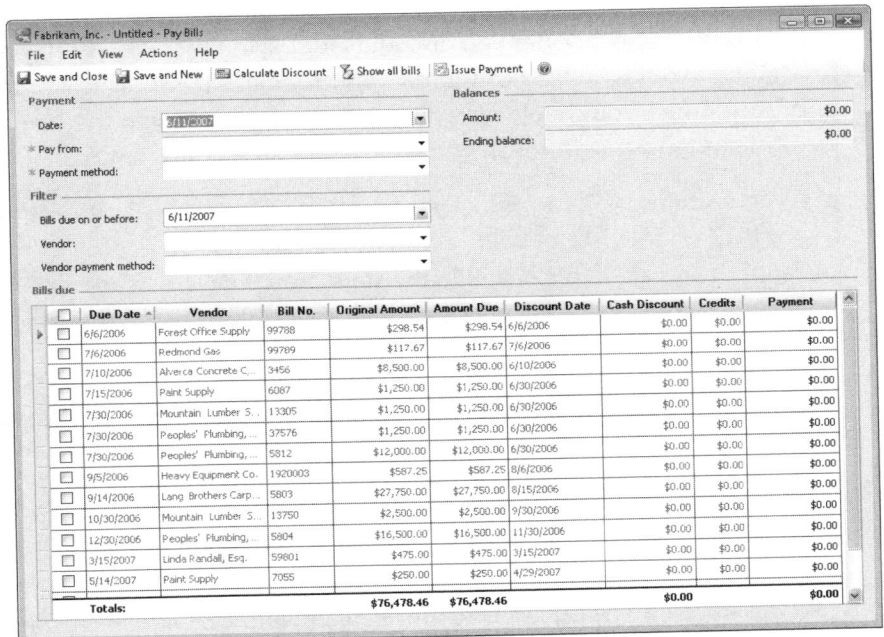

7. In the **Date** field, specify the date on which you are paying this batch of bills (if the date is not the current date).

8. In the **Pay from** list, click **Checking**.

9. In the **Payment method** list, click **Check**.

10. Under **Bills due**, in the **Pay** column, select the check box for each bill you want to pay.

11. Click the **Save and Close** button.

    The Pay Bills form closes.

Taking Advantage of Payment Terms Can Mean a Significant Rate of Return

Your vendors might offer you discounts for paying with cash or paying early. Although your cash flow considerations may make it impractical to take advantage of such offers, you should always consider doing so. Failing to accept beneficial payment terms might mean you are passing up a significant rate of return.

As an example, let's say one of your vendors offers you a 3 percent discount if you pay cash on the date of your purchase. (The normal terms of sale are "within 30 days.") If you elect to pay within the standard 30 days instead of paying cash up front, you effectively pay a 3 percent monthly interest charge—which works out to an annual interest rate of 36 percent!

You'll want to examine each offer closely, and to consider possible cash-flow consequences, but in many cases you will find that passing up payment discounts simply doesn't make business sense. A good way to analyze each situation is to apply the following formula:

D%/(1-D%)x(365/DEP)

In this formula, D% equals Discount Percent, and DEP equals the number of days you paid early. The result of the calculation is the effective interest rate you can obtain by accepting the terms under consideration.

Preparing 1099 Forms for Vendors

The 1099-MISC tax form is used to report certain kinds of income for United States federal income taxes. In some cases, a business needs to prepare this form to report the amounts it has paid to a vendor. The 1099 form records the amounts you paid to the vendor during the previous tax year and the category to which the payments apply.

Most of the information you need to prepare 1099 forms comes from transactions that are recorded in one or another of your expense accounts. When you set up an expense account, you can indicate which 1099 category the account is related to. For example, in an expense account for legal fees, you can specify the 1099 category for amounts paid to an attorney.

Accounting 2007 includes two reports that you can use to help you prepare 1099-MISC tax forms for vendors. The 1099 Summary report shows you the total amount you have paid in each 1099 category. You can double-click a category listed in the 1099 Summary report to reveal detailed vendor records for each category. You can also run the 1099 Detail report directly.

> **Tip** Remember that you don't need to prepare 1099 forms for all the vendors you work with; only those meeting the 1099 criteria. Accounting prepares forms only for the vendors for which you select the 1099 Vendor check box on the vendor record form.

The 1099 Detail report is grouped by tax category. You can use the report as the basis for preparing the 1099-MISC forms for a particular tax year. Each vendor is listed along with detailed information about the amounts the vendor was paid. Only vendors for which you have checked the 1099 Vendor option on the vendor record appear on this report.

You can filter the report by date range and by vendor name. By default, Date Range is set to show all 1099-related transactions. Other entries you can select from the Date Range list to filter the report include This Month, This Fiscal Quarter, and This Fiscal Year. You can also specify a custom time period by choosing dates in the From and To lists.

> **Tip** After you filter the report to show the records for a specific vendor, you can print the report to use as a source for preparing the 1099-MISC tax form itself. To print the report, click Print on the File menu. You can also use commands on the File menu to export the report to Microsoft Office Excel or to save a filtered version of the report.

In this exercise, you will view and filter the 1099 Detail report that you can use to prepare tax forms for vendors.

> **OPEN** the Fabrikam sample company file.

1. In the **Navigation Pane**, click **Vendors**.

2. On the **Vendors** home page, under **More Tasks**, click **Display 1099 Report**.

   The 1099 Detail report appears.

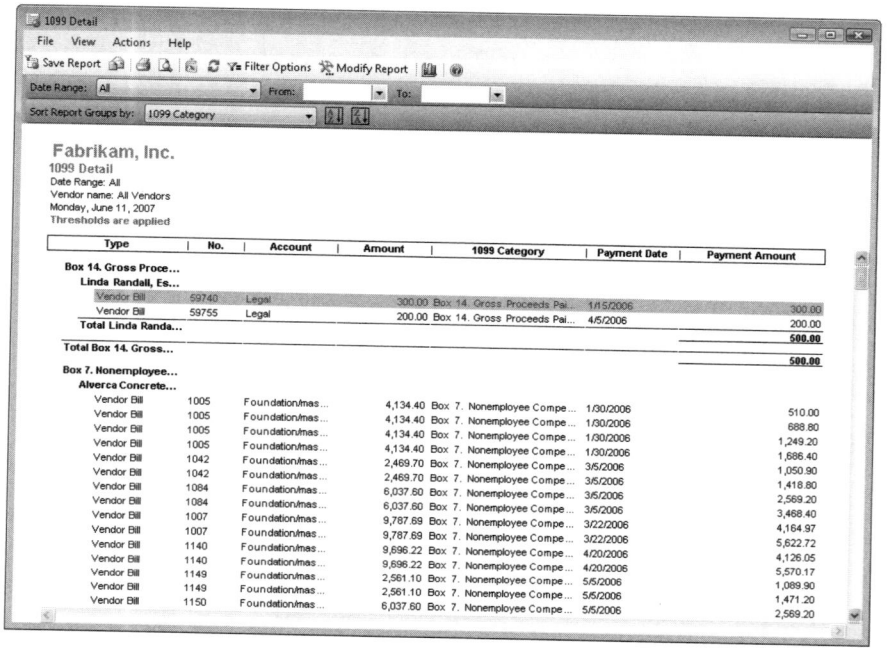

3. On the toolbar, click the **Filter Options** button.

The Select Filter Options dialog box opens.

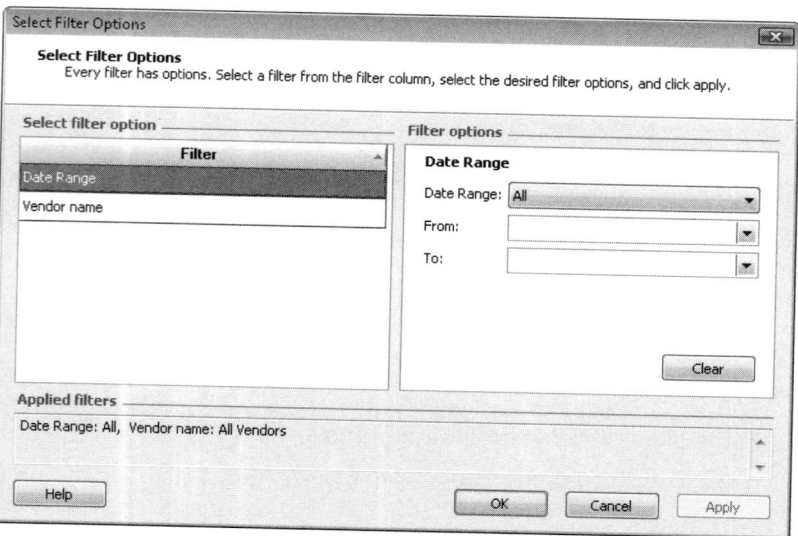

4. Under **Select filter option**, click **Vendor name**.

5. Under **Filter options**, in the **Vendor name** list, click **Selected Names**.

6. Click the **Show Selected** button.

The Select Names dialog box opens.

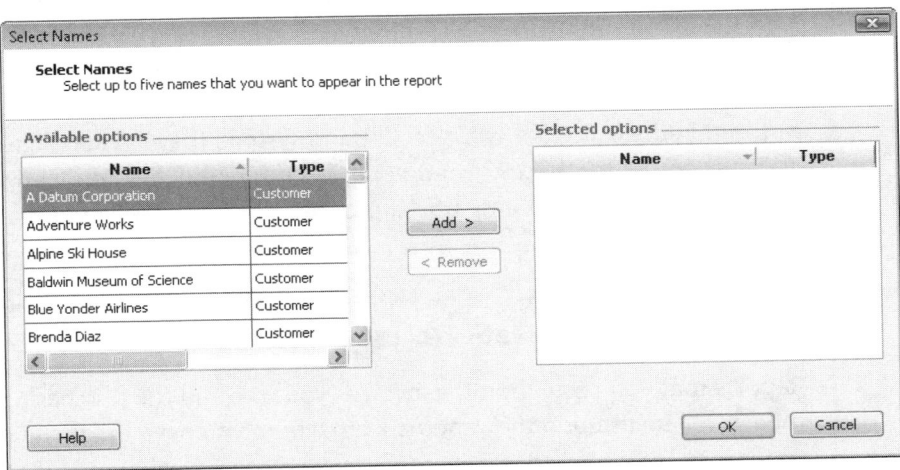

7. Scroll the **Available options** list to display the vendors.

8. Click **Linda Randall, Esq.**, and then click **Add**.

9. Click **OK** in the **Select Names** dialog box, and then click **OK** in the **Select Filter Options** dialog box.

The 1099 Detail report reflects Linda Randall's information.

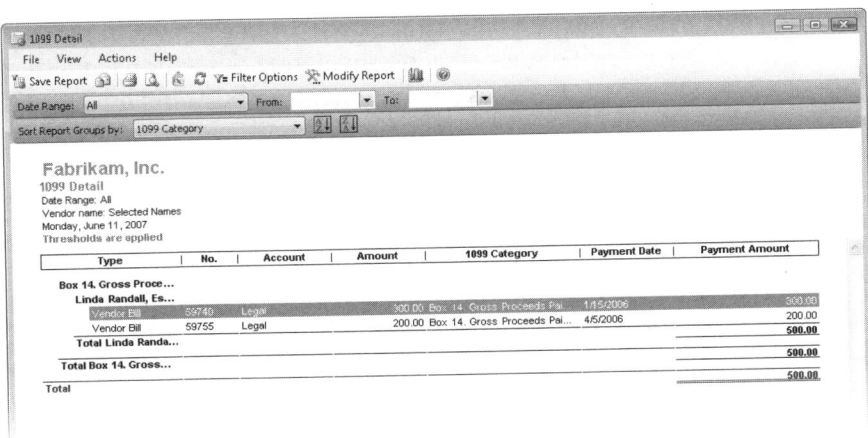

CLOSE the Fabrikam sample company file. If you are not continuing directly to the next chapter, exit Accounting 2007.

Vendor 1099 Considerations

Your corporation must issue an IRS Form 1099 to any unincorporated contractor to whom you paid over $600 in the prior fiscal year. (You also file an IRS Form 1096 with the IRS to summarize the 1099s you issue, to allow the IRS to cross reference the 1099 amounts to the contractor's individual returns.) Independent contractors are also sometimes referred to as consultants, freelancers and other such terms, but, within the context of your accounting system, they are simply treated as a special class of vendor, a "1099 vendor." The Vendor 1099 field on the Detail tab of the Vendor form is used for easy tracking of payments to 1099 vendors.

Reporting Considerations: Purchasing and Vendors

Reports that you base upon the invoices you pay, and the purchasing activity they reflect, will focus upon the vendors from whom you have made the purchases, the terms they have offered, purchase and invoice dates, your payment dates, and the like. Receipt dates and purchase details are particularly important in helping you to properly book the assets you have purchased. Typical "views" by which such information is arranged include vendors, products or services purchased, timing of purchases and receipts, payment due dates, and associated details. Purchasing details drive payment and cash flow reports, accounts payable reports (general listings and, possibly, agings), and underlying detail reports.

To some extent, you will find it important, from a reporting perspective, to intersect vendor invoice details with information about your payments. For instance, the way the vendor matches your payments to outstanding invoices will determine the agings of your remaining unpaid balances, which might impact finance charges that you are asked to pay. In addition, you can review the timing of your payments in contrast to the payment terms offered by your vendors to ensure that you are actually realizing what might be attractive discounts. Among many other uses, year-end reports about your purchasing activities and vendors will help you to ensure that assets are properly classified, that the profits on inventory you have sold are accurately reported (and on-hand inventory is properly valued) and the information you report for your 1099 vendors is accurate and complete.

Key Points

- Vendors are the companies and individuals from whom you order supplies and inventory.
- Vendor transactions are documented through purchase orders, item receipts, and vendor bills.
- You don't need to create a purchase order for every vendor transaction. You can initiate a vendor transaction by entering a bill or by creating an item receipt.
- For some vendors, you need to prepare a 1099-MISC tax form to report the amounts you have paid them during the tax year.

Chapter at a Glance

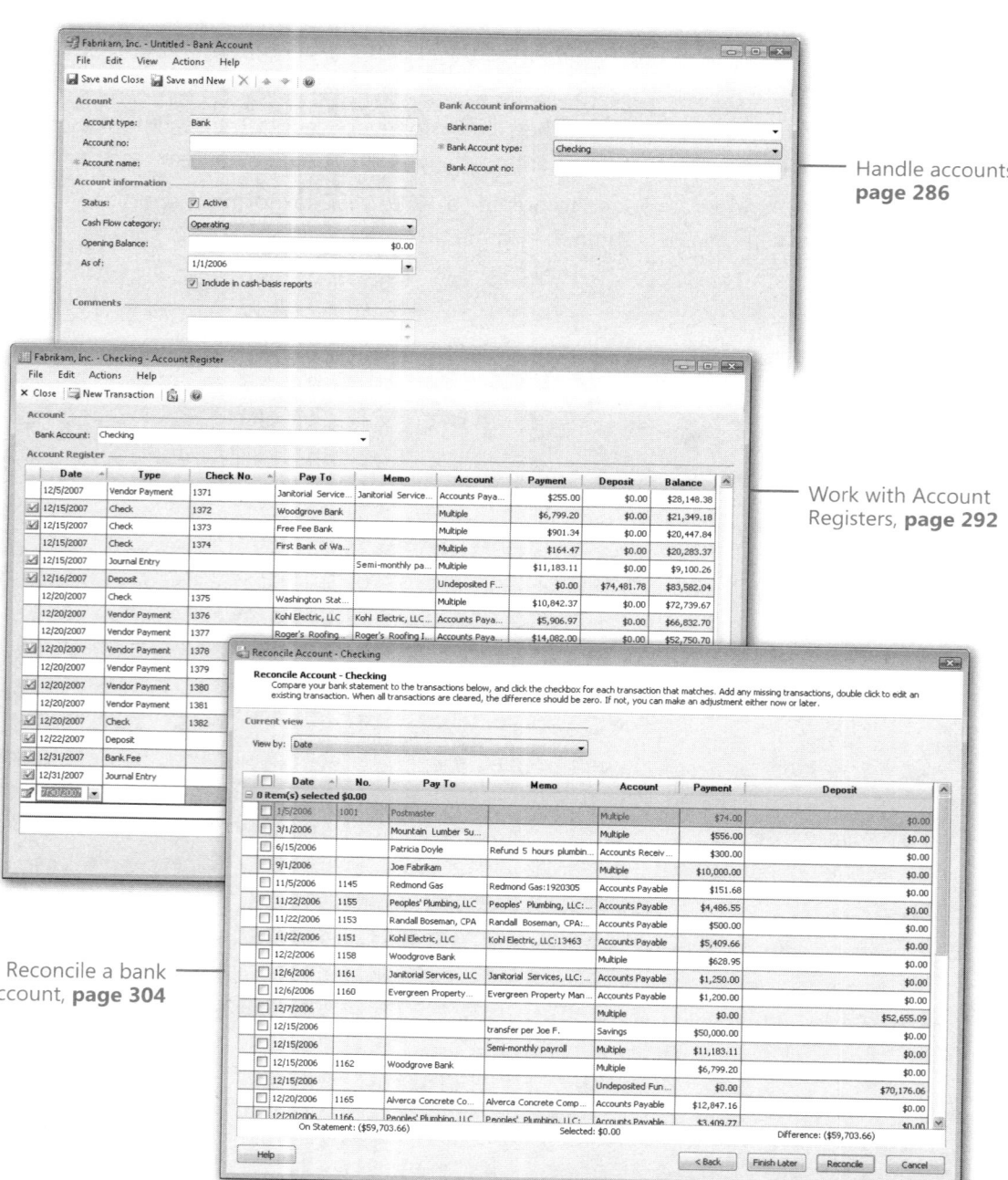

Handle accounts, **page 286**

Work with Account Registers, **page 292**

Reconcile a bank account, **page 304**

14 Managing Bank Accounts and Transactions

In this chapter, you will learn to:

- ✔ Handle accounts.
- ✔ Work with Account Registers.
- ✔ Enter transactions.
- ✔ Reconcile a bank account.
- ✔ Bank online.
- ✔ Accept credit card payments through ADP.

Writing checks to pay this month's bills, depositing checks that you receive from customers, transferring funds between accounts, and recording charges you make to the company credit card are all banking transactions. Keeping accurate records of your banking transactions in Microsoft Office Accounting 2007 is an important part of managing the inflow and outflow of your company's funds.

You can view the activity for each of your bank accounts in an Account Register, where you can also add and edit transactions. You can initiate banking tasks such as writing and printing checks, making deposits, transferring funds, and recording credit card charges, all from the Banking home page.

With Accounting 2007, you can also bank online, provided that you have an Internet connection, and the financial institution where you bank offers online banking. After you set up your accounts for online banking, you can download transactions from your online accounts and match your bank's records with the records you keep in Accounting.

Whether or not you bank online, you need to reconcile your bank accounts. By ensuring that your accounting records are accurate and complete, you gain a clear view of your company's financial position each month, each quarter, and at the end of the fiscal year.

In this chapter, you will learn how to manage banking transactions in Accounting. In addition to learning the steps for essential banking operations such as writing checks, making deposits, and reconciling accounts, you will learn how to set up your accounts to bank online.

> **Troubleshooting** Graphics and operating system–related instructions in this book reflect the Windows Vista user interface. If your computer is running Windows XP and you experience trouble following the instructions as written, please refer to the "Information for Readers Running Windows XP" section at the beginning of this book.

Handling Accounts

In Accounting 2007, you manage your bank accounts and banking operations from the Banking home page, which you can display by clicking the Banking button in the Navigation Pane.

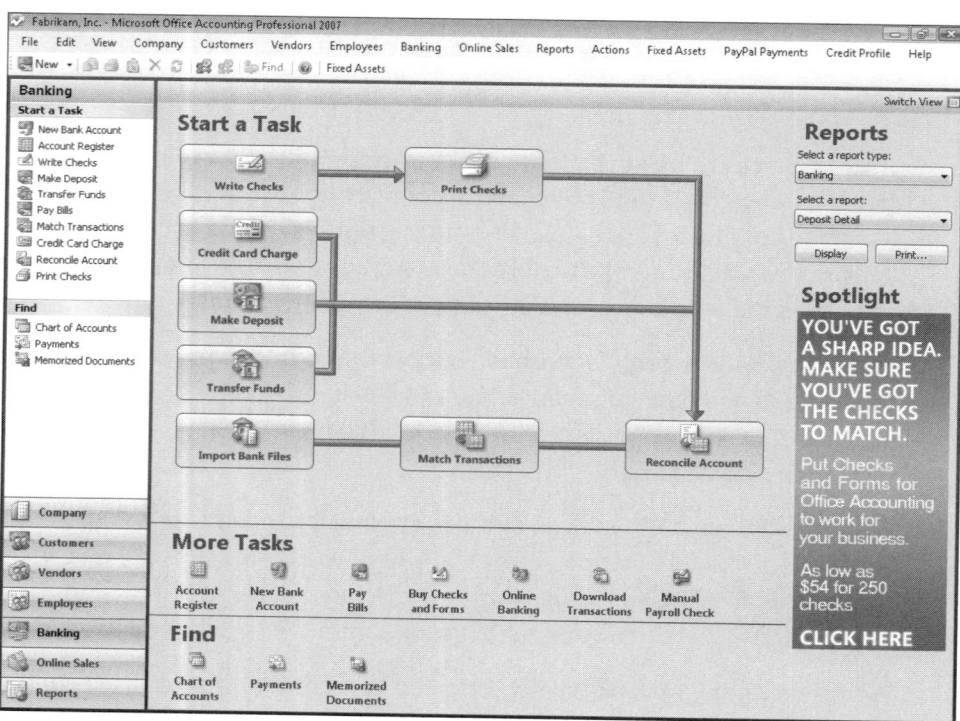

The Banking home page contains entries for standard tasks such as writing and print-ing checks, recording credit card charges, entering deposits, transferring funds between accounts, and paying bills, but you don't have to use the Banking home page to initiate those tasks. If you prefer, you can also start those processes from the Banking menu.

Adding a Bank Account

After you open an account with a bank, you need to enter that account's information into Accounting so that you can record any transactions relating to that account. To create a new bank account in Accounting, display the Banking home page and then, in the More Tasks section, click New Bank Account. A blank Bank Account form opens.

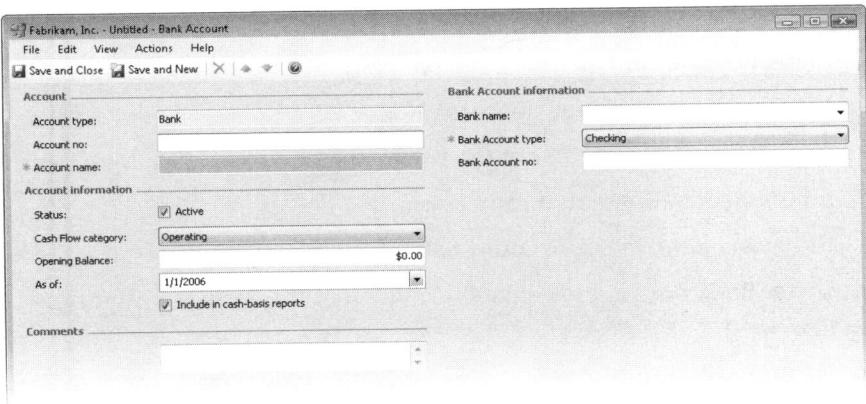

> **Note** If you activated support for foreign currencies by clicking Company Preferences on the Company menu, and then selecting the Use Foreign Currencies check box on the Company tab, the Bank Account form will also contain a Currency list box from which you can select the account's native currency.

Most of the form fields are self-evident. You can find the values for the Bank Account No, Bank Name, and Bank Account Type in the literature the bank provided when you set up the account. In most cases, you should set the Cash Flow Category value to Operating, which indicates that you use the account to manage funds received as customer pay-ments and paid out to cover your company's operating expenses.

> **Note** The other two Cash Flow Category types, Investing and Financing, denote accounts used for other types of transactions. Check with your accountant to determine which category best suits how you plan to use the funds in the account.

When you create the account in Accounting, be sure to enter into the Opening Balance box the amount of the opening deposit you made when you established the account with the bank. You should also enter the day you opened the account in the As Of box.

If you close or stop using a bank account, you should clear the Active check box on the Bank Account form to ensure that you don't accidentally credit additional transactions to the account.

In this exercise, you will add a new bank account to the Fabrikam sample database.

BE SURE TO start Accounting 2007 before beginning this exercise.
OPEN the Fabrikam sample company file.

1. In the **Navigation Pane**, click the **Banking** button.

   The Banking home page appears.

2. In the **More Tasks** section of the **Banking** home page, click **New Bank Account**.

   An untitled Bank Account form opens.

3. Under **Account**, in the **Account name** field, type Main Operating Account.

4. Under **Bank Account** information, verify that the **Bank Account type** box contains **Checking**.

5. Under **Account information**, verify that the **Active** check box is selected.

6. In the **Opening Balance** box, type 500.

7. In the **As of** box, type a date within your current fiscal year.

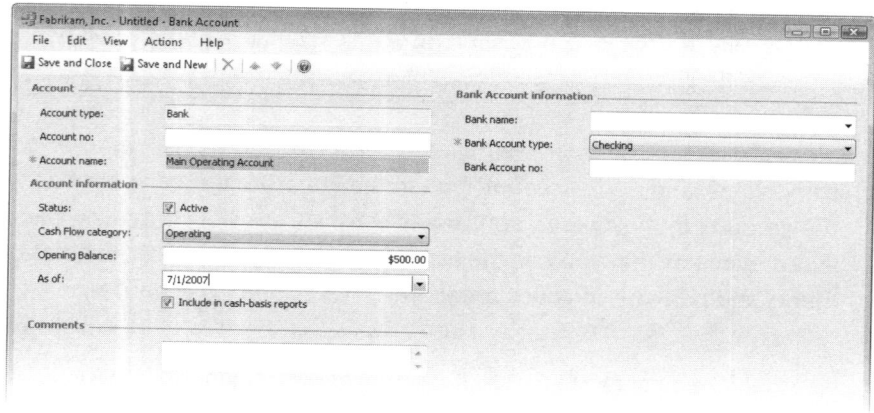

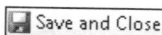 8. On the Bank Account form toolbar, click the **Save and Close** button.

   Accounting saves your new bank account's information.

Viewing and Recording Journal Entries

You will be able to enter most of your company's transactions by using the techniques found later in this chapter, but some of your transactions, such as recording asset depreciation, sales of assets, or entry adjustments require that you or your accountant enter the charge by using the Journal Entries List.

To view the Journal Entries List, point to Company Lists on the Company menu, and then click Journal Entries.

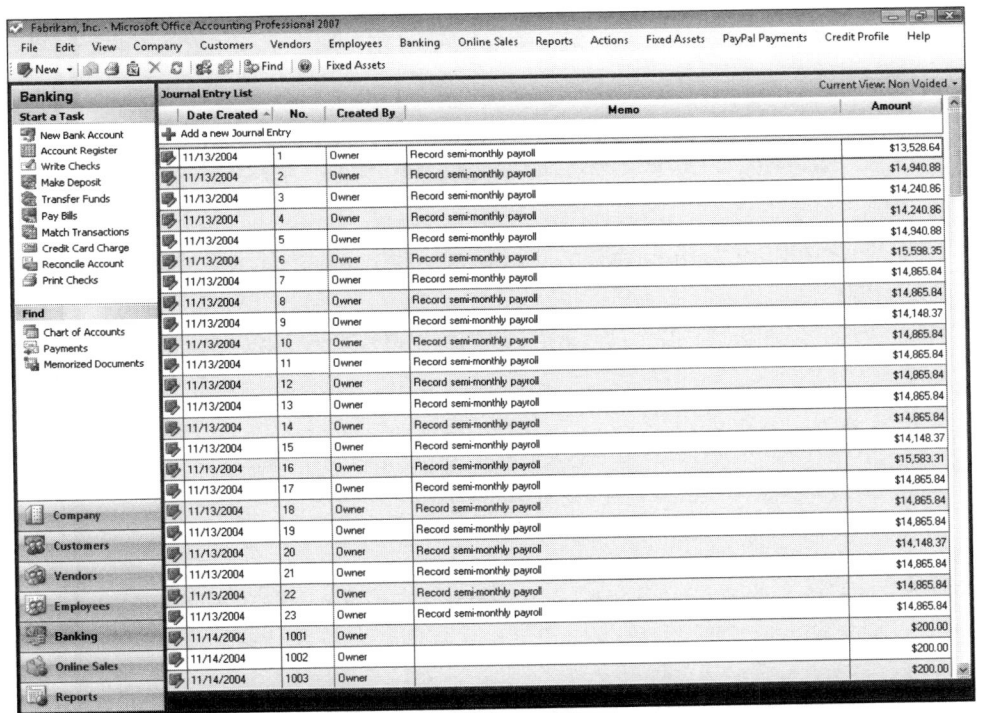

See Also You can sort and filter the Journal Entry List like any other list. For more information on sorting, filtering, and searching in a list, see "Viewing the Item List" in Chapter 5, "Managing Products and Services."

If you want to create a new journal entry, open the Company menu and click either New Journal Entry to record a non-cash transaction or New Cash-Basis Journal Entry to record cash income that's not tied to an existing invoice, bill, check, or other recorded transaction. After you make your selection, the Journal Entry form or the Cash-Basis Journal Entry form opens.

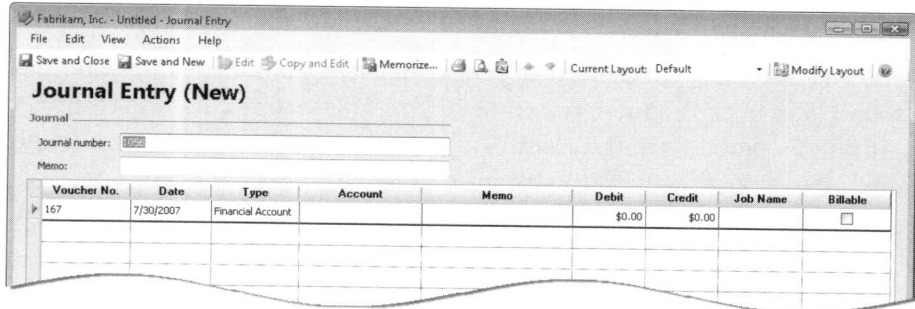

Each journal entry must have a balancing transaction below it. In other words, if money goes out of one account, it must go into another account.

Handling Cash Transactions and Petty Cash Accounting

To record and manage petty cash expenditures, you'll want to set up a petty cash account in Accounting 2007. A petty cash account simply represents an amount of cash that you keep on hand for making small payments. It's an asset account that, as you might expect, has a normal debit balance. Setting up a petty cash account is easy—you simply create an account similar to a bank account, and manually post transactions as they occur.

When you set up the petty cash account, you create an entry to record the transfer of the cash into it. Say you write a check to "cash" from the primary operating bank account: you debit petty cash and credit the operating bank account. When you have expenditures from the petty cash fund, you record them just as you would checks drawn against a bank account—just without the check numbers. (You can use any numbering system that makes sense, if you like.)

When the petty cash account needs to be replenished, you simply create an entry like before—almost as if you are writing a check to the petty cash account. For example, you debit petty cash and credit the bank account the check is drawn upon. The petty cash account itself keeps track of the accounts involved in pay-outs of petty cash, recording debits to those expenses as incurred. Although you will, of course, want to take precautions to safeguard your cash, tracking petty cash in Accounting 2007 is much easier than maintaining a physical petty cash system with slips that you fill out each time a payment is made, which you later record as expenditures to the appropriate expense accounts on a periodic basis.

In this exercise, you will create a cash-basis journal entry to reflect a customer's cash payment for additional work done on their job site.

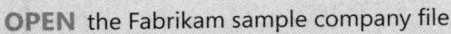 **OPEN** the Fabrikam sample company file.

1. On the **Company** menu, click **New Cash-Basis Journal Entry**.

   A blank Cash-Basis Journal Entry form opens.

2. In the **Memo** box of the **Cash-Basis Journal Entry** form, type On-site payment for pick-up job.

3. In the first grid row, click the cell in the **Account** column, click the arrow that appears, and then click **4100 Cash Income Electrical Services**.

4. In the **Credit** column cell of the first grid row, type 150.

5. In the second grid row, click the cell in the **Account** column.

   Accounting creates a new row and puts the value $150.00 in the row's Debit column, which balances the previous row's $150.00 credit.

6. In the second row, click the cell in the **Account** column, click the arrow that appears, and then click **1005 Undeposited Funds**.

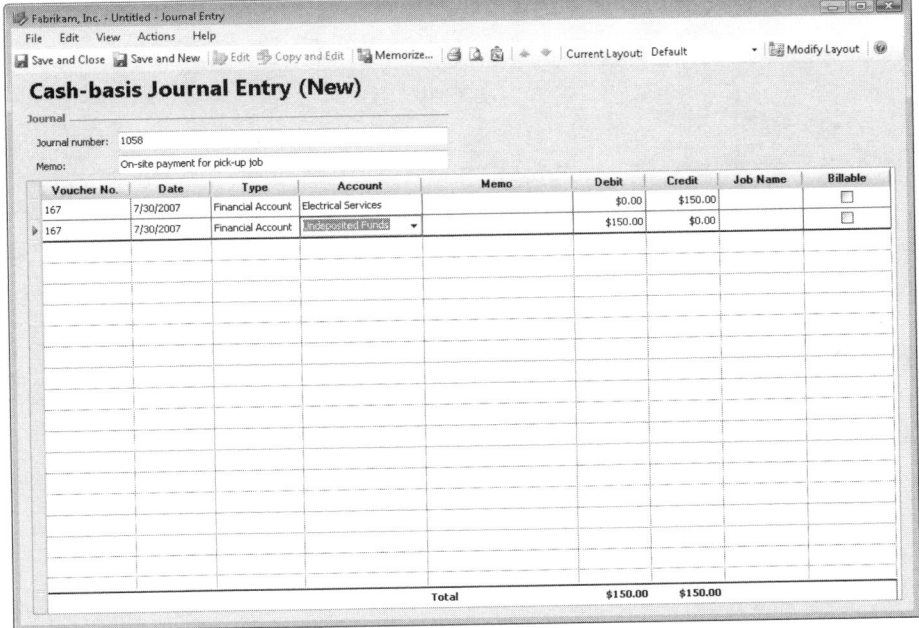

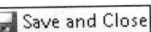 7. On the form toolbar, click the **Save and Close** button.

   Accounting saves your journal entry and closes the Cash-Basis Journal Entry form.

Working with Account Registers

Accounting 2007 maintains an Account Register for each bank account that you define in your chart of accounts. The Account Register displays information such as the date of each transaction, who you paid money to or received money from, the amount of each transaction, and the account balance.

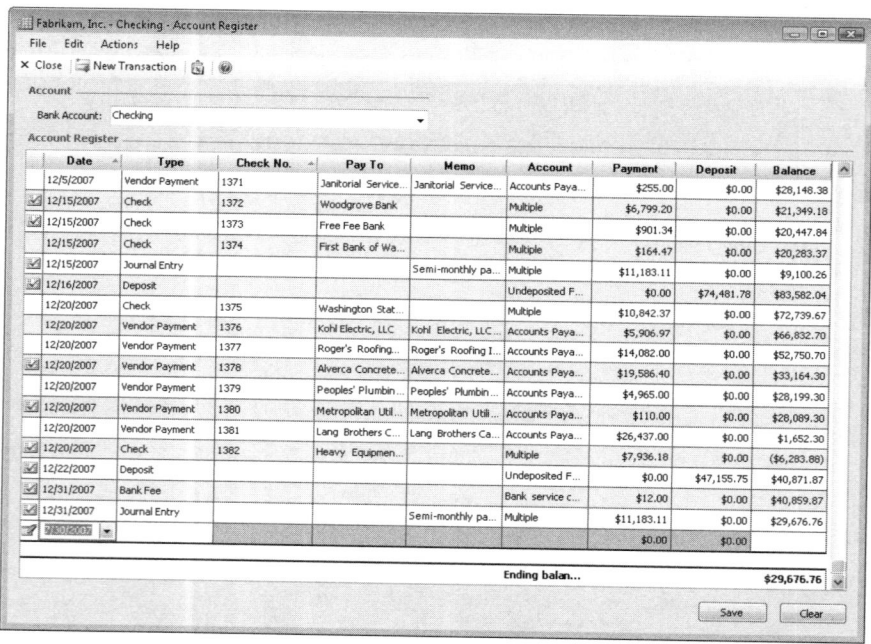

The default order of the items in the register is by date. You can sort the list by clicking a column heading. For example, to group the list so that all deposits are shown together, click the Deposit column heading. The arrow beside the column name indicates whether the list is sorted in ascending or descending order. To see the register for a different account, click that account in the Bank Account list.

> **Note** If you sort the Account Register by a column other than the Date column, the running total shown in the Balance column changes, but the new order does not change the ending balance for the account.

Each transaction recorded in an Account Register is a permanent part of your company's financial records. After you've entered a transaction, whether directly through the register or by writing a check or depositing funds, you cannot delete the transaction. You can, however, edit a transaction or indicate that a transaction is void.

You can also add a transaction by using the Account Register. For example, you can add a transaction to account for interest income that your bank reports or to record a fee that the bank charges for processing checks.

> **Important** You often need to add transactions such as interest income (or a bank fee) when you are preparing to reconcile an account.

Because an account transaction becomes a permanent part of your company's accounting records, you cannot delete a transaction. However, if a transaction is no longer applicable, you can mark it as void.

In this exercise, you will work with the Fabrikam sample company to view the register for a bank account, add a deposit transaction for interest income, and edit and void a transaction.

> **OPEN** the Fabrikam sample company file.

1. In the **Navigation Pane**, click the **Banking** button.

2. In the **More Tasks** area of the **Banking** home page, click **Account Register**.

   The Account Register window opens.

3. In the **Bank Account** list of the **Account Register**, click **Savings**.

   The savings account's transactions appear in the Account Register.

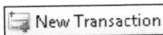

4. On the **Account Register** form toolbar, click the **New Transaction** button.

   The Select Transaction dialog box opens.

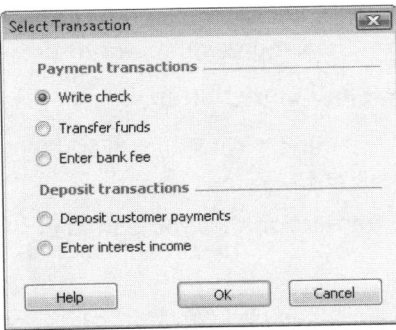

5. Under **Deposit transactions**, click **Enter interest income**, and then click **OK**.

The Select Transaction dialog box closes and the Bank Interest dialog box opens.

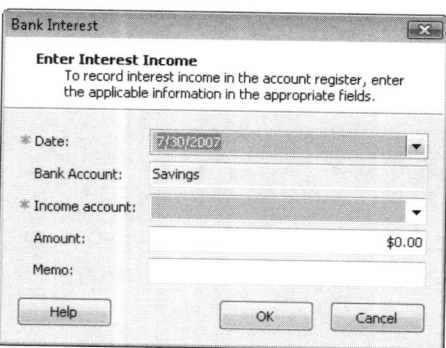

6. In the **Bank Interest** dialog box, keep the current date in the **Date** field. From the **Income account** list, click account 8020 **Interest Income**.

7. In the **Amount** box, type 101.50, and then click **OK**.

    The transaction is added to the Account Register.

8. Double-click the interest income transaction that you created in step 7.

    A Journal Entry form that contains the selected transaction opens.

9. On the **Journal Entry** form toolbar, click the **Edit** button.

> **Important** If you open a transaction in the Account Register that was included on a bank statement that you have already reconciled, Accounting warns you that if you edit the transaction, the account will no longer be reconciled. In some cases, you might have to edit the transaction and reconcile the account again. For more information about reconciling an account, see "Reconciling a Bank Account" later in this chapter.

10. In the **Debit** column for the **Savings** account journal entry, change **$101.50** to $121.00. Make the same change in the **Credit** column for **Interest Income**.

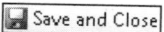

11. On the form toolbar, click the **Save and Close** button.

    If the debit and credit entries do not equal each other, Accounting warns you of this fact and does not let you save the entry.

12. Double-click the interest income transaction that you edited in step 10.

    The transaction appears.

13. On the **Actions** menu, click **Void**, and then click **Yes** to confirm the operation.

Accounting voids the transaction.

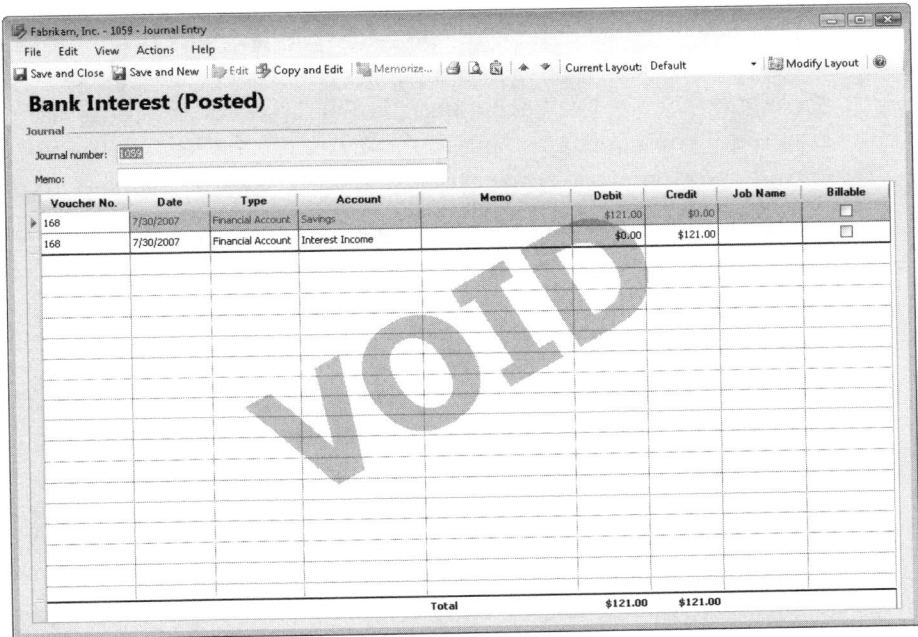

14. On the form toolbar, click the **Save and Close** button to save the transaction record.

    The Account Register window opens.

15. In the upper-right corner of the **Account Register** form toolbar, click the **Close** button to close the Account Register.

Adding a Bank Fee

In addition to interest income, one kind of transaction that you often add to an Account Register is a bank fee. After clicking the New Transaction button at the bottom of the Account Register; choose Enter Bank Fee in the Select Transaction dialog box, and then click OK. In the Bank Fee dialog box, select the account the fee should be charged to (for example, an expense account named Bank Service Charges), enter the amount of the fee, and enter a memo describing the fee.

Entering Transactions

In Chapter 13, "Purchasing from Vendors," you learned how to pay vendor bills. You select the bills you need to pay, the payment account, and the payment method. Accounting then enters each transaction in the Account Register for that account. For example, if you select Checking as the account and Check as the payment method, Accounting creates a payment transaction in the corresponding Account Register.

Not every payment transaction originates from a bill you choose to pay. You can also use the Check form to write a check that you need to enter manually. For example, you might need to write a check to a tax agency, pay your credit card bill, or send a check to a vendor as a deposit on an order you placed.

The Pay To list displays the names of customers, employees, tax agencies, and vendors that you have set up in Accounting. You cannot issue a check to an individual, agency, or company that is not on one of these lists. You can add a company, vendor, or employee to the list of payees by clicking Add A New Payee at the top of the Pay To list, indicating the type of record you want to add, and then filling in the account record. (You cannot add a tax agency directly from the Check form. Instead, you need to use the Sales Tax command on the Company menu.)

When you select a customer, employee, vendor, or agency that is already set up for your company, Accounting adds address information to the Check form. Selecting the To Be Printed check box adds this check to the list of checks that are displayed when you click Print Checks on the Banking home page. If you don't select this option, you can print a check by opening the transaction from the Account Register.

You won't need to add item or expense information to every check you write. However, you can specify accounts or items that a payment transaction relates to. In the exercise that follows, you want a record of the quantity of roofing material that is related to the refund. When you save this transaction, the income account for roofing materials will be reduced by the amount of the check. In other cases, you want to indicate which expense account a specific payment is related to. When you enter item and expense information, the amount of the line items must equal the amount of the check.

In this exercise, you will issue a check and mark the check as one you want to print the next time you click Print Checks on the Banking home page.

> **OPEN** the Fabrikam sample company file.

1. In the **Navigation Pane**, click **Banking**.

2. Under **Start a Task** on the **Banking** home page, click **Write Checks**.

   A blank Check form opens.

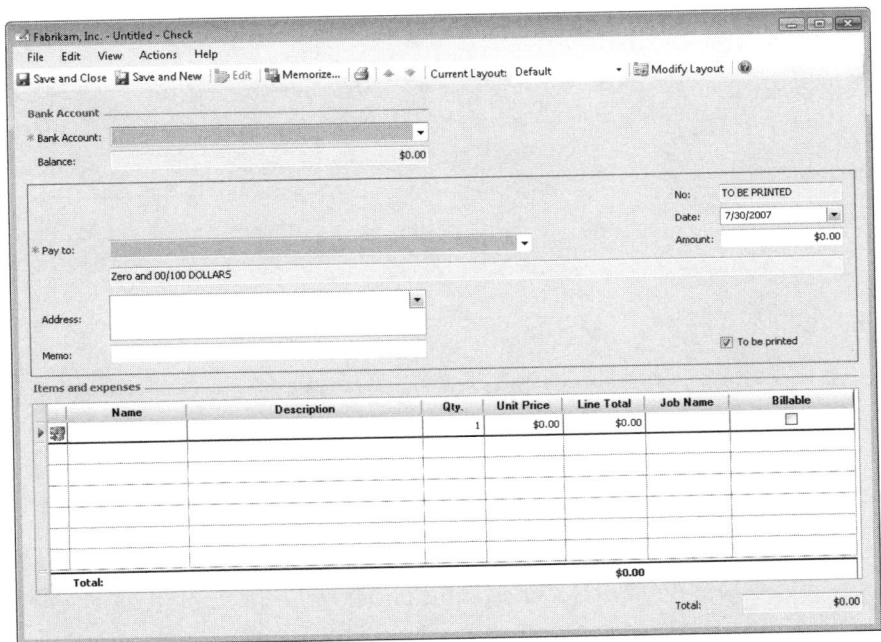

3. Click the **Bank Account** arrow, and then in the list, click **Checking**.

4. In the **Pay to** list, click the customer **Katie Jordan**.

5. In the **Amount** box, type 450.

6. In the **Memo** box, type Refund to customer for materials not used.

7. Make sure the **To be printed** check box is selected.

8. In the **Items and expenses** grid, click in the first column, and then click the **Item** icon.

9. In the first cell under the **Name** column, select **Roofing materials (FF)**.

10. In the **Qty.** field, type 10.

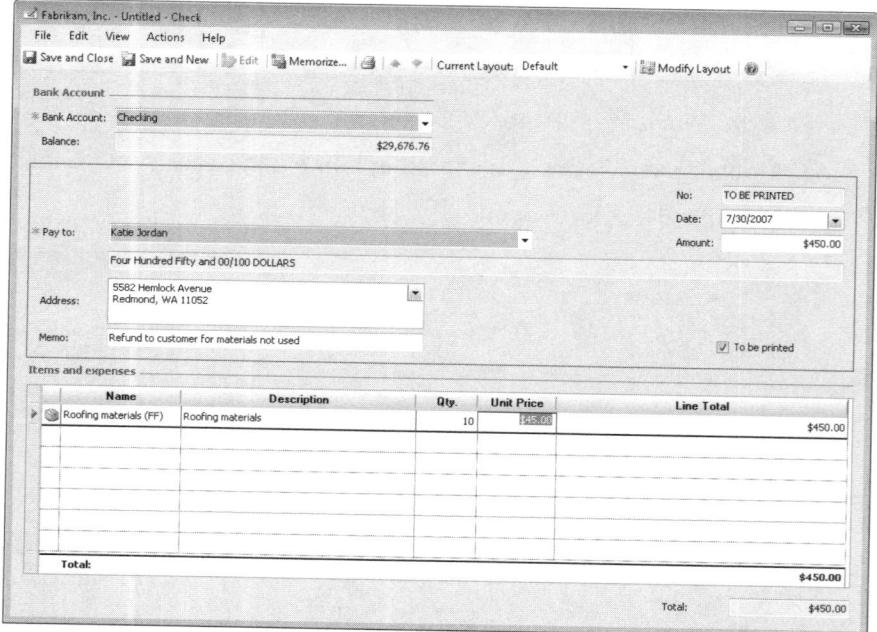

Save and Close **11.** On the toolbar, click the **Save and Close** button.

Printing Checks

You can purchase checks to use with Accounting from a Web site that you can reach by clicking Buy Checks And Forms under More Tasks on the Banking home page. When you are ready to print checks, on the Banking home page, click Print Checks. In the Print Checks dialog box, select the account to use. Accounting keeps track of the number of the last check you printed and fills in the next check number in order. You can enter a different check number if you need to. Select the checks you want to print, and then click Print. In the Print dialog box, select the printer you want to use, change other printer settings as needed, and then click OK.

Recording a Bank Deposit

When you record a bank deposit in Accounting, you first specify the account to which the funds are being deposited. You can then select a customer payment that was previously entered into your company's accounting records or create a new entry for a deposit transaction that is not related to a payment you have already recorded. You can also specify the amount of cash you want to receive back out of the amount you are depositing.

See Also For more information about entering a payment you receive from a customer, see "Receiving Payments into Accounting 2007" in Chapter 12, "Handling Customer Payments."

The items that are displayed in the Payments Received list are customer payments recorded in your company records. You can also add a line item for a deposit not listed as a payment received. The deposit transaction you add, however, must be associated with a vendor or a customer that is set up in your company records or with one of the accounts in your chart of accounts. For example, you can add a deposit related to a refund from a vendor.

In this exercise, you will make a deposit in Accounting by using records from the Fabrikam sample company.

> **OPEN** the Fabrikam sample company file.

1. In the **Navigation Pane**, click the **Banking** button.

2. Under **Start a Task** on the **Banking** home page, click **Make Deposit**.

   A blank Deposit form opens.

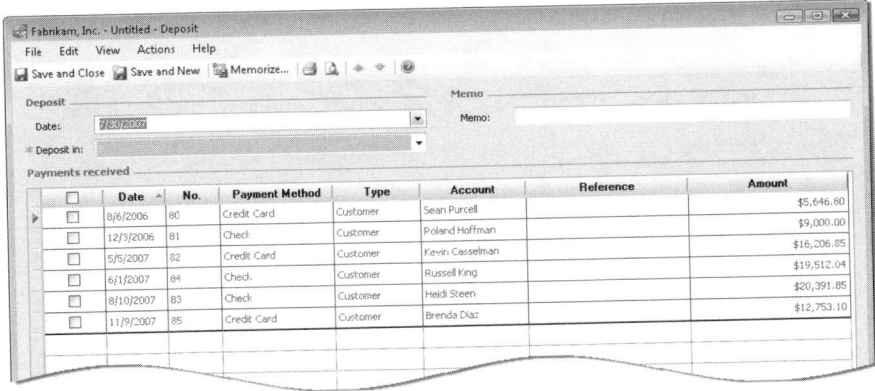

> **Important** If you are using multiple currencies, you must select the currency in which the deposit is denominated before entering any information in the Payments Received grid.

3. In the **Deposit** form, in the **Deposit in** list, click **Checking**.

> **Tip** You can enter a note about the deposit in the Memo field. For example, you could indicate a job name related to the deposit.

4. Under **Payments Received**, select the check boxes for **Roland Hoffman** and **Russell King**.

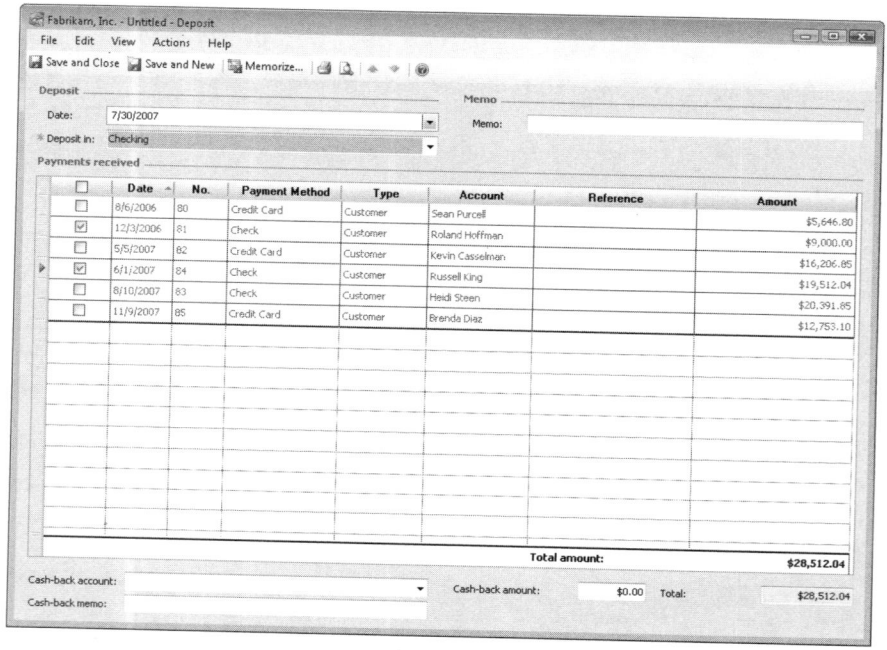

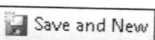

5. On the **Deposit** form toolbar, click the **Save and New** button.

   The two selected deposits disappear.

6. Click the first empty row in the **Payments Received** grid.

   A new deposit row appears.

   > **Note** The deposit row might appear in the middle of the Payments Received grid, depending on the current date and the other payments in the grid.

7. Click in the **Type** cell of the new row, click the arrow that appears, and then click **Vendor**.

8. Click in the **Account** cell, click the arrow that appears, and then click **Evergreen Property Management**.

9. In the **Amount** cell, type 4325, and then press the ⸤Tab⸥ key.

   Accounting adds the line item to the Deposit form and selects it as one of the payments included with this deposit.

> **Tip** If you want to keep a paper copy of the deposit ticket as part of your backup records, on the File menu, click Print.

Save and Close **10.** On the **Deposit** form toolbar, click the **Save and Close** button.

The Deposit form closes.

Managing Dishonored Checks

For reasons ranging from a customer neglecting to reconcile a bank account to outright fraud, you will occasionally find yourself dealing with dishonored checks. A dishonored check is a check that is refused by the bank upon which it is drawn. A bank can refuse a check for many reasons, including apparent physical alterations, mismatched values in the words and numeric amounts on its face, absence of a signature on file that matches the signature on the check, the fact that the check is postdated, and other problems. The most common reason for refusal, of course, is insufficient funds in the account. (NSF is a common acronym for this, stamped upon the face of the check by the bank.)

When you become aware of a dishonored check, you need to adjust the account into which you deposited the check to reflect the change. You void the payment (instead of deleting it) to remove the value of the check from your bank account. This leaves the deposit transaction in place, but flags it as being void, and of no effect on the account balance. It also results in the "reactivation" of the receivable amount against which it was matched—to return the receivable to the books as unpaid. Moreover, you will need to input an entry against the affected cash account for any fees applied by the bank for handling the dishonored check.

Transferring Funds

If your company maintains more than one bank account—a checking account and a savings or money market account, for example—you can transfer money from one account to another. For example, you can keep most of your cash in an interest-bearing account. When you need to pay vendor bills and process payroll, you can transfer the money you need to your checking account. You can transfer funds between any two banking, credit card, or financial accounts except for an inventory account and any account that is tied to a sales tax agency.

> **Tip** If you set up your company to bank online, you can also make account transfers over the Internet.

In this exercise, you will record a transfer of funds between two accounts.

OPEN the Fabrikam sample company file.

1. In the **Navigation Pane**, click the **Banking** button.

2. Under **Start a Task** on the **Banking** home page, click **Transfer Funds**.

   The Transfer Funds dialog box opens.

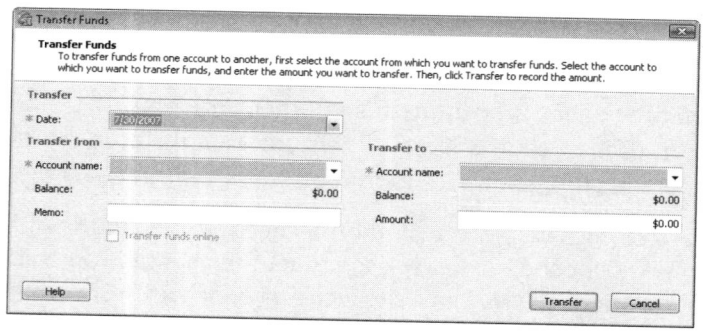

3. Under **Transfer from**, click the **Account name** arrow, and then click **Savings**.

4. In the **Memo** field, type Transfer to fund capital purchase.

5. Under **Transfer to**, click the **Account name** arrow, and then click **Checking**.

6. In the **Amount** box, type 5000.

7. Click **Transfer**.

   Accounting transfers the money from the Savings account to the Checking account, and the Transfer Funds dialog box closes.

Entering a Credit Card Charge

Credit card charges, like payments and deposits in your bank accounts, are recorded in an Account Register through a form that Accounting supplies. In the form, you specify the vendor from which you made the credit card purchase, payment terms, and the items you charged. If your company is set up to use jobs, when you fill in the details of a credit card charge, you can indicate whether an item you purchased is related to a job and whether that item is billable.

See Also For more information about setting up jobs, see Chapter 7, "Managing Jobs."

Many of your credit card charge entries will relate to item purchases. If you need to pay interest on an unpaid balance or a yearly registration fee, you should record the charge as an expense. To record a charge as an expense, click Banking in the Navigation Pane, and then click Credit Card Charge to open a blank Credit Card Charge form.

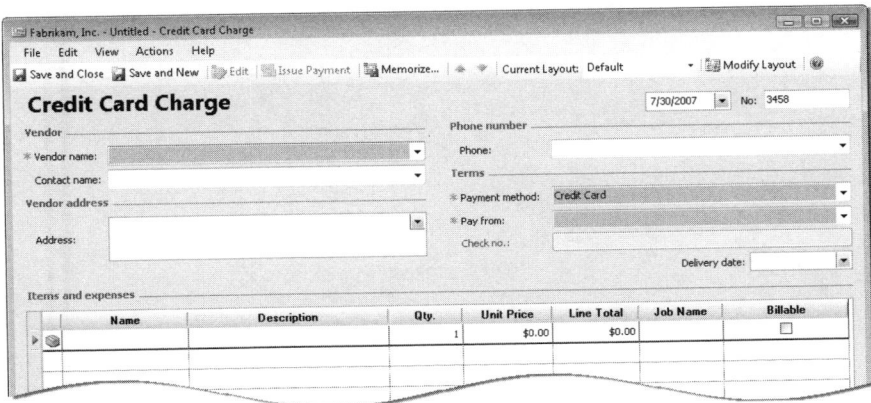

In the Items And Expenses grid, click the marker in the left-most column of the first row, click Expense, and then type a description and price for the expense in the Description and Unit Price fields, respectively.

In this exercise, you will record a credit card charge by using one of the vendors set up in the Fabrikam sample company.

> **OPEN** the Fabrikam sample company file.

1. In the **Navigation Pane**, click the **Banking** button.
2. Under **Start a Task** on the **Banking** home page, click **Credit Card Charge**.

   A blank Credit Card Charge form opens.
3. In the **Vendor name** list, click **Kohl Electric, LLC**.
4. In the **Pay from** list, click account **2540 VISA Credit Card**.
5. In the **Delivery date** field, enter the date when the purchase you are making needs to be delivered.
6. In the **Items and expenses** grid, click the arrow in the first **Name** cell, and then click **Electrical materials (FF)**.

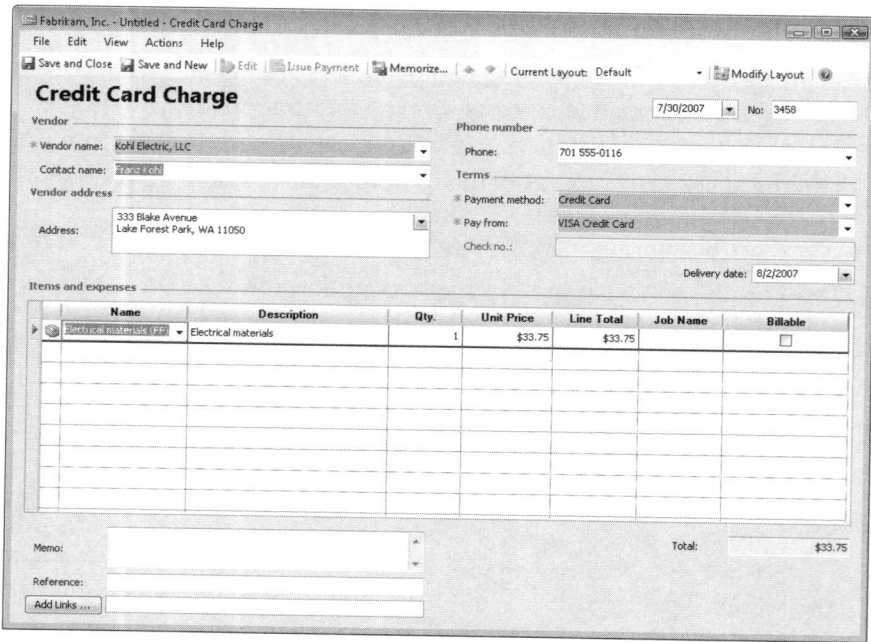

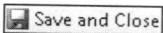 **7.** On the toolbar, click the **Save and Close** button.

You can open the Account Register for the Visa Credit card account and see how this transaction is recorded.

Reconciling a Bank Account

One of the accounting tasks that you need to perform regularly is reconciling your account records with the statements that your bank provides. In comparing your records with bank statements, you can check that each deposit you made was recorded correctly, determine which checks have cleared your account, and review any fees that your bank charged. To completely reconcile an account, you might need to add a transaction to an Account Register to record interest income, for example, or a bank fee.

> **Note** Reconciling bank and credit card accounts is an important part of closing your books at the end of each accounting period. By reconciling your accounts, you can confirm the accuracy of each transaction.

In Accounting, you use the Reconcile Account wizard to list the transactions recorded in an account you want to reconcile.

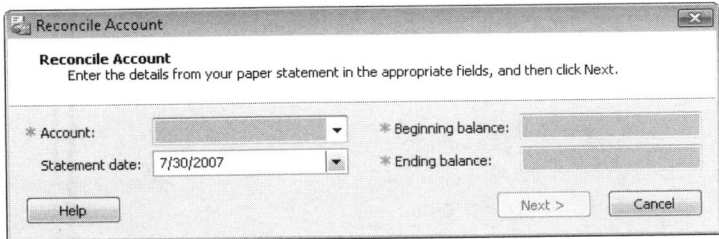

The amounts shown at the bottom of the Reconcile Account wizard in the On Statement and Difference balances change as you select an item. If every transaction is accounted for, and the amounts of each transaction match, the difference will be zero. If the difference does not equal zero, you need to add, edit, or void a transaction so that it does. For example, you might need to enter fees or interest income that appear on a bank statement or adjust the amount of a check that was entered incorrectly. To edit a transaction, double-click the entry for that transaction. To add a transaction, click Click Here To Add A New Transaction, which is located just below the grid.

You can see how transactions are recorded in your company books by reviewing the entries in the Account column. The balancing account for the transaction is the account shown in this column. For example, if a line item is a check, the Account column might show the expense account that was affected by the transaction. If a line item is a deposit, the Account column might show an account such as Accounts Receivable. If more than one account is involved in a transaction, the Account column displays Multiple.

> **Tip** By default, transactions are sorted by date. You can use the Current View list to sort the transactions by type. The Current View list gives you three sorting options in addition to sorting by date: you can list checks and deposits together (either with checks listed first or with deposits listed first), or sort the transactions in the order Deposits, Checks, and Other Withdrawals.

If the reconciliation difference does not equal zero, Accounting displays a message box in which you can click OK to return to the reconciliation at a later point or click Cancel to continue the reconciliation. If the difference is zero, Accounting displays a congratulatory message. Click Display Report to open the Reconciliation Detail report or click Close to complete the reconciliation. You can print the Reconciliation Detail report to review the checks and deposits that have cleared and other details of your bank accounts.

In this exercise, you will reconcile the Fabrikam, Inc. checking account.

> **Note** Accounting generates the Fabrikam sample company file's records dynamically, so you might not be able to reconcile Fabrikam's checking account completely by using the steps in this procedure.

> **OPEN** the Fabrikam sample company file.

1. In the **Navigation Pane**, click the **Banking** button.

2. In the **Start a Task** section of the **Banking** home page, click **Reconcile Account**.

   The Reconcile Account wizard starts.

3. On the first page of the **Reconcile Account** wizard, in the **Account** list, click **Checking**.

4. In the **Statement date** list, type 6/30/2007, or a date within your current fiscal year, as the closing date of the statement to which you want to reconcile your account.

5. In the **Ending balance** box, enter the ending balance from the bank statement you are working from. For this exercise, type 46087.89.

6. Click **Next**.

   The next page of the Reconcile Account wizard appears.

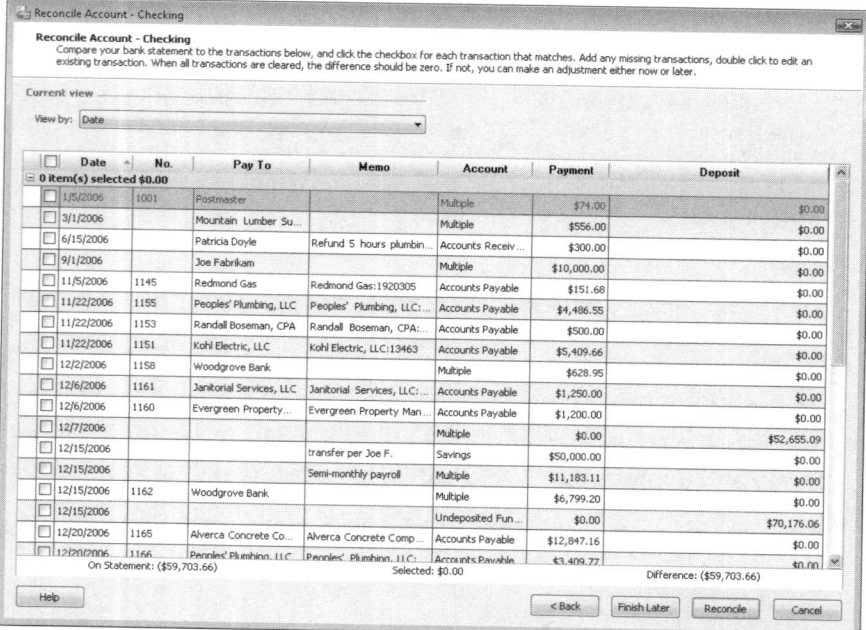

Abandoned Property Considerations

Have you ever had a vendor or former employee fail to cash a check you sent? After you got over the elation of discovering that, yes, it had been months and that, no, they weren't likely to cash the check, what did you do? You might have thought you had a "found money" scenario on your hands.

You probably didn't. The majority of states have substantially adopted the Uniform Disposition of Unclaimed Property Act. (You may have heard of it as "escheat," abandoned property, unclaimed property, or something similar.) If you aren't aware of the act itself, you may know of a similar situation: If you allow a bank account to lie dormant long enough, the bank must turn the balance over to the state. The rules vary from state to state, but the concept generally applies to all "unclaimed" intangible and tangible property. And the bottom line is that failure to report the unclaimed property can result in penalties—as well as demands to turn over the abandoned property, of course. States are becoming progressively more diligent in pursuing what is an appealing revenue stream—especially because it adds to the treasury with none of the negative political press of a tax increase.

There are numerous specifics, depending upon the state(s) within which you live and/or operate your business, but generally, "abandoned property" materializes anytime no activity has taken place (including communications about status or other non-activity) surrounding an account within a specified period of time. The "abandonment" time we're talking about here is typically between three and five years, but, again, each state has its own definitions. And the rules, as you might imagine, differ for various types of transactions, such as deposits, dividends, and distributions of various types. (And, by the way, they also differ for banks and other organizations.)

Although the laws vary, there are several common requirements. You should take (and document) action to find the owners of any property (by sending correspondence to the most recent address you have, asking about uncashed checks, for example). You also have to file abandoned property reports as required in the appropriate state(s). You should investigate the statutes and other rules for the states within which you do business (and within which your customers live, in many cases), to determine the time periods involved, the required dates for filing the associated report(s), the taxing authority (or authorities) with whom you need to file your reports, check-retention policies, and other considerations. In addition to discussing this with your attorney and/or accountant, take a look at the Web site for (or perhaps call or pay a visit to) the taxing agencies involved.

7. Select the check box for each transaction that matches a transaction on your bank statement. For this exercise, select the transactions for check numbers **1371**, **1374**, and **1375**.

> **Tip** To select every transaction displayed in the Reconcile Account wizard, select the check box next to the Date column header.

8. In the lower-right corner of the window, click **Finish Later**.

   Accounting saves your changes and closes the Reconcile Account wizard.

Banking Online

If you bank with a financial institution that supports online banking, you can set up Accounting so that you can work with your accounts by means of an Internet connection. After you set up your accounts for online banking, you can download transactions, reconcile your accounts online, and perform tasks such as transferring funds and paying bills.

Online Banking: Is It Right for Your Business?

Online banking has come to mean various things to small businesses, regardless of the accounting system involved. Online banking, in the simplest sense, gives you the capability to download or import details about your account (typically information about transactions) from your financial institution(s). After you download the information via an Internet connection, you can then load these details into your accounting system. You might also use online banking to direct the bank to transfer money between accounts (such as between your operating and payroll accounts, or to make a monthly payment from checking to a corporate credit card issued by the same bank). Moreover, some online banking systems include online payment (of vendors and suppliers, for example) within the definition of online banking.

Whatever the scope of services you choose to use, there are a few factors to consider before you simply follow the crowd and sign up for online banking. First, consider whether the service or process that is offered truly provides time or cost advantages: Is the "bill-paying service" simply cutting a check and mailing it to the destination (very often the case), while charging you extra to do so? For that matter, is the payment service addressing the needs of the vendor or supplier, for example, in making the payment easy to record correctly through provision of information such as the number of the invoice being paid? (If you constantly have to guide the payee in how to apply your checks, often after initial mismatches, what benefit have you gained?)

When you add layers of communication into the process of managing account balances and paying bills, you might find it hard to resolve issues that arise. Many times, be it in the technical support arena or just plain-old customer service, banks and other organizations these days are finding ways to eliminate the "people" element, one of their highest costs, to save money. That's why they want to "get customers online" in every imaginable way (and to charge additional fees in the meantime, in many cases). Less cost for more revenue is, after all, a great idea from the perspective of the bank and its "partners." But when this highly optimistic scenario hits a snag, or when glitches occur that affect your relationship with suppliers, vendors, or perhaps with taxing authorities (or worse), to whom you are trying to send payments, you might find it hard to connect with a human being who can help you resolve the issue quickly—you're actually more likely to meet with finger-pointing between sometimes aloof or unknowledgeable inhabitants of the various layers. It might turn out, especially if your transaction volume is relatively small, that you experience greater productivity and fewer headaches by "just saying no" to online services that you don't really need.

Setting Up Online Banking

The first step is to work with your bank to set up an online account. As part of this process, you need to define a user name and password that you use to access your online accounts from Accounting.

> **Important** To work through this exercise using your own company, you need an Internet connection and an account that is set up for online banking with your bank. You also need to have set up bank accounts in your company's chart of accounts. For information about setting up accounts, see Chapter 4, "Managing the Chart of Accounts." You can follow most of the steps in this exercise by using the Fabrikam sample company, but you cannot actually download transactions or transfer funds.

In this exercise, you will set up Accounting 2007 for online banking.

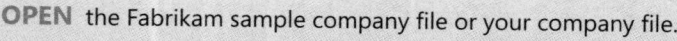

OPEN the Fabrikam sample company file or your company file.

1. In the **Navigation Pane**, click the **Banking** button.

2. In the **More Tasks** section of the **Banking** home page, click **Online Banking**.

   The Set Up Online Banking wizard starts.

3. Read the welcome message. Ensure that you know your account number and the online banking user ID and password for the account. Then click **Next**.

   The Setup Or Modify Online Banking Services page appears.

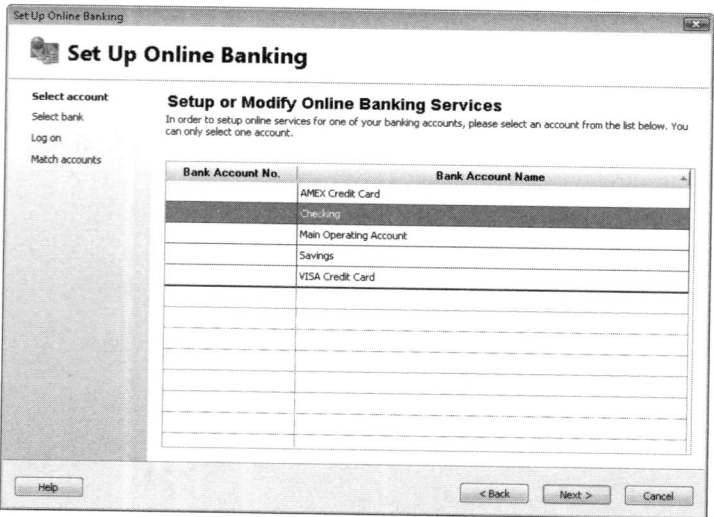

4. Select the account you are setting up, and then click **Next**.

   The Update Financial Institutions dialog box opens.

5. Click **Yes** to have Accounting retrieve the latest list of financial institutions.

> **Note** You can also click No to proceed without updating the list.

6. On the **Select a Financial Institution for Online Services** page, select the bank you use, and then click **Next**. If you don't see your bank listed, click **Refresh** to have Accounting download an up-to-date list.

> **Note** For some financial institutions, a page asking you to log in through the institution's Web site will appear.

7. On the **Log On** page, enter the user ID and password that you have set up with your bank, and then click **Next**.

8. On the next page of the **Set Up Online Banking** wizard, click the **This Online Account Matches** check box, and then select the account in your Accounting chart of accounts that matches the online account set up with your bank.

> **Note** If you are setting up more than one account for online banking, the wizard displays this page again to let you match another account to the correct account in Accounting.

9. Click **Next**.

10. On the **Settings for Downloading History and Balances** page, select the option that specifies the group of transactions you want to download.

    You can download no transactions, transactions that occurred over the past 7 days or the past 30 days, or transactions that have been posted since the date you specify.

11. Click **Next**.

    The Setup Overview page appears.

12. Review the account information, and then click **Close**.

Transferring Funds Online

You can transfer funds online between two accounts that are set up for online banking. To make the transfer, click Transfer Funds on the Banking home page. In the Transfer Funds dialog box, specify the accounts between which you are transferring funds, and then click the Transfer Online check box. When you click Transfer, you will be prompted for your ID and password for the online accounts.

Downloading and Matching Transactions for Online Accounts

After you have set up one or more of your bank accounts as online accounts, you can connect to your financial institution's Web site and download transactions to your company accounts in Accounting. By downloading transactions, you help keep your records in Accounting current with the records at your bank.

After downloading transactions to Accounting, you need to match the transactions in your Account Registers with the transactions that you downloaded. You can match transactions as a step during the process of downloading transactions, or you can download transactions and then match them later.

The Online Banking Summary dialog box displays the online accounts for the bank you selected, the number of transactions that you downloaded, account balances, and the status of the download operation. The information in the Status field indicates whether the connection was successful or whether a problem occurred—for example, if the bank's server is not available.

At this point, you can proceed to match the downloaded transactions to transactions in your Accounting Account Registers or close the Online Banking Summary dialog box without matching transactions. To match transactions at another time, click Match Transactions on the Banking home page.

If one of the downloaded transactions does not match a transaction in your Account Register, select that transaction, and then click Add To Register.

In this exercise, you will download and match transactions.

> **BE SURE TO** set up a bank account and online banking before beginning this exercise.
> **OPEN** your company data file.

1. In the **Navigation Pane**, click the **Banking** button.
2. Under **More Tasks** on the **Banking** home page, click **Download Transactions**. The Connect To Online Banking dialog box opens.

3. Select the check box for the banking institution you want to connect to.

4. In the **User Name** field, type your user name for this bank. In the **Password** field, type your password.

5. Click **Connect**.

   Accounting connects to your bank account and displays the **Online Banking Summary** dialog box.

6. Click **Match Transactions**.

7. Match your transactions to your Account Register, and then click **OK**.

Canceling Online Payments

After you issue an online payment to pay a bill or a vendor payment, you have a period of time during which you can cancel the payment from Accounting 2007. The amount of time is usually between two to three days and depends on your bank or financial institution's payment processing policy. You should verify this policy with your bank.

> **Important** You can cancel an online payment only if you have installed Accounting 2007 Service Pack 1 (SP1). You can download Accounting SP1 from *www.microsoft.com/downloads/ details.aspx?FamilyID=f5a69c78-39a0-4b10-9072-456031457eb5&DisplayLang=en*.

In this exercise, you will cancel an online payment.

OPEN the Fabrikam sample company file.

1. In the **Navigation Pane**, click **Vendors**, and then, in the **Find** section of the **Vendors** home page, click **Vendor Payments**.

   The Vendor Payments list appears.

2. Click **Current View**, and then click **Issued**.

   The Vendor Payments list displays payments that Fabrikam, Inc. has issued.

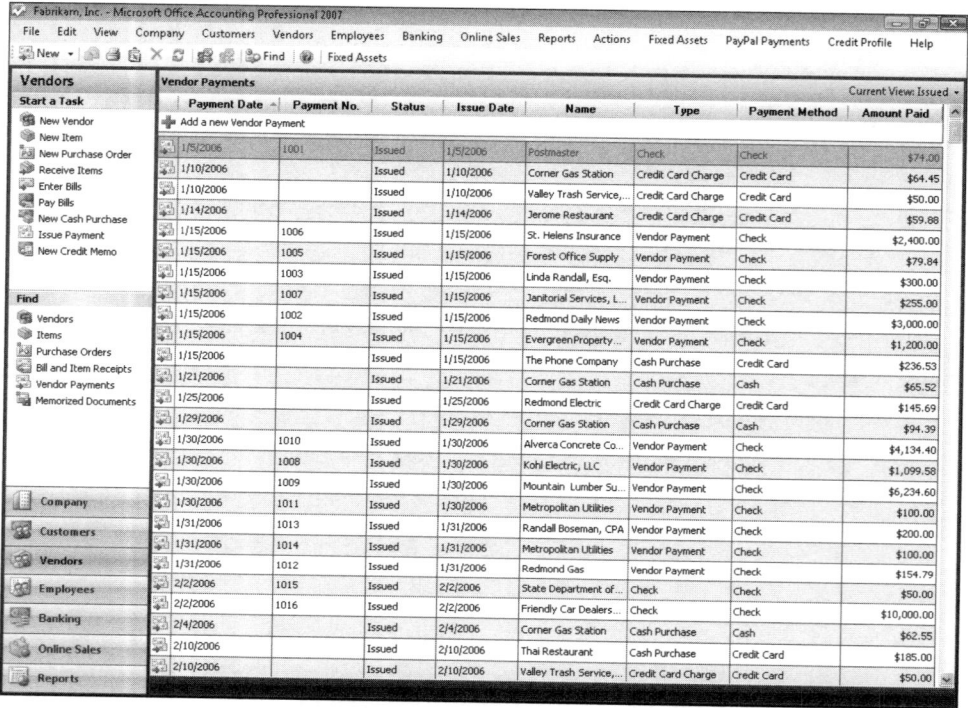

> **Note** All issued vendor payments and paid bills appear as Vendor Payment types.

3. Double-click the online payment you want to cancel.

   The online payment appears in a form.

4. On the **Actions** menu of the form, click **Cancel Payment**.

   The Enter User ID And Password dialog box opens.

5. Enter your information in the **Enter User ID and Password** dialog box.

   One of four messages appears as a result of canceling or voiding an online vendor payment. The messages are summarized as follows:

   ● If the payment cancellation succeeds, you can void the transaction in Accounting 2007.

- If the payment cancellation fails, the message gives the reasons for the failure. You can void the transaction in Accounting 2007, but you should contact your bank to find out whether you can actually cancel the transaction.
- If you void an issued online vendor payment, the message gives you the option to cancel the online payment.
- If you attempt to cancel an online vendor payment that has already been cancelled, the message notifies you that the payment cannot be cancelled.

> **Note** If you void an online vendor payment in Accounting 2007 and the online payment cannot be cancelled, you must record the transaction by creating another payment before you can reconcile the account.

Accepting Credit Card Payments Through ADP

Many customers use credit cards or debit cards to purchase things, particularly when they purchase items online. With Accounting, you can sign up for an ADP merchant account that enables you to accept credit card payments; the ADP service verifies that the customer's card is valid and has sufficient funds to cover the charge. If you bank online, you can arrange to transfer funds from your credit card account quickly.

In this exercise, you will sign up for the ADP service.

> **Important** You must be connected to the Internet to sign up for credit card processing.

> OPEN the Fabrikam sample company file.

1. In the **Navigation Pane**, click **Customers**.
2. Under **More Tasks** on the **Customers** home page, click **Credit Card Processing**.

   The Windows Live sign-in dialog box opens.

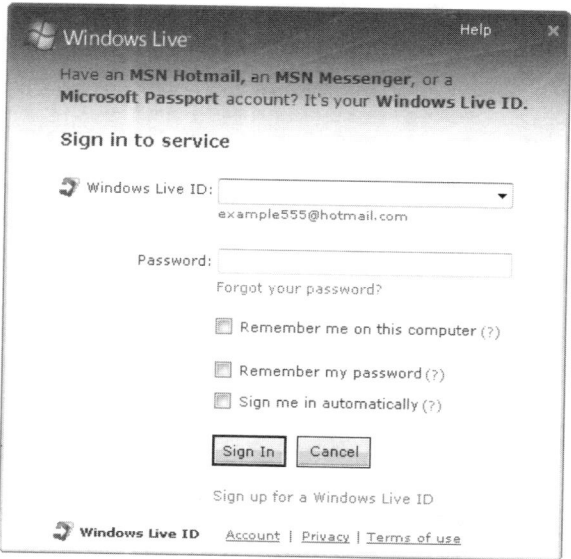

> **Note** If you are running Accounting 2007 on a Windows XP operating system, you will see the Payment Services dialog box immediately.

3. Enter your Windows Live ID and password, and then click **Sign In**.

The Payment Services wizard starts.

4. Follow the instructions in the wizard.

5. When you have completed the wizard, click **OK**.

 CLOSE the Fabrikam sample company file. If you are not continuing directly to the next chapter, exit Accounting 2007.

Reporting Considerations: Bank Accounts, Transactions, and Reconciliations

Reports that you base upon bank accounts will largely focus upon the transactions that take place within those accounts. A check register is itself an account transaction report. These reports can be used in reconciliations, but can also provide myriad views that range from vendors paid to customer payments received, provided that you have created a chart of accounts that supports the detail you need, and reports that point to the "other side" of transaction entries to the bank account(s) involved.

Among "special purpose" reports might be reports to alert you to payments that you have made that, based upon their age and the fact that checks have not been recorded as having come back to the bank, are candidates for abandoned property treatment. Such a report can support follow-up letters to the intended payees, as well as help you to meet the reporting requirements to the appropriate taxing authorities. Other reports might keep you aware of customers whose checks to you have bounced regularly (and have caused you to have to pay banking charges, as well as to spend time and money, perhaps, pursuing payment), or of operating checking accounts that are maintaining higher cash balances than required to meet monthly needs (and which might be candidates for partial monthly transfers to interest-bearing accounts). Other possibilities include reports that support cash-flow forecasting and the like.

The analysis and reporting opportunities surrounding bank accounts offer substantial business intelligence returns. Good reporting of your bank account transactions and balances will help you to understand the cash management component of your operations, among other areas. This affords you yet another way to apply your growing grasp of your overall performance to continuously improve your business.

Key Points

- The Banking home page provides links to common tasks such as writing checks, making deposits, and transferring funds.
- Each bank transaction is listed in an Account Register that you can use to edit a transaction, void a transaction, or add a transaction.
- Reconciling your bank accounts is an important part of closing your books each month and at the end of each accounting period.
- You can set up your accounts to bank online so that you can transfer funds, view transactions, and pay bills over the Internet.

Chapter at a Glance

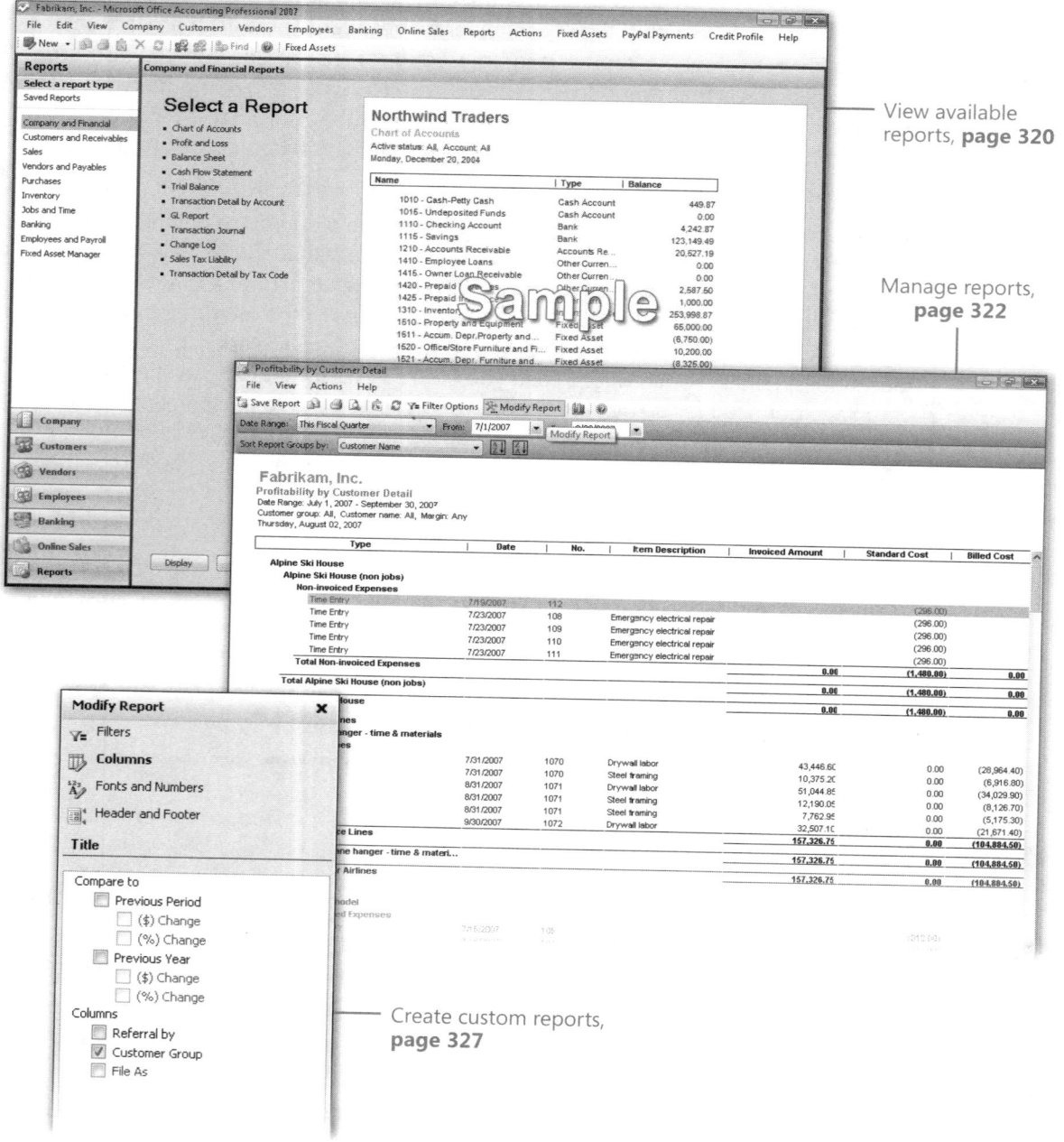

View available reports, **page 320**

Manage reports, **page 322**

Create custom reports, **page 327**

15 Creating Reports to Manage Your Business

In this chapter, you will learn to:

✔ View available reports.

✔ Manage reports.

✔ Create custom reports.

✔ Generate business intelligence from reports.

Accounting records tend to be long lists of journal entries that the average human has a hard time filtering and organizing without help. In Microsoft Office Accounting 2007, that help comes in the form of reports. A *report* is a summary of specific accounting data in a company file, such as item sales by customer or bills from vendors. You can manipulate the built-in reports or create your own to discover the information you need to know to keep your business healthy.

In this chapter, you will learn how to manage the built-in Accounting reports, create and manage custom reports, and generate business intelligence from your reports.

> **Troubleshooting** Graphics and operating system–related instructions in this book reflect the Windows Vista user interface. If your computer is running Microsoft Windows XP and you experience trouble following the instructions as written, please refer to the "Information for Readers Running Windows XP" section at the beginning of this book.

Viewing Available Reports

You can find Accounting reports on the Reports home page, which you display by clicking the Reports button in the Navigation Pane.

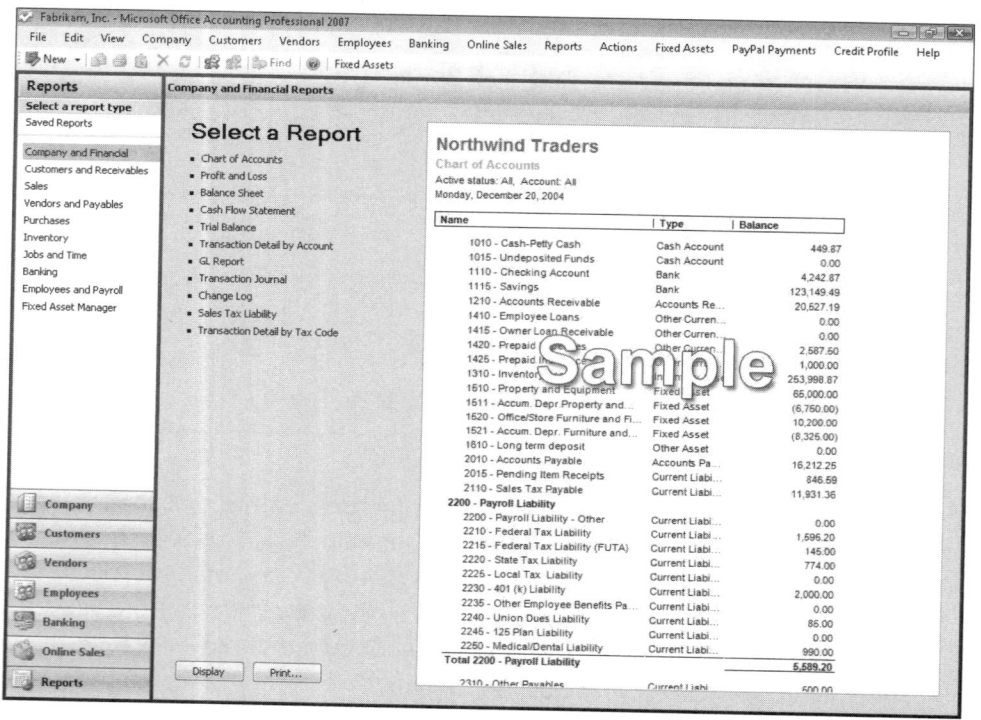

The list of report categories appears in the Select A Report Type panel of the Navigation Pane, whereas the reports available within that category appear in the Content pane. The title of the Content pane changes to reflect the report category that you clicked. From this base of operations, you can display, print, manipulate, and customize your Accounting reports to answer questions about your company and its performance.

Clicking a report name in the Select A Report list in the Content pane displays a sample report that illustrates the type of data the report presents. The sample reports are all drawn from the Northwind Traders company database, which is included with Accounting Professional 2007.

In this exercise, you will view several sample reports.

> **BE SURE TO** start Accounting 2007 before beginning this exercise.
>
> **OPEN** the Fabrikam sample company file.

1. In the **Navigation Pane**, click the **Reports** button.

   The Reports home page appears.

2. In the **Navigation Pane**, click **Vendors and Payables**.

   The Content pane title changes to Vendors And Payables Reports, and the list of available reports changes to reflect the chosen category.

3. In the **Content** pane, under **Select a Report**, click (don't double-click) **Vendor Transaction History**.

   The Vendor Transaction History sample report appears in the preview pane.

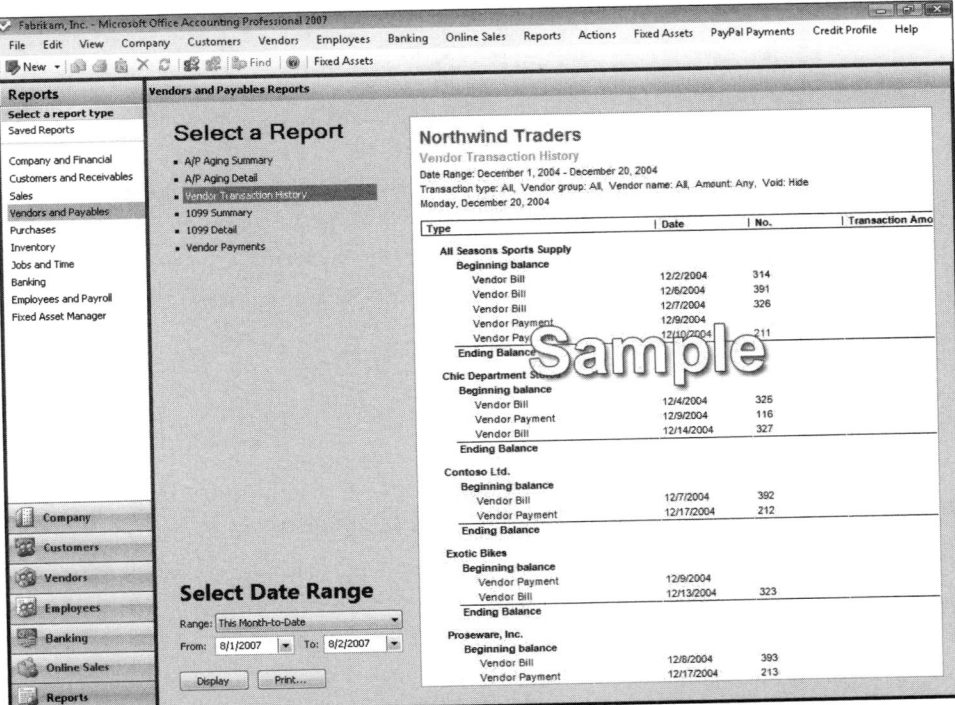

4. In the **Navigation Pane**, click **Purchases**.

The Content pane title changes to Purchases Reports, and the list of available reports changes to reflect the chosen category.

5. In the **Navigation Pane**, click **Purchases by Item Summary**.

The Purchases By Item Summary sample report appears in the preview pane.

Managing Reports

Accounting 2007 comes with a wide range of reports built into the product. Each of these reports is useful for discovering important business intelligence, reviewing past performance, and planning your future ventures. You can analyze your company's performance by viewing and printing the built-in reports as Accounting presents them, or you can focus on specific data within the reports by sorting and filtering the reports' contents.

Displaying and Printing Reports

From the Reports home page, all you need to do to display a report is click a category in the Navigation Pane and then double-click one of the reports that appear in the Select A Report list in the Content pane. If you'd like to filter the report before it appears, perhaps because the report contains a lot of data and takes some time to open, click (don't double-click) the report you want to display, and then use the controls in the Select As Of Date area at the bottom of the Reports home page.

> **Note** For some reports, Accounting displays the Select Date Range controls instead of the Select As Of Date controls.

When you scroll horizontally in a report, Accounting freezes one or more columns on the left to make the report information easier to read.

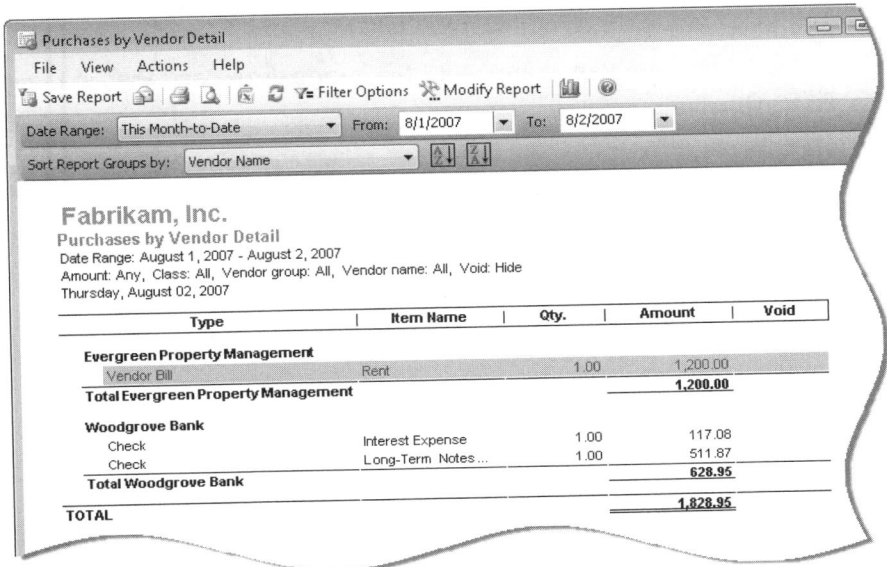

Printing a report is just a matter of displaying the report, clicking Print on the File menu, and using the controls in the Print dialog box to manage the output. If you want to send the report straight to the printer without changing any of your default parameters, you can do so by displaying the report and then clicking the Print button on the Report window toolbar.

In this exercise, you will display and print the Profitability By Customer Detail report.

OPEN the Fabrikam sample company file.

1. In the **Navigation Pane**, click the **Reports** button.

   The Reports home page appears.

2. In the **Navigation Pane**, click **Customers and Receivables**.

   The Customers And Receivables reports appear in the Content pane.

3. In the **Content** pane, click **Profitability by Customer Detail**.

4. In the **Select Date Range** area, click the **Range** arrow, and then in the list, click **This Fiscal Quarter**.

5. Click **Display**.

The Profitability By Customer Detail report opens.

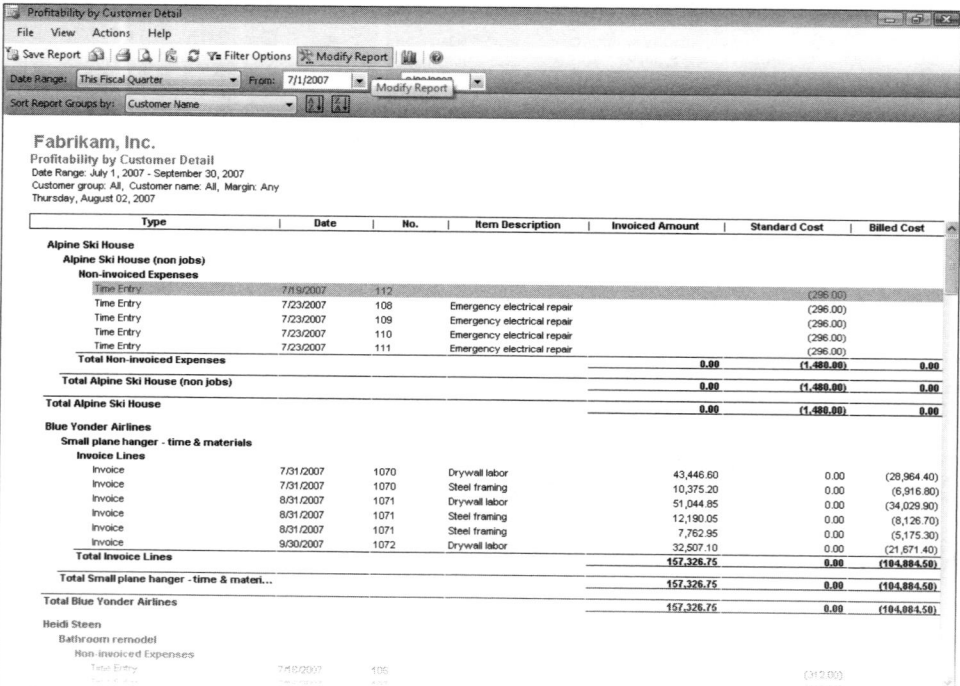

6. On the **File** menu, click **Print**.

The Print dialog box opens.

7. Set your print options in the **Print** dialog box, and then click **Print**.

Accounting prints your report.

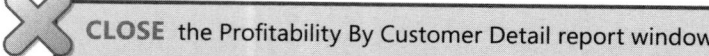

CLOSE the Profitability By Customer Detail report window.

Sorting and Filtering Reports

As with Accounting lists, you can sort a report's records by clicking a column header until you get the sort order you want. Each column header has three sorting positions: unsorted, sorted in ascending order (indicated by an up arrow on the column header), and sorted in descending order (indicated by a down arrow on the column header).

> **Note** Any custom fields you created will appear in the report. You can filter and sort based on those fields as well.

You can filter Accounting reports in three ways:

- By using the controls on the Report window toolbar to select the date range and sorting method for the report.
- By using the predefined filters in the Modify Report task pane, which appears when you click the Modify Report button on the Report window toolbar.
- By using the Select Filter Options dialog box, which appears when you click the Filter Options button on the Report window toolbar.

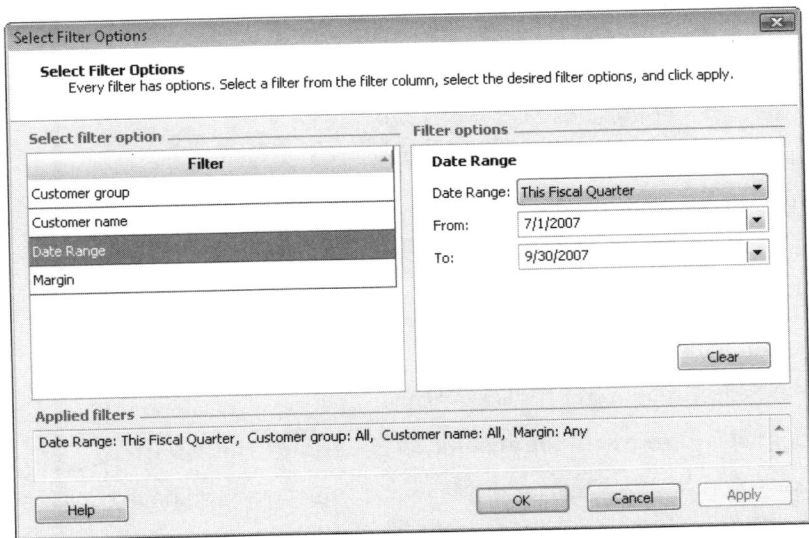

Click the name of the column by which you want to filter and then use the controls under Filter Options in the Select Filter Options dialog box to set the filter's parameters. If you click OK, Accounting filters the report and closes the Select Filter Options dialog box. If you click Apply, however, Accounting filters the report but leaves the dialog box open for you to create new rules or modify existing rules.

See Also For more information about using the filter options in the Modify Report task pane, see "Creating Custom Reports" later in this chapter.

> **Tip** To update a report to include the most recent data entered into your company file, display the report and then click the Refresh button on the Report window toolbar.

In this exercise, you will display and filter Accounting reports.

> **OPEN** the Fabrikam sample company file.

1. In the **Navigation Pane**, click the **Reports** button.

   The Reports home page appears.

2. In the **Navigation Pane**, click **Customers and Receivables**.

   The Customers And Receivables reports appear in the Content pane.

3. In the **Content** pane, click **A/R Aging Detail**.

4. In the **Select As of Date** area, click **Display**.

   The A/R Aging Detail report opens.

5. On the **Report** window toolbar, click **Filter Options**. `Y= Filter Options`

   The Select Filter Options dialog box opens.

6. Under **Select filter option**, click **Balance**.

7. Under **Filter options**, click **Greater Than**.

8. In the **Greater Than** field, type 1000.

9. Click **Apply**.

   Accounting applies the filter rule.

10. Under **Select filter option**, click **As of**.

11. Under **Filter options**, in the **As of** list, click **End of This Quarter**.

    Clicking End Of This Quarter displays customers who will have overdue bills if they do not pay by the end of the current fiscal quarter.

12. Click **OK**.

    Accounting applies the second filter rule in addition to the first rule applied previously.

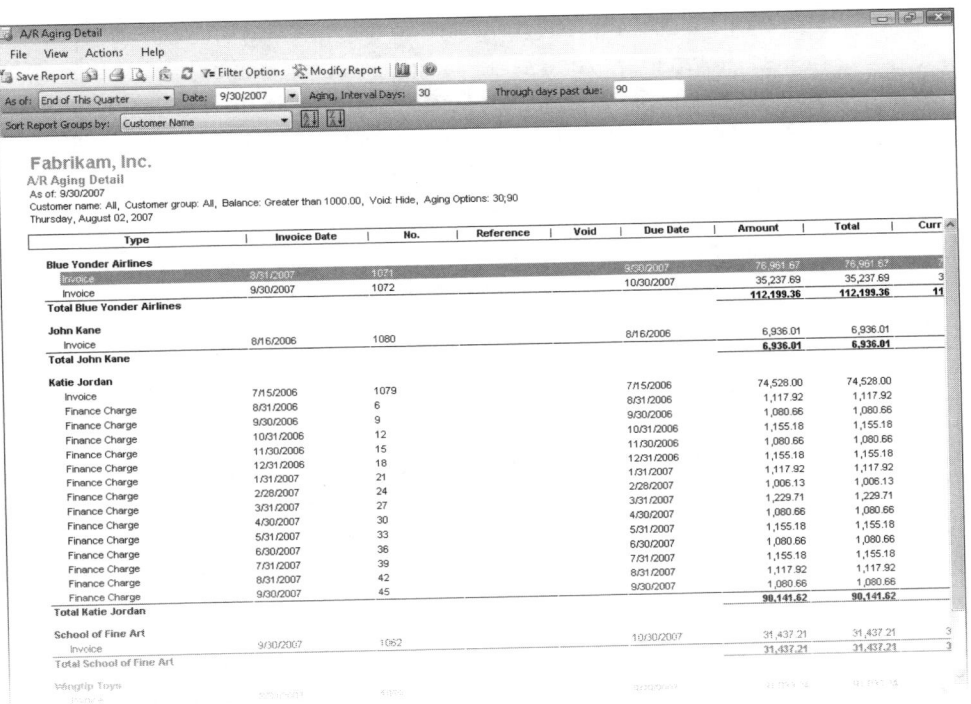

13. Click the **Due Date** column header until it displays a downward-pointing triangle.

Accounting sorts the items within each customer's group, in descending order, by due date.

  CLOSE the A/R Aging Detail report without saving your changes.

Creating Custom Reports

When you create a custom report in Accounting, you actually create a custom version of an existing report. For example, suppose that Fabrikam's construction business is relatively seasonal. The fictional company is situated in the Pacific Northwest, a region that usually gets a lot of rain from January to June. Because construction firms perform less work during the rainy months, the owner should consider creating a custom report that summarizes the work done during the rainy season.

You create a custom report by sorting and filtering an existing report using the techniques shown in "Sorting and Filtering Reports" earlier in this chapter. After the report displays the desired data, click Save Report As on the File menu. In the Save Report dialog box that opens, type a name for the new report, and then click OK. You can display a list of your custom reports by displaying the Reports home page and then clicking Saved Reports in the Navigation Pane.

> **Note** You can save your custom report with the same name as the report on which it is based, but it's better to give the custom report a descriptive name.

One great way to analyze the performance of your business is to compare your revenue and expenditures to those in a previous time period, such as the previous month, or to the same period from the previous year (such as the first quarter of 2007 versus the first quarter of 2008). To add columns to your report that compare report results to those in other time periods, click the Modify Report button on the Report window toolbar. Then, in the Modify Report task pane, click Columns to display a list of columns you can add to your report.

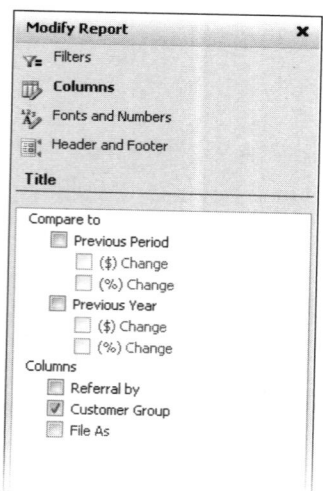

For example, if your report displays sales for June 2007, you can select the Previous Period check box and the ($) Change check box to add columns that display the difference between sales revenues for May and June 2007.

You can change the appearance of your report from the Modify Report task pane in the following ways:

- When you click Fonts And Numbers, the Modify Report task pane lists a series of report areas you can format. Clicking the expand control next to one of the items lists the attributes you can change.

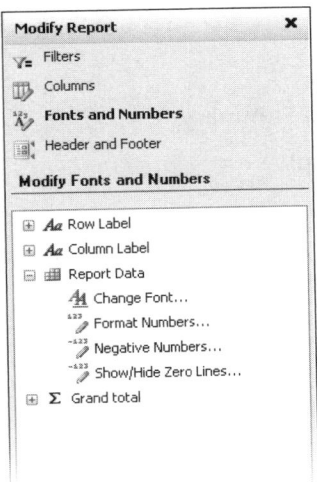

> **Tip** To edit a custom report, you display the report, click the Modify Report button on the report's toolbar, and then use the techniques described in this section.

- The Header And Footer item contains similar controls for your report's header and footer, which appear when you print the report.
- Clicking the Filters item displays a list of pre-defined filters you can use to focus your report's data.

If you want to delete a custom report, click the report in the Saved Reports list, and then click the Delete button on the Reports home page toolbar. (You can't delete any of the built-in reports.)

> **Tip** If you want to create a custom report that isn't based on the data in any single Accounting report, click the Export To Excel toolbar button to export a report or list to Microsoft Office Excel and use that program's capabilities to summarize your data.

In this exercise, you will create and save a custom version of the Sales By Item Summary report.

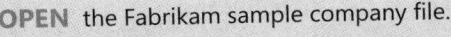

OPEN the Fabrikam sample company file.

1. In the **Navigation Pane**, click the **Reports** button.

   The Reports home page appears.

2. In the **Navigation Pane**, click **Sales**.

   The Sales reports appear in the Content pane.

3. In the **Content** pane, click **Sales by Item Summary**.

4. In the **Select Date Range** area, click **Display**.

   The Sales By Item Summary report opens.

5. On the **Report** window toolbar, type 1/1/2007 in the **From** field, and then type 5/31/2007 in the **To** field.

   The value in the Date Range field changes to Custom, and Accounting filters the report.

 6. On the toolbar, click the **Modify Report** button.

   The Modify Report task pane opens.

7. In the **Modify Report** task pane, click **Header and Footer**.

   The Header and Footer options appear in the task pane.

8. Select the **Footer** check box.

   The Footer(1) and Change Font options become available.

9. Click **Change Font**.

   The Font dialog box opens.

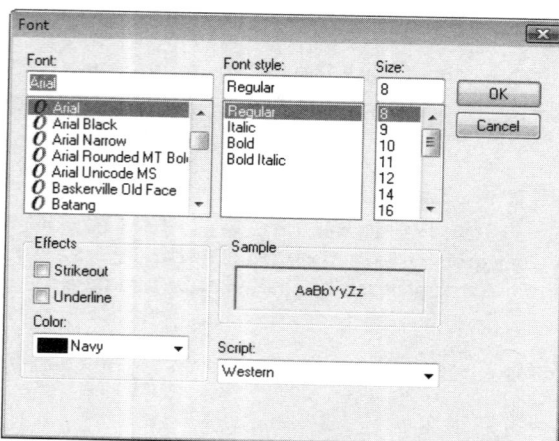

10. Under **Font**, scroll to and then click **Times New Roman**.

11. Under **Font Style**, click **Italic**. Then click **OK**.

    The Font dialog box closes.

12. In the **Modify Report** task pane, click **Columns**.

The available custom columns appear in the Column Properties area of the Sales By Item Summary report.

13. Select the **Previous Year** check box, and then select the **(%) Change** check box.

Columns for the previous year quantity sold, the previous year revenue amount, the percent change for quantity sold, and the percent change of the revenue amount appear in the report.

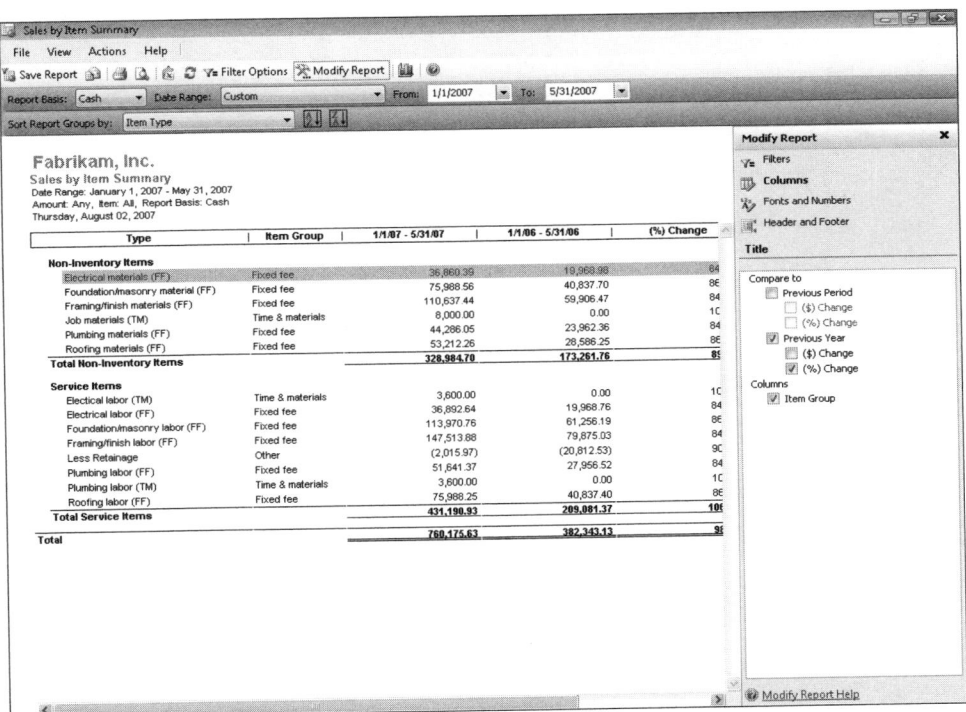

14. On the **File** menu, click **Save Report As**.

The Save Report dialog box opens.

15. In the **Save Report As** field, type Rainy Season 2007. Then click **OK**.

The Save Report dialog box closes.

16. On the **File** menu, click **Close**.

The report window closes.

17. In the **Navigation Pane**, click **Saved Reports**.

The Rainy Season 2007 report appears in the Select A Report Type list in the Content pane.

Generating Business Intelligence from Reports

Businesses must be nurtured to grow, which means that you need to know as much as you can about your company to ensure it remains healthy. The default Accounting reports, plus any custom reports you create, can help you make effective decisions. You should carefully examine each report to understand the information it provides and how that information relates to your business, as well as the information it doesn't provide. Furthermore, you must interpret report data in the context of your business. The built-in reports provide generally useful information, but they can't tell you what that information means to your business. That's where your experience comes in.

Projecting Cash Flow (Professional Only)

One of the central measures of a company's health is the amount of cash it has on hand to pay its bills. Investing large sums in new equipment or supplies when you have a clear plan for growth is one thing, but you should exercise great care if sales slump and you see that you will have a hard time meeting your obligations using cash on hand.

You can discover your cash on hand and projected cash flow from the Company home page, which prominently features the Cash Flow pane.

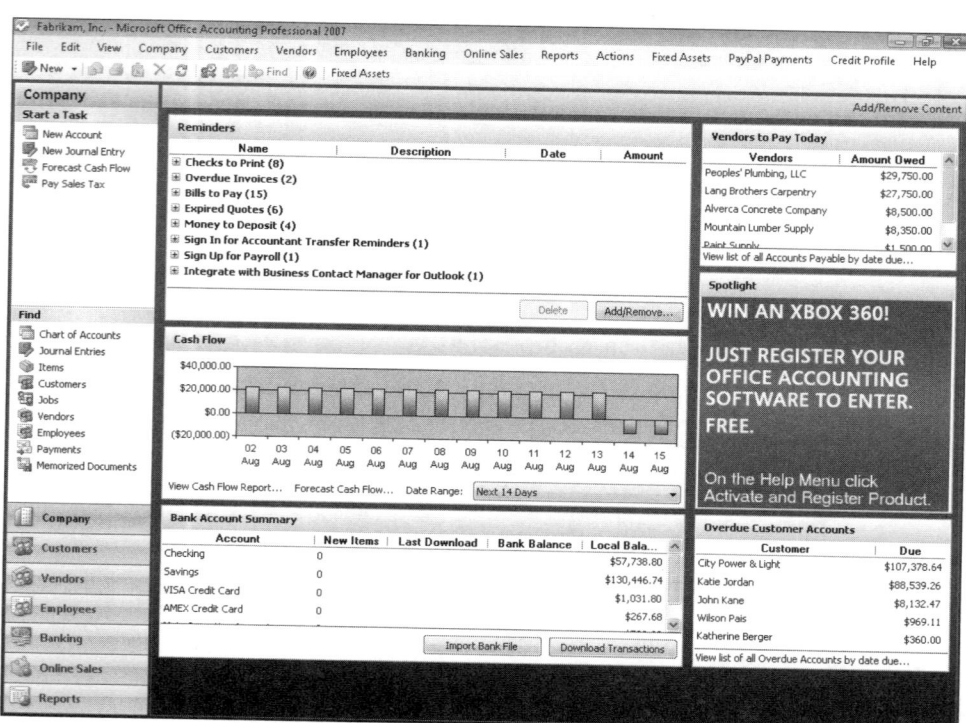

The Cash Flow pane displays your projected cash flow for the period of time displayed in the Date Range list. You can choose to display your cash flow for the next 7 days, the next 14 days, the next month, or the next 2, 3, or 12 months.

If you'd like to see a finer-grained analysis of your company's cash flow, you can click Forecast Cash Flow in the Cash Flow pane. When you do, the Forecast Cash Flow window opens.

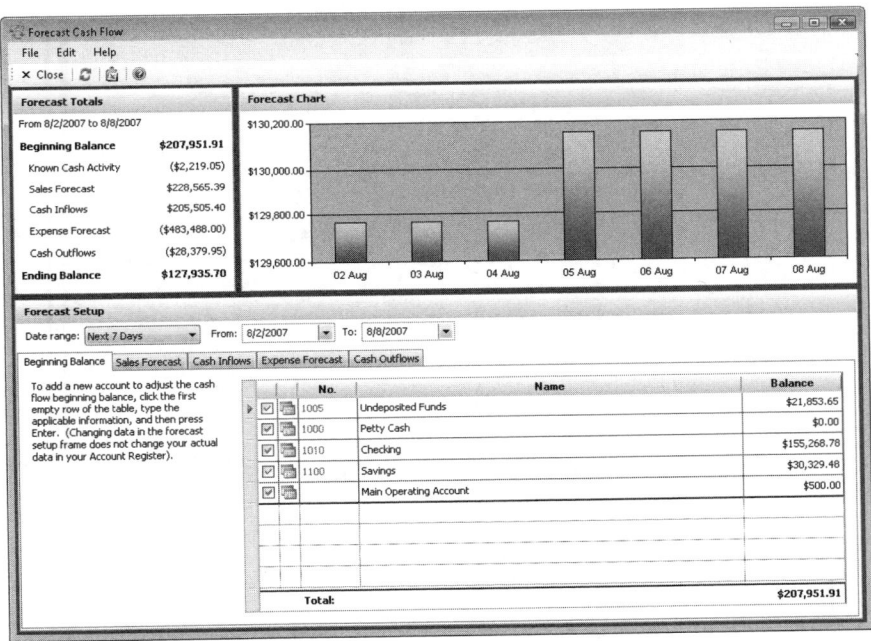

You can find a breakdown of your company's projected cash flow in the Forecast Totals pane, a graphical summary in the Forecast Chart pane, and category details in the Forecast Setup pane. The information in the Forecast Setup pane is particularly valuable in that it enables you to investigate your beginning balance, sales forecast, cash inflow, expense forecast, and cash outflows. Those details can help you decide how you can manage and improve your company's cash flow.

In this exercise, you will discover Fabrikam's cash on hand and projected cash flow.

> OPEN the Fabrikam sample company file.

1. In the **Navigation Pane**, click the **Company** button.

   The Company home page appears.

2. In the **Cash Flow** section of the **Company** home page, click **Forecast Cash Flow**. The Cash Flow Forecast window opens.

3. In the **Forecast Setup** section of the **Forecast Cash Flow** window, click the **Date Range** arrow, and then in the list, click **Next 2 Months**.

   Accounting recalculates the cash flow forecast and displays the results.

4. In the **Forecast Setup** section, click the **Expense Forecast** tab.

   The expenses to be paid appear in the Forecast Setup area's grid.

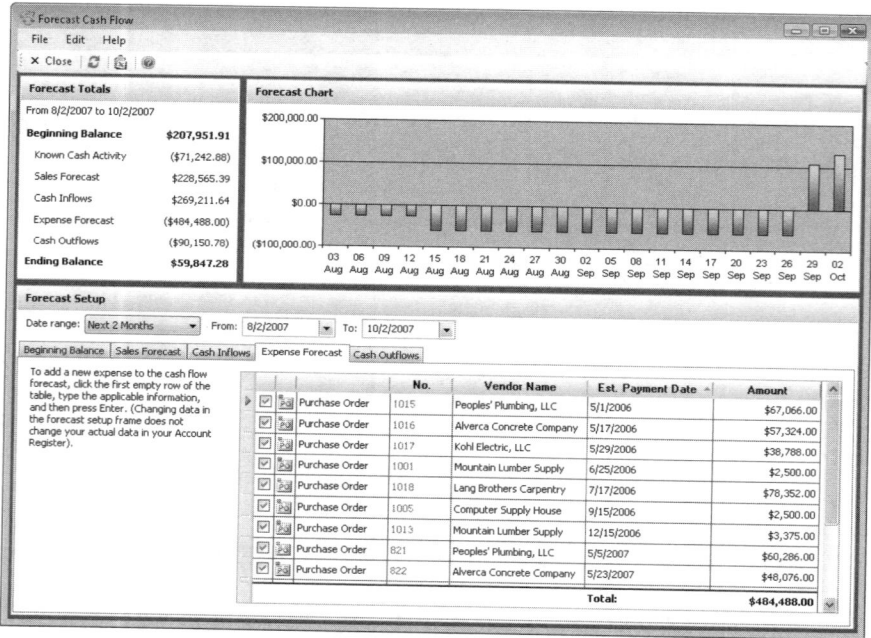

 CLOSE the Cash Flow Forecast window.

Cash Flow Forecasting

When you add a cash flow forecast to the reports library you create, you gain access to critical business intelligence. If you make estimates based upon reliable data, and take into account not only your liabilities but also your commitments, you will be able to count on a realistic and useful forecast. You will be able to use the cash flow forecast to get a clear picture of the sources and timing of cash receipts, as well as the purposes and timing of the cash you can expect to spend.

When you create a cash flow forecast, whether you do so within your accounting system or manually via a spreadsheet, you should focus upon real data (not simply historical data), while at the same time considering information from other sources, including your budget and your overall business strategy. Your cash flow forecast should be arranged in a manner consistent with your financial reports, budgets, and other forecasts, particularly within the context of the level of detail you present, to ensure easy use of this important management and control tool. Your cash flow forecast should resemble the statement of cash flows, one of the most basic financial statements. The sections you create will represent cash flows from operating activities (the largest portion of cash flows for most businesses), cash flows from investing activities, and cash flows from financing activities.

Cash flows from your operating, investing, and financing activities depend upon, and affect, each other in ways that may depend upon the stage of development (and maturity of) the business, conditions that exist within your businesses industry or market environments, and, of course, the general economic environment. For example, a business at the startup stage of the development cycle may witness cash flows generated by financing activities, which, in turn, become available for operating (and perhaps investing) activities of the business. On the other hand, a business at the stage of ongoing, steady-state operations will likely see operating activities providing the cash flows that are forecast for investing and financing activities.

In addition to being designed in a manner consistent with your basic financial reports, it is important that the cash flow forecast presents how cash actually flows. After you assemble the presentation of the sources and uses for cash, you can perform your forecasts and, subsequently, compare the actual cash flows of the business to the cash flows that you have forecast. This will translate to a finely tuned, highly useful tool that, in conjunction with your continually updated estimates and assumptions, will help you to identify cash surpluses and deficits with increasing precision.

Many benefits will accrue from this refined financial planning and control tool. For example, an accurate cash flow forecast will mean that you can take advantage of surplus funds that become available to avoid, or at least to minimize, costs that accrue when you have to borrow to finance your business operations. You can also use your cash flow forecast to assist you in setting aside reserves for substantial expenditures (planned, like fixed assets, or unplanned, like a contingency fund), enacting a strategy to invest in short-term financial instruments with your cash surpluses and to liquidate these securities in times of cash deficits, and other situations. Employing cash surpluses in investments, in expansion of your business, or perhaps both, becomes far more practical after you can be assured, via a sound cash flow forecast, that the cash requirements of the business are anticipated and provided for.

Identifying Your Best Customers

Good customers are hard to find, so it's vital that you identify your best customers and do everything you can to keep their business. You'll have an idea of which customers are the best from your day-to-day involvement in running your business, but you should still take a look at your Accounting data to confirm your opinions.

The Customer Transaction History report is the best report to use to determine your most profitable customers. You might be tempted to use the Profitability By Customer Summary report, which calculates your expected profit by subtracting your costs from the total amount invoiced for each customer. Unfortunately, the Profitability By Customer Summary report doesn't take into account whether a customer actually paid you. According to the Profitability By Customer Summary report, Katie Jordan is one of Fabrikam's most profitable customers, even though she has an outstanding balance of more than $80,000.

In this exercise, you will sort and filter the Customer Transaction History report to identify your best customers.

> **OPEN** the Fabrikam sample company file.

1. In the **Navigation Pane**, click the **Reports** button.

   The Reports home page appears.

2. In the **Navigation Pane**, click **Customers and Receivables**.

   The Customers And Receivables reports appear in the Content pane.

3. In the **Content** pane, click **Customer Transaction History**.

4. In the **Select Date Range** area, click **Range**, and then in the list, click **All**.

5. Click **Display**.

   The Customer Transaction History report opens.

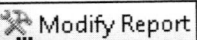

6. On the toolbar, click the **Modify Report** button.

   The Modify Report task pane opens.

7. In the **Modify Report** task pane, click **Columns**.

   The available columns appear in the Modify Report task pane.

8. Select the **Aging (days)** check box.

   The Aging (Days) column appears in the report. You might have to scroll to the right to view the new column.

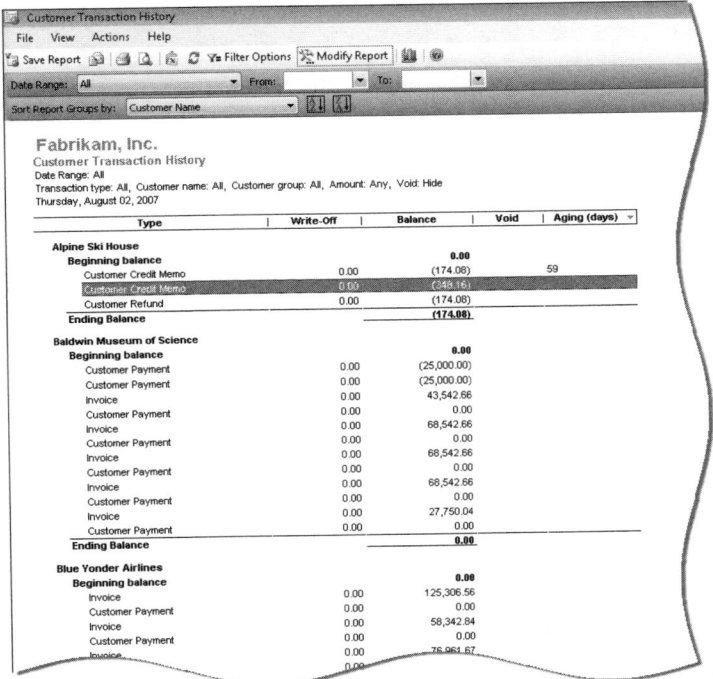

 **CLOSE** the Customer Transaction History report.

Weeding Out Slow-Paying Customers

Many small businesses fail to analyze customer profitability—they simply look at the revenue generated by a given customer's sales and assume that profit will result. But sometimes when you analyze other factors about your customers, such as late payments and pricing concessions you have to offer to keep them, you may discover that your overall profitability will increase when you eliminate the expenses (including interest and administration overhead) that these customers cost you.

When considering customer profitability, and whether to stop pursuing their business, you should identify slow payers as a group, and then carefully consider several things, including the following:

- **Real customer profitability** Does the slow-paying customer group require more support time and cost (due to your attempts to collect or other reasons)? Do they cause you to have to borrow money to meet ongoing expenses, or cause you to be late in your payments to your own vendors and other creditors? Do they cause your business to forgo sales because of inability to restock popular products?

- **Price concessions** Are you giving slow-paying customers price concessions, based upon length of your relationship or for some other reason, in an effort to keep them? Has time passed and rendered their product pricing significantly less than that which you offer new customers? Quantity discounts and other discount types, too, should be considered—are they appropriate for consistently late-paying customers?

- **Discounts and incentives for cash and early payments** Are you offering less-than-optimal (for your business) terms to drive timely payment? (Even if slow-paying customers cannot take advantage of these terms, eliminating their accounts may help to eliminate terms that amount to a high interest loan for you—terms that you may have put in place in the past, but now seek to modify to improve your own financial health.

- **Options for substituting better customers** Can you sell the products or services purchased by the slow-payers to new customers at the same (or perhaps higher, if you're offering the current customers price breaks) prices, and still expect to be paid on time?

● **Impact of losing the customers** What will be the real financial impact of losing the slow-payers, after you factor in the interest and other overhead costs they drive, together with the distraction and frustration that comes with their business?

Just as you can determine who your best customers are (see "Identifying Your Best Customers" earlier in this chapter), and identify aging of individual accounts receivable, you can customize a report to determine which customers make a habit of slow payment. By analyzing the behavior of these customers, and by getting a true sense of their profitability, after you plug their actual costs into the equation, you can often determine that your business is better off without customers who are also using you to finance their operations.

Identifying Underperforming Products and Services

Successful businesses find ways to make their company more attractive to customers. One way to win customers is to improve existing products and services; another way is to offer new products and services. Part of the guesswork in running a business is balancing profits and costs per customer , which means that you must look closely at your costs and your market when you determine how much to charge for your items.

Unfortunately, not all products and services generate the profits required. It's in your best interest to identify those items and drop them from the active list as quickly as possible.

In this exercise, you will identify Fabrikam's underperforming products and services.

OPEN the Fabrikam sample company file.

1. In the **Navigation Pane**, click the **Reports** button.

   The Reports home page appears.

2. In the **Navigation Pane**, click **Sales**.

   The Sales reports appear in the Content pane.

3. In the **Content** pane, click **Sales by Item Summary**.

4. In the **Select Date Range** area, click **Display**.

   The Sales By Item Summary report opens.

5. On the toolbar, in the **Date Range** list, click **All**.

The report summarizes all item sales recorded in Accounting. Electrical Labor (TM), and Plumbing Labor (TM) stand out as low-profit items.

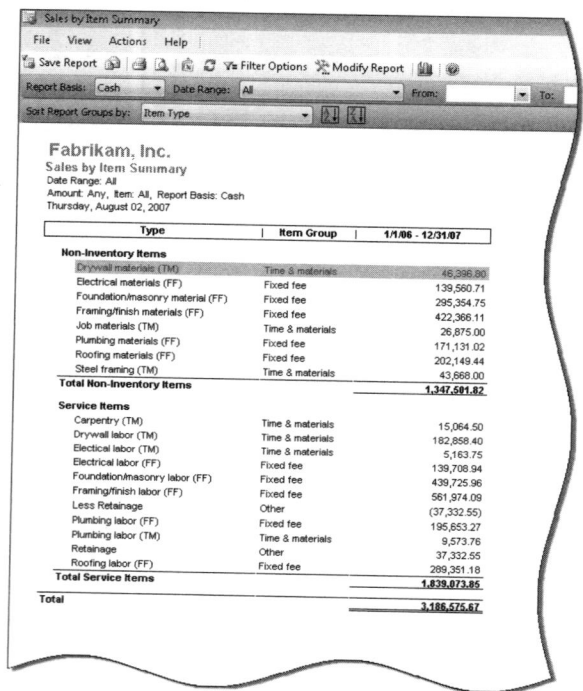

6. On the **File** menu, click **Close**.

> **Note** If a dialog box appears asking if you want to save your changes, click No.

The Sales By Item Summary report closes.

7. On the **Company** menu, point to **Company Lists**, and then click **Items**.

The Item List appears.

8. Click the **Current View** arrow, and then in the list, click **Inactive**.

The Item List displays the items Fabrikam no longer offers for sale, which includes the three low-profit items discovered earlier.

9. In the **Current View** list, click **Active**.

The Item List displays items available for sale.

CLOSE the Fabrikam sample company file and exit Accounting 2007.

Identifying Optimal Product Mix

If you're like most small-business owners, you'll find yourself confronted with product mix decisions on a regular basis. Whether your business builds or buys the products it sells—or even if you sell services, or a mix of products and services to your customers—you will quickly become aware that, to increase your overall margin (without having to increase prices), your objective is to sell more of your higher margin items. At the heart of these product/services mix considerations is the contribution concept. The business intelligence you can generate from well-constructed margin analysis reports can mean taking the guesswork out of reaching and maintaining the ideal mix for your business.

The contribution concept helps you to make intelligent business decisions, such as whether specific products and services should be added (or dropped), whether certain sales territories or customer groups should be expanded (or reduced or eliminated), and whether certain "special orders" should be taken, among other considerations. If you offer only one product or service, these determinations can be pretty simple. But if, like most businesses, you sell a range of different items whose margins vary significantly, working with a "blended gross margin" can become a little more complicated.

Simply focusing your strategy upon selling higher margin products may not be enough to maximize your profitability and return on assets (ROA). Turnover rate becomes an additional consideration. To optimize your mix, you need to measure and control the speed with which each product or service delivers profit to your business, and then to focus upon the products and services that generate cash the fastest. (Many small business owners are surprised to learn that lower-margin products that can be delivered quickly can be significantly more profitable, over time, than higher-margin products with slower turnover.)

To reach and maintain an optimal product/services mix, you need to compare not only simple revenue and margin, but also profitability, ROA, and contribution to the bottom line, for each individual product or service you can offer. Having thus determined the best products and services to include within your growth strategies, you are well on your way to identifying a tentative mix. You can then, of course, refine your mix, on an ongoing basis, to include products and services with higher margins, more rapid turnovers, or both. Well-constructed, frequently reviewed reports support easy tracking of the results of changes you make to your mix, while providing the added benefit of helping you to maintain isolated focus, where needed, upon such specific factors as the effects of pricing, volume, and costs that change over time.

Planning for Traditionally Slow Periods

If your business experiences the "feast or famine" syndrome, or if it exists in a highly seasonal industry and experiences the associated busy and idle periods (such as a business selling locally grown produce), you might be tempted to simply close up shop in the idle periods to attempt to at least save on overhead. These idle periods can often provide excellent opportunities to gain insight to your business, if you use the time to create new custom reports that focus upon specific opportunities for improvement. For example, you can analyze customer margins to identify customers whose behavior and costs make them unsuitable for your business (see "Weeding Out Slow-Paying Customers" earlier in this chapter). You can also invest time in fine-tuning your product/services mix to optimize profitability in busier times (see "Identifying Optimal Product Mix" earlier in this chapter).

In addition to opportunities to generate and analyze new business intelligence about your company, you can invest time in exploring new revenue streams—new products and services that you can add to your mix, with an eye toward analyzing performance after the upcoming sales cycles. Moreover, you might identify new revenue streams that you can exploit in what are traditionally off-peak periods for your business, in effect expanding your sales cycle. To return to our earlier example of a business that sells locally grown produce during the harvest season, let's say that they might import produce items available in other countries when they are not locally accessible. (Perhaps the margins are lower on the imported products, but they might still be sufficient to cover costs and contribute significantly to overall profitability.) An analysis of the contribution of these new streams to the overall, annual bottom line will help you to capitalize on opportunities that make sense, and to reject those that fail to cover their incremental costs or other expenses.

Other Reporting Considerations

In addition to being able to create and customize many basic financial and operating reports out of the box, you should constantly strive to create and use specific "focus" reports that enable you to constantly improve areas of your operations. Customer and product margin analysis, product mix, and cash flow forecasts are great places to start in extending your report library, but a host of industry and market-specific reports could well provide you with the business intelligence you need to exceed the success of your competitors. Industry-specific Web sites and periodicals, as well other resources, abound. Explore these sources of ideas regularly to increase your business' reporting and analysis capabilities.

Key Points

- Accounting reports summarize your data and help you make important business decisions.

- You can sort and filter your reports to focus on time periods, products, customers, and other elements of interest.

- Change the appearance of your reports by using the Modify Report tools available from the report window toolbar.

- You can add calculated fields to compare results from one time period with results from other time periods, such as a month with the previous month or a week with the same week the previous year.

- You can save specific versions of your reports and display them from the Reports home page.

Glossary

account A record of financial transactions, usually grouped around a particular category that helps financial planners determine deductible expenses and taxable income. For example, you would track the cost of professional association memberships, journal subscriptions, and research materials in the Dues, Publications, Books account.

account register A list of transactions for a specific financial account.

accounting The process of recording, classifying, summarizing, reporting, and assessing a company's business transactions. The goal of accounting is to maintain a detailed and accurate picture of the company's performance and health.

accounts payable An account that contains records of monies you owe to your vendors. Microsoft Office Accounting 2007 calculates this account's values from transactions you enter.

accounts receivable An account that contains records of monies owed to your company for the sale of products and services. Accounting 2007 calculates this account's values from transactions you enter.

asset A resource that the corporation owns, such as cash, inventory, or equipment.

back order A reference to an item that a customer has ordered but the item is not currently in stock.

balance sheet A financial statement that summarizes your company's status on a specific date.

cash flow statement A report that describes the amount of money a company expects to have on hand over a period of time.

chart of accounts The list of your company's accounts and their balances.

credit An entry on the right side of an account; debits are on the left. How a credit affects your bottom line depends on the type of account to which it is applied. A credit increases liabilities, equity, or income, and decreases assets or expenses.

debit An entry on the left side of an account; credits are on the right. How a debit affects your bottom line depends on the type of account to which it is applied. A debit increases assets or expenses, and decreases liabilities, equity, or income.

depreciation The amount of value that a physical item, such as a computer or automobile, is assumed to lose over time.

double-entry bookkeeping An accounting method in which transactions are represented as a credit to one account and a debit from another account.

expense An amount spent on products or services related to your normal business operations, such as utilities or wages.

fixed-fee job A job that is undertaken for a set price.

income Revenue generated by selling products and services to your customers.

invoice A request for payment that you send to a customer.

item A product or service that your company offers for sale.

job A multi-part project made up of products and services you deliver over time.

journal entry A record of a transaction entered into an account register.

kit A set of items sold as a single unit.

liability A debt. Something owed, such as accounts payable or income taxes to be paid at a later date.

payment terms The conditions under which customers are expected to pay for products and services.

profit-and-loss statement A detailed statement that describes a company's performance over a period of time. A profit-and-loss statement usually starts with revenues and then covers expenses, but it goes into detail regarding expenses such as the cost of goods sold, operating expenses, taxes, loan interest, and other costs of doing business.

progress invoice A request for payment for a partially completed job.

quote A document that specifies the products and services you agree to sell or provide to a customer, what those items will cost, and the delivery date of a proposed transaction.

report A summary of specific information recorded in Accounting.

sales order A record of a customer's request to purchase an item you offer for sale.

sales tax code An entry that reflects the tax an authority levies on a transaction.

support list A list that Accounting creates to track customers, items, and other important business data.

time-and-materials job A job that bills the customer for actual time and material expenses incurred while performing the job.

user account A user name and password combination that allows employees to enter and view data in Accounting.

vendor A company or individual from which you purchase products or services.

XML A text-encoding standard that enables you to store data about a document's contents within that document.

Index

Numbers

A

About the Authors

Curtis Frye

Curt Frye is a freelance writer and Microsoft Most Valuable Professional for Microsoft Office Excel. He lives in Portland, Oregon, and is the author of eight books from Microsoft Press, including *Microsoft Office Excel 2007 Step by Step*, *Microsoft Office Access 2007 Plain & Simple*, *Microsoft Office Excel 2007 Plain & Simple*, and *Microsoft Office Small Business Accounting 2006 Step By Step*. He has also written numerous articles for the Microsoft Work Essentials Web site.

Before beginning his writing career in June 1995, Curt spent four years with The MITRE Corporation as a defense trade analyst and one year as Director of Sales and Marketing for Digital Gateway Systems, an Internet service provider. Curt graduated from Syracuse University in 1990 with an honors degree in political science. When he's not writing, Curt is a professional improvisational comedian with ComedySportz Portland.

William E. Pearson III

William E. Pearson III has an extensive background working as a CPA, internal auditor, financial analyst, controller, and management accountant. He is the founder of Island Technologies Inc., where he consults on and implements business intelligence solutions. Bill is well known in the international business intelligence community through his articles and other publications.

Acknowledgments

Creating a book is a time-consuming (sometimes all-consuming) process, but working within an established relationship makes everything go much more smoothly. In that light, I'd like to thank Sandra Haynes, the Microsoft Press Series Editor, for inviting me back for another tilt at the windmill. I've been lucky to work with Microsoft Press for the past seven years, and always enjoy working with Valerie Woolley, a Project Editor at Microsoft Press. She kept us all on track and moving forward while maintaining her sense of humor.

I'd also like to thank Jean Trenary of Online Training Solutions, Inc. (OTSI) for shepherding the book through the production process and completing the project with a careful proofread. My fellow Microsoft MVP Mitch Tulloch did a great job as technical editor, Jaime Odell kept me on the straight and narrow with a thorough copy edit, Lisa Van Every brought everything together as the book's compositor, and Joan Preppernau kept an eye on quality throughout the process. I hope to work with all of them again.

—Curtis Frye

Additional Resources for Home and Business

Breakthrough Windows Vista™: Find Your Favorite Features and Discover the Possibilities

Joli Ballew and Sally Slack
ISBN 9780735623620

Jump in for the topics or features that interest you most! This colorful guide brings Windows Vista to life—from setting up your new system; accessing the Windows Vista Sidebar; customizing it for your favorite gadgets; recording live television with Media Center; organizing photos, music, and videos; making movies; and more.

So That's How! 2007 Microsoft® Office System: Timesavers, Breakthroughs, & Everyday Genius

Evan Archilla and Tiffany Songvilay
ISBN 9780735622746

From vanquishing an overstuffed inbox to breezing through complex spreadsheets, discover smarter ways to do everyday things with Microsoft Office. Based on a popular course delivered to more than 70,000 students, this guide delivers the tips and revelations that help you work more effectively with Microsoft Office Outlook®, Excel®, Word, and other programs. Also includes 'webinars' on CD.

Look Both Ways: Help Protect Your Family on the Internet

Linda Criddle
ISBN 9780735623477

You look both ways before crossing the street. Now, learn the new rules of the road—and help protect yourself online with Internet child-safety authority Linda Criddle. Using real-life examples, Linda teaches the simple steps you and your family can take to help avoid Internet dangers—and still enjoy your time online.

The Microsoft Crabby Office Lady Tells It Like It Is: Secrets to Surviving Office Life

Annik Stahl
ISBN 9780735622722

From cubicle to corner office, learn the secrets for getting more done on the job—so you can really enjoy your time off the job! The Crabby Office Lady shares her no-nonsense advice for succeeding at work, as well as tricks for using Microsoft Office programs to help simplify your life. She'll give you the straight scoop—so pay attention!

Microsoft Office Excel 2007: Data Analysis and Business Modeling

Wayne L. Winston
ISBN 9780735623965

Beyond Bullet Points: Using Microsoft Office PowerPoint® 2007 to Create Presentations That Inform, Motivate, and Inspire

Cliff Atkinson
ISBN 9780735623873

Take Back Your Life! Using Microsoft Office Outlook 2007 to Get Organized and Stay Organized

Sally McGhee
ISBN 9780735623439

What do you think of this book?

We want to hear from you!

Do you have a few minutes to participate in a brief online survey?

Microsoft is interested in hearing your feedback so we can continually improve our books and learning resources for you.

To participate in our survey, please visit:

www.microsoft.com/learning/booksurvey/

...and enter this book's ISBN-10 number (appears above barcode on back cover*). As a thank-you to survey participants in the United States and Canada, each month we'll randomly select five respondents to win one of five $100 gift certificates from a leading online merchant. At the conclusion of the survey, you can enter the drawing by providing your e-mail address, which will be used for prize notification only.

Thanks in advance for your input. Your opinion counts!

*Where to find the ISBN-10 on back cover

Example only. Each book has unique ISBN.

www.microsoft.com/learning/booksurvey/